THE DARK SIDE OF ISAAC NEWTON

SCIENCE'S GREATEST FRAUD?

Godfrey Kneller portrait 1689, used with kind permission

'If we evolved a race of Isaac Newtons, that would not be progress. For the price Newton had to pay for being a supreme intellect was that he was incapable of friendship, love, fatherhood, and many other desirable things. As a man he was a failure; as a monster he was superb.'

Aldous Huxley[1]

THE DARK SIDE OF
ISAAC NEWTON
SCIENCE'S GREATEST FRAUD?

NICK KOLLERSTROM

PEN & SWORD
HISTORY

AN IMPRINT OF PEN & SWORD BOOKS LTD.
YORKSHIRE - PHILADELPHIA

First published in Great Britain in 2018 by
PEN AND SWORD HISTORY
an imprint of
Pen and Sword Books Ltd
Yorkshire – Philadelphia

ISBN 978 1 52674 054 0

Printed and bound in the UK by TJ International,
Padstow, Cornwall

Typeset in Times New Roman 10/13 by
Aura Technology and Software Services, India

Pen & Sword Books Ltd incorporates the imprints of Pen & Sword
Archaeology, Atlas, Aviation, Battleground, Discovery,
Family History, History, Maritime, Military, Naval, Politics, Railways,
Select, Social History, Transport, True Crime, Claymore Press,
Frontline Books, Leo Cooper, Praetorian Press, Remember When,
Seaforth Publishing and Wharncliffe.

For a complete list of Pen and Sword titles please contact
PEN & SWORD BOOKS LIMITED
47 Church Street, Barnsley, South Yorkshire, S70 2AS, England
E-mail: enquiries@pen-and-sword.co.uk
Website: www.pen-and-sword.co.uk

Or

PEN AND SWORD BOOKS
1950 Lawrence Rd, Havertown, PA 19083, USA
E-mail: Uspen-and-sword@casematepublishers.com
Website: www.penandswordbooks.com

Contents

Preface.. 6

Glossary of terms 13

Commended Bibliography 14

Chapter 1   Ecce Homo.. 15

Chapter 2   To Unweave The Rainbow.................................... 45

Chapter 3   The Gravity Of The Situation.............................. 68

Chapter 4   The Mythic Equation 110

Chapter 5   The Hollow World Of Edmond Halley............... 124

Chapter 6   The Crushing Of Hooke.................................... 133

Chapter 7   The Intractable Moon.. 147

Chapter 8   The Duel With Leibniz...................................... 179

Chapter 9   'Restorer Of Solid Philosophy' 215

Chapter 10   Jason, The Golden Fleece, And the Turning
                Of The Zodiac 234

Chapter 11   Gold, Wealth and Empire 246

Appendices.. 254

Select Bibliography.. 272

Notes 274

Index 293

Preface

There is a need today for a demythologised life of Britain's greatest scientist. In the last century, all of the weighty, the insightful, the memorable Newton-biographies have sprung from across the ocean – as if the transferring of the remains of Newton's Jermyn Street abode to Massachusetts, where it was reconstructed in 1913, had perchance exerted some effect upon America's academic life. By contrast, the British biographies since that of the Scotsman David Brewster, composed in 1830, have been slight and uninspired.

It will be said, has not Professor Richard Westfall achieved just this in a 900-page tome? Does not his biography include and encompass all the latest findings, and do so far more comprehensively than any endeavour by this writer can hope to do? His achievement is certainly a milestone – and yet, as he has admitted, there opened up a gulf between himself and his subject while researching his hopefully-definitive textbook until, in the end, the old superman image more or less just reappeared in his textbook, alive and well. To give but one example, Westfall commented on the first mention of the celebrated apple myth appearing not less than 60 years after its supposed occurrence, in the year prior to the death of his subject. He averred that this 'does not lessen the credibility of the event'[1] Anyone who can keep a straight face while declaring that a 60-year gap between what was supposedly a main event of a lifetime and its first mention to another, has merely succumbed to the spell of a national myth.

The huge mass of unpublished Newton-manuscripts was fully analysed and made publicly available only in the late twentieth century. This is a fact as relevant to theological heresy and alchemic belief of our subject, as it is to the question of whether or not he discovered the law of gravity. For whatever reason, mythic images have prevailed over historical truth for a very long time, in a manner that hard-boiled science historians would never normally have tolerated. Call it reverence, call it tradition, but for whatever reason it has long been hard to see the man behind the demi-god image. Today's secular society no longer has the same need for an image of the scientist-seer to weld together religion and science as did the eighteenth and nineteenth centuries, and so should be able to view these old myths more impartially.

Something of a revolution in the perception of this historical figure did take place over those decades, stimulated by tercentenary celebrations on both sides

PREFACE

of the Atlantic of the great events in question; events from the 1660s onwards, culminating in 1687 when the grandiose *Principia Mathematica* appeared. These celebrations seem now largely over and the torrents of publications from the Newton heavy-industry have quietened down into mere rivers. Seven large volumes of Newton's Correspondence and eight even larger volumes of his Mathematical Papers now weigh down the library shelves – or used to; I guess they are now packed away in basements – and these enable myth to be checked against fact in a manner scarcely possible hitherto. At last one can tell the story with little fear that it will have to be greatly altered tomorrow, by some decisive new revelation.

Then there came the full publication of the correspondence of John Flamsteed, Britain's first Astronomer Royal. One has the impression that most of the vital information has now surfaced. To give an example, Dobb's survey of Newton's alchemy seems likely to remain the standard reference on the subject, not least because poring over half a million words in manuscript is a time-consuming task. The modern experts on Newton's alchemy, Betty Dobbs and Karen Figula, were probably more informed about the matter than anyone has ever been, even including Newton's confidantes in the art, Locke and Boyle. Similar comments could be made about Newton's theological work, where Westfall's biography has given what was the first thorough and reliable account of Newton's theological position. One only has to compare it with Manuel's *The Religion of Isaac Newton* published in 1974 which is relatively slight in its comments, to see how much more has been included. The theological heresy kept as a dark secret for so long, so that it could be officially denied by Brewster's two-volume biography, can at last form an organic part of a biography. Some interest has developed in the apocalyptic date which Newton finally ascertained, of 2060, from Jerusalem manuscripts, harped upon in a 2003 docudrama by the BBC. His unpublished theological ruminations are now mainly up online, thanks to Rob Iliffe's work.

The Sussex University 'Newton Project' has now put much of the Correspondence online, as well as some alchemical and theological works, plus a large number of secondary sources, i.e. books about Newton. This must bring us into a closer immediacy with the subject, for most of us who cannot travel to these libraries.

In these pages will be found a graphic, blow-by-blow account of how England's greatest scientist *failed* to discover the law of gravity. This is a startling new perspective, which challenges the 'official mythmakers'. Either it is radically mistaken, or it demands that past biographies be thrown away. This is a book for people who enjoy coherent, logical reasoning *with a bit of maths* woven into it. If, for example, mv^2/r for centripetal force is not your scene, or causes you pain, then this may not be the book for you! We seek for the concept of genesis, of where and with whom an idea (such as differential calculus) first began, and to do that we will have to scrutinize the maths now and then.

THE DARK SIDE OF ISAAC NEWTON

A thematic presentation has been used, assigning a chapter to each of the main subjects developed by Newton. A work concerned with demythologising required such a structure, to allow concentration on one subject at a time. The first, biographical, chapter examines some aspects of a complex and at times thoroughly devious character which thereby emerges. There is no chapter as such on his three decades of alchemical research partly because he made no public statements on the matter. More attention is here given to the lives of those from whom he stole credit, viz Hooke, Leibniz and Flamsteed, as they have hitherto had the 'virtue' drained out of them to create the mythologized, demigod Newton-image.

I hope that Chapter Three will not be too strenuous or protracted to read through, as I grapple with the great error of centuries, and correct it. It is there necessary to criss-cross the timeline several times from different points of view to receive the complete picture.

If there is one earlier biography similar in spirit to the present opus, it was L.T. More's 1934 opus, published in New York, though admittedly such a pre-war opus has now become quite outdated by the mining of all the unpublished manuscripts which has since occurred. Then there was Manuel's startling Freudian profile of 1968 from Cambridge, Massachusetts, after which in 1980 came Westfall's mighty opus from Indiana university, followed by the scarcely shorter *In the Presence of the Creator* by Gale Christianson, New York 1984 (though I haven't read it). On optics, I.A. Sabra's opus composed at Harvard is likely to remain the definitive word on the subject (1975, reprinted 1981), and Bernard Cohen's *The Newtonian Revolution* from Harvard in 1980 is not a text one lightly disagrees with. The recommended bibliography given below includes these. One hopes the reader will appreciate the refreshingly short nature of this list. In our text, a 'main sequence' of biographies, those of Brewster, More, Manuel and Westfall, will be referred to from time to time.

Two British names will be invoked below as expert opinion, one of the twentieth century and the other of the nineteenth, both of these being mathematicians who attained a remarkable empathy for their subject; Augustus de Morgan, and Professor Whiteside. Disagreement with their judgements will indeed be rare and yet, on occasion, will take place. I offered to edit the essays of Professor D.T. Whiteside, the acknowledged world expert upon Newton's mathematical works, and his views will be much referred to in what follows. The collating of Whiteside's essays assisted in focussing my mind upon the deep and multifold issues involved.

In whatever form, the theme of our tale has to feature in the education of a scientist. I have endeavoured to compose a narrative of interest to the general reader. The saga of how Leibniz discovered the calculus and his dire clash with the British Royal Society is always worth retelling. Here I have not gone to the extreme of A.R. Hall in his *Philosophers at War* concerning the calculus dispute, where he stated initially that he would not discuss the mathematical aspects of calculus – and didn't! Not even in footnotes, so that the reader is never really sure what 'it' is that is being discussed. One does require a minimal amount of mathematics to anchor the meaning, which cannot be avoided. A great advantage of studying seventeenth-century science and no later, is that one can quite readily apprehend its mathematics. Footnotes are comments that may be helpful or of interest, while end of chapter references may not be. They may expand on diverging expert opinions over the matters related, which would disrupt the flow of text to insert.

The onward-rolling tercentenary process has seemed like a living thing, as it reactivated each stage of Newton's life, causing papers and books to be published, conferences to be held, TV programmes etc., three hundred years later. Now things have gone very quiet as the great and mighty Newton-experts of the last century have all passed away. So, I here dust off some old manuscripts and offer them to the public! Six million words have to-date been posted up on the Newton-Project of Sussex University managed by Rob Iliffe, in a rather chaotic fashion, which may help to make obscure alchemical or theological texts more inaccessible. The entire correspondence seems to be up there, though letters written in Latin (not uncommon in those days) are there still in Latin. A lot of the old biographies are up there. The project has now moved to Oxford, with Iliffe having lost his collaborator(s).

The science historian habitually portrays merely one half of a character, namely that which contributes towards 'progress'. I have tried to avoid doing this. As an example of the science historian's dilemma, we may consider the character of Galileo, though he is not included in our tale. He is sent a gold chain by the Dutch government. It is a reward for his application for a prize, for a method to determine longitude. He found four moons of Jupiter, and from their orbits the time could be computed on a ship, if one had them plotted in tables. Admittedly this would be tricky on a tossing ship, yet they gave him the prize. The Inquisition, however, wouldn't let Galileo receive the prize and so it was sent back. That is a story, part of a hero-image. On the other hand, one could tell of his studies of his own horoscope, and how Galileo juggled with the ascendants from two possible birth-times. Was he Leo or Gemini? In the end he decided one was more flattering.[2] Now, should this be missed out? It certainly does get missed out. 'Wholly and frighteningly modern'[3] he might be, but are we distorting the character by omitting such?

Edmond Halley is known for his prediction that a comet would return. He noted that some stars had moved, plotted mortality statistics – and already the reader yawns. But what did Halley himself see as his most significant discovery?

That can readily be answered from a portrait in his mature years, when he was Astronomer Royal, as he is shown holding a piece of paper on which his discovery is inscribed, his insight into the very structure of the earth. It was hollow. It was hollow and inhabited within. Now, one may ask, why have biographies of Edmund Halley tended to omit this? The answer is evident enough, that Halley's hollow-earth theory had a fertile future in science-fiction, fantasy and amongst certain strange sects, and so was viewed as undesirable. Actually, his view was a logical deduction from the 100 per cent overestimation of lunar mass in the *Principia*. Halley's hero-worship of Newton did not permit him to question the veracity of the bizarre computations whereby his master reached the conclusion, of an ultra-dense Moon, even though he could not follow them – but, we are now getting entangled in details which should be spelt out in due time.

Robert Boyle, the 'Sceptical Chemist', seems to have been the only chemist known in history to proclaim that he was ignorant as to what the elements were; also known for the law which his assistant Robert Hooke more or less pointed out to him as his candid account intimates. His action in causing the repeal of the statute prohibiting the manufacture of gold by alchemists, should be a matter of historic interest. By having a word with his parliamentary friends, he caused a new statute to be proclaimed, in the first year after the 'Glorious Revolution' of 1689, which repealed the strict law prohibiting alchemists from 'multiplying' gold. The expansion of trade required more gold, and it was hoped a method of his might produce some. Three centuries of history books have largely omitted Boyle's serious belief that he had witnessed the making of gold by an alchemist.[4] Such matters tend to be excised from the history books, as not well according with a conception of progress.

We live in the age of the specialist, but these characters in our tale remain fascinating just because they were not such. They were polymaths. They had no single 'ism' or 'ology' which defined their existence. Christopher Wren was an astronomy lecturer at Oxford, who became London's chief architect after the Fire of London. The reverend John Flamsteed had a parish to look after as well as being Astronomer Royal. An account should capture this. The modern specialist is a dangerous person, mastering merely one sliver of knowledge which may be very effective, but which lacks an overall framework of meaning. As knowledge has become more specialised, meaning has become lost amidst fragmented disciplines which cannot speak to each other.

The period involved was the heroic age of science, before that sadly enfeebled being, the specialist, came upon the stage. In Restoration England the key characters moved around the new reality-concepts as they were being created, before the new physics had taken shape. We go behind the official myths to the real fears and hopes, the vision and the treachery.

PREFACE

At the centre of stage moves the maestro, with his genius and his God, with his anti-Baconian mould of having no discernible interest in applied science (as we would nowadays say), who produced a book comprehensible to four or five mathematicians in Europe, and fate moves with him. When he confronts a king, resisting his mandate, the king (James II) flees the country a year later. As he moves to the Mint, the Bank of England is founded. When he becomes President of the Royal Society, it is the foremost scientific society in the world. When he forms an enemy, he wrecks the death of such as well as the life. As he visualised his own life somewhat in biblical terms, so an echo here will be permitted – as part of his own self-image, if nothing else. He surely was, as Bernoulli described him, the 'restorer of solid philosophy.'

We here claim that he did *not* invent, conceive, discover, or even explain the law of gravity – however, he applied it. Likewise, he did not formulate, conceive, or use what we know as Newton's Second Law of Motion. But, looking on the bright side, he did formulate a law of cooling, as well as an inverse *cube* law of gravitation, for which he rarely gets credit, whereby tidal forces of the Sun and Moon vary inversely as cube of distance. He used this in his tide computations, otherwise only discovered in the next century by the great French mathematicians. He was in one sense the first to 'square the circle' with some competition from Leibniz, as we'll see. Glorious myths swirl endlessly around the hero and glitter with images of what never happened.

With apologies to Galileo, the three characters that were used so effectively in his dialogues – Salviati, Sagredo and Simplicius – have been resurrected from the pages of his *Two New Sciences*. They emerged, three and a half centuries later and still as argumentative as ever, to turn up at chapter endings and dispute over sundry points. They insisted on appearing, perhaps by way of complaint that the chapters had been unduly dogmatic or that other viewpoints had not received adequate expression. If the main endeavour of these pages is to stimulate informed debate, there seemed no reason to object to their appearance.

By way of assisting the reader in following the turbulent politics of the day, we here list the six monarchs and a Lord Protector who came and went during Sir Isaac Newton's life (1642-1726), and their dates of accession to the throne:

House of Stuart:	Charles I 1632 (beheaded in 1649)
	Interregnum 1649-1660
	Charles II 1660
	James II 1685
	William and Mary 1688
	Queen Anne 1702
House of Hanover:	George I 1714

The Dutch William of Orange became co-regent with Mary Stuart by a special Act of Parliament in 1688, as he declared that he was not prepared to remain a mere consort to the Queen. Georg Ludwig of Hanover came to England as Prince George, the consort to Queen Anne, and he later became George I of England in 1714, of the 'Hanover' dynasty. Caroline of Ansbach became Princess of Wales, and wife of the future George II, when she moved to London with the house of Hanover in 1714.

Glossary of terms

Achromatic	A lens of two types of glass, to minimise chromatic abberation, viz. colour artefacts seen round the edge of the lens.
Apogee	Each month the Moon is then furthest from the Earth.
Apse line	Long axis of the lunar orbit, joining Perigee and Apogee positions.
Baricentre	Common centre of gravity of Earth and moon
Eccentricity	Measure of the elongation of an ellipse.
Ecliptic	Plane in which the earth orbits the Sun.
Epicycles	Imaginary wheels in the sky used by astronomers before Kepler
Evection	Horrocks devised an elliptical method for coping with this largest of the lunar inequalities, originally detected by Hipparchus.
Medician stars	Four satellites of Jupiter, discovered by Galileo
Nodes	Points where the Moon crosses the ecliptic, twice monthly
Perihelion	When Earth draws nearest to the Sun each year.
Precession	The motion, one degree per 72 years, of the Vernal Point against the stars.
Principia	Philosophia Naturalis Principia Mathematica' published in 1686. In English the word order reverses as 'Mathematical Principles of Natural Philosophy.'
Quadrature	The half-moon positions.
Rectilinear	Motion in a straight line
Saros	A close synchrony of major lunar cycles, every 18 years, 11 days: Halley realised it would predict eclipses.
Sesquialterate	In a ratio of three to two, here alluding to Kepler's 3rd law of planetary motion.
Sidereal	Motion against the fixed stars. A sidereal day is four minutes shorter than the solar day.
Sidereal period	Time for one orbit measured with respect to the stars, 27.3 days for the Moon.
Vernal point	Sun's position at the spring equinox, in the zodiac.

Commended Bibliography

BAILY, F. *An Account of the Revd John Flamsteed*, 1835
CHAPMAN, A *The Preface to John Flamsteed's Historia Coelestis Britannica*, Greenwich Monographs, 1982
COHEN, I. B. *The Newtonian Synthesis*, 1980
DE MORGAN, A. *Newtonian Essays,* 1914
HALL, A. R. *Philosophers at War*, C. U. P., 1980
HALL, R. *Isaac Newton, Adventurer in Thought*, 1992
ILIFFE, R. *The Cambridge Companion to Newton*, 2016
MANUEL, F. A *Portrait of Isaac Newton*, 1968
MORE, L. T. *Isaac Newton, a Biography,* 1934
SABRA, I. A. *Theories of Light from Descartes to Newton,* 1975, 1981
WESTFALL, R. S. *Never at Rest*, 1980
WHITE, M. *Isaac Newton, The Last Sorcerer*, 1997

One has qualms about including the volume by White, with its crackpot title. And yet, it may be the only book on this list likely to have been perused within your circle of acquaintances. The others are only likely to be read by science historians; they belong more firmly in the past. The two films that can be viewed online -

> *The Secret Life of Isaac Newton* – Full documentary, 2014: 1.4 m views.
> *Newton the Dark Heretic* BBC2 2003 (focused upon a possible 2060 date for 'the end of world', in a Jerusalem manuscript)

will both tend to endorse Mr White's image, in seeking as ever for the 'real' Newton. You can only do that, by reading this.

Chapter 1

Ecce Homo

Shall the great soul of Newton quit this earth,
To mingle with the stars; and every Muse,
Astonished into silence, shun the weight
Of honours due to his illustrious name?
But what can man - even now the sons of light,
In strains high warbled to seraphic lyre,
Hail his arrival on the coast of bliss.

James Thomson,1727, 'To the Memory
of Sir Isaac Newton'

The 19-year old Isaac Newton started life at Trinity College as a sizar – a Cambridge term for a student who must earn his keep by performing menial tasks, functioning as a valet and emptying chamber-pots. And yet his mother was wealthy. To quote Westfall, his mother 'now begrudged him an allowance at the university that she could have afforded easily. Though her income probably exceeded £700 per annum, Newton's accounts seem to indicate that he received at most £10 per annum ... Despite her wealth she forced her son to be a sizar.'[1]

The young undergraduate student did have enough capital, however, to lend out money with interest. Lending or borrowing money between students was a violation of the Trinity College rules.[2] Papers preserved from this time show in neat columns how much his fellow-students owed him. Later, when he became the most distinguished of British scientists, *nobody* came forward from his student days to claim that he had known Newton then. One finds no other reference to his fellow-students than via this practice of usury. If he had sufficient money to lend it, then why did he need to practice usury? For a student who maintained so low a profile there is little else one can ask about these early days.

At his mother's home in Woolsthorpe, Newton had been surrounded by servants – who had, it appears, been relieved at his departure. Manuel, in his colourful opus, *A Portrait of Isaac Newton*, argued that a deep bond of affection must have existed with his mother; after all, a psychological study requires of its subject a close relationship with *someone* in a lifetime. This case has been well rebutted by Westfall, and chiefly for the above reason, that Newton's mother was wealthy yet sent her son to college as a sizar, but also because his mother abandoned him at the tender age of 3 to be brought up by his grandmother so that she could live with another man. His father died before he was born.

In his psychoanalytic study of the great scientist, Manuel found significance in some early school notes made at Grantham grammar school. These were translations from the Latin, and included sentences chosen in the manner of free association, with phrases like:

> 'A little fellow.
> He is paile.
> There is noe roome for mee to sit.
> What imployment is hee good for?
> What is hee good for?
> He is broken
> The ship sinketh.
> There is a thing which trobeleth mee.
> He should have been punished.
> No man understands mee.
> What will become of me.
> I will make an end.
> I cannot but weepe.
> I know not what to doe.'

Concerning this dismal choice of sentences for a Latin exercise, Manuel comments:

> 'In all these youthful scribblings there is an astonishing absence of positive feelings. The word 'love' never appears, and expressions of gladness and desire are rare. A liking for roast meat is the only strong sensuous passion. Almost all the statements are negations, admonitions, prohibitions. The climate of life is hostile and punitive.'

But, for an abandoned child, left to be brought up by his grandmother, they are understandable. Were the student loans his only means of relating to his fellow-students?

Some recollections of his student days were given by Newton. With Dr William Briggs, an undergraduate at Corpus Christi, he recalled dissecting an eye together. In the kitchen of Trinity, he recalled cutting the heart of an eel into three pieces and noting how they went on beating in unison together. An early optical experiment was performed at this time, where he stared at the sun continually and then noted the after-images formed, and then had to 'shut himself up in the dark for several

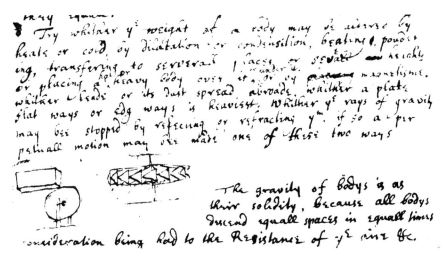

Sketches of perpetual-motion machines by the twenty-year old Newton: 'Try whether … ye rays of gravity may bee stopped by refracting or reflecting them, if so a perpetuall motion may be made one of these two ways.' c.1664.

days' before his eyes recovered. Later, he inserted a bodkin 'betwixt my eye and ye bone as neare to ye backside of my eye as I could', in order to observe the coloured circle images formed as he moved the bodkin about. One can only repeat the comment in a tercentenary volume, 'The reader is urged not to attempt to replicate this experiment.' (*Let Newton Be!* p.35)

His notebooks of the time show a keen and developing interest in natural philosophy. He mulled over a perpetual motion engine which harnessed the flow of gravity. If the downward flow of gravity-ether could only be reflected up again, somehow, or perhaps refracted, then one could generate perpetual motion. His student notebook shows a gravity-turbine sketch, powered by the flow of the reflected gravity-ether! His belief at that time was that, to quote Westfall, 'gravity (heaviness) is caused by the descent of a subtle invisible matter which strikes all bodies and carries them down' – a view which he later developed in his 1675 letter to the Royal Society.

Coming up to college in 1661, Newton was elected to a scholarship in 1664 and so ceased to be a sizar. Did he have a cat for company in those days, which grew fat on the meals he forgot to eat, a story from his niece Catherine Barton? It sounds unlikely. In 1667, he was elected a Fellow, which involved swearing to take holy orders in Trinity College. There is some irony here, as Newton was shortly to reach his heretical conviction that the Trinity did not exist. The great Watchmaker up above, he realised, took a dim view of the whole notion. It was, he came to realise, the arch-heresy of the whole of Christendom! In 1669, he accepted the post of Lucasian professor of mathematics, and dwelt for a further 26 years in Trinity College.

In the 1680s, he had an assistant Humphrey Newton (no relation) who gives interesting recollections, among them that Newton kept a huge pile of guineas by his door, as many as a thousand he estimated;[3] the purpose of which, surmised Humphrey, was as a test of his honesty. This youthful lending and hoarding of money foreshadows his later decades of work with Britain's currency. Also, Humphrey Newton recalled that, while walking in the fellows' garden, Newton was in the habit of inscribing figures on the ground with a stick, a somewhat Archimedes-like posture. 'If some new gravel happened to be laid on the walks, it was sure to be drawn over and over with a bit of stick, in Sir Isaac's diagrams; which the Fellows would cautiously spare by walking beside them...'[4]

There are perhaps two letters in the correspondence of Isaac Newton – seven bulky volumes of it – which seem to show an actual interest in another human being. One of these is a letter composed in May 1669 for a certain Francis Aston, giving sage advice about travel, and how to comport oneself when abroad, of what to inquire about, and so forth. The letter was never sent, a salient fact which Manuel omitted to note in his analysis thereof, and was as Westfall observed more or less copied out from another's advice on travel. Observed Westfall, 'The eloquence of the letter lies in its uniqueness. It is the only personal letter to or from a peer in Cambridge in the whole corpus of Newton's correspondence. In its uniqueness, it adds colour to the portrait of isolation in Stukeley's ... anecdotes.'[5]

There was a traditional tale that Isaac Barrow, the first to hold the post of Lucasian mathematics lecturer at Cambridge, resigned in 1669 so that Newton could have it. This was dismissed by Whiteside as 'sentimental gloss' in 1970, arguing that Barrow's resignation was more likely to have been motivated by a desire to acquire the post of Master of Trinity, to which he was appointed soon after. Persons holding the Lucasian chair were debarred from applying for such other posts.[6]

That same year, Barrow had notified John Collins of a powerful new opus by Newton, *De Analysi*, saying that its author was 'very young... But of an extraordinary genius and proficiency in these things'. *De Analysi* concerned the binomial expansion and methods of treating infinite series, but also it gave indications of something later to be called 'fluxions'. The sight of this work was enough for Barrow to recommend Newton for the Lucasian chair.

John Collins functioned as a clearing-house for mathematical correspondence. In the wake of the Great Fire he played a vital role when so many books had been burnt and mathematics was hardly a priority for reprinting as far as the publishing houses were concerned. He became the mathematical advisor to Henry Oldenburg, secretary of the new Royal Society. From the moment when Collins received *De Analysi*, the name of Newton began to be known.

Newton typically demanded the manuscript back and refused any inquiries for further details, but word got about by Collins making a copy thereof, without the author's knowledge or permission, and sending brief summaries of its contents to various mathematicians. Later, he showed his copy of the manuscript to one or two people, including Leibniz in 1676. Collins and Barrow finally abandoned their attempt to persuade Newton to allow his *De Analysi* to be published as a supplement to Barrow's *Opera*, which came out in 1670. *De Analysi* finally saw the light of day in 1711, by which time all its brilliantly original steps were but historical curiosities.

As mathematics lecturer, Newton could empty a hall. '... Oftentimes he did in a manner, for want of Hearers, read to ye Walls,' recalled Humphrey Newton, a trait which may remind one of Kepler, as mathematics teacher at Graz, or indeed of Flamsteed in his Gresham lectures. Westfall found a paucity of references to anyone who recalled attending his lectures over the years. Only two persons ever came forward to claim the kudos of having heard Newton's Lucasian lectures in Trinity when he had become famous throughout Europe. William Whiston, Newton's successor in the Lucasian Chair at Cambridge, could just about recall having attended the lectures, stating in his *Memoirs* that he 'understood them not at all'. Collins was in 1670 trying to persuade Newton to publish a formula on interest rates which he had computed: Newton replied that it could be published provided his name wasn't on it, for otherwise, 'It would perhaps increase my acquaintance, ye thing wch I chiefly study to decline'.

In 1676, Collins wrote to Newton asking him whether he would say more about his method in *De Analysi*, and received the reply, curious for a Lucasian mathematics professor, that he would be no more troubled on the matter and that he wished he could withdraw even those things he had previously given out (Nov. 8th). He added, in a telling phrase, '... It's plain to me by ye fountain I draw it from, though I will not undertake to prove it to others', *and he didn't*. Collins was asking about the brilliant methods of handling infinite series revealed in this opus – but posterity was to be more concerned with certain comments made en passant therein about what could be taken for, what somewhat resembled, the differential calculus. The dismissive reply to Collins left futurity with the hardly resolvable dilemma as to whether he really was in possession of a brand-new method superior to anyone else's, that of Leibniz in particular, and merely wished to keep quiet about it; or whether, as De Morgan concluded, he had developed fluxions as an innovative approach but was then unsure as to its rigour, and but for Leibniz would have left it lying amongst his mass of unpublished papers.

The poignant tale of Newton's phantom dog 'Diamond' occurs here: 'Most readers know the tradition of his dog Diamond,' wrote De Morgan (Essays,1914, p14.) The said dog one day knocked over the candle in his master's study and some papers on optics caught fire, and a distraught Sir Isaac then entered crying, 'O Diamond, Diamond, thou little knowest the mischief done!' By 1677, he might have decided to compile his optical notes for publication, then destroyed by a fire from a candle falling over. Could that account for the great delay in publishing his optical works, despite it being one of his earliest interests? Though the dog Diamond apparently never existed, the story indicates the popular need for an incident of some human interest about England's greatest scientist, which is otherwise hard to come by.

As member of parliament, only one remark of his is recorded; the request that a window be closed. The reader will find it strange, that so introvert a character as has here been depicted should be chosen to represent Cambridge in parliament. This is somewhat of a mystery. It can only be described as an act of genius, that when the ink of the *Principia* was barely dry in March of 1687, Newton should turn his attention to the religious-political crisis confronting his university, as King James attempted to foist a Catholic representative into a key university office, and that he should so distinguish himself as to be elected a year later to the brand-new parliament, in the wake of Britain's 'Glorious Revolution'. A letter of his urged 'an honest Courage' which could 'save ye University'. It was a success, and the next year King James fled the country. Newton remained in the 'Convention Parliament' for three years. He dined in 1688 with William of Orange, a month before William was proclaimed the consort of Britain's new queen.

The Mark of the Beast

Newton's earliest manuscripts on theology date from 1672. Prior to that, his comments on the deity seem as if made about some close acquaintance; for example, in his student notes on Descartes which commentators call '*De gravitatione et equipondere fluide*', he finds that he cannot endure the relativity of motion implied by Descartes' system, where everything swims around in vortices. He objects that in such a world, God would not be able to determine where Jupiter had been a year ago:

'If the place of the planet Jupiter a year ago be sought, by what reason I ask, can the Cartesian philosopher define it?... And so, reasoning as in the question of Jupiter's position a year ago, it is clear that if one follows Cartesian doctrine, not even God himself could define the position of any moving body accurately and geometrically...'

Some framework of absolute space was needed, for the Almighty to determine His co-ordinate system!

A year or so later, in 1669, we find an implicit reference to his deity in his explanation of how 'infinite equations' work, how one can sum a series having an infinite number of terms, even though the human mind could grasp only a small number of them. His *De Analysi* explained:

'this new method [of analysis] can always perform the same by Means of infinite Equations. For the reasonings in this are no less certain than in the other [viz., finite, ordinary equations]; nor are the Equations less exact; albeit we Mortals whose reasoning Powers are confined within narrow limits, can neither express, nor so conceive all the Terms of these Equations as to know exactly from thence the Quantities we want...'

The assigning of definite values for the converging infinite series he was developing involved reference to his deity, not subject to human limitations, the great computer-brain up above.

Newton's remoteness from others contrasted with the close relation he enjoyed with his deity. In the privacy of his study he thundered: '... Ye earth with them that dwell therein began to worship ye Beast and his Image...', the Beast being the Holy Trinity. To quote Westfall, 'The mere thought of trinitarianism, the "false infernal religion", was enough to fan Newton into a rage.' He saw it as idolatry, 'ye sordid worship in sepulchres of ye Christian Divi... Ye adoration of mean and despicable plebians in their rotten reliques,' and denounced corrupt monks. While writing the *Principia* he was decoding the Apocalypse, or at least this carried on throughout the 1680s. He searched for the pure unsullied Father-God religion as Noah had handed it down. By 1675, the fervour of his belief stood in the way of ordination. This was the accepted condition for his cushy job with only a very few lectures expected per term. Trinity College after all produced bishops, what else did it do?

Four times previously he had asserted his orthodoxy under oath at Trinity College but declined to do so again. In early 1675, he wrote to Oldenburg, secretary of the Royal Society, saying he requested to be excused his subscription, 'For ye time draws near yt I am to part with my Fellowship...' At the last moment, the Merry Monarch was prevailed upon to grant a royal dispensation, altering the terms of the Lucasian professorship, so that henceforth it required no taking of holy orders. It is believed that Isaac Barrow, the previous holder of that post, obtained this dispensation for Newton.

His entry into parliament demanded from him deception and secrecy over the burning issue of religious belief. His Arian heresy (denial of the Trinity) absolutely prohibited the tenure of public office. Even so, while in parliament he boldly composed *Two Notable corruptions* of scripture, these being the passages in the fourth gospel where the Trinity is apparently referred to, (especially 1 John 5:7) and had the nerve to send it to John Locke in 1690 – who it seems did share his shocking and unmentionable opinion – with directions that it be published in Holland, without authorship. This treatise referred to 'the hot and superstitious part of mankind' as adhering to the Trinitarian phantasm – i.e., the whole of Christendom! The more coolly logical part one assumes was to follow him in revering the new *deus supra machina,* his 'Pantocrator' God-over-All, who definitely never had a Son equal to Himself.[7] Later, realising just in time that its publication would spell the mere erasure of his career, he stopped it. These fears were well-founded: as was later discovered, the Dutch publishers had rightly surmised the author of the treatise.

The true religion of the patriarchs he traced back, reconstructing the original temple of Noah and his sons; there had been a fire in the centre, illuminated by seven lamps... 'The true religion was the most rational of all till the nations corrupted it,' Newton wrote. Christ was more a prophet like Moses than the agent of a new dispensation. 'All peoples worshipped one god whom they took to be the ancestor of all the rest,' Westfall explained. 'They described him as an old and morose man and associated him with time and with the sea...' (p. 352) This was all expounded in great detail in a treatise *Theologiae gentilis origines philosophicae,* composed in the 1680s, which Newton then realised that he could never publish. Westfall, whose initial studies of this period were theological, has dealt with this subject very competently, being probably the first person to do so. He described the *Origines* as 'the first of the deist tracts', deism being the religious system associated with the rise of Newtonianism in the eighteenth century. It rejected the Trinity.

In 1698, an Act for the Suppression of Blasphemy and Profaneness again forbade anyone disbelieving in the Trinity from holding public office. Newton tried once more for parliament, on the strength of being knighted by Queen Anne (in 1705) for his services to the Mint. At Cambridge, he met with hecklers objecting to 'Occasional Conformity', which was the accepted practice whereby dissenters qualified for full civil rights by taking the sacraments only once a year. 'No scene could have shaken him more,' comments Westfall. 'Only on his deathbed did he venture finally to refuse the sacrament.' Newton gave money for bibles to be distributed for the poor, a sage precaution.

William Whiston, Newton's successor to the Lucasian chair in Cambridge, scuttled his own career by speaking out against Trinitarianism. He was expelled from his lecturing post, it being clear to those in the know from whom had acquired that belief. Newton was understandably alarmed as to what Whiston might do next, and so we are hardly surprised that in his memoirs Whiston said of Newton that, 'He was the most fearful, cautious and suspicious Temper, that ever I knew'.

Whiston had only to name Newton as the source for his Arian heresy and the latter's future would have been jeopardised. Here was Whiston's view as to how he fell out of favour with Newton:

> 'But he, perceiving that I could not do as his other darling Friends did, that
> is, learn of him, without contradicting him, when I differed in Opinion
> from him, he could not, in his old Age, bear such Contradictions, and
> so he was afraid of me the last thirteen years of his life.'[8]

To Whiston belongs the credit of persuading Newton to publish a mathematical work. His *Arithmetica universalis* appeared in 1707, the substance of his Lucasian lectures on algebra, and was highly praised by Leibniz in an *Acta Eruditorum* review. Whiston gained no thanks for this. Newton complained continually about the title and supposed errors in the text and declined to have his name appended to it, though everyone recognised the author. In 1732, this widely-read opus was reprinted in three European cities: Leiden, Milan and Paris.

'A nice man to deal with'

A correspondence took place on a scriptural note between the eminent Whig philosopher John Locke and Newton in 1702. Locke sent a commentary on a bible text concerning baptism, hoping to receive some advice thereon. As the months passed and no reply came, he wondered whether he had in some way offended Newton, or were the commentaries not approved of? Instead of asking the question directly, Locke requested his cousin to deliver a note in person, cautioning that:

> ... I would fain discover the reason for his long silence. I have several reasons to think him truly my friend, but he is a nice man to deal with, and a little too apt to raise in himself suspicions where there is no ground; therefore, when you talk to him of my papers, and of his opinion of them, pray do it with all the tenderness in the world, and discover, if you can, why he kept them so long, and was so silent. But this you must do without asking him why he did so, or discovering in the least that you are desirous to know... And therefore pray manage the whole matter so as not only to preserve me in his good opinion, but to increase me in it; and be sure to press him to nothing, but what he is forward in himself to do.'

It seems that Newton had disagreed with Locke over the scriptural passage and so had not replied. The situation showed, More believed, 'Newton's inordinate sensitiveness and jealous personal pride, that a tried and trusted friend of Locke's reputation and character should have felt it necessary to counsel such elaborate precautions and so entrust another to find out the cause for not returning some loose papers.'[9] Locke never again met up with Newton.

A Bag of gold for Cheyne

George Cheyne was a Scottish mathematician who published an unduly advanced treatise on integral calculus, as a consequence of which his mathematical career came to an end. Inspection of Cheyne's opus, *Rules of the inverse method of Fluxions* must, in Whiteside's view, 'have given [Newton] a severe fright'.[10] Appearing in Scotland in 1703, this treatise very competently reviewed not merely British calculus, such as it was, but also the great strides forward which had been made on the Continent. This incident was the goad which finally drove Newton to publish his treatise on fluxions in 1704, entitled *De Quadratura Curvarum,* oddly appended to his *Optics.*

Dr Cheyne met his hero Isaac Newton in 1702, hoping to be instructed concerning his *Rules,* but was startled to have the latter merely place a bag of money in front of him. 'Dr Cheyne refused – both in confusion – but Sir I. [would] not see him afterwards', rather briefly recorded John Conduitt. Cheyne had admitted to being in need of financial aid for printing his book. Yet there was more to this scene than mere confusion over an offer of assistance. The great Swiss mathematician Johann Bernoulli declared Cheyne to be '*versé profondement dans cette matière*' after perusing a copy of the opus.[11] Could that have been a threat, which had to be dealt with?

George Cheyne, who practiced as a physician, was all too aware of the shortcomings of his opus, stating (to David Gregory[12]):

> 'This paper will be certainly incorrect, because I have none to inform [me] of my mistakes & none is fit to correct his own errors... Necessity, which begets so many bad authors... Has forced me to let my paper go and now I am about printing it.' Yet he was unprepared for the sustained attack on his treatise from Abraham De Moivre, appearing in 1704. 'It was, there can be no doubt, de Moivre's overriding purpose - on direct instruction from Newton himself... thoroughly to discredit Cheyne's character in the eyes of contemporary mathematicians.'[13]

Cheyne thereafter renounced mathematics. For a verdict on this skirmish we quote Whiteside:

> 'De Moivre, and Newton in his shadow, won the battle inasmuch as Cheyne, rightly soured by the squabble, thereafter withdrew from such 'barren and airy studies' for the more real and rewarding realms of medicine and religion. But the victory was an empty one. For all that Cheyne's talent was indeed mimicry rather than original expression, British mathematics in the early 1700's was not rich enough in men even of his secondary calibre that it could afford to have Newton and his aides so harshly and selfishly crush it.'[14]

De Quadratura Curvarum emerged as the first published Newtonian treatise on fluxions, having been composed a decade earlier in 1691/2 (not in the 1670s as was later alleged[15]) and its preface contained the vague but ill-humoured comment, 'And some Years ago I lent out a Manuscript containing such Theorems, and having since met with some Things copied out of it I have on this occasion made it public...' which experts believe was directed at Cheyne. Whereas the continental giants Leibniz and Bernoulli had followers who developed their calculus methods, Newton had none – he could only stand as a lone mountain peak.

A passion for Fatio?

In the fiftieth year of his life, Newton sent a letter showing concern for another human being. Fatio de Duillier, the Swiss 'mystic and mathematician' as Whiteside referred to him, had resolved to dedicate his life to promoting the work of Newton. He had shown his credentials by initiating the calculus controversy the year before, with the poisonous words, 'which idea [of the differential calculus] itself came to him [Leibniz], it seems, only on the occasion of what Mr Newton wrote to him on the subject'. (Letter to Huygens, 18.12.1691). Fatio became convinced he had a theory for the cause of gravity, which in the event did not see the light of day. He was mentioned in the mathematics text *De Quadratura* for a theorem he had developed, which was a near-unique honour, and he was in the early 1690s compiling a second edition of the *Principia*, though this did not materialise. It was a close relationship. 'I intend to be in London ye next week and should be very glad to be in ye same lodgings with you. I will bring my books and your letters with me,' wrote Newton in 1689.[16] 'Undoubtedly a passive homosexual' was the rather daft diagnosis of Peter Lancaster-Brown (*Halley's comet and the* Principia p.82), and Manuel opined on 'something sinful in his affection for Fatio which his censor could not cope with'. Fatio was the one person who overcame Newton's habitual remoteness; even Halley could not do that.

A letter was received by Newton from Fatio one day, in which the latter claimed to be sinking into a mortal illness, having not long to live. It expressed his fond affection and a grateful farewell; but then, rising above mere self-pity, the letter commended his brother to Newton as one able to serve him just as well as he, Fatio, had had the good fortune to have done. An agitated reply was immediate:

> 'Sr
> 'I have ye book & last night received your letter wth wch how much
> I was affected I cannot express. Pray procure ye advice & assistance
> of Physicians before it be too late & if you want any money I will
> supply you. I rely upon ye character you give of your elder brother &

> if I find yt my acquaintance may be to his advantage I intend he shall have it, & hope yt you may still live to bring it about, but for fear of ye worst pray let me know how I may send a letter &, if need be, a parcel to him, & pray let me know his character more fully, & particularly whether his genius lyes in any measure for sciences or only for business of ye world. Sr wth my prayers for your recovery I rest - etc.'

Concern for Fatio's welfare moves seamlessly into the option of getting to know the brother should Fatio pass away, and requests for more practical details on how to do this. Fatio had caught a slight cold and was soon well again.

Would Fatio like to move up to Cambridge from London, as the air would be better for his health? urged a 1692 letter from Newton. This proved impossible so another letter said, 'I must be content to want your good company,' adding that 'I fear you indulge too much in fansy in some things,' a propos of Fatio's interpretation of bible prophecies: sound advice though the latter seems not to have taken it, judging by the way he ended up in the stocks at Charing Cross some years later. He had become the secretary of a religious sect of undue 'enthusiasm', the Camisard prophets.

One letter of Fatio's which ends 'please burn this' described a secret alchemical recipe. The close liaison between these two men ended abruptly under the shadow of Newton's approaching nervous breakdown. To quote Westfall on this mysterious episode, 'It is unlikely that we will ever learn what passed between them in London. Their relation ended abruptly, however, never to be resumed ... The rupture had a shattering effect on both men. Newton rebounded from his breakdown, but Fatio effectively disappeared from the philosophic scene forever.' (p.538) Fatio left the community of natural philosophers to which he had for a while seemed to belong, and joined a French religious community, which perhaps better suited his volatile temper. His only slight further role in our story lies in the stimulus he gave to the calculus controversy.

Lord Halifax and the Mint

'Being fully convinced that Mr Montague upon an old grudge wch I thought had been worn out, is false to me, I am resolved to have no more to do with him,' Newton wrote to Locke in 1692, an indication that Montague should be viewed as one of the few people in some degree close to him, or at least less remote than others. Yet it cannot be maintained, as Voltaire so shockingly suggested, that as Chancellor of the Exchequer, Montague promoted Newton to his mint position merely because he was in love with his charming niece Catherine Barton. She was only sixteen when Newton was appointed Warden of the mint and clearly Halifax had not then laid eyes upon her.

In 1679, Charles Montague entered Trinity College, acquired an M.A. by a royal mandate and became a fellow. In 1687, Newton referred to Montague as 'my intimate friend' in a letter to Halley. Montague hired a mathematician to try and teach him enough mathematics so that he would be able to understand the *Principia,* but the effort was in vain. In 1696, Montague offered Newton a job at the mint, while it was passing through a crisis of recoinage, explaining that the job 'has not too much businesse to require more attendance than you may spare'. He was later to explain his motive as, 'He would not suffer the lamp that gave so much light to want oil.' Montague had become President of the Royal Society by the time he offered Newton the job of wardenship of the Mint.

If it was intended as undemanding work, events made it otherwise. The diarist John Evelyn noted, for May 1696, 'Money still continuing exceeding scarce, so that none was paid or received, but all was on trust, the Mint not supplying for common necessities,' and that was the month Newton started work at the mint. All old coinage had to be melted down and the nation became critically short of currency because of the recoinage through the summer of 1696. Work started at four in the morning and continued through till midnight, with fifty horses turning the mills to press out the new coinage. Over two million pounds sterling in new coinage was minted that year, a most dramatic time for Newton to enter his new career. The coins were made of silver and difficult equations had to be balanced because, if the value of the metals in the coins exceeded that of their nominal value, they would be melted down by sundry persons; while if they had insufficient silver in them, foreign markets would not accept them as currency. Yet, all this great struggle was in vain, the grand recoinage of many millions of pounds sterling was doomed, because the silver had after all been undervalued; the new coin was melted down by city goldsmiths 'almost as fast as it issued from the Mint' to quote Westfall. (p.567) Legislation poured out of parliament to try and halt the destruction of the new currency, but in vain.

It was too noisy to live on the premises of the Royal Mint, adjacent to the Tower of London, and Newton's handsome salary of £500 per annum purchased a house on Jermyn Street, near to St James' church, Piccadilly. He lived there for more than a decade. After the move to London, he hardly ever attended the Royal Society meetings for the remaining years of the seventeenth century. He went to church services at St James. In these days he became familiar with John Conduitt, who was later to marry his niece, inherit his job as Master of the Mint, and attempt the first biography, though this last ambition was not realised.

To Charles Montague, President of the Royal Society, was delivered Newton's reply to the challenge of the French mathematician, Johann Bernoulli, put out to test the pulse of the European mathematicians with regard to the new calculus of motions. Bernouilli published the problem in the German *Acta Eruditorum* in June 1697, and by December, no-one but Leibniz had solved it; Leibniz suggested publishing it in French and British science journals (the *Philosophical Transactions* and *Journal des savants*) to see if anyone could solve it before the next Easter, and the story goes that Newton received the problem in January one day after returning from a hard day at the Mint, and stayed up till four in the morning to solve it. 'As the lion is recognised by his print,' Bernouilli said, so he recognised the authorship of the solution, though it was submitted anonymously. The kindly reader will no doubt credit Newton's assertion that he solved the challenge on the same day as he received it. The one other person who submitted a solution was the French Marquis de l'Hôpital, the man who had composed the very first textbook on calculus But we come to this in Chapter 8.

Blood flows at the Tower

To some it has seemed inappropriate that the very representative of English science should spend three decades of his life employed at the Mint. 'The high priest of science was translated to the Temple of Mammon,' complained De Morgan. The science of economics is regarded as having begun in the 1690s, and the first paper notes were floated then. One smells a Newtonian flavour to what was then happening at the Mint, as a machine was for the first time employed to stamp out the new coinage, to foil the clippers. They had been obtaining silver by cutting small portions off the edges of the coins. By automating the procedure, the coins all looked identical, and this became more difficult.

The crisis at the Mint pertained to matters of weight and density. The coinage gathered in only had about half its proper density, i.e. massive nationwide pilfering of its silver content had been going on. Newton argued that the coins should be cast with 20 per cent less silver in them, but most, including John Locke, argued that it was imperative to keep a full silver content in the coinage, to maintain its value and credibility. Paper money was starting to be used while Newton was Master of the Mint, a position to which he was promoted in 1699 at a salary of around £1500 a year. His income varied because it was a defined fraction of the currency created each year. By 1698, £1 million in paper notes were in circulation.

The so-called 'Glorious Revolution' of 1688 locked Britain into a long war of attrition against France and massive new taxes descended onto the land to maintain a standing army, larger than any known hitherto, costing '£5 million and more each year'. Many of these novel tax systems blossomed in the fertile mind of Charles Montague. The 1690s were a period of industrial boom for Britain, and by 1716, London succeeded Amsterdam as the centre of world trade.

In 1701 Sir Isaac wrote, 'But though paper credit be a sort of riches we must not use it immoderately. Like vertue it has its extremes. Too much may hurt us as well as too little.'[17] England was the only European nation to succeed in creating paper credit in the early eighteenth century. It produced around £15 million in paper banknotes when it owned no more than £12 million in bullion, i.e. gold and silver. Amsterdam, London's great rival as a trading centre, did not produce bank notes in excess of its deposits of bullion until 1781. One may surmise that the gravitas of the Master of the Mint played some part in this difficult exercise in credibility. The banknote promises to repay in gold and will do so provided not everyone asks for it at once.

By changing the concept of currency from its concrete meaning into an abstraction, new power was obtained on which British trade could expand. Newton witnessed a million pounds being transferred to the bank of Amsterdam to pay for the British standing army without any gold being moved. We are here well into the modern world, where it is hard to say exactly what money is or just how it behaves, but our lives revolve around it.

It was surely appropriate that Newton presided over the manufacture of paper money. In the seventeenth century, abstractions came to be accepted as real, like gravity where no-one could comprehend how it could be exerted across the immensities of space, yet it somehow did so, and like atoms which no-one could see but of which everything was made. Natural motion was defined as a kind which never happened and could never be seen anywhere, as in the First Law of Motion and even white light, the very symbol of purity, was now somehow a mixture of rays differentially refrangible. Nothing was any longer what the senses seemed to indicate. Even mathematics, cast for millennia in the elegant mould of Greek geometry, was convoluting itself into fluxions which few could understand – 'the ghosts of departed quantities' Berkeley called them, or 'the art of numbering and measuring exactly a Thing whose Existence cannot be conceived' to quote Voltaire. Sensory experience was not just left behind, it was excised from the real world and wrapped up into 'sensoria' by John Locke![18]

Banks were beginning. Earlier in the century one kept one's gold at home; after all, where else was it safe? Merchants had kept their gold in the Tower of London which seemed fairly safe, until the king took it; Charles I seized £120,000 of theirs from the Tower in 1640. Then later, Charles II filched £1,500,000 from the goldsmith-bankers via their account with the Chancellor of the Exchequer, wiping out many small savings. After this trauma it was evident that a monarch-proof savings account was needed, and so the Bank of England was founded in 1694, two years before Sir Isaac arrived at the Mint. In 1697, there were just 25 public banks in Europe.

We are now in a quite different world from that of a mere century earlier, when the Chancellor of England Lord Burghley had written to the famed alchemist Kelly in 1591, at the court of King Rudolf at Prague, urging him to return home to England, because more gold was urgently needed to finance a foreign war. Or, if he could not come in person, the letter asked, could he at least send a small portion of his powder of multiplication? (Letter of Lord Burghley of 1591)[19]. Kelly had declined. But now, progressive thinkers realised, far from needing more gold, paper money could be printed.

Concerning the prosecution of those caught counterfeiting money, to whom no mercy was given, the following comments from Manuel's psychological study may be quoted, as pertinent to other disputes in which Newton became embroiled:

> 'In the Mint Newton was gratified with the exercise of naked power over his fellow creatures... Newton was not wholly delivered from the bondage of his anger by ranting at prisoners, for there was an inexhaustible font of rage in the man, but he appears to have found some release from its burden in these tirades in the Tower... for more than three decades the colossal wrath of Isaac Newton found victims in the Tower. At the Mint he could hurt and kill without doing violence to his scrupulous puritan conscience. The blood of the coiners and clippers nourished him.'[20]

As a picture, it invites comparison with Lord Macaulay's depiction of Francis Bacon, who interrogated persons while they were being stretched out upon the rack, likewise in the Tower of London.[21] Macaulay described Bacon as employing the rack to extract 'confessions' from persons for crimes they had not even committed, but nothing of the sort could be suspected in the case of the Master of the Mint. These stern interrogations in the Tower of London by Britain's leading natural philosophers may be metaphors for the new attitude towards nature, whereby her secrets were henceforth to be extracted.

'The Charming Bartica'

Mystery surrounds the place of residence of Catherine Barton, the noted London beauty and niece of Isaac Newton, during the decades when she resided in London. Did she live with the dissolute Lord Halifax for ten years and manage his household affairs, and if so was there a private marriage? Or was she chastely and demurely residing with her uncle all the time, as Halifax's official biographer would have it, and indeed, as Newton's official biographer David Brewster would also have it? Manuel declared that 'The riddle of the Newton-Catherine-Halifax relationship is insoluble' *(op. cit.*, p.259). Augustus de Morgan's version of events, which involved a secret marriage, could only be published posthumously by his wife, Sophie.[22]

Brewster and de Morgan corresponded on this matter, the former declaring the subject to be 'the most disagreeable portion' of his entire biographical study. Once Halifax died in 1712, the entire relation of Newton to Flamsteed altered, because the pillar of the former's support at court had melted away. In consequence, Flamsteed was able to take concrete steps to regain his astronomical data books which Newton and Halley had stolen from him, and also to gain possession of the publication of his data which Halley had brought out without his permission and against his will. Quite suddenly, the tables were turned. We return to this matter later, noting now merely an unusually strong bond between these two Whigs. Private scandal was indeed widespread during Newton's life over the Barton-Halifax affair, yet de Morgan was convinced that no 'dishonour' was involved.

The poet Dryden eulogised over Catherine Barton:

'At Barton's feet the God of Love
His Arrows and his Quiver lays,
Forgets he has a Throne above,
And with this lovely Creature stays.
Not Venus' Beauties are more bright,
But each appear so like the other
That Cupid has mistook the Right
And takes the Nymph to be his mother.'

Yet his ode on the untimely death of Halifax (who succumbed to a fever at fifty-four) lamented about 'thou, O Virgin-widow, left alone'. The biography of Halifax referred to her as being a widow before she became acquainted with Halifax, as its mode of accounting for the appellation 'Mrs'. This was in error, de Morgan pointed out, as she had never before married. Conduitt's memoirs referred to her dwelling for twenty years at her uncle's house while in London, which, de Morgan observed, left ten years of her three decades' life in London unaccounted for; she had moved to London in 1696.

It is pleasant to picture the two dwelling in the same household, the Master of the Mint and the society beauty, the former who made no bones about his lifelong virginity, who never showed any interest in the opposite sex, and the other who told Jonathan Swift the risqué tale of the countess who wanted to be buried by minions of Diana. As related by Swift, it involved a countess whose will declared that she was to be borne to her grave by bearers and a priest who were alike virgins; and so, after her death, lay unburied! Swift particularly relished this tale, as he did numerous others she told him. 'I love her better than anybody...' he told his diary, when complaining that he did not see her very often, owing to political difficulties as he was a Tory while she and Halifax were Whigs. Should a play about Sir Isaac come to be written – better that is, than Bernard Shaw's dismal effort – one feels sure that this domestic scene in Jermyn Street would provide somewhat more than comic relief. It would show the picture of Halifax hanging up in the President's study, that being the first sight the seventeen-year old Catherine had of him when she arrived into the busy metropolis of London.

Private marriages were, de Morgan explained, much more frequent in those days, and Halifax, as one whose rise or fall depended wholly upon popular opinion was not in a position to make a second marriage owing to the circumstances of his first. Already he had been ridiculed for marrying an elderly duchess in order to extricate himself from an ecclesiastical destiny and launch himself on a Parliamentary career – 'under the tutelage of a venerable matron,' as one broadsheet had it – and she died in 1698 leaving him with a convenient amount of ready cash. He thus could not well have survived society comment had he been seen to marry a lady twenty years younger than himself.

Society comment appeared however in no uncertain terms in the form of *The Memoirs of Europe* of 1710, a scandalous book of society gossip which sped through several reprints. It cast events as having taken place in ancient Rome, so that Halifax's abode was described as a palace by the Thames of lavish luxury and wanton debauchery. Its authoress, a Mrs Manley, knew Halifax's history intimately and 'cynically recounts all the scandals of his private life' to quote More. The Roman emperor who represented Halifax fumed that 'the charming Bartica' insisted that he marry her:

> 'I love her dearly, and have lavished myriads on her, besides getting
> her worthy ancient parent a good post for connivance. But would you
> think it? She has other things in her head, and is grown so fantastic
> and high she wants me to marry her, or else I shall have no more
> truly; 'twas ever a proud slut.'

Our scene now shifts to the Kit-Kat club in London in the year 1703, where Halifax was toasting a lady with, as was there the custom, some verse inscribed on a glass with diamond. Replete with imagery of the Mint, it read:

> 'Stampt with her reigning Charms, this Standard Glass
> Shall current through the Realms of Bacchus pass;
> Full fraught with beauty shall new Flames impart,
> And mint her shining Image on the Heart.'

Catherine Barton moved to Halifax's house in 1706, de Morgan concluded, as it was that year he made his will where all his jewels plus £3000 went to her, 'as a small token of the great Love and Affection I have long had for her' plus an annuity of £200 to Isaac Newton. Halifax's biography described her as having been 'Super-intendant of his domestic Affairs', but adds that as she was 'young, beautiful and gay', rumours could not but spread. Shortly prior to his death in 1713, Halifax altered his will making out £5,000 to her, plus Bushey Park (just north of Hampton Court) with a furnished lodge in it, 'as a small Recompense for the Pleasure and Happiness I have had in her

Conversation'. That comprised one-fifth of his whole estate. Flamsteed wrote in his sardonic manner to Sharp, he had left it to her 'for her *excellent conversation.'*

De Morgan also found Swift's *Journal to Stella* to be indicative, where Catherine is mentioned about twenty times. Swift visited her at her 'lodgings' and likewise visited Halifax at his 'lodgings' but never both together. As they were both his closest of friends, de Morgan concluded, it appears that he had been asked to be discreet. The notion of him dropping in regularly to the Master of the Mint's home is not very credible, as indeed it seems likely that they never met.

When Halifax died, Newton wrote to a relative of 'The concern I am in for the loss of my Lord Halifax, and the circumstances in which I stand related to his family,'[23] which de Morgan saw as fairly conclusive evidence, as the author of this note was one careful of words. The Barton family cherished the connection, and Catherine's first cousin had two children named Catherine and Montague. What became the 'Portsmouth Collection', the main compendium of unpublished Newtoniana, was passed down through the Barton-Conduitt lineage.

The President Laughs

> 'There is a story that only once was Newton known to laugh, when someone asked him what use he saw in the *Elements* of Euclid.'[24]

There are two or three occasions on record, in the 84 years of his life, when Newton laughed. A comparison may here be made with the morose Philip IV of Spain, who is said to have laughed but three times in his life. The first such occasion was recalled by Humphrey Newton who assisted Newton at Trinity: 'I never saw him laugh but once' he related, and that was after he had loaned an acquaintance a copy of Euclid. The acquaintance asked what use its study would be to him, 'upon which Sir Isaac was very merry'.

A second occasion came much later, when Newton in his old age was relating to Conduitt how he came to construct the reflecting telescope which he invented. Conduitt recorded, 'I asked him where he had it made, he said he made it himself, & when I asked him where he got his tools he said he made them himself & laughing added if I had staid for other people to make my tools & things for me, I had never made anything of it...' Here one feels is the honest pride of the mathematician who is also a fine mechanic (Westfall p.233). He was proud of the tin-arsenic alloy he had devised for the reflecting mirror – one of the several practical outcomes of his years of chemical researches, another being his employment at the Mint where he had to be able to discern true from debased currency.

His last laugh came when 84 years old, the year of his death, as he was preparing the third edition of the *Principia.* In conversation with Conduitt, he explained how a comet might be swallowed up by the Sun and thereby cause it to explode. So what would happen to us, an alarmed Conduitt inquired? The sudden heat death of the earth as the sun flared up would be the result, after all did not the Earth show the remnants of previous catastrophes? It might happen soon, perhaps next time one of the comets came round! The bright supernovae seen by Kepler, Tycho Brahe and Hipparchus, stars which flared up in unnatural brilliance for a short while and then vanished, were, the aged President believed, due most likely to comets impacting upon them. Conduitt recalled:

> 'That he could not say when this comet would drop into the sun. It might perhaps have 5 or 6 revolutions more first, but whenever it did it would so much increase the heat of the sun that this earth would be burnt and no animals in *this earth* could live. That he took 3 phaenomena seen by Hiparchus, Tycho Brahe & Kepler's disciples to have been of this kind, for he could not otherwise account for an extraordinary light as those were, appearing all at once among the fixed stars ...'[25]

The comet he had in mind here was the dreadful one of 1680. Of it one German scholar had written:

> 'I tremble when I recall the terrible appearance it had on Saturday evening in the clear sky, when it was observed by everybody with inexpressible astonishment. It seems as though the heavens were burning, or as it the very air were on fire... from this little star stretched out such a wonderful long tail even an intellectual man was overcome with trembling; one's hair stood on end as this uncommon, terrible, and indescribable tail came into view.'[26]

In such close proximity, was not some calamity bound to happen soon? Newton showed Conduitt its periods of returning as given in his *Principia*. If he meant to imply by certain phrases that it was due to fall into the Sun, Conduitt inquired, should he not make it clearer to readers? After all, it concerned them. The *Principia* did not deal in speculation, he replied, 'and laughing added he had said enough for people to know his meaning.'

Distinction

His whole life was one continual series of labour, patience, charity, generosity, temperance, goodness and all other virtues, without a mixture of any vice whatsoever,[27] noted James Conduitt. Here one can only quote Gjertsen, that 'The undiluted hero worship offered him by Conduitt is likely to have formed the basis for an agreeable relationship.'[28]

His interests in art, music and poetry can be summarised briefly, all too briefly. Concerning the Earl of Pembroke's famous collection of statues, he remarked that Pembroke was 'a lover of stone dolls'. He never diverted himself with music or art, recalled Conduitt, but it seems that he did once visit to an opera. 'The first act, said he, I heard with pleasure, the second stretched my patience, at the third I ran away.' The English classics – Chaucer, Spenser, Shakespeare and Milton – were absent from his shelves. Of poetry, Conduitt recalled that 'in later years he had so ill an opinion of poets that you could not do any man a worse turn with him than to say he was a poet. He always imagined that poetry was a study so very contrary to mathematics.'[29] (Such an attitude is reminiscent of the attitude to poetry of another great scientist, Charles Darwin, whose autobiography confessed, 'For many years now I have been unable to read a line of poetry.') In the court of George II, he had the tedium of having to listen to Handel playing the harpsichord; when 'Newton, hearing Handel play the harpsichord, could find nothing worthy to remark but the elasticity of his fingers.'[30]

The Bishop of Rochester, Francis Atterbury, took exception to Conduitt's reminiscence of Newton's 'lively and piercing eye', writing to a friend that:

> 'In the whole air of his face and mien, there was nothing of that penetrating sagacity which appears in his composures [i.e., portraits]. He had something rather languid in his look and manner, which did not raise any great expectations in those who did not know him.'

On the other hand, Bishop Burnett said that Newton was 'the whitest soul he ever knew'.

England bestowed its grandest honours upon him: Scholar of Trinity College; Fellow of Trinity College; Lucasian professor of Mathematics; Fellow of the Royal Society; Member of Parliament; Warden of the Mint; Master of the Mint; Knight; Justice of the Peace; and finally President of the Royal Society. And yet, the dark column of his mathematical power and genius appears to us as flawed by his inability to relate to other people. His biographer Sullivan observed, 'He seems to have been impervious to the arts... His understanding of other people seems to have been practically non-existent'. (p.244) Almost his only close relationships with people were with those whom he hammered into their graves, with the relentless and implacable fury of the Old Testament deity exterminating an enemy, and these three victims were the geniuses to whom he owed the most. In the process of so doing, he trod the ways of deception, and the many portraits of him painted through his life depict all too well the transformation wrought upon his being by so doing.

THE DARK SIDE OF ISAAC NEWTON

His prime interests were always with the non-living, the inorganic – from chemistry to coinage, from physics to theology – and his deity created a world that could as well have been uninhabited.

Let us conclude with Frank Manuel's closing remarks in his perceptive pschoanalytic study:

> 'The overwhelming question remains whether Newton's science, which gave him great power and little wisdom, can in some other incarnation bestow that wisdom upon his fellows. For the times are not yet fulfilled.'

A very English myth

The first account of a gravity theory having dawned upon Newton in or around the plague year of 1666 was related to William Whiston in 1694, twenty-eight years after the event, as Newton was emerging from his nervous breakdown. A later account was related to Pemberton, which version did involve a garden. Dryden had composed a poem about the year 1666, heralding it as the 'Annus Mirabilis,' and much had been expected of it. These initial versions have in common with the Genesis story, that no apple is there mentioned.

Accounts of the apple myth burgeon after Newton's death. Its very first mention comes from Stukeley the antiquarian, from a visit he paid to the octogenarian President when in the last year of his life. Stukeley journeyed out to the little village of Kensington, wherein the President was ensconced for the last few years of his life as his ailing lungs needed its fresh air. Away from the bustle and grime of London, he could concentrate on mapping out the precise design of the Temple of Solomon, in accord with the dimensions given in the Book of Ezekiel – an indication to the Creator no doubt of the kind of reception he had in mind in the Hereafter.

The President was back on speaking terms again with Stukeley, after a few years of ostracism due to the latter standing for a post in the Royal Society without full Presidential approval. Stukeley had just completed a thorough field study of Avebury and Stonehenge, had become the first secretary of the Society of Antiquaries, and was promoting his romantic concept of 'the Druids'. No doubt he was keen to expound on his concept of the 'Druid cubit' of 20.8 inches, or perhaps he was there interrupted by the ageing President, reminded of a dissertation of his upon the Sacred Cubit of the Jews, in which he had proved... What was it now? Appended to the *Chronology of the Ancient kingdoms* was a ground-plan for the temple of Solomon scaled in 'sacred cubits', which were '21½ inches, or about 22 inches', so perhaps the President felt that Stukeley's cubit measure was about right.

That very year, Stukeley was moving up to Grantham as a clergyman, the town of Newton's schooldays, so we may be sure they had much to talk about. No doubt Stukeley kept off the subject of the £20,000 which Sir Isaac had recently lost in the South Sea Bubble,[31] as likewise he avoided mention of his new scheme for the reform of astrology. But he may well have discussed his leading role in London's Masonic Lodge, frequented by so many of the Fellows of the Royal Society.

In a Kensington garden, over a cup of tea, that antiquarian heard the apple tale emerge *for the first time* in all its neo-biblical charm and simplicity. This was in the year 1726. Stukeley composed the first British biography of Newton, using material collected by Conduitt, who had intended to compose one but never got round to it.

The next year, when Sir Isaac Newton died, two written accounts sprang up of the apple myth, one by Voltaire, in his first collection of essays in English, who cites Catherine Conduitt as his source for it, and the other by one Robert Greene, who says 'that Martin Folkes had told him about Newton and the apple' – 'the gossip Martin Folkes' as De Morgan called him.

An amusing article 'Newton's Apple' by de Beer and McKie[32] gave a resumé of the legends, and castigated Brewster for having cast doubt on the story in his biography. Having ascertained to their satisfaction that the story derived from Newton himself, via Stukeley, the two authors regarded this as having settled the matter beyond all possible dispute. If anything, their survey established the converse. If a man only mentions what he presents as the key event of his life *sixty years* after it has supposedly happened and one year before he dies, that does not establish its veracity but rather more the opposite.[33]

For comparison, the German chemist August Kekulé waited some thirty years after his great discovery of the structure of the benzene ring before claiming that the idea had come to him as a dream while staring into the fire, and this interval is regarded by modern scholars as too large to be credible; especially since his notes around the time when he first presented the benzene ring concept, somewhat later than his alleged date for the 'ring' dream, show no sudden insight, but a gradual development of his idea. What now looks very much like being a completely fabricated myth formed by the ageing Kekulé has been endlessly quoted as showing how the scientific creative process works. A further painfully relevant aspect of the Kekulé story, is that it has now been suggested that the motive for his invention of the fireside-dream myth was that of avoiding an otherwise embarrassing priority claim from a colleague.[34]

The first Newton biography appeared in the year after his death, 1727, composed by the secretary of the French Académie des Sciences, Fontenelle. Relying mainly upon notes sent to him by John Conduitt, it is the only biography which lacks the apple myth. That primal myth was yet unborn – despite which, Fontenelle deemed it 'certain' that his subject had made his grand discoveries by the age of 24, i.e. in the year 1666.

Let no reader fear that mere bickering by this writer will eclipse the immortal tale, so universally known that the mere image of an apple falling can evoke it, which has grown into the very emblem of scientific inspiration and sunk deep roots in the national psyche. As a part of the English heritage, the apple story remains perennial. It has been psychoanalysed.

In the bold claim of the magazine *Garden Answers*, the apple falling on his head 'caused him to discover gravity'. Whatever the sources and reality of the story, it does have extraordinary popular purchase. Indeed, the British Post Office could presume complete public familiarity with the image of the apple as denoting Newton, and thus use it as an appropriate emblem for the stamp which marked the *Principia* tercentenary.

> 'It is precisely the popular appeal of this myth which should draw us back to it for closer scrutiny.... Is there not something marvellously reassuring about that tale? Nature quite literally knocks us on the head with the required knowledge! The story bespeaks an amazing integration between humanity and the natural world. And what better endorsement could there be for the potential of the 'gentleman scholar'? In addition, it is fundamentally a pastoral image, as are so many other cherished images of Englishness, including the paintings of Constable: it is, thereby, associated with that touchstone of Englishness - the countryside.
>
> This simple and often repeated tale resonates because it is so reassuring. Amidst the insecurities generated by nuclear technology and the big moral questions posed by molecular biology, genetic engineering, and the new reproductive technologies, it offers a more peaceful image of the generation of scientific knowledge – one which is fundamentally without conflict.'[35]

The old man died, but the tree lived on, in the family garden at Woolsthorpe: his tree, the apple tree, beneath which he may indeed have, as he later recollected, computed the area under a hyperbola to 52 decimal places – and has the world yet recovered from it, one may ask? In the 1820s this venerable tree was finally blown down by a storm, and some branches were chopped up into logs, one of which was presented to the Royal Astronomical Society, where it resides in a glass case to this very day.

DISCUSSION

Salviati: Why, the character of this creator of modern science, this hero of the English race, this Promethius of the modern age, has here received a scurvy treatment. Let me draw your attention to his deep humility, shown in the memorable remark he made at the end of his long and eventful life:

> 'I don't know what I may seem to the world, but, as to myself, I seem to have been only like a boy playing on the sea shore, and diverting myself in now and then finding a smoother pebble or a prettier shell than ordinary, whilst the great ocean of truth lay all undiscovered before me.'

Sagredo: And yet, Salviati, should we not pause awhile before accepting a third-hand quotation only published a century after the death of its supposed author – one who moreover never visited the sea-shore in his life? I admit it is one of the two most often-quoted lines attributed to Sir Isaac – the other being his phrase about standing on the shoulders of giants.

The words have a poetic ring to them quite unlike the authentic quotations from Sir Isaac. It seems that they first saw the light of day in some *Anecdotes* of a Joseph Spence in 1820. The source given was one Michael Ramsay who is said to have picked it up from Samuel Clarke or Fatio de Duillier when he visited London in 1730. Nothing resembling it occurs in the biography by Fontenelle, and he was sent the sayings and memorabilia of Newton as collected by John Conduitt, a very reliable source. It is the sort of edifying remark he would hardly have failed to include, had it been available. From Tower Bridge Newton would have viewed a polluted Thames lapping against merchant vessels, but as for pebbles on the sea-shore – I'm not convinced.

As to his humility, what about the Royal Society custom initiated by Sir Isaac, of having a mace placed on the high table while he was presiding over its meetings, with none but himself and a couple of secretaries allowed at that table? I believe that occasionally distinguished foreign visitors were permitted to attend at this high table as well. Then he proposed in addition having a couple of butlers attired in a special livery in waiting at the doors, but it seems the Royal Society baulked at this. And, what about the seventeen portraits for which he posed during his lifetime, did that show humility?

Salviati: It is too sweeping to claim that Newton had 'no imaginative understanding of other human beings'. Why, he mingled with a host of distinguished characters in post-Restoration high society, and people came from abroad just to see him. For a comment showing genuine psychological insight into another's predicament, allow me to point out his remark about how monks of old used to cope with temptation. Monks who fasted in isolation, he remarked, 'arrived to a state of seeing apparitions of women... and of hearing their voices in such a lively manner as made them often think the visions true apparitions of the Devil tempting them to lust'. Far from avoiding temptation, he concluded, 'these men ran themselves headlong into it'. The proper solution to such temptation, he observed, was to avert the thoughts by some other employment. I find this rather insightful.

Sagredo: That quotation indeed sums up his attitude towards the gentle sex. But, have I rightly understood you? Is your one instance of Sir Isaac manifesting an 'imaginative understanding of other human beings' to be found in his private jottings about Mediaeval monks? One may have doubts about the use of unpublished notes to derive such views: as the saying goes, he who takes a dead man's unpublished notes with a view to publication has added a new terror to Death. Didn't he leave enough in the public domain for us to assess his legacy? For the president of a society whose motto was '*Nullius in Verba*' (no trust in words), I would say he left rather a lot.

Salviati: That is an odd opinion, as nine-tenths of Newtonian manuscripts now perused by scholars are unpublished. Why, his published material is a mere tip of the iceberg. Do you wish to put back the clock to before the Sotheby's sale of 1936, when scholars were groping in the dark about how his genius unfolded? He burnt various documents before his death, no doubt personal matters deemed unsuitable for the eyes of others, which legitimises scholarly perusal of his unpublished work.

Sagredo: Now you mention it, his priority claims did tend to depend upon bringing out unpublished manuscripts from many years ago, and then having some acolyte testify to having seen them.

Salviati: Another noble trait of Newton's not mentioned by the author was his generosity, well-recalled in the Fontenelle biography, towards relatives, to aspiring mathematicians and indeed to people in various walks of life who wrote to him.

Sagredo: He did become wealthy – one only has to recall the £20,000 he lost with the South Sea Bubble of 1720 – and he bestowed his money where it would be appreciated. One colleague of his who needed financial assistance fairly desperately was the reverend John Flamsteed, so that he could employ calculators to expedite his work and not have to waste his own time continually taking on pupils for lessons; it was within Newton's power to procure such a grant, and whenever Flamsteed was asked how his work was coming on he replied that progress was slow on account of his lacking assistance in performing the computations. Newton never procured for him one penny. One cannot imagine Part III of the *Principia* without Flamsteed's superb data as its basis – from the angular sizes of the planets to the motion of Jupiter's moons, from his comet data on the 1680 comet to the Moon's motion – and yet he never responded to Flamsteed's piteous appeals for funding.

Simplicius: I am impressed by the temperance of his diet, whereby he abstained from tea or coffee, took no tobacco or snuff, and partook of wine or ale only at mealtimes. His regular breakfast consisted merely of sweetened orange peel boiled in water and some bread and butter. Also, I gather he became somewhat vegetarian in his later years. Doubtless this moderate diet and abstention from drugs contributed to his robust good health and longevity.

But, I fear that you two are missing the key to Sir Isaac's character, whereby that he saw himself as an interpreter of the Divine Plan, living on the eve of the fulfilment of the times. I mean, anyone who discovers so much about the universe must feel themselves to be close to the Maker, just as Neils Bohr used to tell Einstein that he must 'stop telling the Lord what to do'. In an age racked by civil war and 'enthusiasms' and millenarian prophets, which had only just stopped burning women on suspicion for witchcraft, his grand synthesis gave a superb image of political stability, of law and order. He could reveal that the Catholic Church as the Antichrist had only so many years left to go and deduce it from his simple principles of prophecy interpretation. His extensive decoding of the apocalypse may not have been published, but didn't it have a major effect on his circle of freethinking deistic colleagues?

Salviati: Well, perhaps, but let us not forget that he would not permit any discussion of theological matters to take place under his presidency of the Royal Society. They were kept in a separate realm.

I suppose that you have in mind Lord Keynes' 'Last of the Magi' ephitet in his tercentenary address to the Royal Society – what has been described as an 'unfortunately memorable phrase'.[36] The great economist alleged that Newton 'was not the first of the Age of Reason. He was the last of the magicians ... the last great mind which looked out on the visible and intellectual world with the same eyes as those who began to build our intellectual inheritance rather less than 10,000 years ago.' What twaddle! For myself, I regret that Lord Keynes did not address the matter of how paper money, the National Debt and the Bank of England came into being at more or less the moment in time when Newton arrived at the Mint. Then we might have learnt something.

Say what you like, he was a character who maintained an integrity in whatever he did, who did things thoroughly and who normally succeeded in whatever he set his hands upon. Just look at the way the membership of the Royal Society started to climb once he became its President: it kept steadily increasing because of the fine image he gave to the Society.

Sagredo: But, he was treacherous.

Simplicius and Salviati: What! How can you say such a thing?

Sagredo: I'm afraid so. Just look at those devious eyes in the portraits. He always had to be The Source, and so in the end could not acknowledge the genius of others.

To give an example, look at how he behaved over the pact with Flamsteed on the Moon data in the 1690s. He had repeatedly promised Flamsteed in writing not to make any public use of that data without first gaining the latter's permission – just as Flamsteed had been asked to promise the same thing with regard to the table of atmospheric refraction that Newton had supplied him with. Flamsteed's reason for this was straightforward, that he was in the process of improving his lunar data by recalibrating his fixed star co-ordinates on which the lunar data depended, so might wish to make corrections before anything went into print.

Then, Flamsteed discovers that the mathematician David Gregory has received some Newtonian pages to be printed on *Theory of the Moon* based on his data, published in 1702. He has not been informed about the matter, let alone asked for permission, nor can he find any trace of acknowledgement of where all the Moon-data came from in the article. And to cap it all, Gregory is given a story by Newton in 1698, that Flamsteed's Moon-data table was really Halley's, as he (Newton) had seen it in Halley's handwriting at Greenwich! Thereby he excused himself for using the data without any acknowledgement. That I find truly staggering.

Salviati: Well, perhaps it *was* Halley's data.

Sagredo: Not a chance. He hadn't the apparatus, let alone the patience. Flamsteed's diary records that he spent the best part of 1695 in collecting Moon data for Newton. There was no other astronomer in the world capable of taking readings to such accuracy in minutes and seconds. It was the very reason Greenwich observatory was set up, to gain the more accurate Moon-data. Halley would turn up at Greenwich now and then, attempting to pry some more lunar or planetary data from him, and I think Flamsteed normally tried to oblige; after all, Halley had helped him substantially in setting up Greenwich as an observatory in the early days, but the idea that he took lunar data from Halley just isn't feasible. One regrets that Brewster should have reported the story as true[*] – and indeed as the grounds for the Flamsteed-Halley rift – had been caught in act of forgery! The victims of Newtonian perfidy have had their names blackened by future historians – such was their fate.

---

[*] Lunar data used by Newton: David Gregory wrote, 'Newton often told me, but especially in December 1698, that these tables [Flamsteed's lunar ones] were first made and computed by Edmond Halley, and communicated to Flamsteed, and published by him without the knowledge of Halley, and that this theft was the origin of the eternal quarrels between Halley and flamsteed. Newton said he had seen the handwriting of Halley.' Brewster, Vol. II, p.166. (see also Cohen, Intro. to Variorum Principia edition, 1971, p.176). For Flamsteed's comment on this rumour, see his letter to Colson, 10.10. 98, (in Correspondence, Vol. IV): 'Mr Halleys [table] could be of no use to him, because he [Halley] used the Tychonic places of the fixed stars to rectifie and state the Moons by.' The old positions of the stars from the Tycho Brahe era were too inaccurate for any *Principia* computations.

Simplicius: Why, this is a shocking tale, but it strains my credulity as lacking a motive.

Sagredo: I thank you for raising that issue, Simplicius. Around mid-1695, the Cambridge mathematician had to accept that his grand ambition of accounting for the Moon's motion – what today's mathematicians would describe as a three-body problem – by his theory of gravity was making very little progress. Edmund Halley had spread it far and wide that he was engaged upon the problem, so the eyes of the world were upon him, but all he could come out with was a slight rejigging of the rules or 'equations' that Flamsteed was using.[37] As a north-country astronomer, Flamsteed was very familiar with the work of Horrocks, indeed he was its prime exponent and was known to have improved upon it, as the best approach available to lunar prediction.

But, Newton let his improvement of the Horrocks-rules be printed, with a proclamation by Gregory that they were derived from his theory of gravity, and some exaggeration of their predictive accuracy. A person capable of assessing these rules was John Flamsteed. And so it was that after 1695, he started to treat Flamsteed as a mere nuisance.

Salviati: I'm not surprised he fell out with that crotchety and irritable old character.

Sagredo: In other aspects of his life, one finds the same pattern. When calculus was discussed, he had to hope no-one would realise his claim to have first written his *Principia* in fluxional terms and then re-cast it geometrically was a complete fabrication to bolster a priority claim. When politics arose, he had to hope none of his deist disciples would let the cat out of the bag that he fervently disbelieved in the Trinity, a heresy which absolutely barred entry to British politics. When the subject of gravity came up, he had to deny that Hooke had suggested the law and a great deal more besides both to him and to the Wren-Halley coffee house meetings; telling Halley that Wren had mentioned it some years before Hooke, which he hadn't. In the same way, when social mores were the issue, he had to hope that no-one would notice the affair his niece was having with the great courtier Lord Halifax, the key to his political power.

Simplicius: Enough, Sagredo! At times your tongue seems to run away with you. You should blush to make such accusations against this paragon of modern science. In that heroic age of science, he sought for a unity in knowledge, and found it.

The three characters first appeared in Galileo's 'Dialogues concerning Two World Systems', where Galileo's view was expressed by Salviati, Sagredo was an informed layman, and Simplicio was a dyed-in-the-wool Aristotelian. Salviati and

Sagredo were the names of persons known to Galileo, while the third of Galileo's characters was named after Simplicius, a commentator on Aristotle whom he admired excessively, in Galileo's view. They were accustomed to meet at a house in Florence for their historic trialogues. In the present discussions, Salviati has matured into a science historian[38] but it is Sagredo who gives expression to the author's view. Simplicius seems to have forgotten his Aristotle and now plies the trade of a mathematics schoolteacher.

Chapter 2

To Unweave The Rainbow

I would like your opinion about Huygens' explanation of light, assuredly a most brilliant one since the law of sines works out so happily.

Leibniz to Newton, 7 March 1693

A 'New Theory of Light and Colours'

Glowing with the praise received for his new telescope from the Royal Society – the 'catadioptrical telescope' as he named it – the 30-year old Isaac Newton, Fellow of Trinity and Lucasian Mathematics professor, intimated that he could also, if they so wished, deliver a work on optics. This had been the topic for his first course of lectures from the Lucasian chair, in the Lent term of 1670, and though it nowadays seems an odd thing for a mathematics lecturer to tackle, he was merely following in the footsteps of Isaac Barrow, who had recommended him for the post. Barrow's lectures had covered received theories of optics, such as Kepler's 'Dioptrics' and Descartes' theory of the sine law of refraction, and the dispersion of white light into coloured refractions. For the latter, Newton was to coin the word, 'spectrum'. Kepler's treatment thereof, one may add, showed a thin white line in the middle of the spectrum.

Much earlier, in 1664 as a mere undergraduate student, his interest had been awakened by such mathematical issues as, what was the ideal contour for a convex lens? A spherical shape gave a somewhat blurred focal point, and in telescopes with two lenses together, much detail at the edges was lost. And then what about the colours of the rainbow? In 1668, he purchased a prism at a summer fair, perhaps that of Stourbridge. He also looked at what we now call the interference patterns of light, for Robert Hooke's *Micrographia* of 1665 had described how coloured rings appear through thin films; nowadays called 'Newton's rings'. What about the spacing of these rings? Descartes' sine rule meant that light must somehow be amenable to mathematical treatment.

There were, he explained in his lectures, five main colours formed when sunlight refracts through a prism, and these were blue, green, yellow, orange and red, and perhaps some others. Did not such phenomena show that light was formed of corpuscles, and could not this also account for the colour rings around the lens? Refraction meant that red corpuscles were stronger, or perhaps bigger, because they bent less than the blue on being refracted, he concluded. The coloured rings in thin films were periodic, as Hooke had shown. The young Isaac was excited to find that the squares of the diameters of these light and dark circles followed an arithmetical progression. He could never manage, however, to account for these rings and their sequence of hues by means of his (wholly mistaken) corpuscle theory.[1] One may add, that his particle theory was a modification of Descartes' view, that light was composed of ether-particles, which moved differently according to their colour.

Supposedly from his belief that refracting telescopes could not be much further improved, owing to lens refraction difficulties at higher magnifications, he built his radically original reflecting telescope, which gave X40 magnification – 'this prodigy of art' as John Flamsteed called it.[2] The skill was in casting and polishing its smooth, concave mirror, and if one or two unsatisfactory attempts had been made hitherto in constructing a reflecting telescope, they had failed on this. Isaac Barrow carried this brilliant invention to London in December 1671, where it caused a sensation and met with royal approval. Barrow had earlier been employed at Gresham College as a mathematics lecturer before being appointed to the chair at Cambridge, (the Royal Society was situated at Gresham College, located where the Barbican now stands) so this seemed appropriate. There was a deeper connection with Barrow, because it was he who taught or passed on to Newton what later came to be known in more general forms as the methods of integration and differentiation (though in a geometric form). Prior to the arrival of this telescope, only a few mathematicians in the Royal Society had heard of Newton through John Collins, a mathematical correspondent who functioned as an advisor to Henry Oldenburg, Secretary of the Royal Society.

In reply to their queries, Newton happily sent on to the Royal Society the ratio of copper, tin and 'white Arsenic' whereby he cast the mirror, which was optimal he had found at 12:4:1. 'Bell metal' was no use he explained to them because although it had a fine reflectance, and could be white enough if the arsenic powder was added in, it bubbled on solidifying so the surface was useless (it contained silver which absorbs oxygen from the air upon melting). His recipe became known as 'speculum metal'. It had the drawback of tarnishing after a few weeks and so the telescope was not of great practical utility. For this reason, reflecting telescopes were hardly developed prior to the 1740s – they required a silver film to be precipitated onto a concave parabolic glass surface, and the chemistry required for this was not available any earlier. The two reflecting telescopes that Newton built reflected some 16 per cent of incident light.

He would also let them have a 'Philosophical discovery' of his about light, which had caused him he said to design his telescope, adding modestly that it was 'in my Judgement the oddest if not the most considerable detection wch has hitherto been made in the operations of Nature'.

The Seeds of Discord

In his paper on the theory of light which he submitted to the Royal Society in 1672, Newton explained that what he was here proposing was not conjectural, or probable, but merely certain. This was not quite the Baconian approach which the twelve-year old Royal Society of London was endeavouring to foster, so its Secretary Henry Oldenburg decided to omit from its journal the *Philosophical Transactions* the polemical section, which read:

> 'A naturalist would scarce expect to see the science of those (colours) become mathematical, and yet I dare affirm that there is as much certainty in it as any other part of optics. For what I shall tell concerning them is not an hypothesis but most rigid consequence, not conjectured by barely inferring 'tis thus because not otherwise, or because it satisfies all phenomena (the philosophers universal topic) but evinced by the mediation of experiments concluding directly and without any suspicion of doubt.'

In other words, if anyone disagrees I shall be *very* angry.

Hooke, for whom candour was a more pronounced virtue than tact, was a referee and was shown the unexpurgated version. As he saw it (quoting the Israeli science historian Zev Bechler):

> 'this was raving nonsense. No theory in physics could possibly be "a most rigid consequence" of experiments, "concluding directly and without any suspicion of doubt." Theories were never "necessary." So the greatest part of his review letter was an attack against this apparent dogmatic naiveté of the newcomer. Newton never succeeded in convincing Hooke, nor anybody else for that matter.'[3]

The First Wave-Particle Debate

What the bold newcomer proposed in this 'Philosophical discovery' was nothing less than that white light itself was composed of the different hues into which it was split by refraction. Pure colours meant those which could not be split up any further by refraction, while mixed colours were produced by blending these pure colours,

47

e.g. orange or green. He found 'The most surprising and wonderful composition was that of whiteness: white light is a confused aggregate of rays imbued with all sorts of colours.'

This was, he admitted, hard to imagine. Light, '... Produceth in our minds the phantasms of colours', showing that he was au fait with the Cartesian outlook whereby colours were produced in the mind by mechanical agitations etc in the outside world, in contrast with Aristotle's view that colour was inherent in the objective world. So white light was composed, on his theory, not of the colours themselves, but just the rays. But what were the rays? This was no concern of his, was the austere reply. An answer to that would be a mere hypothesis, and Newton was not concerned with such.

This was no mere theory or hypothesis, its author explained, like Descartes' view that light consisted of ether particles, or like Hooke's view in his *Micrographia* that light was a wave-effect rippling through the ether; why no, it was a statement of what could be directly observed from experiments. But could it? People found it an impressive but hard to follow piece of theorising. 'To the same degree of Refrangibility ever belongs the same colour, and to the same colour ever belongs the same degree of refrangibility' was his 'Doctrine' (refrangibility means refractive index). In the next breath he added that the very same colours could also be formed by mixing light, for example red plus yellow light gave orange, and 'orange and yellowish green makes yellow.' Did that conflict with his earlier affirmation that colours were specific to a refractive index? He concluded that '... It can no longer be disputed ... Whether Light be a Body.' A particle model of light was fairly clearly implied in this first paper on light, even though its author was claiming – as a few persons objected – that there was no need to discuss such an assumption. Two successive issues of the Philosophical Transactions carried, first his theory of colours, and next his telescope design.

The critique of Robert Hooke appears to this writer (though not to many others) as fair, helpful and constructive for an up-and-coming new member of the Society. It praised his fine and careful experiments, pointed out the theoretical weaknesses and suggested where further work could be done. Hooke was not sure that further improvement in refracting telescopes should be written off owing to chromatic aberration: 'the Difficulty of Removing that inconvenience of the splitting of the Ray and consequently of the effect of colours, is very great, but not yet insuperable'. The author of the paper was fortunate in having so comprehensive an evaluation of his thesis, by one of a different theoretical disposition. Hooke was perplexed by the notion that all the colours produced must be already present beforehand in the white light, which seemed to him a gratuitous assumption:

> 'I doe not yet understand the necessity; noe more than that all those sounds must be in the air of the bellows which are afterwards heard to issue from the organ-pipes.'

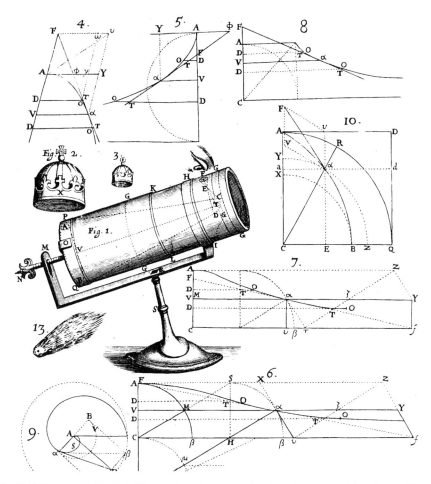

The Phil Trans. of March, 1672 showing the new reflecting telescope, with John Wallis' maths in the background.

He would be quite willing to consider a particle model for light, if only some empirical evidence could be brought forward in support of it and invited Newton to do so. This was a reference to Newton's claim that 'it could be no longer disputed... Whether Light be a Body'. This reply was not published in the Royal Society's journal.[4]

Initially with clenched teeth Newton replied merely, 'I... Am glad that so acute an observer hath said nothing that can enervate any part of it,' adding, 'You shall very suddenly have my answer'. 'Very suddenly' turned out to mean three months later, when a fifteen-page reply was received by Oldenburg. Like a refrain of fury, Hooke's name was repeated twenty-five times, in 'a paper filled with hatred and rage', as Westfall called it (p.247). Could one not print the paper without mentioning the names of persons disagreed with, delicately replied Oldenburg (the secretary's job *was* trying at times), because (in noble words) 'those of the R. Society ought to aime at nothing, but the discovery of truth, and ye improvemt of knowledge, and not at the prostituting of persons for their mis-apprehensions or mistakes'? After brooding over the matter for two weeks the reply came, 'I understood not your desire of leaving out Mr Hooks name...'

To start with, Newton was furious with Hooke for indicating that further development of refracting telescopes to overcome the aberration problems might be feasible:

> 'The first thing that offers itselfe is lesse agreeable to me, & I begin with it because it is so. Mr Hook thinks himself concerned to reprehend me for laying aside the thoughts of improving Optiques by Refractions. But he knows well yt it is not for one man to prescribe Rules to ye studies of another...'

This whole reply was printed in the *Transactions* with Hooke permitted no further comeback, which must have done nothing to improve his migraine attacks.

Next, the reply firmly denied that any 'hypothesis' was being proposed. Hooke was, it fumed, 'ascribing an hypothesis to me which is not mine'. In his critique, Hooke had said:

> 'But grant his first proposition that light is a body, and that as many colours or degrees thereof as there may be, soe many severall sorts of bodys there may be, all which compounded together would make white...'

This was the theory implicit in Newton's colour paper, which Hooke was spelling out and calling it a hypothesis, and further asserting that it was not certain but merely possible. Newton here claimed that this hypothesis 'is not mine', but in the *Principia* and then more definitely in the *Optics* just such a particle model of light was to be argued.

Next, Newton's reply evaluated Hooke's wave-model of light, which 'I am mistaken if there be not both Experiment and Demonstration to the contrary'. Hooke was an early proponent of the wave-theory of light and Huygens acknowledged him as a forerunner, when his wave-theory emerged in 1690. This wave-model Newton first summarises as, 'the vibrations which make Blew and Violet are supposed shorter then those wch make Red and Yellow...' Against this (correct) theory his objection was that light could only travel in straight lines, demonstrating that he had not then come across the phenomenon of diffraction.

The initial 'New Theory of Light and Colour' dealt solely with the reflection and refraction of light. Interference was known since 1665 with what posterity called 'Newton's rings' but had not formed part of the debate so far; evidently it was a different kind of phenomenon from the 'rays differently refrangible' of his prism experiment, if only because the colour sequence was in reverse. A rainbow had blue as the most refracted hue at the top, with red at the bottom, while for the interference rings the blue is smallest and nearest the centre while the red ring is largest. As Hooke first brought optical interference phenomena to the attention of the Royal Society so he was also the first to point out the phenomenon of diffraction, and he did so in direct reply to Newton's challenge concerning his wave-theory.

A Shaken-up Hooke

Writing to the President of the Society, Lord Brouncker, Hooke said of his reading of the reply from Newton:

> '(I) should have done it with much more pleasure had I not thereby understood that somewt that I had sayd in my first paper had given offence to one that I had noe thought much lesse any Designe to disoblige: and if there is any thing therein that any way savours of incivility or reproach I doe heartily begge his pardon and assure him twas innocently meant. The truth is I never intended it for Mr. Newtons perusall which if I had might possibly have been more choice in my expression, and have taken more time in the penning thereof. for I doe assure your Lordship I had not above three or 4 hours times for the perusall... For twas to fulfil your Lordships commands not any concern of my owne that made me give your Lordship my opinion of Mr. Newton's Theory.'

He is still in a state of near-incredulity that open-minded debate over differing explanations should cause offence:

> 'But I was so far from imagining that Mr. Newton should be angry that I cannot yet believe that he is or will be soe for any concerne in a philosophicall Dispute wherein certainly if anywhere a freedome & liberty of Discoursing and arguing ought to be Tollerated.'

Concerning the matter of telescope improvement by the study of refraction and how his words had been interpreted by Newton:

> 'I misunderstand myself if my words would bear either interpretation which were these. I am a little troubled that this supposition should

make Mr Newton lay aside the thought of improving telescopes & microscopes by refraction since tis not improbable but that he that has made soe good an improvement by reflection would have done more by refraction &. I think I neither reprehended him nor prescribed Rules to his studys.'

Hooke then gives (June 1672) to Lord Brouncker the first account of diffraction in the English language, in support of his wave theory of light. It concerned 'the seeming Impossibility which he [Newton] hath fixt on the fundamentall supposition'. With a beam of sunlight entering a darkened room, and a razor blade held up across it, so that the ray falls on a screen:

> 'your lordship plainly saw, that the Light of the sun did Deflect very deep into the shadow ... I am very confident he (Newton) will ascribe that deflection of ye Rayes neither to Reflection nor Refraction.'

This confidence turned out to be unmerited because, Newton, once he heard about it, was going to persist in explaining the phenomenon by refraction for all the rest of his days.

In these letters of Hooke there are two references to scientific authorities. 'Occam's razor' from William of Occam (Ockham in Surrey); '... supposing it wholly useless to multiply entities without necessity' he says, over his doubt about Newton's affirmation that there pre-existed an indefinite number of colour-rays in white light. Then on the more general issue involved, the very principle of the scientific method, Hooke reaffirmed his belief from the great Lord Bacon:

> 'I see noe reason why Mr. N should make soe confident a conclusion that he to whome he writ did see how much it was besides the business in hand to Dispute about hypotheses. For I judge there is noething conduces soe much to the advancement of Philosophy as the examining of hypotheses by experiments & the inquiry into Experiments by hypotheses, and I have the Authority of the Incomparable Verulam to warrant me.'

There is no anger or malice in his response to the fairly savage attack to which he has just been subject.

The above-quoted letter by Hooke was never sent to Newton. Its conciliatory tone might have done much to pour oil on troubled waters, quite apart from informing him of the existence of the phenomenon of diffraction, as a direct reply to his 'Demonstration' against the wave-theory. The Royal Society, given a clear answer by the Society's expert on the matter, omitted to forward it.

The Debate Continues

The opening words of Grimaldi's *Optica* of 1665 were:

> *'Lumen propagatur seu diffunditur non solum Directé, Refracté, ac Reflexè, sed etiam alidquodam Quartomodo, DIFFRACTE.'*

> (Light will propagate in straight lines, can be refracted and reflected, but as well as these it can also be diffracted.)

Since that initial account of diffraction by Grimaldi, one further major property of light had been described, with which a theory of light had to grapple, namely interference, with Hooke's discovery of what came to be called, 'Newton's rings.' Then there was the discovery of a velocity to light – reported by Roemer to the Paris Academy of Sciences in 1676, from the phasing of the satellites of Jupiter in their eclipses – which greatly stimulated such theorising. Also, Iceland spa crystal disclosed the phenomenon of polarised light to Huygens, however this contributed little to the theoretical debate in England. Reflection and refraction were plausibly argued on both the wave and particle theories.

The Newtonian particle-theory had what Whiteside has called the 'ineluctible corollary that the speeding light-corpuscle must move faster in a denser medium than in a thinner one.'[5] Was this credible? The *Principia* was to explain it, but it seemed an odd thing for corpuscles to do, and it was to be nearly two centuries before Foucault demonstrated that the reverse was the case. In the case of interference and diffraction, it is difficult to see how anyone could perceive them in terms other than a wave theory.

The Reverend John Flamsteed took a common-sense view of the new theory of colours; he used the refractive index values as given by Newton's optics paper simply because they were more accurate than others. He viewed this aspect of Newton's paper as quite original. In one of his 1681 Gresham lectures he stated:

> 'Concerning the proportions betwixt ye sines of the sayd angles, few Authors agree with each other by reason that they are difficult to be observed. The usual way of observeing is by the prisme or triangular glasse.'

Sunlight thus split up appears:

> 'spread over with different colours which as Mr Newton has well showne prove that the raies of light are of different formes & that ye severall sorts are proper for representing severall colours; now

before this discovery of his, those that made experiments by the prisme for ye measures of reflections were doubtfull on which part of the Coloured oblong image of the Sun they ought to pitch.'[6]

A down-to-earth interpretation of Newton's colour theory by Britain's only professional astronomer! He found the refractive index value of 14 to 9 given by Newton for glass to be more accurate than the 3 to 2 ratio given by Descartes. Concerning the theory involved, however, he rightly surmised that, 'I rather think that the raies of light move not so swiftly thru ye prism as in the free aire'. (to Collins, 17.4.72)

The 1672 paper had a central experiment or *'experimentum crucis'* – a phrase taken from Hooke's *Micrographica,* where the coloured interference patterns were so called, because of the 'crucial' fact about them that they could supposedly not be interpreted by reflection or refraction. This *'experimentum crucis'* involved two prisms; a thin beam of sunlight in a darkened room was split by the first prism, and then a screen having a narrow slit allowed just one part of the spectrum to pass through onto a second prism. The 'crucial' observation was supposed to be that no further change of colour could be seen in any splitting of the light by the second prism. A leading French experimentalist of the seventeenth century, Mariotte, with impeccable credentials as a natural philosopher, found that he could not replicate the experiment, and thereby blocked the spread of Newton's colour theory in France. In the case of red light, the *'experimentum crucis'* worked adequately, Mariotte found, in that red stayed red once obtained and would not change into anything else, but for purple he was led to reject Newton's experimental result; his second prism would split up the purple into red and even some yellow.

The Newtonian theory could account for red and yellow light adding up to orange, but not that red plus blue should make purple. Later on, Newton joined up the two ends of his spectrum rather unaccountably to form a ring. Spinning this ring around made the hues blend into white light.[7] With the modern physiological theories of colour receptors in the eye we can appreciate how the extreme end of the blue/purple blends into red, though this is at the other end of the spectrum if arranged by wavelength. For Mariotte, what he saw refuted the theory; his second prism modified the purple to give what was supposed to be right at the other end of the spectrum, namely, red.

Another Frenchman Lucas reached similar conclusions. His comments were subtle, as would be expected from a Jesuit priest who lectured in mathematics. He appreciated the eloquence and force of logic in the argument. He found somewhat circular the claim that light consisted of rays differently refrangible, where the rays were seemingly defined just by their different refractions. He suggested some other possible light experiments to the Royal Society, doubted whether the *experimentum crucis* was quite so crucial, and persistently saw red when purple light was re-refracted, inferring, as did Mariotte that this refuted the theory in question. Newton's replies degenerated rapidly into sheer abuse:

'But since you know not how to make these separations, I perceive you never yet saw any of ye Primary colours about which you have written so much, nor know what they mean.'(6.3.77)

Touching here is David Brewster's account of how his hero dealt with the correspondence arising from the optics paper. 'No personal invective ruffled his equanimity; no vulgar jealousy roused his indignation.'[8]

Christiaan Huygens, the 'doyen of European science', declared that Newton had not solved 'the great difficulty of explaining by mechanical physics wherein this diversity of colours consists'. The reply to Huygens was such that the latter would not dispute any more. Huygens 'was not used to being addressed as a delinquent schoolboy' to quote Westfall. Altogether, Newton answered about a dozen letters about his new theory, after which he threatened to withdraw from the Royal Society. Despite the great acclaim both for his telescope and for his optical theory, the business of having people disagree with him was just too much. He withdrew into isolation and alchemic studies.

In early 1675, Newton was up in London and attending a Royal Society meeting, where as it happened Hooke was holding forth on a phenomenon of diffraction which he had discovered. Newton made the remark that this seemed but 'a new kind of refraction', to which Hooke replied, 'that though it should be but a new kind of refraction, yet it was a *new one*'.

Newton's conviction that diffraction was but a variant of refraction turned up in the *Principia*, where a sharp edge, such as the razor blade Hooke used, was credited with a force around it which 'refracted' the light as it passed around.

A Sevenfold Theory

In 1675, Newton re-emerged from his solitude with 'an hypothesis explaining the properties of light' sent off to the Royal Society, after having ascertained from preliminary letters from Oldenburg that this would definitely not involve him in disputation. Whereas with his 'New theory about light and colours' of three years earlier hypotheses had been categorically dismissed, here they were burgeoning. Here was a radically new theory, that there were *seven* colours of the spectrum, and that the ratio of their refrangibilities (i.e., refractive indices) was as the intervals of a music scale! The paper told lyrically how:

'as the harmony and discord of sound proceed from the proportion of the aerael vibrations, so may the harmony of some colours... And the discord of others... Proceed from the proportions of the aethereal.'

But didn't that resemble Hooke's view which had so annoyed him a few years earlier, that 'as there are produced in sounds several harmonies by proportionate vibrations, so there are produced in light several curious and pleasant colours, by the proportionate and harmonious motions of vibration intermingled'?[9]

An extra colour that no-one could see[10] was added in to the six colours of the rainbow, because seven was the perfect number, greatly enhancing the credibility of his theory. The number seven signified completion, wholeness, harmony. As there were seven Days of Creation, as Apollo's lyre had seven strings,[11] as Wisdom had built seven pillars, as there were seven days in the week – so, henceforth, there were to be seven colours in the rainbow. It was a master-stroke, indeed his great master-stroke, in optics. As his theorising sank deeper into quagmires of irreconcilable contradiction, as Light obstinately refused to shape up in accord with his corpuscle model, as that upstart at the Royal Society persisted in giving experimentally-based reasons to refute his proposals – then, from the depths of his alchemic studies, he reached for something stronger than reason. He forged a mythic image and was immortalised by it. Understandably, this 1675 letter to the Royal Society had a rhapsodic tone – 'pulsing with the rhythms of the presocratic philosophers' as Manuel described it. It was the letter about how 'nature is a perpetual circulatory worker'. Amidst these dream-visions culled from the embers of the Western alchemic tradition, he seemed to realise that the scale of music lined up with that of the rainbow. But, we may wonder, has he by then adopted a wave-theory of light?

The measurement of the velocity of light by Roemer from the motion of the satellites of Jupiter was reported in 1676, and its enormously high value shot to pieces the viability of Newton's refraction hypothesis. Back-of an-envelope computations of his estimate the impossibly large force that would have to apply at the boundary where refraction occurred, instantaneously to alter its velocity. However small a mass his light particles had, that high speed gave momentum values that were impossibly high. This is the most likely explanation of the non-publication of his optical papers, until his mature years in 1704.

To return to that number of perfection, seven. What Newton called 'the whim of the spheres' had long gone – seven crystal spheres, from the Moon out to Saturn, which had revolved so harmoniously for two millennia, powered by angel intelligence – and instead there were six planets a-swirling in the solar vortex. Also, seven metals were then known to chemists, no more and no less. For example, in all editions of Lemery's *Cours de Chemie,* running through the first half of the eighteenth century, the number of metals which exist remains fixed at seven. Zinc was discovered via brass-making as a metal in its own right in the early eighteenth century, as was platinum imported from the New World, and these finally broke the mould of millennia. The effect on Newton's subconscious of years of dealing with chemical/alchemical texts where the recipes involved the time-honoured planetary glyphs for the seven metals, should not be underestimated.

Later on, the *Optics* of 1704 came to be composed in seven discrete sections. Book One contains two parts, Book Two is divided into four parts while Book Three is single. As well as seven colours of the rainbow, *Optics* also described seven complete sets of 'Newton's rings' counted around a lens, where the first set of rings had seven discrete colours. At the time of its composition, claimed Castillejo[12], Newton was also composing a design for Solomon's temple which was sevenfold in structure. *Optics* also enjoyed a triple eight motif, with Part one of Book One having eight definitions, eight axioms and eight propositions, recalling the eight 'definitions' of the *Principia*. This 24-fold motif is repeated four steps later, with the third part of Book II being divided into 24 propositions. Thus *Optics* had a numerological undercurrent; helping out, as it were, when the sterner attempts at scientific theorising broke down.

Some doubted whether the music scales did well accord with the optical data; however, as the colours formed a continuous band, the appropriate divisions were not difficult. *Optics* employed musical scales to account for interference rings:

'Newton was forced to carry out a series of *ad hoc* mathematical calculations, in order to make his experimental data fit the mathematical theory. Different arrangements of just intonation [the scales of music] ratios were therefore given in order to make the musical division approximately correct in each case.'[13]

The first theoretical explanation of the sine law of refraction was made in 1687, in the *Principia*. It assumed an attractive force at optical boundaries, which speeded up the light corpuscles as they crossed over. The first *correct* theoretical explanation of the sine law of refraction was given in 1690 by Christiaan Huygens in his *Traite de Lumiere*, as today learnt by every physics student.[14] Huygens there unveiled the quite different implications of the two rival hypotheses:

'I will finish this theory of refraction by demonstrating a remarkable proposition which depends on it; namely, that a ray of light in order to go from one point to another, when these points are in different media, is refracted in such wise at the plane surface which joins these two media that it employs the least possible time: and exactly the same happens in the case of reflexion against a plane surface. Mr Fermat was the first to propound this property of refraction, holding with us, and directly counter to the opinion of Mr Des Cartes, that light passes more slowly through the glass and water than through air.'[15]

Leibniz, writing from Hanover, asked Newton's opinion. It was the only letter Leibniz ever wrote directly to him and it arrived just as the latter was drifting towards his nervous collapse. '*Illustri Viro!*' it began; as one mathematician to another, could he not sense the elegance and inner coherence of the new theory?

> 'Now as you have thrown most light on precisely the science of dioptrics by explaining unexpected phenomena of colours, I would like your opinion about Huygens's explanation of light, assuredly a most brilliant one since the law of sines works out so happily.'[16]

Several months later, a reply came. First it commented on gravity, placing its author as it were at the centre of the universe, 'since all phenomena of the heavens and of the sea follow precisely, so far as I am aware, from nothing but gravity acting in accordance with the laws described by me...'

Then on the question about Huygens, the reply was succinct, 'As for the phenomena of colours... I conceive myself to have discovered the surest explanation.'

That was a post-nervous breakdown reply, a breakdown which marked the end of his creative, scientific life – except only for the development of his lunar theory.

On the Shoulders of Giants

Let us return to the two events of 1671/2, the invention and the theory, noting the close liaison between the two. The idea for a reflecting telescope was then a hundred years old and had been discussed by various writers. Newton took his design from James Gregory's *Optica Promota* of 1663, adding a deft design feature of his own concerning the eyepiece position. His was the first such telescope to be constructed, and as mentioned it was useful for a few weeks before the mirror tarnished. Its highly competent design earned Newton a fellowship with the Royal Society, but it was of no practical value.[17] Westfall omits to inform his readers of this fact, leaving them in a state of perplexity as to why his hero should not have used his own discovery in preference to a refracting telescope.

The theory of the 1672 optics paper compares with that of an opus published in Prague in 1648, *Thaumantias, Liber de Arcu Coelesti* by Marci de Kronland. Here too, a prism dissected a sunbeam, and Marci isolated the monochromatic rays. He too passed these through a second prism placed behind the first, concluding, 'a coloured ray does not change its colour by a renewed refraction'. Some of Marci's conclusions were:

> 'Theorem XII The different colours are produced by different refractions.
> 'Theorem XVIII The same colour cannot proceed from two different refractions, and the same refraction canot produce more than one colour.

'Theorem XX If a coloured ray is refracted, this does not change its colour.'

These are strikingly similar to the conclusions of the *New Theory of Light*. The original feature of the 1672 paper was its employment of the 'minimum deviation' formula for prism refraction, whereby the angles of refraction could be accurately computed.

The different refractive indices of spectral colours were probably first measured by the Englishman Thomas Harriot (1560-1621) at the turn of the seventeenth century, who in the view of Lohne had understood Snell's law before anyone else. He used prisms made of glass and filled with water to observe the dispersion of a ray and described how the rainbow was formed by double refraction in a raindrop. His works remained largely unpublished, because his atomism was regarded as too shocking, but they were circulated in manuscript.[18] Hariott corresponded with Kepler who had come to hear of his optical discoveries, sending him three letters on the subject. The early Royal Society tried to find Harriott's manuscripts in vain and concluded that they had been lost; however, they turned up in the next century.

History of science books have routinely deprived Hooke of credit for interference and diffraction, both of which he described for the first time in England.[19] They neglect to state that Newton's new telescope did not in any useful sense work, and normally indicate to the unsuspecting reader that Newton was the first person to resolve light into its spectral hues. Despite his incomprehensible theory as to how 'Newton's rings' work (by 'fits of easy transmission' – not mentioned in this account, in an attempt to keep the story reasonably straightforward) and despite his first mentioning them in print only a decade after Hooke, his name has been attached to them. Thomas Young, in the early nineteenth century, discussed how 'Newton's rings' viewed as an interference phenomenon supported his new wave-model of light:

'This, I assert, is a most powerful argument in favour of the theory which I had before revived: there was nothing that could have led to it in any author with whom I am acquainted, except some imperfect hints in those inexhaustible but neglected mines of nascent inventions, the works of the great Dr Robert Hooke...'[20]

The Achromatic Anomaly

What *could* have been further developed at the time was the 'achromatic' lens for telescopes, constructed from two types of glass ground so that they fitted together and which could overcome the problem of 'chromatic aberration', which then limited the magnification obtainable from any telescope. This was a major item in

Hooke's disagreement with the colour theory. If light consisted of 'rays differently refrangible', it was supposed to follow that a lens could not be constructed which held the colours together as they passed through instead of splitting them up. To quote Bechler:

> 'The new reflector was at once elevated from a mere technological breakthrough... to that of visible proof of the supremacy of his new theory over the old theories of light.'[21]

There was a problem here in that Hooke had already outlined how such a compound lens might be designed. *So, also, had Newton,* and he was thereby placed in a strange dilemma. He was claiming that his reflecting telescope was designed to overcome a theoretical barrier to further progress in refractor telescopes. Should he agree that Hooke's advice was probably correct – always an irritating business – or, should he persist in his (mistaken) attitude? He took three months in replying to Hooke (having said to Oldenburg that his reply would come 'very suddenly'), while he drafted no less than five replies which are still extant. One of them is three times the length of his final reply. These drafts have only recently been analysed, and reveal their author swaying indecisively between on the one hand agreeing with Hooke and revealing that he *could* mathematically show the design principle for an achromatic lens, and on the other hand claiming that such a design was an impossibility. The reader is at last in a position to understand why the opening of the long reply note to the Royal Society, above-quoted, was on this theme, and why it simmered with such fury. Later on, Newton's *Optics*, to quote Bechler, 'lowered the curtain on the possibility of fabricating a workable achromatic lens'.[22]

It is an awesome tribute to Newton's power and influence that no such telescopes were built in Europe prior to 1750. In 1749, the brilliant French mathematician Leonhardt Euler published his solution for constructing an achromatic compound lens, entirely ignoring the relevant theorem of *Optics* which argued its impossibility – the notorious 'dispersion theorem' in, part II of Book 1. Euler was then criticised by the London optician John Dollond for attempting 'that which so long ago has been demonstrated impossible'. A few years later, Dollond was grinding the first achromatic lens, taking up where Hooke had left off. Telescopes could start improving again.

Aftermath

Apart from blocking the development of telescope technology for nearly a century, and preventing the acceptance of Huygens' correct wave theory of light for slightly longer, what else was new? *Optics* of 1704 described an improved form of the prism refraction experiment, with a lens in front of the prism, so that each of the different spectral colours were brought to a focus on the screen, which was the prototype of the modern spectroscope. Equally fine were the 'Newton's rings' experiments, which measured the thickness of the layers producing the rings as Hooke had not managed to, and did so very accurately, and under different types of monochromatic light. The experiments were most impressive, and the theory of light was original, though not true. One scholar has evaluated 'the more rigid style of the *Optics* and the greater sense of certainty that it bears' compared with the earlier *New theory about light and colours* and concluded that:

> 'The youthful confidence of the newly appointed Lucasian professor that he would found a new mathematical science, a science of colour, had been frustrated. As brilliant as we may judge Newton's optical work to be, by his own standards he had not fully succeeded, and the *Optics* remained a patchwork of mostly thirty-year-old writings with internal contradictions and no underlying mathematical structure... The success of the recently completed *Principia*, I believe, gave him the confidence - even arrogance - to return to his earlier optical work and attempt to give it a veneer of certainty which was simply not there.'[23]

Optics, presented by Newton to the Royal Society from his position of its president in 1704, scarcely had a *theory* of light that was true, in that it could be verified by agreed procedure. Unlike the *Principia,* which re-cast the physical universe, its theory stood in an uneasy liaison with the optical phenomena at least of interference and diffraction. In search of instruction, we quote from Thomas Kuhn:

> 'Newton's new theory of light and colour originated in the discovery that none of the existing pre-paradigm theories would account for the length of the spectrum.'[24]

Experts have perceived the optics debate of the seventeenth century from very differing perspectives. Two accessible discussions of Newtonian optics for the general reader are *Never at Rest,* Westfall's biography of Newton, and Sabra's *Theories of Light from Descartes to Newton*, but these disagree greatly in their relative perspectives; what one sees as a scientific discovery deduced from experiment, the other views as a dogma which was never verifiable.

Professor A.R. Hall, in his *History of Science 1500-1800* treats the topic as if the discovery of the splitting of white light by a prism into colours were fairly comparable to the analysis of a chemical compound into its constituent elements.

This we may call the analytical approach. Historians of science normally adhere to some such viewpoint; thus Professor Westfall declared:

'Whereas the modification theory held ordinary sunlight to be simple and homogeneous, Newton demonstrated that it is a heterogeneous mixture of what he called difform rays, rays differing in refrangibility, in reflexibility, and in the colour they exhibit.'[25]

On this view, sunlight is a composition of different rays.

Is white light so composed? An intensity spectrum of white light will display a continuous level band, while that of a coloured light rises to a peak at a specific wavelength. Does this mean that white light contains an aggregate of radiations, of all different wavelengths, blended together? The question re-arose in the nineteenth century when the French physicist Louis-Georges Gouy showed mathematically that it was *not* necessary to assume that white light *contained* waves of all spectral frequencies: rather, he asserted, a prism or diffraction grating *produced* the differentiation.[26] Gouy and Lord Rayleigh debated with Henri Poincaré on the subject. To quote from a modern textbook on light, this demonstration by Gouy:

'... Raises the question whether Newton's experiments on refraction by prisms, which are usually said to prove the composite nature of white light, were of much significance in this respect. Since white light may be regarded as consisting merely of a succession of random pulses, of which the prism performs a Fourier analysis, the view that the colours are manufactured by the prism, which was held by Newton's predecessors, may be regarded as equally correct.'[27]

The science historian A.I. Sabra developed this theme in his opus *Theories of Light from Descartes to Newton*:

'Gouy showed that the motion of white light can be represented as the sum or superposition of an infinite number of waves each corresponding to one of the spectrum colours. As it happens, the composed motion in this representation turns out to be a single *pulse,* such as that produced by a pistol shot or an electic spark. Using Fourier's theorem it can be shown that the Fourier analysis of such a pulse yields a continuous spectrum such as that produced by a dispersive apparatus... the regularities produced by the dispersive apparatus (for example, the prism) would not exist in a real or physical sense in white light.' (p.280)

Sabra's argument concluded polemically enough that:

> 'It will be seen that Hooke's ideas, in a polished form developed, no doubt, beyond Hooke's own expectations, were later introduced into optics to replace the Newtonian conception of white light.' (p.252).

Sabra here quoted Hooke in his reply to Newton's theory as saying:

> 'I can in my supposition conceive the white or uniform motion of light to be composed of the compound motions of all the other colours, as any one straight and uniform motion may be composed of thousands of compound motions... but I see noe necessity of it.'

... as being an anticipation of the modern view. It needed the Fourier analysis theorem before any necessity for the argument could be perceived, Sabra pointed out.[28]

Westfall repeats several times that Hooke 'failed entirely to come to grips with Newton's experimental demonstration of the *fact* of heterogeneity.'[29] What fact was that? With that phrase he has endeavoured to evade some quite complicated assumptions.

DISCUSSION

Sagredo, Salviati and Simplicius are watching a rainbow.

<u>Simplicius</u>: ... Four, five, six. No, I can't see seven colours either. But what of it? It was the incomparable genius of Newton which showed that white light is made up of all spectral colours, and with the development of the wave theory of light it became clear that each colour corresponds to a given frequency. This was the beginning of modern optics, and the start of the modern analytical aproach to nature. Why, his theory of refraction could account for even the angular width of a rainbow.

<u>Sagredo</u>: I always have difficulty in grasping what Newton's *New Theory* of 1672 actually said. I've a copy of it here. His theory tried to distinguish primary and secondary colours – but, the attempt was locked in a self-contradictory definition system. One of its propositions was, 'To the same degree of refrangibility ever belongs the same colour, and to the same colour ever belongs the same degree of refrangibility,' in other words a one-to one equivalence between hue and refractive index.

THE DARK SIDE OF ISAAC NEWTON

Simplicius: Fine. So, what's the problem?

Sagredo: Another proposition read, 'There are therefore two sorts of colours. The one original and simple, the other compounded of these. The original or primary colours are, red, yellow, green, blue, and a violet-purple, together with orange, indigo, and an indefinite variety of intermediate gradations.' There is an irresolvable contradiction here, because a single hue of green for example could be either a primary or a secondary colour. If it came from splitting up white light then it was a primary colour, original and simple like these fine rainbow hues. If on the other hand it were formed by mixing yellow and blue (as the paper claimed it could be), then it would be compounded.

Salviati: That sounds like semantic quibbling. It seems to me that the Newtonian theory was not about observed colours as such, but about light *rays*. It really needs to be defined by two 'nots': it was *not* about a 'hypothesis', such as what a light ray might be made of, because that would be speculative and he wanted to avoid speculation; but equally it was *not* about colours as we see them, because for the mechanical philosophy colours were no part of the outside world: they were merely formed within one's 'sensorium', located in some corner of the brain, and were subjective. In other words, the *New Theory* was proposed within a framework of Cartesian dualism.

Simplicius: You've lost me now.

Salviati: A lot of people were puzzled. It claimed to be a demonstration with mathematical certitude and so could not contain anything merely speculative, such as a 'cause' for the phenomena. His theory had the practical goal of showing why his reflecting telescope was preferable to the usual lens telescopes; if light rays from the stars were composed of 'rays differently refrangible', then it followed, or so he claimed, that the use of lenses must be of a rather limited value for telescope design...

Sagredo: We digress somewhat. His original definition of a primary colour, with its one-to-one correspondence to refractive index, led logically to an unlimited number of such colours. A spectrum shows a continuous gradation of colour, so there is no logical limit to the number of such – which left him wide open to the devastating criticisms of Huygens and Hooke. Hooke's citing of Occam's razor was entirely appropriate, for a theory which led to an indefinite number of 'primary' colours. The whole development of his colour theory was an attempt to answer these criticisms.

Incidentally, his reply to Huygens' criticism here actually contains a joke, I believe the only one in sixty years of correspondence. Huygens had suggested that there might be only two primary colours, instead of an indefinite number, and had even had the effrontery to suggest that white light could be formed by mixing two colours together, instead of requiring all the spectral hues as Newton's *New Theory* had claimed to be necessary. The reply was: 'No man wonders at the indefinite variety of waves on the sea or sands on the shore, but should they all be of but two sizes it would be a very puzzling phaenomenon. And I should think it as unaccountable if... [there should be] but two sorts of rays.'[30] Further remarks in that letter caused Huygens to avoid further correspondence, saying that its author defended himself *'avec tant de chaleur.'*

Simplicius: You mean that his *Hypothesis* of three years later, where the number of spectral colours became seven, was an attempt to escape from a rather useless definition which gave him no limit to the number of primary colours?

Sagredo: Precisely. The eighteenth century tended to see the Newtonian theory as holding that there were seven colours in the spectrum. But it remained unclear whether white light was supposed to be composed of three, seven or an indefinite number of different colours – or rather, strictly speaking, modes of ray corresponding to them.

Simplicius: I get a bit lost with this theory. What that classic experiment of 1672 actually achieved was a more accurate measurement of refractive index than previously, by measuring the angles separately for each colour at the prism's minimum deviation position. It seems that Thomas Hariott did make such experiments earlier in the century, but no-one seems to have heard about them, so effectively we may take Newton's precise measurements in this experiment as the first of such.

Salviati: Yes, and the word 'spectrum' was first coined in that 1672 report; prior to that 'spectral' only referred to ghosts! I am reminded of Kepler's innovative use of the word 'focus' to describe a centre of an ellipse or parabola: previously as a Latin word it signified just the hearth of a home where a fire was. These new words show great changes in human experience. Newton was the first really to *see* what has ever since been called a 'spectrum.'

Day Two

Sagredo: Yesterday, I almost understood the Newtonian *New Theory of Light and Colours*. It seemed to make sense while you were explaining it, Salviati, but then later I lost it. Do you mind if we go over the argument one more time? Newton made the claim that the conclusion of his theory was 'evinced by the mediation of experiments concluding directly and without any suspicion of doubt.' What was that conclusion?

Salviati: That white light was not pure, but was compounded.

Sagredo: Of what?

Salviati: That did not concern him.

Sagredo: Perhaps this reply, which so baffled Huygens and Hooke, as it still baffles me, was what is called a 'phenomenal' approach, which refrains from looking at causes. But his theory also said, or concluded, '... It can no longer be disputed... Whether Light be a Body'. Throw this in, *as an assumption*, and I can make sense of it. He would then simply be saying that there was a mixture of light-particles in a ray of white light, as there are loaves in a basket or raisins in a cake. I can't see why he objected to Hooke pointing out that this was an assumption which he had made, not a conclusion.

Yesterday, Simplicius justified the theory by referring to the modern wave-theory of light. With the development of the wave theory of light, he said, it became clear that each colour corresponded to a given frequency. This startled me. Just look at the row which erupted when Thomas Young proposed a wave theory of light – even though he had used Newton's measurements as given in *Optics* to demonstrate it. It quite terminated Young's scientific career. He was obliged to move on to other matters, like medicine and deciphering the Rosetta Stone. In France the grip of Newtonian orthodoxy was not quite so rigid and there Fresnel carried Young's theory forward, using interference phenomena, until eventually it was accepted. Now, let me ask you, Salviati, whether Newton did at any time embrace a wave-theory?

Salviati: Hmm. He did make remarks which sound rather like a wave-theory, in his 1675 *Hypothesis explaining the properties of light*. He was trying to explain his 'Newton's Rings' experiments, where you will recall he measured the thickness of circular colour-rings with extraordinary accuracy for different single hues of light. There he debated the well-established analogy of light with sound, and derived an equivalence between the seven colours of his spectrum and the seven notes in a musical scale. Everyone knew that sound was a wave phenomenon. But, that 1675 theory was ether-based, and later with the *Principia* he came to reject all ether-type theories. After that, explaining interference phenomena wasn't easy! A definitive modern survey by Sabra found that Newton always considered all forms of the wave hypothesis for light to be false.[31] Perhaps that answers your question?

Sagredo: The ring experiments were indeed awesome in their precision, but none of the theory was valid. After all, who could take seriously 'fits of easy transmission' to explain the coloured rings? What was valuable was the *attitude* of analysis he was showing towards the phenomena of optics, rather than particular – if you'll excuse the expression – theories of light. History of science textbooks always talk as if a discovery had been demonstrated by that 1672 experiment, and as if critics like Huygens and Hooke simply failed to realise the fact. But its subject-matter was not given a scientific basis until Young in 1801 proposed that there were three types of colour-receptor in the eye. The only scientific and correct theory of the time about light was knocked into oblivion by Newton's theory, and that was Huygen's wave-theory of 1695.

Salviati: Sagredo, these tirades of yours about how history should have been grow tedious. The mathematics of the day was just not up to coping with a Huygens-type wavefront as a model for the propagation of light. Also, Huygens saw light as a longitudinal wave, not a transverse wave as it actually is, so it's doubtful whether it was a 'correct' theory. Then there was the phenomenon of rectilinear propagation...

Simplicius: I beg your pardon? May I point out, Salviati, that the 1672 paper was composed in a lively and readable style, and the Royal Society evinced genuine pleasure upon having it read to them, as recorded in the thanks conveyed by Mr Oldenburg to its author. This was a far cry from the later style of 'glacial remoteness' which that illustrious author later developed.

Has it occurred to you that the optical theories of Hooke, Huygens and Sir Isaac all agreed on one point? They all viewed yellow as a primary colour – though they may have held different views on what was meant by 'primary'. Hooke and Huygens concluded that there were only two primary colours, yellow and blue, chiefly from observations on the transmission of light through coloured liquids. They were all wrong, because as Thomas Young showed, yellow isn't one of the three primary colours, but rather strangely comes from mixing beams of red and green light.

Salviati: Ha! Well, I'm glad they all agreed upon something.

(They walk off, arguing.)

Chapter 3

The Gravity Of The Situation

'I began to think of gravity extending to ye orb of the Moon'

Isaac Newton, in 1718

In 1666, as London went up in flames and the Black Death raged, Newton watched, or so he said, an apple fall. It was in Woolsthorpe at his mother's house, in that summer when he developed the theory of calculus and split up light into its spectral hues. It has become the best known of scientific inspirations, even though modern scholarship finds some doubt over its veracity. We now journey back three and a half centuries to that decisive moment when Heaven and Earth were united by a new physics, and sniff about for the story of what really took place.

Coffee at St Paul's

Towards the end of the 1670s, the scientific minds of Europe were grappling with 'the great unanswered question confronting natural philosophy, the derivation of Kepler's laws of planetary motion from the principles of dynamics'.[1] Edmond Halley, Robert Hooke and Christopher Wren met at the St Paul's coffee house to discuss such matters (the Sir Christopher Wren tavern now stands on the spot). Apart from his eminence as an architect, Wren had reformulated the Cartesian laws of motion, which the historian Sprat of the Royal Society gave precedence over all his other achievements. (Cartesian refers to the theory of the French philosopher René Descartes.) From a member of this group came the *first formulation* of the principle of universal gravitation: Robert Hooke.

Secretary of the Royal Society and one of its founder members, and Professor of Geometry at Gresham College, Hooke wrote in November 1679 to Newton, that in his view:

> 'all Coelestial Bodies whatsoever, have an attraction or gravitating power towards their own centres... But that they do also attract all other Coelestial bodies that are within the sphere of their activity...'

68

THE GRAVITY OF THE SITUATION

And then in his next letter of January 9th, 1680 he formulated the inverse square law of attraction:

> 'my supposition is that the Attraction always is in a duplicate proportion to the distance from the Center Reciprocall.'

The group had to acknowledge that none of them had the mathematical ability to show how such a principle would give an elliptical orbit.[2] For this reason Hooke wrote to Newton at Cambridge, to sound out his opinion of the matter. He sensed – and quite rightly, as it turned out – that this was the man to sort out the matter. This he would have done with some trepidation, as still smarting from the barbed remarks Newton had directed towards him over a debate concerning the latter's theory of colours.

One thing led to another and eventually Sir Isaac had come out with his remark, 'If I have seen further than others it is because I have stood on the shoulders of giants'[3] in 1675, a remark quoted wholly out of context down the centuries as showing humility, but actually a taunt about Hooke's short and hunchback figure.

Had there been anyone else Hooke could have written to about the matter, we may be sure he would have done so, but he resolved that the man who had invented the binomial theorem and developed a theory of colour was the man for the job, reclusive and irritable though he might be. His first letter received the dismissive and off-putting reply that Newton did not wish to be troubled with matters of 'philosophy' as he had other things on his mind; and the second received no reply. Hooke was later to claim that his first letter was sounding out Newton, as to whether he had any such idea on the matter, and so did not state the inverse square principle. Four years later, Halley went to visit Newton at Trinity College, Cambridge and extracted from the latter the claim that he was able to demonstrate how an inverse square law of attraction would generate an elliptical orbit.

The question arises as to why the discovery of this law is universally credited to Newton. Four years later, in August 1684, Newton's mind started to work on his *Principia*, somewhat as a result of his comet investigations and triggered by a visit of Halley. From then to the spring of 1687, the mighty chains of mathematical deduction were forged whereby the 'System of the World' was laid out, according to Matter and Motion, Inertia and Gravity.[4] The fact that Hooke knew that he could not demonstrate how Kepler's laws could be derived from the inverse square law of gravity,[5] is hardly relevant to the question of priority.

Not while the priority dispute was raging, but in his old age, Newton recalled that as a young student the idea had come to him in 1666, while comparing the motion of an apple to that of Moon; leaving biographers the task of explaining why he had said nothing about the matter to anyone for the next eighteen years – even when written to on the subject by the Secretary of the Royal Society. He was an introvert character they explained, which was true enough. The computation he then attempted used an inaccurate estimate of Earth's diameter and so did not link together Moon and apple,[*,6] and so he put the idea aside, they explain. Voltaire told this story and it has been repeated ever since. *The myth was born.*

There are one or two objections to this story,[**] for a start the notes which Newton made on his copy of Wing's *Astronomia Brittanica*, an astronomical textbook of the time, in 1669. These show his acceptance of the Cartesian vortex theory, a theory entirely incompatible with his own theory of gravity, which was in fact demolished lock, stock and barrel by his theory when it did emerge – although it took the French a hundred years to appreciate the fact. Descartes' theory viewed the planets as carried round the Sun by a swirling vortex of invisible matter; it all worked through pressure and not by attraction. Newton's notes on his copy of *Astronomia* refer to the *pressure of the solar vortex upon the terrestrial one*; and they queried whether the Earth's 'endeavour of receding' from the Sun might affect the Moon's orbit, 'unless the Moon also shares in the same endeavour'.

Such an 'endeavour of receding' is what would now be called centrifugal force. Today, physics students still get rapped over the knuckles with a 'Not centrifugal force- centripetal force!' The former is somewhat more intuitively evident; if, for example, a bucket is swung round on a string it appears as if the bucket is experiencing a pull away from the centre, a 'centrifugal' force. The concept of gravitation in contrast was a centri*petal* force pulling towards a centre. It was a more abstract idea and required the development of the concept of inertial motion: uniform motion in a straight line, found neither in the physics of Aristotle nor – in quite this form – in that of Descartes.

To formulate this principle required a remarkable degree of detachment from the world of experience, for such motion is nowhere observed, *ever*; uniform motion in a straight line without any force acting upon the body. It requires one to envisage a

---

* The 1666 myth: It is generally agreed (See Westfall, 'Newton's Marvellous Years,' Isis 1980 71 p117) that this memory relates to a document dated around 1669 printed in 'The Correspondence of Isaac Newton, Vol I, p 299-300. The essence of the computation there presented is a comparison of the force from the spinning of the earth ('conatus recendi' or centrifugal force), whereby weights are slightly decreased at the equator, with the force on the Moon due to its spinning. An inaccurate figure is indeed used for the earth's diameter, but there is no hint in the paper that anything failed to match up and was put aside for this reason. As Bernard Cohen well expressed the matter: 'Later on, after Newton had learned how to analyze orbital motion in terms of the action of a centripetal force on a body with an initial component of inertial motion, and had written the Principia, he interpreted his early calculations *as if* they were essentially the 'moon test' described in the scholium to prop. 4, bk.3, o the Principia.' (1980, p.240)

** Gravity theory: The great significance of Professor D. T. Whiteside's re-evaluation should be acknowledged, as the editor of the monumental eight-volume *Newton's Mathematical Papers*. His here-relevant argument is found in 'Before the Principia,' *Jnl. for the History of Astronomy*,1970,1,5-19 and in 'Newton's Lunar Theory: From High Hope to disenchantment,' *Vistas in Astronomy*,1976,19,317-328.

perfectly empty universe, with one sole object moving through space. It would then perform this inertial motion in a straight line. No-one could tell this because there would be no ruler and clock, and if there were, then the motion would no longer be in a straight line, because gravity would make it curve.

What is nowadays known as Newton's First Law of Motion, was first formulated in 1674 by Robert Hooke[*] in the words:

> 'That all bodies whatsoever that are put into a direct and simple motion, will so continue to move forward in a straight line, till they are by some other effectual powers deflected and bent into a Motion, describing a circle, ellipsis, or some other more compounded Curve line.'

from a lecture of his entitled, 'An attempt to prove the motion of the Earth'. This law or axiom is essential for explaining how a body moving in a circular orbit is in fact accelerating towards the centre – and only then can one begin to infer an inverse square law of gravity.

Vim centripetum appello. were the bold, opening words of the text he composed for Halley, in November 1684, which has come to be known as *De motu* – 'I will call "centripetal" that force which...'[**] Here was the utterly new concept, a force pulling circular motion *towards the centre.* That would be his force ... of gravity.

An Enduring Obsession

Let us look more closely now at the crucial years when the gravity of the situation began to dawn upon the scientific minds of Europe, and at the irritation of Isaac

---

[*] Descartes on first law of motion: Normally the textbooks credit René Descartes with first formulating the principle of inertial motion in a straight line, which has become known as Newton's First Law of motion as learnt by every physics student. However, Descartes' philosophy had space everywhere filled with matter so that motion could only be that of the whole of the matter in a closed path or vortex. Descartes' description of the circular motion in the heavens, was as being in an inertial path, of 'quies philosophica,' scientific rest. It is questionable whether Descartes could have applied a 'first law' of motion to such circular orbits. Perhaps nobody did prior to Huygens' analysis of centrifugal force. The relevant statements by Descartes were in two parts: that what was once moved, would continue to move, and that straight line motion was natural. He did not state that such motion would be of uniform velocity, as did Hooke in the passage quoted. See, A. Gabbey, 'Force and Inertia in Seventeenth-Century Dynamics,' in 'Studies in History and Philosophy of Science,' 1971, 2, 1, p.1-67

[**] For a nine-page tract which might be what he gave to Halley in December 1684, see Whiteside, *'Preliminary manuscripts of Isaac Newton's 1687* Principia,*'* CUP 1989, pp.3-11; for the English translation see Whiteside, , *Math Papers VI* 1974 'The fundamental De motu corporum in gyrum.' Halley presented the document to the Royal Society on 17 December.

Newton at being troubled thereby, just at a time when his years of alchemical experimentation seemed to be getting somewhere.

'His fires were almost perpetual,' observed his assistant Humphrey Newton, 'the transmuting of metals being his chief design...' This had been his major activity since 1678, performed near the east end of Trinity College chapel. One substance Newton then used extensively was sal ammoniac, ammonium chloride, which he found 'an aid to the elixir'.

A heavenly insight came to him: 'I understood that the morning star is Venus and that she is the daughter of Saturn and one of the doves...' which his diary records as 10 May 1681. A week later, on 18 May: 'I perfected the ideal solution. That is, two equal salts carry up Saturn... Then the eagle carries Jupiter up... At last mercury sublimate and sophic sal ammoniac shatter the helmet...' The planetary names are here alluding to the metals associated with them: Jupiter, tin; Saturn, lead; and Venus, copper.

'Neptune with his trident leads the philosopher into the sophic garden' is a note belonging to this period. These dream-images have a marvellous levity to them, as if the right hemisphere of his brain were protesting at what the other half was about to get up to. 'I made Jupiter fly on his eagle' – a cry of triumph recorded on 23 May 1684 (sublimation of tin, presumably). These dying embers of the Western alchemic tradition were then to fade out thereafter, and his alchemic furnace was to expire, as a different kind of inspiration took a hold of him, from August of that year. After that, Jupiter was definitely not flying on his eagle.

During these years of gazing into the flames, when strange mysteries were – or perhaps, were not – revealed to him, he was in correspondence with Robert Boyle about whether transmutation could be effected so as to overcome the shortage of gold required for the expansion of currency. 'If those great pretenders bragg not,' he said, referring to Hermetic Philosophers, there were mysteries 'not to be communicated without immense dammage to ye world'.[7] He was to return later to this theme, when Robert Boyle succeeded in repealing the stern and centuries-old decree prohibiting the multiplication of gold, i.e. he made transmutation legal! In 1404 alchemic transmutation to make gold (called, the 'Craft of Multiplication') was sternly prohibited by Henry IV, as being a crime against the Crown. That statute was repealed in 1689 in the first year of William and Mary's reign: citizens were allowed thenceforth to produce gold by any means, including the 'craft of multiplication,' but upon one condition - any such gold produced 'be from henceforth employed for no other use or uses whatsoever but for the increase of monies,' i.e. it had to be brought straight to the Royal Mint.

It must be said that Robert Boyle rather disappointed Newton after that and failed to come up with the goods. Intimations by the Father of Modern Chemistry that he was able to make gold proved to be shall we say a youthful enthusiasm.

THE GRAVITY OF THE SITUATION

The researches of Rob Iliffe have provided a relatively full picture of the ultimate issues with which Newton was grappling through the winter of 1679/80,* such that he met the approaches of the Royal Society's Secretary with polite but firm declination to become involved in its doings, on account of his great distance from 'philosophy'. He was busy decoding the apocalypse, and this was involving him in some intense discussions with his colleague Henry More (also from Grantham), the Cambridge Platonist.[8]

More composed his *Apocalypsis Apocalypseos* in the latter half of 1679 and sent out copies as New Year's gifts around the beginning of 1680. A letter which he wrote to John Sharp in August of 1680 alluded to his and Mr Newton's 'agreement in Apocalypticall notions'. It was by no means uncommon in Restoration England, for themes in the books of Daniel and Revelation to be assigned a political relevance, especially in relation to Roman Catholicism, added to which, in 1679 the strange hysteria of the Papish Plot had gripped the nation. More's letter to Sharp described his gift to Newton of a copy of his new book, adding that in discussion Newton had seemed much to approve of his views, in the expression of which '...he seemed to be in a manner transported'.[9]

Newton returned from Woolsthorpe Manor on 27 November 1679, two months after the start of Michaelmas term, starting his first response to Hooke on the next day, and over the next month or so, read More. Iliffe reconstructs 'at least three conversations' between More and Newton over this brief period, during which it became evident that More was greatly mistaken in supposing a concordance of views. The disagreement revolved around the seven vials and seven trumpets of the Book of Revelations, and their link with historical epochs of time. The extensive marginal comments which Newton added to his copy of More's book show him arguing against 'synchronising the trumpets and the vials'. An in-depth debate about history, the apocalypse and the millennium was ongoing between the two, which remained cordial although both had deeply held though differing convictions. Newton's was related to his disbelief in the Trinity, which he had carefully to conceal, and through which he became immersed in studying theological movements of the fourth century, as the period when the doctrine of the Trinity became established.

The early 1680s also found Newton continuously occupied with his alchemical researches that involved metal sublimations, especially involving the volatile metals tin and antimony, and ammonium chloride (sal ammoniac). The latter is a

---

* For the theological debates between Newton and Henry More around this time, as a result of the latter's *Apocalypsis Apocalypseos* appearing towards the end of 1679, see R.Iliffe, 'Making a Shew: Apocalyptic Hermeneutics and the Sociology of Christian Idolatry in the work of Isaac Newton and Henry More', in *The Book of Nature and Scripture*, edited by J.Force and R.Popkin (Dortrecht, 1994), 55-88.

salt that will readily sublime on heating, and he viewed it as 'the key to the art' and 'an aid to the Elixir'.[10]

An in-depth correspondence with Thomas Burnett about how God had created the world again shows his adherence to vortex-theory. The latter's forthcoming *Telluris Theoriae Sacra* of 1681 was soon translated into English as the *Sacred Theory of the Earth.* Newton had evidently been sent a pre-publication draft, the text of which made no allusion to vortex-motion. His first letter to Burnett suggested that the work should take account of 'ye pressure of ye vortex or of ye Moon', as having worked formatively upon the Earth over the course of time. This *downward pressure exerted by the Moon* he pictured as having formed hills and valleys in the course of time. 'Note the allusion to the Cartesian theory of vortices', added the editors.

Burnet's reply rejected this view. It quoted Newton's remark about formative processes as having taken place 'by ye pressure of ye vortex of ye Moon upon ye waters' and suggested that Newton should adopt a more bible-based, Mosaic account of Earth's early stages. A second letter to Burnet in January 1681 returned to this theme, despite Burnet's scepticism: 'the pressure of ye Moon or Vortex etc may promote ye irregularities of ye causes of ye hills'.[11] The letter carried on for six pages describing the exact manner in which the world was created – underscoring the way in which theological issues were uppermost in Newton's mind over this period.

These considerations help us to evaluate what did and more importantly what did not transpire, over the crucial winter of 1679/80. Enough has now been said to indicate a direction of interest, such that when Newton replied to Hooke's letters of 1679/80 saying that he did not wish to be troubled with such matters,[12] the simple meaning of such replies can be accepted.

Two Comets

A huge comet turned up in the autumn of 1680 and provides us with a good opportunity to see who believed what in this crucial period. It disappeared into the sunrise in November and then reappeared in the sunset moving away from the Sun in December two weeks later, with its tail having swung round into the opposite direction, so it was visible in the evening sky instead of the morning sky. Newton we now find writing to Flamsteed about the latter's outlandish belief that the 'two comets' seen were in fact one and the same![13] The Astronomer Royal was of the persuasion that the comet had gone up to the Sun, turned around, and then come back again on the other side of the Earth. Somewhat as the Greeks of old had failed to apprehend that Hesperus the Evening Star and Lucifer the Morning star were one and the same planet, Venus, so was the single nature of this comet not appreciated – except by the canny Astronomer Royal.

THE GRAVITY OF THE SITUATION

By what means could the Sun effect such a pull? It was some kind of magnetic force, surmised Flamsteed, who was not much given to theoretical speculation. This could hardly be the case, replied Newton in a long letter, concerning 'ye question of two Comets', for the Sun was hot, and heat destroyed magnetism, and therefore he thought it unlikely that any magnetic force could be pulling the comet round, and so he did not accept the theory that the two comets seen in the sky separated by a two week period were but one. He then expounded at length as to how his computations, based on observations of Mr Halley, did not concur with the notion of a single comet turning up twice.

It is certainly noteworthy that the Reverend John Flamsteed was the sole person to realise that the 'two comets' were one, and that it had merely reappeared after passing very close to the Sun. In fact, this comet had turned around far more sharply than any previous comet, because of the extreme proximity of its orbit to the Sun![14] Not until 1685 did Newton concede that the two comets had been one and the same, in a letter to Flamsteed. The correspondence points to the absence of a theory of universal gravitation in Newton's mind, fifteen years after he is supposed to have discovered it. Instead, Newton's letter alluded to the motion of the solar vortex: accepting hypothetically the notion that there was just one comet, he explained that it would have to have swung around the Sun, i.e. gone behind it, and not in front as the astronomer had supposed, because of the *direction in which the solar vortex was rotating.*

Various manuscript drafts exist of that letter, which show Newton alternating between two possible modes of explaining the comet's path – if he were to grant the astronomer's case that there was just one comet not two; either the Sun's magnetism, or its huge ether-vortex swirling around it. Those were the only two options! That letter sent in February 1680 was only a couple of months after his correspondence with Hooke.

One notes with some relief the cordial tone of his letter to Flamsteed, which is signed, 'your affectionate friend & servant'; a far cry indeed from the terrible hammer-blows which Newton was to administer to Flamsteed in his later years, so that when the latter's magnum opus, *Historia Coelestis* eventually emerged, much of its preface had to be supressed – because its theme was Newton's treacherous and duplicitous behaviour![15] We come to this later.

Like an augury, what later came to be called Halley's comet, turned up in 1682, but we have no record of what Newton thought about it, as his correspondence does not allude to it. The new physics had not yet begun to suggest itself to him, no true thought of cometary orbits had yet arrived! Comets were a riddle, because their tails fanned out away from the Sun, and so seemed to show the opposite of a gravitational attraction by the Sun. Halley, espying it with his telescope set up in Highbury, had no inkling that he was destined to be immortalised by it some years later, when it occurred to him that it was the very one depicted in the

Bayeux tapestry and which returned at regular 76-year intervals; the only bright, periodic comet.

That comet was totally within the ecliptic i.e. the plane of the solar system, so it was seen as within the zodiac[16] in the night sky, BUT it was moving in the reverse direction to all of the planets. This soon signified to Robert Hooke that no ether-vortex could exist, or at least that this comet was mysteriously unaffected by any such (Cartesian) ether-vortex. In that case, what could be carrying it round, in an opposite direction?[17] As to whether Newton in those years was also troubled by such thoughts, the historical record remains silent.

Let's summarise Newton's response to the two quite dramatic comets that turned up in these formative years. There were three letters which Flamsteed sent to him over December 1680 to February 1681 about the comet making that very close perihelion passage around the Sun, enclosing his data for the Cambridge mathematician, and *only after the third* does he get a reply. Newton ponders the question of 'ye two comets' in some depth in several letters. He admits the possibility of some 'magnetical force' whereby the sun pulls the comet around it, but then decides *not* to accept that view, because he does not agree with the astronomer but rather believes that there were two separate comets. For the second 1682 comet, known to posterity as Halley's Comet, which lit up the night sky, there is no record of any comments by Newton – no correspondence with anyone. Halley recorded it and Hooke held forth about it in his lecture from which we have quoted, about how it was going in the reverse direction to any solar-vortex ethers carrying the planets around and developing his theory of gravity. Newton, engrossed in his theological and alchemic studies, declined to be involved.

A Visit to Cambridge

Coming to 1684, when Halley went to visit Newton at Cambridge,[18] the traditional story (here regarded as largely fictional) has Halley asking him what orbit would be generated by an object orbiting under an inverse square law. 'An ellipse,' he replied. 'How do you know?' quoth the astonished Halley. 'Because I have calculated it,' replied Newton, but said he had mislaid the computation. He promised to send it to Halley, who duly received it in the post later that year, along with various other propositions, all called '*De Motu*'. The story is accompanied by quips as to how while others were seeking for the law of gravity, Newton had mislaid it. This story has been fed to generations of science students; it has endured for centuries! The contrast is not lost between the serene power of the great mathematician and the vain babbling of Hooke, who could not prove what he asserted.

What Halley actually received, three months after his visit, was hardly a solution to his 'inverse square problem', but rather a tract containing material for the course of nine lectures over the Michaelmas term. What ended up in the *Principia* was a theorem which said that *if* an object orbited around another in an ellipse, with a stationary centre of mass at one focus, *then* a force varying inversely as the square of the distance can be derived.*

This was not what Halley had been supposedly astonished to hear that he could perform, namely prove or deduce that such an orbit must be elliptical.

In other words, an honest reply would have been, 'Sorry, but nobody can do that. Give me several months and maybe I will be able to demonstrate the converse – namely that, given an elliptical orbit, an inverse square law of attraction can be inferred.'

The problem of deducing an elliptical orbit from the inverse-square law, always proposed as the reason for conferring the laurels upon Newton rather than Hooke, was beyond the capability of, not merely the coffee-house trio, but of *any* mathematician in the seventeenth century. Eliptical maths is hard because it involves a *varying* acceleration. Not before 1710 was such a thing demonstrated, by the mathematician John Bernoulli.

The well-known 'apple-Moon' computation given in the *Principia* – which related the same gravity principle to the Moon's orbit as to the fall of an apple – used circular motion to test an inverse square principle. Such a circular orbit has a constant acceleration, directed towards the centre. We will endeavour to show how no computation of the acceleration due to gravity may be found anywhere in the *Principia*. To cite a (strictly fictional) account in a physics A-level textbook, 'About 1666, at the early age of 24, NEWTON discovered a universal law...' etc, and then, he was disappointed to find 'that the answer for g was not near the observed value...'[19]

His actual 1685 Moon-apple computation is of the form, that an object on earth falls 15 feet in one second, while the Moon 'falls' 15 feet in one minute, there being here a scale factor of 60 reflecting the Moon's distance of 60 Earth-diameters. (See Appendix) Newton did not (we here argue) have the concept of acceleration, as developed by the next generation of Continental mathematicians using the Leibnizian calculus.

Moving from the clear equations of mathematics to the murky realm of human psychology, one assumes that, when Sir Isaac was informed of a problem which

---

* To quote I. Bernard Cohen on this ever-controversial issue, 'What Newton proved, however, in *De Motu* was not that if the attractive force varies as the inverse square of the distance, then the orbit will be an ellipse; rather, he proved the converse, namely, that if the orbit is an ellipse, then the attractive force must vary inversely as the square of the distance.' ('Contemporary Newton Research,' Ed. Bechler, Reidel, 1982, p.84.) A US physicist (Robert Weinstock) has argued that no such proof (given an inverse square law, an elliptical orbit will be the consequence), such as Newton claimed to be able to give to Halley, is to be found in any edition of the *Principia*, and that such a proof was first given by Bernoulli to the Paris Academie in 1710. See *The Newton Handbook*, Gjertsen, p.501-2 ('the inverse problem of central forces').

Robert Hooke could not solve, having been previously irritated by Hooke's presumption to doubt or at least wish to debate his theory of optics, he – *if* the story is true – lied to Halley. He asserted that his demonstration was somewhere mislaid. Biographers find no difficulty in believing the story, because it fits in with later attempts to paint Hooke right out of the picture, and with the notion that Newton had worked it all out long ago.

What actually happened in 1684 can be reconstructed quite simply. In February, Christopher Wren offered a prize of a book to anyone, i.e. to Hooke or to Halley, if they could within two months explain what an inverse square law of attraction had got to do with Kepler's first law of planetary motion, i.e. ellipses. Hooke's mathematical ability was not well capable of dealing with ellipses in this context. In either May or August Halley visits Newton at Cambridge. In August, Newton's alchemical furnace goes out and his chemistry notebook ceases to show any more experiments. We may surmise that something important had then occurred to him, such as an approach to the problem which Halley had brought. His Michaelmas term notes show him grappling with the matter, and by October, his ellipse work was in 'almost definitive form'.[20] On a *second* visit in November, Halley recalled that he saw 'a curious treatise '*De Motu*'.[21] The copies extant date from around January 1685.

This story has the defect that it shows nothing superhuman, but merely a mathematician taking the best part of a year to solve something which no one else could do. Accordingly, it was remembered *as if* the matter had all been worked out years before. Every Newton biography and every history of science has accepted this story despite the complete absence of documentary evidence for its having been derived earlier.

The first '*De Motu*' documents (early 1685) contain no trace of the apple-Moon computation, though this was the crowning glory of Newton's achievement.[22] Is it likely that a treatise on dynamics and the force of gravity, this prelude to the *Principia*, kept as a secret what he had developed years earlier? For no less is implied by the normal telling of the story. It is simpler by far to assume that this linking of gravity between sky and earth occurred in 1685 – the greatest achievement of his life – and that it was the dawning of this realisation which inspired Newton to compose his magnum opus over the next couple of years.

Halley's Diplomacy

A character who can go carousing with Peter the Great in London, as well as get on with Sir Isaac is, as the biographer Manuel so rightly observed, 'flexible'.[23] When the first volume of the *Principia* arrived, the Royal Society, little appreciating what was to come, had just spent its last penny on a marvellous illustrated encyclopaedia of fish. Edmond Halley therefore gallantly offered to foot the bill. A problem arose when it was observed that themes on which Hooke had been lecturing and giving demonstrations for twenty years, such as the motion of pendulums in relation to gravitational force, were treated without acknowledgement being given. Hooke protested; *his* gravity theory had been taken over, he said.

Thereupon Sir Isaac threatened to withhold the third part from the world, to which the first two were merely the prelude, in fury describing Hooke as 'another that does nothing but pretend and grasp at all things...'[24] Confronted by this heroic bringing-down-the-tablets-of-revelation-and-threatening-to-smash-them posture, Halley, realising that British science confronted by brilliant continental geniuses like Leibnitz and Hooykaus, could ill afford to be without such a tome, decided to approach Sir Isaac in the only manner he allowed anyone to get near to him; sycophantic adulation.

22 May 1686, Halley to Newton: '[Mr Hooke] says you had the notion from him, though he owns the demonstration of the Curves generated thereby to be wholly your own...,' concerning the 'decrease of gravity being reciprocally as the squares of the distances from the centre'. This is a modest enough claim by Hooke, with no uncertainty in the historical record over the justice of Hooke's claim.

Then, in his highly diplomatic letter to Newton, in which he served as the midwife for the *Principia's* third volume, while endeavouring not altogether to betray his old friend Hooke, Halley wrote:

> 'I must beg your pardon, that it is I, that send you this ungrateful account (of Hooke's pretentions); but I thought it my duty to let you know it, *that you may act accordingly*, being in myself fully satisfied, that nothing but the greatest candour imaginable is to be expected from a person, who has of all men the least need to borrow reputation.'[25]

Candour? From Newton?

There are three components of the *Principia* for which acknowledgement of Robert Hooke as the source should have been made but were not: the universal theory of gravitation by an inverse square law of attraction; the 'first law of motion'; and the oblateness in the shape of the earth, whereby it is wider at the equator.[26] Despite the disappearance of so many of the crucial Hooke documents immediately after his death, there is little doubt that these fundamental themes were derived from him. Of other issues one cannot be so definite; for example, Hooke gave lectures and demonstrations on pendulums, conical and oscillating, in relation to the force of gravity, and ascertained how these varied in different latitudes as timekeepers; all of which ends up in the *Principia*. He spoke of how the Moon faces the earth on account of its gravitational pull, and in a general way of how its gravity pull causes the tides. However, he gave no mathematical demonstration of how two tides a day result thereby and so quite rightly the credit goes to Newton. The notion was far from self-evident. Bacon had dismissed the notion that the Moon caused the tides as had Galileo, and Descartes had come out with the opposite notion, that when the Moon was overhead the *pressure* of its vortex pushed the seas down![27]

Returning to the scene after the Part Three of the *Principia* had been received by the Royal Society, and a crushed Hooke was sitting over his cup of coffee in amazement, realising that another of vastly superior mathematical abilities had successfully muscled in on his gravity theory. His protests – according to Halley – met with the riposte that he should have consolidated his claim by putting it in a more substantial form. 'Sayd Newton the veryest knave in all the house,' records Hooke's diary for July 3, 1689.[28]

Isaac Newton's Theory of Gravitation

We now have a slight surprise for the reader; something which he or she may never have heard of before. Scarcely described in histories of science, this arcane matter, which we now bring forth into the light of day is – Newton's theory of gravitation. He proposed it in the year 1676, to the Royal Society. It was registered but not published, which meant that all the Fellows and only them, could read it.

We've seen how, in the back of his copy of Wing's *Astronomia Brittanica*, Newton commented upon Kepler's third law. It is often claimed that around this year, 1669, he deduced that this law showed an inverse square principle, as if this were some early apprehension by him of the law of gravity. What his notes actually show here is 'a complicated theory of solar, terrestrial and lunar vortical interaction to "explain" the principal inequalities of the weaving orbit of the Moon'[29] where Kepler's third law applies to Earth, Mars, Jupiter and Saturn, but not for Venus and Mercury, whose orbits are *too perturbed by proximity to the solar vortex*; for these, their 'endeavour' of receding (*'vis centrifuga'*) does not vary as the inverse square of their distance from the Sun. The terrestrial vortex (which holds the Moon) he views as 1/43rd part as strong as the solar vortex. Clearly all this has nothing whatever to do with a theory of gravitation. His notes on this Wing textbook are in Trinity College library, Cambridge.

How strange that scholars can read these early manuscripts and yet believe that their author had already formed the hypothesis that was to be suggested to him in 1680 by Robert Hooke, but such is the case for *all* books printed on the subject prior to Bernard Cohen's opus of 1980, which was in essence a digest of Tom Whiteside's insights.

Isaac Newton, as a newly-elected Fellow of the Royal Society, held forth for some three pages describing how his theory worked. Let us not confuse it with that which he later stole off another. Whereas Newton scholars burrow about in unpublished manuscripts prior to 1685 in their attempts to follow up Newton's later reminiscences of what he had done as a young man, and are more often than not guilty of using mere gossamer bridges of speculation in the reading of meanings plainly absent from the text – we shall be giving the reader the plain and simple meaning of a public statement, confidently sent forth by a young Fellow of Trinity at the height of his powers.

Our account will be fully in accord with Newton's dominant interest through this decade, the 1670s; his alchemic researches. Newton scholars present their theories as if there were two quite different persons under one skin; the one laying the foundations of dynamics and the patron saint of the Age of Reason, and the other endlessly searching for the Green Lyonne, the Philosopher's Gold and so forth. There was but one person, who developed:

> 'so may the gravitating attraction of the earth be caused by the continual condensation of some other such like aetherial spirit, not of the main body of phlegmatic aether, but of something very thinly and subtilely diffused through it, perhaps of an unctious, or gummy tenacious and springy nature.'[30]

The notion came to him while observing how a lens on his table when rubbed would attract little bits of paper, 'yet would the papers as they hung under the glass receive some new motion, inclining this way or that way, according as I moved my finger'. He surmised that there must be some subtle ether causing this, which was a fair enough way of referring to static electricity, and that the *ether of gravity* was of a different kind.

As 'nature is a perpetual circulatory worker', so this gravitational ether circulated, and condensed when it reached the ground, thereby pulling things downwards. His was a totally vitalistic and proto-alchemical theory, whereby:

> 'the vast body of the earth, which may be everywhere to the very centre in perpetual working, may continually condense so much of this spirit as to cause it from above to descend with great celerity for a supply.'

Its 'gummy, tenacious nature' enabled it to get a grip on objects as it bore swiftly downwards, not easy one imagines for an invisible and intangible substance. A quantitative statement here appears, as would indeed be expected from such an author, which in view of later claims he made about this theory should be noted. Following directly on from the previous quote, he asserts:

81

> 'in which descent it may bear down with it the bodies it pervades with a force proportional to the superficies of all their parts it acts upon...'

In other words, the larger the surface of body, the greater the force of gravity acting upon it. Readers will recall that Galileo had refuted some such notion.

After condensing, this gravity ether descends into the bowels of the earth to be refreshed, and then arises until it 'vanishes again into the aetherial spaces'. Also the Sun did:

> 'imbibe this spirit copiously, to conserve his shining, and keep the planets from receding further from him.'

How odd that a theory which accounted for so many mysterious phenomena did not become better known. It explained why the Sun kept shining, why the planets did not fly away, and why big objects fell down more forcefully than small objects. As well as explaining the so-mysterious pull downwards to which this sublunary realm is subject, it could also account for the planets being kept apart, for, as oil and water did not mix:

> 'the like unsociableness may be in aetherial natures, as perhaps between the aethers in the vortices of the sun and planets.'

Let us imagine ourselves back into the period of the mid seventeenth-century to see what Newton's original new theory was trying to explain, in terms of the dynamic dilemmas involved. For ages, Aristotle's homely, four-element theory had been accepted, which said that things made of 'earth' and 'water' fell downwards while anything composed of 'air' and 'fire' tended to move upwards. Bacon had banned Aristotelian explanations on the grounds that they were *mere words*: and thus the above instance merely said that things fell down because it was their nature to do so. In its place, Descartes' theory had become popular, but had a major drawback of having no concepts of matter, weight or solidity: the sole difference between matter and empty space was in the shape of particles! The world had been drained by Descartes of all properties except those of geometry, i.e. *shape* and *extension*. He had vortices of little particles which might account for the revolution of planets around the Sun, but why on earth should things fall downwards?

Thus, Isaac Newton's theory of gravitation was an account in terms of 'ethers' to account for why things fell downwards. It was a *qualitative* theory in that the several ethers were different in nature. Its tenor was well expressed by Manuel: 'one feels a powerful primitive animism in which the eathereal substance becomes alive'.[31]

82

THE GRAVITY OF THE SITUATION

In the year 1679, somewhat before the correspondence with Hooke began, Newton had written to Robert Boyle with a different angle on his ether-gravity theory – which it seems he was quite proud of, having perused no small amount of alchemical documents by this time. It is quite likely that this was a response to Boyle writing to him the year before, revealing or hinting at the secret of transmuting gold.

This letter written to Robert Boyle in February 1679 discerned that 'ye cause of gravity' was to be found, not as earlier in a flux of downward-rushing particles, but rather in a static gradient of texture in his aether, moving from grosser particles above to subtler ones below. That gradient *extended to Earth's centre*:

> 'from ye top of ye air to ye surface of ye earth and again from ye surface of ye earth to ye centre thereof the aether is insensibly finer and finer.'

Because of that gradient, any body suspended in this aether-gradient would 'endeavour' to move downwards. He thereby made clear that its gravity-field continued down through Earth's crust as far as Earth's centre. Somehow there were *holes* in the ether of different sizes, so that the finer ether could somehow move through the grosser ether... It was nothing less than the very 'cause of gravity' which an excited 37-year-old Newton revealed to his colleague. It had the radically originally feature that it worked by a push, which could readily be understood, not a pull.* [32]

These ether-based theories gave a *physical cause* of gravity, without any action-at-a-distance. Only after Halley's visit was such a quest abandoned and instead he developed a mere mathematical description. We are here a long, long way from the '*hypotheses non fingo*' that the mature President of the Royal Society was heard to mutter when people complained that they could not apprehend how an inverse square principle was supposed to work across the wide reaches of the universe. [33]

---

* She there redated the *De Gravitatione* manuscript to the 1680s and showed how it had developed out of an earlier text 'Of Nature's obvious laws and processes of vegetation' dating from the early 1670s. [This text may be perused at the 'Chymistry of Isaac Newton' site] His special new gravity-ether there appeared, which *gave objects weight* by pulling them downwards: 'But in its descent it [the ether] endeavours to beare along with bodies it passes through, that is makes them heavy & this action is promoted by the tenacious elastic constitution whereby it takes ye greater hold on things in its way, & by ts vast swiftness.' Dobbs, *Janus* p.264; discussed by William Newman in 'A Preliminary Assesment of Newton's Alchemy', *The Cambridge Companion to Newton*, Ed Iliffe, 2016.). Years earlier, Hall & Hall (1962, p.70) had placed it back in the 1660s. Scholars have generally accepted this redating, eg: 'Most scholars (myself included) had fixed its date of composition no later than 1673. Nevertheless, Dobb's claim is persuasive if not decisive.' (J.E.McGuire, in *Rethinking the Scientific Revolution*, Ed. Ostler, M., 2000, p.271)

Perhaps in the early 1680s – the date is uncertain[34] – he wrote some notes concerning Descartes, which scholars call '*De gravitatione et equipondere fluide*' (their opening line):

> 'Gravity is a force in a body impelling it to descend. Here, however, by descent is not only meant a motion towards the centre of the Earth but also towards any part or region... in this way if the conatus of the aether whirling about the Sun to recede from its centre be taken for gravity, the aether in receding from the Sun could be said to descend.'
> (Hall & Hall, p.148)

We note the Aristotelian flavour of gravity being a force *in* a body which makes it descend, also something resembling the converse of gravity which was 'levity' in the Aristotelian scheme of things. The ethers tended to move *away* from the Sun, in the huge solar vortex, they were pulled away from it, so he mused to himself, by something resembling the pull of objects downwards on the surface of the Earth.

This theory is, it should be stressed (in opposition to what will be read in Newton biographies), wholly in accord with *all* his written documents, published or unpublished, prior to 1685, in that it is proposed within the context of vortex theory, which as we've noted had to be demolished in order finally to argue his *Principia*: then, he emptied out the heavens by introducing the void and something absolutely new began.

A manuscript dated to 1681 was unearthed by professor Whiteside, and shows Newton still believing that an ether-vortex pulls the planets around the Sun: '*Materiam coelorum fluidam esse [et] circa systematis cosmici secundum cursum Planetarum gyrare*' (loosely translated as, 'The fluid material of the heavens is flowing around and makes the planets turn'). On that basis, Whiteside made his claim that even after 1680 Newton still adhered to the Cartesian vortex theory.[35]

It was an original theory, being unique in explaining gravity by means of a push instead of a pull.

Robert Hooke's Theory

Hooke's first statement of a gravity principle extending throughout the solar system appears in 1664 in his *Micrographia*, in the section entitled, 'The Vale of the Moon'. The different planets each had their own centres of gravity he argued, and the mountains on the Moon indicate that it, too, possesses gravity. He there rejected the vortical theory of Descartes.

THE GRAVITY OF THE SITUATION

In 1666, Hooke read to the Royal Society some papers about his experiments with gravity,* where weights were carried to the top of Westminster Abbey, and then lowered into a mineshaft, to see how their weight altered as his theory predicted it should. These he concluded (rightly) were too inaccurate to demonstrate any perceptible change in the weight due to the variation in gravity, and he concluded with the vital insight that a pendulum clock would be sufficiently accurate to detect such a variation, over a period of time. We find him in correspondence with sea-captains, taking pendulum clocks he gave them to see whether they went slower at the equator. Later on, Edmond Halley was to detect that in equatorial latitudes clocks go slower, from which the bulge of the Earth at the equator was deduced. Of the decrease below the Earth's surface he said:

> 'But in truth, upon considering the nature of the theory aright, we may find that (supposing the theory true, that all the constituent parts of earth had a magnetic or attractive power) the decrease of gravitation is almost 100 times less than a grain to a +pound, at as great a depth as 50 fathom.'[36]

This isn't quite accurate but shows he had a theory for computing the matter. His assumption was that 'a body should lose somewhat of its gravitation, or endeavour downwards, by the attraction of the parts of the earth placed above it', which is correct.

1666 deserves to be remembered as the year when one man, Robert Hooke, started to think of gravity as linking together the heavens and earth. 'I have often wondered, why the planets should move about the sun according to Copernicus' supposition...' he said to the Royal Society, in a lecture discussing how orbital motion could be regarded as compounded of a central attractive force towards the Sun and a straight-line inertial tendency. But that another man, Isaac Newton, also in that year had such thoughts, is most doubtful. One hesitates to mention Sir Isaac's nervous breakdown of 1693; when so beside himself was he that he even accused John Locke of trying to 'embroil him with women'; but his recollection of having discovered the theory around the year 1666 is *first heard* of in the year following the nervous breakdown, i.e. 1694.

---

* On 21 March of that year Hooke reported his gravitational experiments to the Royal Society, whereby a distinction between mass and weight was implied, and where future experiments with spring balances and pendulum clocks were recommended. On 23 May of that year he first proposed to the Royal Society that the motion of the planets be resolved into two components, radial and transverse, in a lecture entitled: 'On the Inflection of a Direct Curve by a Supervening Attractive Principle.' According to Patterson ('Hooke's Gravitational Theory and its Influence on Newton,' 'Isis,' 1949, 40 p333), 'Thomas Young at the beginning of the nineteenth century recognised the importance of Hooke's May lecture, and in his historical catalogue placed it as the earliest listing under the heading 'Central Forces

The coffee-house trio would have had various occasions for debating this issue, e.g. the publication in 1673 of a work by Christiaan Huygens, a brilliant Dutch astronomer, about how to compute centrifugal force in circular motion. Combined with Kepler's third law, this gave fairly readily the principle of an *inverse square* principle of attraction whereby the Sun pulled the planets. Ah, but could anyone link this to the first law derived by Kepler, which specified that the motions had to be elliptical?

One would have much liked to be a fly on the wall for some of those discussions, of which so little is recorded, and that irrevocably polarised by the storms and loyalty-tests which followed later. How did Hooke endeavour to express his understanding of the difference between inertial and gravitational mass, which caused him to invent the spring balance and stimulated his development of the pendulum clock? What were the grounds for his asserting an inverse square principle - was it just by way of analogy with the magnetic force experiments he had been conducting? Christopher Wren (then undergoing an astonishing transformation from Oxford astronomy professor to London's chief architect) had one gathers a few ideas upon the modifications required to Descartes' axioms of uniform motion.

In his 1674 opus *An Attempt to Prove the Motion of the Earth* Hooke refers to Wren as 'the incomparable mathematician' so he had clearly found these discussions illuminating. A diagram of Hooke's from the year 1666 is here shown, concerning

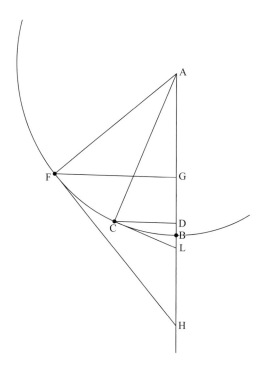

the resolution of circular motion into radial and tangential components. This 1674 work formulates a general principle of gravitation for terrestrial phenomena and the motion of the solar system but does not specify an inverse square principle, merely that the attractive power must decrease with distance. In the late Seventies, his theory develops in two notable ways. Firstly, the records of the Royal Society show him experimenting with the force of magnetic attraction and how it decreases with distance; in such an empirical, Baconian manner he may have arrived at his inverse square principle, which the coffee-house trio was to debate at length.

The other development – the first practical application of Hooke's theory of gravitation – was his *Cometa* of 1678, where he proposed the new notion that comets returned owing to being pulled round the Sun, as opposed to the earlier notion that they went in a straight line – 'which is a very new opinion' as Samuel Pepys recorded in his diary.[37] Hooke surmised several possible orbits, such as, 'if further we will admit it to move in an ellipsis...' Such an ellipse he explained might even lie in a plane perpendicular to the ecliptic.[38]

The culmination of Hooke's theory appeared in 1682, with a theoretical justification for the inverse square principle of gravitation given before the Royal Society, written up with the title *Of Comets and Gravity*.[39] His bold hypothesis, surely the grandest yet formulated before the Royal Society, was that throughout the universe there existed 'an active principle, which I conceive universal to all solid bodies in Nature, and that is, of a Gravitation or Power of attracting similar solid bodies towards their centres'.[40]

His argument wove between the physics of an earth which moves round the Sun, still a fairly new idea, to comets and why their tails point away from the Sun – quite a tricky matter to explain. His theory is shown to be better than the old theories of vortices or crystal spheres because of the way comets move about the solar system, in a quite contrary direction than the planets. Discussing how the comet of 1664 passed between Earth and Mars, he concluded triumphantly:

> 'Those that hold solid Orbs,[41] will afford it no room, nor those that hold *Vortices*. Those that suppose Demons, may suppose what they will, but to little purpose.'

That comet, he explained, had moved retrograde with respect to the planets 'in-between Earth and Mars'.[42] He alluded to the very recent comet of August 1682 in this context, as also having been retrograde, or rather he says he will discuss this question. Hooke seems to be the only person who realizes, at any rate in the UK, that comets are moving in the solar system in the wrong direction with regard to the supposed solar vortex – that is what he here means by 'going retrograde'. This is what nullifies that ether-vortex theory, he explains. But he doesn't realize that the two 1679/80 comets were one and the same, only Flamsteed gets that.

Gravity has to be universal, he explains, because all the other planets we can see are spheres, and moreover they are spinning round, as too is the Sun. They are spherical in shape because gravity is pulling their matter in towards the centre and were it not for that gravitational pull, their parts would fly outwards due to the axial spin (p.178).

Space must offer zero friction to the motion of bodies, Hooke explains – which argument gets soaked up into Part II of Newton's *Principia*, without any acknowledgement. Whatever occupies the vast expanse of the universe must be:

> 'so fluid, as hardly to be able to hinder the Motion of any Solid through it, much less of a Body of any considerable Bulk or Magnitude.'

Gravity applies to any body in proportion to its 'weight' he explains, irrespective of shape or whether it is solid or liquid. (Today we would say 'mass'). And the attraction is as *inverse square* of distance simply because of the three-dimensional nature of space. Using the analogy of some sort of effluvium radiating out through space, he explained:

> 'For this Power propagated, as I shall then shew, does continually diminish according as the Orb of propagation does continually increase, as we find the Propagation of the Media of Light and Sound do also... And from hence I conceive the Power thereof to be always reciprocal to the Area or Superficies of the Orb of Propagation, that is duplicate of the distance.'

His exposition of the inverse-square nature of the gravity force followed on from his lecture-series on light in the previous year, where he had derived the inverse square law for light intensity geometrically using conical space elements – an example of what Hooke called 'Physics geometrically handled'.[43]

There was no-one else in Europe capable of making such a statement. Robert Hooke deserves to be accredited as *the* discoverer of the theory of gravitation, which he developed between 1666 – when lowering masses down a well in Surrey he strove to measure their decrease in weight – to 1682, when his theory was fully formed. Only one further development remained and that was his comprehension, between 1683 and 1687, of the oblateness in the shape of the earth and how it lessened slightly the force of gravity at the equator.

The above argument concerning the 'Orb of Propagation' is analogous to that later used by Michael Faraday for how electrostatic force decreases from a point as the square of distance. As the area of the surface of a sphere is $4\pi r^2$, so in unit area of such a sphere's surface, the concentration of lines of flux (or however one pictures it) must vary inversely as the square of the distance, for exactly the same reason as light and sound intensity decrease through space inversely as the square of the distance. Indeed, in the previous year (1681) Hooke had explained how light intensity falls of as the inverse square of distance from source in similar terms.[44]

The Conception and Birth of 'Newton's Theory of Gravitation'

The reader will groan, 'Not another Bacon-Shakespeare controversy!' But, the psychology of the creative process is surely of greater interest than a mere demi-god superman image left over from the Age of Reason. We can now locate the two moments in time, which we may allude to as the conception and birth, of Robert Hooke's theory of gravitation, within the mind of Isaac Newton. Its birth-process may have gone somewhat transcendentally beyond what was imagined by Robert Hooke and yet we stick to this phrasing.

The conception occurred as already discussed on 9 January 1680 and its birth sometime in 1685 when Newton achieved the epochal and monumental linkage of the sidereal lunar period to the rate of fall of objects on Earth. He showed that the rate at which the Moon 'fell' towards Earth was to the rate of fall of objects on the surface of the Earth, inversely as the square of their distances from the centre of the Earth.

An extract from Hooke's diary for the period in question[45] shows his sanguine, effervescing brain, ever-teeming with new ideas:

1679

Oct.27 About attraction.
Nov.8 At Mans. Sir Chr. Wrens. He told me that he had found to make a circle equall in periphery to Ellipse, about centrall attraction.
Dec.1 Letter from Newton.
Dec.5. Wrote to Mr Newton.
Dec.7. Newton's letter.
Dec.9. Sent letter to Newton
Dec.24 Read Newton's letters to Boyle at Garways, Battersby.

1680

Jan 3. Examined Theory.
Jan 4. Perfect Theory of the Heavens.

Excited by it all coming together in his mind, he put pen to paper on 6 January to Newton, even despite the latter having said in his previous two replies that he did not have any interest in 'philosophy'. All the major components of the new synthesis are assembled – except one. It never occurred to Hooke that what Galileo had demonstrated, that bodies fell so that their speed increased equally per equal increment of time, could be linked to the Moon's revolution against the stars, its 'sidereal' path, using the centrifugal force formula shown by Hooykaus. Equally, and contrary to several centuries of tradition, it had not at this time occurred to Newton. The latter had at this time *no inkling* that he was destined to become known for a theory of gravitation, other than the one he had proposed.

In his previous letter Hooke had proposed the notion of a universal force of gravitational attraction and had broached the all-important concept of circular motion being composed of two components, a straight line 'inertial' component and a radial force towards some centre. Diagrams survive showing how Hooke had lectured on this subject: in opposition to the Cartesian notion that the vortical orbits were 'inertial' motion. In this letter he started by asserting the universal inverse-square law of attraction, seeing it in terms of Kepler's second law,[46] and asserting that such a formula would give stable elliptical orbits, 'Which I conceive doth very Intelligibly and truly make out all the appearances of the heavens.' There were two specific purposes of this correspondence for Hooke: one was to try and revive Sir Isaac's now-dormant interest in 'philosophy', and the other was to seek his counsel, as one with an admitted superior mathematical ability, to ascertain quite generally what kind of curves would be generated by such a supposition. In the previous letter Hooke had also referred to a ball rolling about in a bowl, where the attraction towards the centre decreased with the distance from the centre, and Newton in reply had drawn a diagram, with which Hooke had agreed.

Next, Hooke raises the subject which he reported to the Royal Society back in 1666, of how such a force of attraction would decrease could one go into the earth: it would gradually decrease, he suggested, like 'a body moved in a concave Sphaere where the power Continually Decreases the neerer the body inclines to a horizontall motion...' Newton was later to show by his integral calculus that the force decreased linearly with distance from the centre.[47] This is important because a few years later, when entering into his condition of self-delusion, or perhaps just lying, he was to assert repeatedly that Hooke in this letter had said that gravity below the surface of the earth decreased as the *square* of the distance from the centre, which it does not within the earth, but only above it; Hooke in this letter distinguished these two things. Hooke's initial gravity computation of 1666 had estimated how much a weight would decrease upon taking it down a mine.

The letter comes on to the assumption which has to be made in using the inverse square law for astronomy, that the forces act as if from the centres of the planets:

'But in the Celestiall Motions the Sun Earth or Centrall body are the cause of the Attraction, and though they cannot be supposed mathematicall points yet they may be Concieved as physicall and the

> attraction at a Considerable Distance may be computed according to the former proportion as from the very Center.'

Next his breezy letter reports to Newton how Edmond Halley found at St. Helena[48] that a pendulum at the top of a mountain went slower than at the bottom, 'which he was much Surprised at, and could not Imagine a reason. But I presently told him...' This he links to how bodies will be slightly lighter near the equator, 'the Circular motion being swifter', and to the problem of standardising time measured by pendulum clocks, at different latitudes and altitudes.

Hooke's early researches were on the difference between mass and weight, whereby an ordinary balance (which measures mass) would be no use for such gravity experiments, so that he invented the spring balance and developed the pendulum clock. Over the years, he had lectured on all these subjects, and had quite probably (in Lohne's view) shown how Kepler's third law was related to the inverse square principle, though the first and second laws remained to baffle him. Now it had all come together in his mind and he was simmering away but could not make the link to ellipses.

If surmise may be permitted, Sir Isaac would have said to himself 'Good Lord, supposing he's right? What did I say, a "sticky and unguent nature"?' The contrast between this theory wholly consonant with the latest developments in dynamics owing to Hooke's conversations with Halley and Wren, and his own alchemical and metaphysical theory would have been too great for him to cope with and so he did not reply to the letter and decided to forget the whole thing.

That turned out to be impossible, for the heavens did not permit it. A comet, possibly the biggest ever recorded in Flamsteed's view, blazed across the night skies – and again he formed a totally erroneous opinion. If a comet disappears in the early morning sky going towards the Sun, then reappears two weeks after in the evening sky going the other way, then how, the modern reader will wonder, could one not realise the two were one, having gone around the Sun? A simple answer would be that such motion is not well compatible with vortex theory, which up till now Newton had had no reason to question. We've seen how, even after Hooke's letters to him proposing an utterly different scheme, a clearly dateable manuscript by Newton exists for 1680/81 accepting still the vortex theory.[49]

His one reply to Hooke on the subject of dynamics was to propose a query about how objects would fall downwards from a great height and be deflected by the rotation of the Earth – which we have not discussed, wishing to keep the story as straightforward as possible – but suffice to say his conjecture was erroneous, as Hooke was advised when he discussed it with other Royal Society members. So, around the years 1684-5 it would have dawned on him that Flamsteed had been right all along about the comet going round the Sun. He would have perceived that *all* his statements to others on matters of dynamics had been completely mistaken:

his unguent-and-sticky-texture gravity theory of 1676; his dynamic conjecture to Hooke; and then his argument to Flamsteed about the comet. This would have irritated him and thereby stimulated him into trying to get something right. In these years, he collected comet-path data, with help from Halley, and came to the conclusion that their paths were either parabolae or ellipses, although with a very large eccentricity. The heavens were turning up the very stuff of his mathematics lectures! Did Halley's comet start the Newton brain turning over, the one that is known to history?

His breakthrough came in 1685, after he had been stimulated to work on the subject by visits from Edmond Halley, when we have the first evidence for the 'apple-Moon' computation – centuries of mythologising notwithstanding. Once he had performed this, he began to realise that he had the power to re-cast the universe. The void, hitherto seen only at the tip of a mercury column, he now projected through all the vast immensities of space. The universes both of Descartes and of Aristotle had been *full*, with substance of one kind or another. He became able to relate both the first and third law of Kepler to the inverse square principle, and the second to what is nowadays called the conservation of angular momentum. The proto-calculus which he had been mulling over for years began to activate in his mind, so that he could formulate the law as an attraction between all the *particles* in the universe, and integrate this to give the attraction for planets. Then, as we've seen, the beginning called *De Motu*, blossomed forth into the *Principia,* the most incomprehensible masterpiece ever composed.

Through all past history till that moment, the lunar sidereal orbit had had a purely *astral* significance, measuring the Moon's position against fixed stars, a zodiac or whatever. Sir Isaac detached it from this astral reference and utilised it in a previously unheard-of way, for creating a new science of mechanics. With admirable simplicity, he ignored all of the baffling irregularities of the Moon's motion, and just took a circle for its orbit. A simple ratio of 60 is applied to the distance ratios as to the time ratios. *

At this time he was composing an obscure treatise on the religion of ancient Chaldea[50], and 60 was the Chaldean number base, so perhaps this gave him the idea of the factor of 60. It one of those acts which, once it has been accomplished, is very difficult to see why no-one thought of doing it before.

With regard to why so rudimentary a calculation (as it may appear to us) did not occur to anyone before, it may help to note that Galileo never showed any interest in computing the acceleration due to gravity, i.e. the amount by which velocity would increase each second during free fall. Science historians will tend to assume that he did this, or even infer the value he ought to have reached from his experiments: but he didn't.[51]

---

* As the modern lunar-distance figure is 60.27 Earth-radii, his figure of 60 was within ½%; however, the computation of lunar orbit needs to be performed using the common centre of gravity of the Earth-Moon system, and that smaller orbit-radius gives him a larger computation error of around 1%, see Appendix 4.

In this 'annus mirabile' of 1685 two other implications of the 'apple-Moon' test unfolded before Isaac Newton. One was his integral calculus method of demonstrating that the attraction of the earth acts *as if* all the mass were concentrated at its centre before he could show that he had no cogent grounds for doing *any* Moon-test, because the test employs distances measured from Earth's centre. The other conception was that of 'absolute space'. Rotational acceleration and velocity are not relative but are measured by an absolute frame of reference. This is rather mysterious. Why should the Moon's *sidereal* period be taken? What have the stars got to do with the gravity of Earth?

He came to forget food or sleep, as his muse hammered out the new mechanics, until, in March 1687, the *Principia* was completed, and he sent the last volume to the Royal Society, of which Samuel Pepys was then President.

The Blossoming of Self- Delusion

On 20 June 1686, Newton composed, in a letter to Edmond Halley,[52] *five grievous lies.* This letter is in a sense the most significant he ever wrote and is required reading for insight into its author's character.

It was in reply to a missive from Halley, which expressed the hope that 'candour', indeed 'the greatest candour imaginable' would be forthcoming from him, as has earlier been mentioned, and that he might 'act accordingly' in response to Hooke's claims that he had been addressing the Royal Society for twenty years about gravity. Sir Isaac did indeed act accordingly, in a most decisive fashion, but not as Halley had in mind.

With the preface that the whole matter was 'a frivolous business' and that this account was only 'so far as I could remember, for 'tis long time since they [i.e., his letters to Hooke] were writ, & I do not know that I have seen them since', he makes the following points:

> (1) 'That what he told me of the duplicate proportion was erroneous, namely that it reached down from hence to the centre of the earth.' At no point did Hooke suggest this to Newton or anyone else, as Halley could readily have checked. His lettters clearly indicate a different principle in subterranean realms, as has been quoted. This accusation is thrice-repeated in his letter to Halley, then again in the next letter. If Hooke believed such a thing he would indeed have been as incompetent as the history books say he was.

> (2) Of the duplicate proportion (ie, $1/r^2$) 'he told it me in the case of projectiles.' The statement in Hooke's letter which has been quoted

was *universal* in context and not limited to projectiles. The law is clearly irrelevant to the case of projectiles, because for the distance a projectile goes up or down the variation in the acceleration due to gravity is negligible.

(3) Of his earlier correspondence with Hooke 'in my answer to his first letter I refused his correspondence... Could scarce persuade myself to answer his second letter; did not answer his third.' He is now pretending that his letters to Hooke were written in a mood of contempt, that he already knew more about the theory than Hooke pretended to do and so forth. All Newton biographies accept this retrospective view, as to how Hooke failed to comprehend that he could not help but irritate and annoy Newton by his presumption, etc.

(4) Further, when Christian Huygens published his *Horologica* in 1673, Newton wrote him a letter, and mentioned 'the forces of the Moon from the earth, and earth from the Sun', which 'shows that I had then my eye upon comparing the forces of the Planets arising from their circular motion, and understood it.' Newton biographers (More, Rigaud) cited this recollection as evidence of a Moon-test performed before 1673. It is more difficult for modern biographers to do this, now that his correspondence has all been published and evidently the letter in question had nothing whatever to do with forces between planets, merely giving a (totally inaccurate) estimate of the ratio of the *distances* Sun-Earth and Earth-Moon.[*] The Dutch editors of Huygens' complete works have pointed out[53] that no such argument about gravity appears in the letter to Huygens.

(5) Newton alluded to his unguent-and-tactile-ether theory which he submitted to the Royal Society, averring that therein:

'I hinted at a cause of gravity towards the earth, sun and planets, with the dependence of the celestial motions thereon; in which the proportion of the decrease of gravity from the superficies of the planet (though for brevity's sake not there expressed) can be no

---

[*] A follow-up letter (27th July, Correspondence, II, p.446-7) states 'ye greatest distance of ye sun from ye earth is to ye greatest distance of ye moon from ye earth, not greater then 10000 to 56....' As the true ratio is 10000 to 25.7, the error is 120%. He again quoted this part of the letter in his note to Halley of July 1686. The ratio found in one of his 1669 papers as 559½ to 100000, ie just the same.

other than reciprocally duplicate of the distance from the centre,' a breathtaking act of self-deception.

After such shockingly fictional claims, the letter then changes tack, as if assuming that Halley would decline to believe any of the foregoing - as might well have been the case:

> 'But grant I received it [the gravity theory] afterwards from Mr Hooke, yet have I as great a right to it as the ellipsis... I do pretend to have done as much for the proportion [i.e., the inverse square law] as for the ellipsis, and to have as much right to the one from Mr Hooke and all men, as to the other from Kepler.'

He has added the rigour of demonstration to the ellipse laws of Kepler as to the gravity law of Hooke, he is now saying. No-one has disputed this. The bile of his letter now spills over into a slur against Kepler: 'For as Kepler knew the orb to be not circular but oval, and guessed it to be elliptical...'

The next paragraph follows on logically from the foregoing, and consists of the threat to suppress publication of the third volume of his *Principia*, now that Halley has already committed himself personally to the cost of printing the first two. He regrets the difficulty in selling the two volumes alone, which he explains ought now really to be called, '*De Motu Corporum libri duo*,' though he appreciates that this does not sound very exciting. This behaviour he explains with a slur against philosophy: 'Philosophy is such an impertinently litigious lady, that a man had as good be engaged in lawsuits, as have to do with her.'

Halley is caught! The decision he cannot even discuss with anyone else, for so much hangs upon the cover-up to which he is summoned, not least his own finances (from his wedding-dowry). Edmond Halley came to understand that the rise of his own career was bound up with Newton's. Whatever amazement he may have felt over the arguments of the letter, his discussion of them with others or with Newton will cost him not less than his capital outlay on a book which he knows would not sell; quite apart from the general upset of his colleagues in London. No wonder that Halley is the one person to get such high praise in the *Principia*: 'the acute and universally learned Mr Halley'.[54]

After composing this letter, Newton discovers that there is more of his bile to come, and added a postscript longer than the letter. He there suggested that Hooke might have obtained his views on gravity from the copy of Newton's letter to Huygens deposited at the Royal Society, 'and so what he wrote to me afterwards, about the rate of gravity, might be nothing but the fruit of my own garden'. The sole mention of gravity in that letter was a comment upon the Moon facing the Earth,[55] which Hooke had years earlier discussed in a comparable context. He adds, 'And it's more than I can affirm, that the duplicate proportion was not expressed in that

letter'. We can make that affirmation; there was no such allusion in the letter –
Newton's argument here is again deceptive.

Finding his fury against Hooke to be unabated, he accused:

> 'This carriage towards me is very strange and undeserved [i.e., asking
> for some credit]; so that I cannot forbear, in stating the point of justice,
> to tell you further, that he has published Borell's hypothesis in his own
> name; and the asserting of this to himself, and completing it in his own
> name, seems to me to be the ground of all the stir he makes. Borell did
> something in it, and wrote modestly.* He has done nothing...'

Like a beast in agony through being pierced by a barb it cannot remove, Newton is
twisting and turning over the fact that Hooke comprehended the whole significance
of an inverse square law of attraction for gravity years before he did. Later on, he
will resolve the strain through a process of self-delusion using a mock-biblical
story of the Apple and the Fall. In this letter he is alternating between claiming he
had it first, then suggesting Hooke's priority was nothing remarkable because it was
known by others, e.g. Borelli. In a previous letter he had asked Halley to check up
with Christopher Wren because he, Newton, seemed to remember that back in 1677
he had a conversation with Wren in which the latter had seemed to comprehend
the significance of an inverse square law, and wanted to use Wren's memory of
the occasion to support his priority claim. Halley checked this up with Wren, and
replied to Newton – in the difficult reply he had to make – in the negative, though
phrased in his usual tactful manner.

In 1666, Giovanni Borelli had published *Theory of the Medician Stars*[56], the
latter being the name Galileo gave to the moons of Jupiter he had discovered.
Borelli, as a mathematician, proposed that a combination of three forces were
required to explain planetary orbits: one a 'natural instinct' pulling them towards
the Sun; the next in opposition to this a receding tendency -i.e., centrifugal force;
and then a sideways force pulling the planet along in its orbit, coming from the
Sun's rays. By contrasting such a three-force model, one can see how far Hooke had
come in comprehending that only one force was required, a central one, together
with a principle of rectilinear[57] inertia. Hooke lectured that year to the Royal
Society on orbital motion and the principle of gravity, as already discussed. Newton

---

* The character referred to in this postscript 'Bulliandus' is strangely accredited with formulating an
inverse square law of gravitational attraction - thus: 'Now if Mr Hooke, from this general proposition in
Bulliandus, might learn the proportion in gravity, why must this proportion here go for his invention?'
Historians have failed to find any such principle asserted by 'Bulliandus' (Ismael Bouillaud), who held
a neo-Aristotelian view of 'inner strivings' which held the planets in their courses, as he had rejected
the Cartesian system; thus, Koyré says, 'I have to point out, however, that Bullialdus does not assert
the inverse square law of attraction...' (Isis,1952, 43,p.336) His opus was published in 1645 in Paris.

discovered, around 1669, how to compute centrifugal acceleration ('endeavour of receding') for planetary orbits, and also made a computation, by how much the force of gravity at the equator would be decreased owing to the Earth's rotation. Only two of these three, Hooke and Borelli, made public their views in this period, and 'in stating the point of justice' it has to be said that the writings of Borelli and Newton at this time contain no suggestion of a general principle of gravitation.

We now go back to a period of a few years earlier, to when Isaac Newton was an honest man. Scant though are the recollections of human encounters with him, and even fewer are the recollections of his having any interest in other people, one feels that he would then have looked one straight in the eye, without duplicity. He had written the words '*Isaacus Neutonus - Jeova sanctus unus*' as an anagram of his own name,[58] (the date is not known exactly) but this view had not yet blossomed in any unduly offensive form. On our reading his correspondence with Hooke is sincere and respectful.

The Newton biographies treat these letters as Newton later claimed they were, as entirely deceptive and concealing the fact that Newton then understood the whole theory of gravity so much better than did Hooke himself that he was embarrassed by the latter's simplistic comments. They accept Newton's later claim with no shred of documentation that just after these letters he derived the first and second laws of Kepler from his inverse square principle. Westfall in his biography – in the preface of which he advises readers that it took twenty years to write – states this as if were but a matter of fact.[59]

It is hardly remarkable that a man fresh back from Lincolnshire where he managed the funeral arrangements after the death of his mother should confess to Hooke that he was:

> 'almost wholly unacquainted wth what Philosophers at London or abroad have of late been imployed about. And perhaps you will ye more to believe me when I tell you yt I did not before ye reciept of your last letter, so much as heare (yt I remember) of your Hypothesis of compounding ye celestial motions of ye Planets, of a direct motion by the tangt to ye curve & of ye laws & causes of springyness, though these no doubt are well known to ye Philosophical world.'

The 'hypothesis of springyness' was what is nowadays called Hooke's Law. We find other expressions of gratitude such as 'I cannot but return my hearty thanks for your thinking me worthy of so noble a commerce & in order thereto francly imparting to me several things in your letter'. Or again:

> 'If I were not so unhappy as to be unacquainted with your Hypothesis above mentioned (as I am wth almost all things which have of late

been done or attempted in philosophy) I should so far comply wth your desire as to send you what Objections I could think of against them if I could think of any.'

The letter concludes by saying he is attempting a new design of his reflecting telescope and promising that 'If I do any thing you may expect to hear from me'. It is signed 'Your humble Servant', as Hooke had likewise finished his. There is no trace of irritation or malice, still less of superiority, which historians advise us was present. Hooke replies with a very tactful and encouraging letter, hoping that his interest in 'Philosophy' may revive by-and-by, adding 'And I know that you that have soe fully known those Dilights cannot chuse but sumetime have a hankering after them and now and then Desire a tast of them'. (The spelling mistakes are said to be due to his amanuensis.)

Are we to believe that, returning from his mother's funeral arrangements, he was suddenly stimulated to solve the relation of Kepler's first two laws to an inverse square principle, then put it aside and told no-one about it? This is what his biographers wish us to accept. Our view adheres rather to the plain historical record, that as soon as he had obtained a solution to this problem, at Halley's prodding, it was at once communicated to the Royal Society by Halley, at the end of 1684. There is no historical evidence that the problem of elliptical orbits so much as interested Newton before he realised of his own accord that the comet trajectories were elliptical. After this revolutionary discovery – if the phrase may be excused – then the geometrical problem of computing the orbit size, perihelion, nodes, inclination to the ecliptic and eccentricity for a comet's path seized a hold of him and he began for the first time to think in the manner of which history tells.

'For a man to achieve what is expected of him,' wrote Goethe, 'he must esteem himself greater than he is. This we readily put up with, provided he does not carry it to absurd limits.' The carrying to absurd limits was in a sense desired by the Royal Society. As President, Newton became its focus, in a manner absolutely different from the free and open collaboration amongst equals in the earlier days when Hooke did so much to bring it together. His rise was its rise. The linking of science to religion in the eighteenth century needed the plaster-cast image of him as demigod, as Pope wrote:

'Nature and Nature's laws lay hid in night;
God said, let Newton be! and all was light.'

As it happened, this coincided with Newton's own self-image. The deeply paranoid and secretive tendencies which his puzzled biographers note developing after the *Principia* was published – which should after all have been his moment of glory and made him a happy man – as if he felt people were trying to persecute him, was a quite different being from the younger man, and is to be expected as guilt resulting from so terrible an act of treachery and deceit, which he could discuss with no-one.

What is generally called his nervous breakdown occurred in 1693, when he (it seems likely) had to be supervised for a while by Trinity College staff. Far from agreeing with his biographer More that 'the only permanent effect of his illness [i.e., his nervous breakdown] was a certain lassitude of mind and unwillingness to engage in creative work,' we are driven to see an all-too-permanent effect of his derangement as a myth created, of an apple in a garden: Conduitt recalled in his memoirs that in 1694, Newton told him the story of how he began to think of his gravity theory back in 1666 when staying at his mother's. Of what he had in fact been pondering in those early years he most kindly gave credit to 'Wren, Hooke and Halley'. In the *Principia,* it is acknowledged that these persons had observed that an inverse square law could be derived from Kepler's third law, and that is all. The manuscript had 'Wren, Halley and Hooke' and Halley, ever the diplomat, had reversed the order. This derivation, which need have no particular connection with a principle of gravity, had occurred to several people and as we have seen was done by Newton on or around 1669. Thus he has achieved a complete psychic swap-over with Hooke, digesting a theory Hooke had been developing for over twenty years, without a trace of acknowledgement, and handing Hooke credit for what he himself managed. To what extent Hooke achieved that for which he was credited remains unsure.

Newton's equals became his opponents. Leibnitz, Hooke and Flamsteed were the great scientific geniuses of the age to whom he owed so much, and how did he treat them? Let us also consider his attitude to Kepler, whose achievements were hardly inferior to his own. Do we find any mark of respect towards Kepler in the *Principia*, any statement that there was no-one to whom he owed more?*

Do we so much as find acknowledgement that he discovered the first and second laws that bear his name? We do not. Kepler had developed a vitalistic, magnetic theory of what held the planets in their places, which is not normally described in terms of vortices, yet he is cited together with Descartes as persons who had espoused the vortex theory. The entire Part II of the *Principia* is dedicated to demolishing the vortex

---

* The three published versions of Newton's *Principia* and the preliminary manuscript drafts contain no mention whatever of Kepler's magisterial contribution to the science of motion. Not only do the printed pages of Newton's great book fail to list Kepler among the inventors of dynamical principles and concepts; there is not even an attribution to Kepler of the discovery of the whole set of three major laws of planetary motion. Kepler appears in Newton's *Principia* only as an astronomer, primarily an observer of comets, and he is mentioned in passing as the admitted discoverer of only the third of the Keplarian laws of planetary motion, the harmonic law.' I. Bernard Cohen, 'Kepler's Century' in 'Four Hundred Years, proceedings held in honour of Johannes Kepler,' *Vistas in Astronomy,* Oxford, 1976, p.6. Kepler viewed the force involved as 'of an intangible nature, closely related to light and magnetic force,' and therefore 'Every planetary body must be regarded as being magnetic, or quasi-magnetic; in fact, I suggest a similarity, and do not declare an identity.' (to Maestlin in 1605) *Occult & Scientific Mentalities in the Renaissance* Ed. Brian Vickers, 1984, pp. 150-151.

theory. In such manner did Newton's mind dismiss as a possible rival one whose genius matched his own. In contrast, the philosopher John Locke, who declared that his goal was but 'to be employed as an under-labourer in clearing the ground a little' for 'the incomparable Mr Newton'[60] was sufficiently deferential to be accepted as a friend.

A doctored 'letter to Huygens'

The letters sent to Halley in June and July of 1686, staking Newton's claim to have discovered of the law of gravity, alluded thrice to views expressed in a letter which he had sent to Christiaan Huygens in Holland years ago, in 1673. We've noted how these views were wholly absent from the letter which Huygens had actually received. It had been sent to Huygens via Oldenburg the Royal Society's Secretary, he had transcribed it. *But,* the views alluded to by Newton are present in the copy of the letter held by the Royal Society.

The first letter sent to Halley averred that Newton just happened to have a copy of this old letter, from thirteen years ago, and it had:

> '...added out of my aforesaid paper [i.e., the 1675 letter to the Royal Society] an instance of their [the laws of motion] usefulness, in comparing the forces of the moon from the earth, and earth from the sun; in determining a problem about the moon's phase, and putting a limit to the sun's parallax, which shows that I had then my eye upon comparing the forces of the planets arising from their circular motion, and understood it.'

Then a second letter to Halley five weeks later quoted a part of its opening paragraph, and explained: 'Now from these words its evident yt I was at that time versed in the Theory of ye force arising from circular motion, & had an eye upon ye forces of ye planets.'[61] Then on a third occasion of bringing this passage to Halley's attention, it was even suggested that Hooke could have derived his knowledge of gravity theory therefrom, by perusing the copy kept in the Society's correspondence.

The passage alluded to was not present in the letter received by Huygens. The letter in Newton's handwriting as sent to Oldenburg for transcription is now in the Royal Society's archives.[62] The two are identical, except for the omission of this key passage. The editor of the Huygens Oeuvres commented (in translation):

> 'We see that Newton's main argument in favor of his priority with respect to Hooke consists in the passage of his letter to Huygens ... It will be noticed that this passage is missing in our text, that is to say in the copy that Oldenburg transmitted to Huygens. It is difficult

to explain such an important omission, as being absolutely contrary to Oldenburg's habits. All copies of the letters that Oldenburg sent to Huygens have been recognized as accurate, and only in rare exceptions does Oldenburg omit a sentence.'

The editors of Huygens' *Oeuvres* ruled out the possibility that Oldenburg had himself decided not to send the text, which constitutes the latter half of the opening paragraph of the letter, on the grounds that he only omitted odd phrases and some concluding remarks, as omissions which would have had Huygens' blessing. They concluded that some instruction must have been given to the Royal Society's secretary, of which no trace survives: 'What is the hand which has withdrawn from the eyes of Huygens the reflections of Newton on the centrifugal force?'[63] What Oldenburg had written to Huygens a propos of this copied letter, was merely: 'I find myself obliged to give you a copy of it, which I shall do in English as I received it,' which hardly sounds as if he had decided to omit the bulk of the first paragraph.[64]

Louise Patterson in 1950 wrote that 'The Royal Society copy in which it [the gravity argument] does appear is an edited copy. The Huygens letter therefore... provides very dubious evidence on Newton's behalf.'[65] The letter which Huygens actually received in 1673 merely said:

'I am glad, that we are to expect another discourse of the Vis Centrifuga, which speculation may prove of good use in Natural Philosophy and Astronomy, as well as in Mechanics'.[66]

It cited as an example, that the Moon faced earthwards owing to 'ye greater conatus of ye other side to recede from it' – a similar answer had been given to this question in his c.1669 document, discussed above.[67]

The moon kept facing Earthwards *because of* a centrifugal pull on its far side, which pulled it away from the Earth. That perspective was *negated by* his later theory of gravity, indicating that he was then nowhere near it.

We must turn to an appreciation of the life of Robert Hooke (1996) to hear a straightforward judgement here, endorsed by no British science historian:

'Later authors have supported Newton's claims [to have discovered gravity theory by himself] by quoting this passage from a copy of his June 23rd letter [of 1673, to Huygens in Holland], reposited at the Royal Society. But Huygens' editors have proved with photostatic copies that the passage concerning gravitation does not appear in Huygens' copy of the letter. The Royal Society copy, therefore, must have been doctored to produce the desired effect.[68] Newton gained his vast reputation, therefore, partly by planting evidence to establish priority, if not by himself, at least by his followers. He became less than civil to Hooke and always refused to give him credit for his most productive ideas. Hooke was deeply saddened and hurt by this neglect of one of his greatest achievements.'[69]

Changing Perspective

Only in 1952 was Hooke's letter of 9 December 1679 to Newton *stating the principle of universal gravitation* published.*

This stimulated Louise D. Patterson to argue for a re-evaluation of Hooke's work. This has been a major source for the present study.

The entire argument here presented hinges on the affirmation by D. T. Whiteside in 1970:

> 'Let me insist that Newton's extant manuscripts contain, before 1684, not a single reference, explicit or implied, to a centri*petal attractive* force used to account for the constraining of the vortical matter into a circular orbit from a straight-line inertial path. Nor do they exhibit factual evidence of *any* 'Moon test' made by Newton at *any* time before the middle 1680s in the simple numerical form suggested by Newton himself to Desmaizeaux in 1718 -in a context (of priority squabbles) where it was to his considerable advantage to assert that such a test had in fact taken place.'[70]

This is a negative statement, embracing the fifteen million or so extant words penned by Sir Isaac, and affirming that they do not corroborate the memory of their own author. For one reason or another, perhaps including religious factors, it took some centuries for this conclusion to be attainable. If someone other

---

* An Unpublished Letter of Robert Hooke,' A.Koyré, Isis, 1952, 43, p.312-337. The re-emergence of this long-lost letter was accompanied by a commentary by Prof. Alexandre Koyré, which denied that Hooke there comprehended the principle of universal gravitation which he was there proposing. His commentary described the contents of the historic letter in the very terms in which Newton years later explained its meaning to Halley! Koyré wrote, 'As for the inside of the earth.. it was only when Hooke - erroneously - asserted that the inverse square law was valid even there...that Newton applied himself to solving the problem.' One would not normally expect a distinguished science historian writing about his own subject, seventeenth-century astronomy, to confound a celestial and a subterranean reference. When publishing the historic letter, one might have supposed that the plain meaning of its content would have had more force than the reminiscences of the person to whom they were addressed six years later. In fact Hooke explained in this letter that the inverse square law was *not* applicable below the surface of the earth. His sentence containing the inverse square law linked it to Kepler's second law of planetary motion. Koyré's attitude is shown in the way he described how various persons 'claim' or 'argue,' whereas, 'Newton tells us...'

than the person who had just edited the massive eight volumes of Newton's mathematical works had made such a remark, then little notice might have been taken.

There is however one point upon which we are obliged to diverge from Whiteside. It concerns what happened around 1679/80, after Newton had returned to Cambridge having overseen his mother's funeral arrangements:

> 'We may choose or not to take his [Newton's] word that he had already, in the winter of 1679/80, obtained a proof of what Halley sought (even though he could not reproduce it for him).'[71]

We have no such choice. Two reasons have here been given as to why that is the case. His letter to Flamsteed in February 1680 about the comet, was phrased in terms of the rotating ether-vortex around the Sun, which pulled or pushed upon the comet. That was Newton's proposal, whereas Flamsteed had advocated some magnetic force. And secondly, his letters to Thomas Burnett starting in December 1680, alluded to the whirling ether-vortex around the Moon that pushed down upon the earth – just as Descartes said – causing hills and vales to be formed. Neither of those positions are in the slightest degree compatible with the theory of gravity which Hooke was trying to tell him about. Then also, if you want to believe that his *De Gravitatione* was composed in the 1680s, that too expresses Newton's ether-vortex view: 'if the *conatus* of the aether whirling about the Sun to recede from its centre be taken for gravity:' we saw how this is centri*fugal* force, pulling the huge ether-vortices *away* from the Sun.

It may be helpful to summarize some key events over this period, while Newton was proclaiming his adherence to an ether-vortex gravity theory:

- Letter to Boyle about gravity theory February 1679
- Newton buries his Mother June 1679
- Returns to Cambridge from Woolsthorpe November 1679
- Correspondence with Hooke December 1679
- Letter to Flamsteed about the comet February 1680
- Decoding the apocalypse with Henry More 1680 first part
- Letters to Thomas Burnett, about how Earth was created: Dec. 1680, Jan 1681.

The arrival of Halley's comet in 1682 bisected the life of Newton. Claims that he had formulated *any* principles of scientific gravitational theory before its advent are unfounded. He had investigated in an inconclusive way the 'endeavour to recede' of circular motion in relation to Kepler's third law, but that is about all.

The argument that Hooke lost his right to credit for the theory because he had not published it, as Halley records Royal Society members saying to him, implies that Leibnitz should have been given sole credit for the invention of differential calculus. In fact, however Hooke did present his inverse square law of universal gravitational attraction, in the autumn of 1682, to the Royal Society, though as we'll see his extensive treatise on the matter seems only to have been published posthumously. The historical record is alas unclear at this critical juncture.

A comparison may be made with the adoption of' fluxion' notation *after* the *Principia* had emerged – as used by British mathematicians for the next two centuries. To quote Whiteside:

> 'As Newton never himself forgot (though he tried cleverly by various ingenious turns of phrase to hide from his contemporaries), the standard dotted notation for fluxions was invented by him only in mid - December 1691.'[72]

The deception was confounded by his claim that he had first carried out the *Principia* computations in a calculus form and later re-cast them into their arcane geometrical style, a story accepted by every biographer and it would seem just about every history of science up until Whiteside's publication of the complete mathematical works, when the affirmation could be made that no trace of any such reworkings existed. This is here of interest as showing Newton's tendency to claim that he was working with an idea a lot earlier than he in fact was. It was made in the context of a bitter and ferocious attempt to divest Leibnitz of credit for his discovery of the method of calculus.

At last we are able to evaluate what really happened in the months following that catalytic visit to Cambridge by Edmond Halley. In the words of John Lohne:

> 'Halley had to wait three months till he got - not the deduction - but a tract containing material for a course of nine lectures ... We may indeed be grateful that there was a problem Newton could not solve, and so was forced to write and publish his Principia.'[73]

He pointed out the still-controversial fact that:

> 'What Newton proved, however, in De Motu was not that if the attractive force varies as inverse-square of the distance, then the orbit will be an ellipse; rather, he proved the converse, namely, that if the orbit is an ellipse, then the attractive force must vary inversely as the square of the distance.'[74]

The mathematics of elliptical motion was never going to be easy. What Newton gave to Halley as *De Motu*, had a cumbersome *three-dimensional* construction, a proto-integral calculus that did just about look like a proof.* He had been asked to provide a demonstration where the starting-point was given, viz Kepler's law of elliptical motion, as likewise was the end-point that had to be reached, viz an inverse-square law of centripetal force. Nobody is ever going to say 'Aha!' upon perusing his proof.

Years later – nobody is quite sure when – Newton was composing a 'System of the world' which was an alternative version of Book III of his *Principia*, or a less mathematical version. He there alluded to persons who had got the *wrong* answer about gravity:

> 'The later philosophers pretend to account for it either by the action of certain vortices, as Kepler and Descartes; or by some other principle of impulse or attraction, as Borelli, Hooke, and others of our nation.'[75]

Hooke is bracketed with Borelli, Kepler and Descartes as 'later philosophers' who had got the wrong answer! One is here shocked by the deceptive logic, whereby the man who had first pointed out the theorem to him is dismissed.

While Newton never in his life troubled to visit the seaside to see how his tidal theory was working, Hooke was corresponding with sea-captains about their problems in locating position and whether they would take one of his curious new clocks with them. The 'Crushing of Hooke' (Chapter 6) has repercussions for the way in which the merits of pure versus applied science is assessed, in that a book of extreme abstractions which no-one could fully understand was given a more exalted status than any applied scientific work.

DISCUSSION

Sagredo, Salviati and Simplicus sit in a garden. An apple falls.

<u>Sagredo</u>: Why, this is a new story of the discovery of gravity, and one moreover which seems to be true. It has always seemed odd to me that discoveries concerning

---

* The late E.J.Aiton was one of the few science historians who really understood the mathematics involved. He described the proof of the Kepler area law given in *De Motu* as 'mathematically unsound' on the grounds that the summation of the infinitesimal changes was not accomplished rigorously. Concerning its inference that, in an elliptical orbit, the centripetal force varies as the inverse square of the distance, Aiton wrote: 'Once again this argument leaves unresolved the logical difficulties inherent in the approximation of a continuous force by a sucession of impulses' (E.Aiton, *The Vortex Theory of Planetary motions,* London, 1972, 103-4.) Such difficulties, reflecting the limited range of integral calculus methods then available, may help us to discern that the proof was first accomplished, in a difficult and laborious manner, in the autumn of 1684 and not earlier.

light and weight should have been made concurrently, as these two things are opposite in their natures. Put them twenty years apart and it makes sense, I can understand it at last.

Salviati: No, I cannot accept this, and moreover I am profoundly shocked by your attitude. To quote the scholar J. W. Herivel:

> 'The assumption that there was no true test of the law of gravitation during the plague years argues for a degree of duplicity on Newton's part, both in casual conversation with Whiston and Pemberton... and in his unpublished account in the Portsmouth Draft Memorandum, [which] is difficult to credit.'[76]

We are here discussing the greatest scientist who ever lived, and one regarded as having a high ethical standard. Furthermore, Sagredo, you are too much in the habit of dismissing the unanimous weight of scholarly opinion, which in this case has accepted for three centuries that Kepler's laws were recast in terms of the new dynamical concepts, which decisively altered natural philosophy, around the end of 1679. Not only Westfall, Herivel and Cohen, but even Whiteside has not questioned this.

Simplicius: Quite so. And there is a Newton-document written not later than 1669 which clearly linked Kepler's third law to an inverse square force principle, and also it compared the Earth's pull on the Moon to the centrifugal force of the Earth's rotation. This paper was shown to the Scottish mathematician David Gregory, who later testified that in it, 'all the foundations of his philosophy are laid: namely the gravity of the moon to the earth, and of the planets to the sun... In fact all these are... subjected to calculation'.[77] It's a well-known fact that his computation had to be laid aside merely because the estimated size of the Earth was then too small. He finished the computation much later on, when the Earth's size was better known. That's good enough for me. Sir Isaac was no liar, and I thank you for saying so, Salviati.

Sagredo: Let's calm down a bit. In fact, perhaps we had better change the subject or I shall be in danger from you two. (Picks up apple) Tell me, do either of you experience any difficulty in crediting the apple story, not mentioned by Sir Isaac prior to 1726?

Simplicius: Certainly not. Patrick Moore described it as, '... The story of the falling apple - which is particularly interesting because it seems to be true'.[78] Are you trying to dismiss this story learnt by every schoolboy as a mere fable?

THE GRAVITY OF THE SITUATION

Sagredo: In his student notes on Descartes, composed in the late 1660s, we find him discussing gravity. He said that this concept could apply equally to objects falling down towards Earth, as to the ethers receding away from the Sun, that is to the force pulling them away from the Sun. The old levity-gravity balance was plainly still there. In the common-sense Aristotelian picture, some things tended to move upwards, things of air and fire, as they experienced the opposite of a downward gravity pull. It makes sense after all to visualise two forces opposing each other, doesn't it? This old view was still found in Leibniz' *Tentamen,* composed in 1687, where levity and gravity counterbalanced each other in the smooth running of the solar system. Not before the autumn of 1684, was the universe re-cast so that gravity applied to all things, so that whatever exists, has weight. In the first definition of the first book of the *Principia* we find the words *massae, pondus, densitate* and *quantitas materiae* are all interlinked – it is a meditation upon mass and weight, as a starting-point for the whole argument.

Most people who have looked at that page which so impressed David Gregory have drawn your conclusion from it, Simplicius. It is a text resembling those optical illusion images, which seem to alternate between two quite different pictures. Gregory's testimony upon it bears witness to the extent to which Sir Isaac could impose his version of the past on others. That text said nothing of a gravity pull of the Sun on the planets, as Gregory alleged, but merely of a force with which the planets recede from the sun.[79] Likewise no pull of the Earth upon the Moon was mentioned, but only a centrifugal force (or '*conatus recendi*' as they called it) of the Moon *from* the Earth. And, as Bernard Cohen noted, its author did not even hint that the earth's gravity might extend to the moon.[80] It did indeed link the third law of Kepler to an inverse-square centri*fugal* force, that is a tendency to recede; but others such as Huygens had managed that also, at much the same time, and it wasn't very evident what led on from there. It was a result which fell out of the mathematics of the cube and square powers of the Kepler law, without much difficulty.

I query the accepted notion that Sir Isaac sat on his results for years out of sheer reticence or lack of interest. If he withheld something, that meant it was imperfect or not ready. As for Salviati's suggestion that the inverse-square law of attraction and Kepler's first law were welded together and then just mislaid somewhere until Edmond Halley came along - well, surely, we can recognise this as a mere school physics myth. As soon as he had derived that result, Edmund Halley was sent it. And what he did over the winter of 1679/80 was just what he told Hooke – absolutely nothing. He attended his laboratory furnace and probably pondered some theological heresies of the fourth century.

Our author's argument here is well-grounded upon Newton's *honesty*. At this time, the alchemical or 'Hermetic' phase of his life, he was a straightforward chap.

Little enough interest in other people to be sure, unless you could key into his current interests as Thomas Moore the Platonist was able to do, yet he was honest. His polite but resolute lack of interest in the blandishments of the Royal Society's new secretary Robert Hooke about the New Philosophy was just that and was not something else as he later tried to maintain. There is no way that what Salviati is claiming could have taken place at that time, without this correspondence being radically deceptive. Is there?

Salviati: Using your argument, then no more had Robert Hooke reached a theory of universal gravity by the time of, say, his *Cometa* in 1678.[81] In that work, an analogy with magnetism led him to restrict gravity so that it did not fully apply to comets. As I recall, he there suggested that after coming close to the Sun, comets could somewhat lose their gravity as a magnet lost its magnetism, and therefore moved away from the Sun because they had acquired some levity from the Sun's light; rather charming really, but definitely not universal gravitation.

Simplicius: We should not marvel, that everyone was still accepting the power of levity as the opposite of gravity, in the 1670s. The tails of comets were plainly being affected by something opposite in nature to the Sun's gravity, because of the way they always streamed out away from the Sun, and Hooke was trying to explain that. It also intrigues me that the 1680 comet came so close to the Sun, a mere fraction of the solar radius, almost the closest that has ever been recorded! This meant that it was swung violently round to go almost back on its own course - at just the time when the minds of Europe were becoming ready for the motion of universal gravity. It also happened to pass by either side of the Earth, coming in at one side as a comet of the evening sky, and reappearing the next week in the morning sky. How strange!

Sagredo: In those days, astronomers were just getting used to the notion that comets existed in space, instead of being mere sublunary meteors somehow drawn up into the higher reaches of the air – the age-old view until the times of Kepler and Tycho Brahe. In that lecture by Hooke to which you referred Salviati, he says that some still believed that comets were sublunary, which meant that they had been produced by the earth. I do agree with Simplicius that the comets of 1680 and 1682 altered the whole debate, once it dawned on people that they had been turned around in their motion by the Sun. Prior to them, there was genteel debate as to whether comets moved in straight lines or in some great circle, but that was all. Then, for about five years hardly anyone could believe that the 'two comets' of 1680 were the same. There was no precedent for a comet to be reversed in its trajectory by the Sun like that. Cassini, Halley, Hooke, Newton – none of them believed it!

THE GRAVITY OF THE SITUATION

Salviati: There is a world of difference between conjecture and demonstration, and science has progressed not by hunches, but by rigorous logic. Hooke was a person who almost achieved a great number of things. He threw out suggestions on all sorts of topics and didn't follow them up. The stark fact is, that in the seven years between making his key suggestion to Newton on 9 January 1680 and the *Principia* emerging, Hooke did nothing to substantiate or develop his assertion.

Sagredo: I will admit that every book written on the subject concurs with your view – except that older books had not heard of the 9 January letter. And yet, in your 'nothing' I find a comprehensive ten-page lecture. Did not Hooke present and elucidate his inverse-square theory on three or four occasions in public, at a time when no-one else in the world espoused it? Plus his letter to Newton of 1680 which he read to the Royal Society; plus a long lecture he gave to the Royal Society of 1682, as well as his comments to Wren and Halley in 1684. One regrets that the Royal Society did not see fit to publish this audacious account of universal gravitation. No doubt it would have been regarded as too speculative. Hooke's argument given for the inverse-square law was quite cogent, based on the three-dimensional nature of space, and followed on from his lectures on the inverse-square attenuation of light intensity in the previous year. That is the reason for the law being inverse-square, there surely is no other. But, if you refuse him credit for the law on the grounds that he failed to demonstrate it, then why are you crediting Newton with the binomial theorem which he produced in 1675? He never proved that at all, but merely said that it worked - as indeed it did!

Salviati: Your view leaves much scope for conspiracy theories; but, having checked through all the Notes and Records of the Royal Society for the 1680s, I'm afraid I rather doubt whether Hooke ever did come up with such a grand explanation. There was just one note for 14 February 1683 which said, 'Mr Hooke brought in a method of explaining the cause of gravity, an account of which he was to give in writing.' One assumes he never did, any more than when Wren put him on the spot a few years earlier.

Simplicius: What a pity that the credit for these fine discoveries could not have been shared out, instead of arguing so.

Chapter 4

The Mythic Equation

'The clear formulation of the differential law is one of Newton's greatest achievements,' wrote Albert Einstein. Dare one ask, what law was that? A notion of Newton's second law of motion, concerning acceleration as being proportional to force, will tend to form in the reader's mind at this point.[1]

Official Mythmakers Cover the Tracks

One tends to find with Newton historiography that that old myths forged in the Age of Reason do still endure, so that the achievements of eighteenth century Newtonianism are placed at the feet of a seventeenth century figure who had never heard of them. Generations of schoolchildren have been taught about Newton's computations concerning 'g' and still are, even though use of this measure of an acceleration due to gravity is absolutely foreign to all three editions of the *Principia* and indeed any other mathematical opus of Newton.

Since Galileo's treatment of falling bodies, acceleration had been a topic for discussion and experiment. It would be wholly a-historical to suppose anyone then had the conception of acceleration as a numerical value – although historians do just that. Galileo discovered that the ratio of velocities of two falling bodies were in proportion to their times for which they have been falling; but, as Bernard Cohen has pointed out, the writings of Galileo do *not* contain any statement saying that:

$$V \; \alpha \; kt,$$

where k would be a constant of proportionality between velocity and time, i.e. the acceleration, from which a value of 'g' could be derived.[2] Galileo also discovered that the ratio of distances fallen were as the squares of the times. Similar comments could be made concerning the Dutchman Christiaan Huygens' treatment of centrifugal force published in 1673, which is normally described in terms of acceleration in circular motion – and it is indeed convenient to summarise what he showed in such terms. However, we need to guard against the importing of modern concepts back into a past before they had been conceived.

Contrary to most textbook accounts of the matter, we shall find that the distinction between *momentum* as the product of mass and velocity (generally referred to as 'motion' or 'quantity of motion') and *force* as the product of mass and the rate of change of velocity is an achievement of the eighteenth century – and to the continent of Europe only, as far as the beginning of that century is concerned. It is all too easily assumed that Newton accepted or used acceleration as rate of change of velocity, as if that were given in the *Principia.* None of the three editions of the *Principia* employ a quantitative concept of acceleration. This has vital implications for the history of the differential calculus.

No 'g' Computation

Westfall, in his epic biography of Newton, *Never at Rest,* refers to 'Galileo's figure for the acceleration of gravity'.[3] Galileo had no such figure, nor did the concept ever occur to him. Westfall routinely refers to Newton's measurement of 'g', by which he appears to have in mind the distance an object falls in one second when dropped. This distance is numerically equal to ½g, but conceptually it is quite different. Distance is after all a very different thing from rate of change of velocity. To take one more example, an article on 'Newton and the Law of Gravitation' by Rosenfield[4] discussed the apple-Moon computation with the words, 'One expects this acceleration to be the same as that for a freely falling body. This step was not difficult to make for Newton.' He never took that step.

Had the *Principia's* illustrious author formed in his mind the notion of rate of change of velocity, then there are several key passages where it would have been useful. The 'apple-Moon test' which he computed in 1685 is one, concerning the relative pull of the Earth's gravity on the Moon compared to objects on its surface, which appears near the start of Book III of the *Principia* – well described by Westfall as 'the lynchpin of the entire argument for universal gravitation;'[5] one might assume that it would also appear in his second law of motion, first composed late in 1684 for his '*De Motu'*.

The historic 'apple-Moon test', linking gravity's pull on the Moon to that on the proverbial apple, is referred to by Westfall as 'Newton's g computation', and if even so distinguished a scholar thus describes it, then one can hardly blame the many physics textbooks which have used such language. In fact, the *Principia's* computation did not employ even velocity, the first differential of motion, let alone acceleration, the second. What it said was that the distance the Moon 'fell' in one minute towards the Earth was the same as the distance which an object on Earth falls in one second. The ratio is a factor of 60, between minutes and seconds, and this is the ratio of the distances from Earth's centre, as the Moon is 60 semidiameters of Earth away. The third edition of the *Principia* encumbers this computation with various correcting factors designed to make it appear as accurate to 1 part in 3000 but the basic argument is unchanged. An Appendix describes the steps of this historic computation in more detail.

Let's go back to a publication from tercentenary celebrations of the *Principia*, which narrates the classic, the irresistible, but fictional tale of this achievement:

> 'Newton calculated the acceleration towards the Earth which the 'lunar apple' would experience if it was very near to the Earth's surface. This turned out to be exactly the same as the acceleration of ordinary falling bodies near the Earth's surface.'[6]

The narration of this event has been much improved by being relocated in time at Cambridge of 1685 rather than Woolsthorpe in 1666,[7] due to the researches of Professor Whiteside and one hopes that a yet further improvement may some day come about through realising that it involved no computation of acceleration or anything resembling it. That tercentenary publication continued:

> 'Newton recognised that all forces cause acceleration, and that if the force is doubled then so is the acceleration.'

This again giving the quite misleading impression that some measure of acceleration exists in the *Principia*. The book may come near to such; it does come near to such, and the casual reader seeking to penetrate its arcane geometry may readily mistake its arguments for such; especially in for example Propositions 32-29 of Book I, discussed below.

The Second Law

Turning to the Second Law of Motion one finds a yet more brazen emendation of its content by historians. Gillespie's *The Edge of Objectivity* roundly asserted:

> 'By Newton's second law of motion, force is measured as the product of mass times acceleration.'[8]

Gillespie's cutting edge of objectivity did perhaps not extend as far as reading what the *Principia* actually said, which was merely that[9] 'change of motion is proportional to the motive force impressed'[10] – and no more. As this has been the most persistently and radically misunderstood sentence in the entire *Principia* down through the centuries, it may be worth contemplating its seven words of Latin, *'Mutationem motus proportionalem esse vi motrici impressae'*, his second 'Law' in the first Book. An earlier definition (in Book 1) explained that by 'quantity of motion' was meant the product of mass and velocity. A formulation of the Second Law of Newton in 'Men of Mathematics' by E.T. Bell is all too typical, and states that 'rate of change of momentum is proportional to the impressed force.'

We may quote just one more illusory account from a history of mathematics:

> 'Newton never made the statement that force equals mass times acceleration. His second law says F=d(mv)/dt and Newton was far too cautious a man to take the *m* out of the bracket.'[11]

Newton never put it into the bracket, he never differentiated 'mv'. Quite apart from the Leibnizian calculus notation [d(mv)/dt] which he clearly wouldn't have used, he simply never formulated the concept of rate of change of momentum. This was accomplished on the other side of the Channel and half a century later – while British mathematicians were loyally stunting their development by adhering to the Newtonian dot-notation.[12]

What is the power that nourishes these blooms of fantasy? The first author above has clearly made a conscious effort to get through to what was really said in the second law, but has ended up with something quite different, *very* different. The entire statement of the law consists of ten words of plain English. Without answering the question, we proceed.

Clearly what is actually said in the *Principia* is relevant to the genesis of calculus in the seventeenth century. Bernard Cohen pointed out that 'Newton does not say here "rate of change of momentum",... Despite the many scientists and historians who have alleged that this is what he meant.'[13] He continues, 'Newton was perfectly aware that continuous forces produce continuous accelerations' - which is acceptable, if taken in a quite general sense.

To return to the *Men of Mathematics* version of events, its author asserted, 'The most important thing for mathematics in all of this is the phrase opening the statement of the second law of motion, *rate of change*.'[14] Had such a phrase indeed been present, migrating through a time-warp from the mid-eighteenth century, it would have sealed forever the debate as to who invented the calculus.[15] This grasp of rate of change of momentum, the author blithely continues, 'gave him [Newton] the master-key to the whole mystery of rates and their measurement, namely the differential calculus.'[16] This misconception is a *central illusion* normally found in *all* accounts of the genesis of differential calculus. Did his second law of motion refer to the rate of change of momentum? Had it done so, that would clearly imply that its author comprehended and was using the notion of rate of change of velocity.

No doubt related to this is the notion that Newton first composed his *Principia* using the differential calculus, but then re-wrote it in its obscure geometrical format. Newton himself made that claim during the great calculus dispute as we shall see. It was doubted by the great nineteenth-century Newton scholar Augustus de Morgan but only definitively refuted by Whiteside in the 1970s, after a thorough perusal of all the available manuscripts, and nowadays books on the subject are coming to accept her judgement.

As a general comment, one may note that Newton's early and largely unpublished work on fluxions from 1665 onwards, terminating more or less after the circulation of his masterly *De Analysi* manuscript in 1669, generally employed letters to signify fluxions rather than the dot notation which he first published in 1693. With the dotted notation a second differential is an easy matter, while use of a letter to denote a 'nascent' or fluxional quantity does not so readily encourage the forming of a second differential.*

First Formulation of F=MA

Who first defined the concept of acceleration in quantitative terms? That's easy to answer; in 1700, the French mathematician Pierre Varignon published his formula:

$$\text{acceleration} = dds/dt^2$$

which looks very much like its first quantitative definition.[17] (where 's' is distance, 't' is time and 'dd' represents the second differential in Leibnizian terms). Varignon was a disciple of Leibniz and a go-between in the great dispute. 'There is glory enough in the discovery for both of you' he wrote to Leibniz, but alas his humane attitude could not prevail. Later on in 1737 the brilliant mathematical genius Leonhard Euler *invented* the formula F=mdv/dt in a couple of treatises.

'In neither of these places did he ascribe the law to Newton' commented a puzzled historian,[18] discussing Euler's achievment: this scholar found it baffling 'how Euler could believe that his principle was new,' as it appeared evident to him that this principle had already been formulated in the *Principia*. That as we have seen, is far from being the case. Euler boldly claimed that his

---

* A more thorough treatment of the velocity of a falling body was given in propositions 39-41 of the *Principia*'s Book 1. A modern restatement of the computations there involved were given by Tom Whiteside, he explained that these sections provide 'an excellent illustration of Newton's infinitesimal method in the *Principia.*' (D.T.Whiteside, 'The Mathematical Principles Underlying Newton's Principia,' 1970, p.16.) In his restatement Whiteside used the formula dv/dt, ie rate of change of velocity with respect to time, and discussed how these sections 'establish' that an '"instantaneous' acceleration' resulted from a central force. Such terms may be OK as modern reformulations of the meaning, *provided* one is clear that they are quite absent from the text. Proposition 39 establishes that the time taken by a body in falling is proportional to the area under a certain geometric curve. (see Figure) These propositions discuss acceleration in a geometrical manner, giving no hint that a quantity dv/dt might exist.

principle embraced 'all principles previously given, defining natural motion'. As the President of the Berlin Academy of Sciences, Pierre-Louis Maupertois, so rightly declared:

> 'The force multiplied by the instant of its application gives the increment of velocity. From this principle Mr Euler derives the laws of communication of motion by a sublime and rigorous analysis.'

Here indeed is the first formulation of F = MA - but, don't expect to find that in a history book. [19]

The whole subject is enveloped by a miasma of myth, which indeed gives the subject its charm. Perhaps one day it will all be cleared up and then cease to be interesting. For example, in *Mathematics in Western Culture* (1977) Morris Kline states:

> 'It was by solving a famous differential equation that Newton was able to deduce Kepler's laws so readily.' (p.257)

Merely replace 'differential' by 'integral' and the statement is correct! Newton ascertained the necessary truth of Kepler's second law for an object moving in a central forcefield by an *integration* procedure and was thence able to deduce the first (ellipse) law.

The dilemmas spring from the curiously half-born nature of differential calculus in the *Principia*. In its many rules and principles of reasoning there is no statement of a method which we would call calculus. It is almost present therein, the infinitesimal changes and motions are all there, blurring the classic edges of the old geometric style, but it had not yet detached itself from the geometry to become the algebraic process which we call calculus.[*]

---

[*] On this perplexing issue, the following quote concerning Newton's unique geometrical style may be helpful. A book review by Nauenberg of Guicciardini's *Isaac Newton on Mathematical Certainty and Method* (2009) concludes with:

> Newton's quixotic quest to establish the calculus purely on geometrical grounds, 'the venerated language of the Ancients,' Guicciardini tells us, 'was a failure. He tried to reformulate his analytic methods of discovery into a synthetic form, a form in which all reference to algebraic analysis is suppressed -- the equation is neglected -- and the purity, unity and beauty of geometry [is] recovered,' and concludes that these views 'determined Newton's approach to publication, shaped his relationships with his acolytes, and influenced his strategy in his polemic with Leibniz.' Guicciardini's book should become essential reading and an invaluable resource for anyone with a suitable background in mathematics who is interested in the history of the development of the calculus in the 17th century, and in the important role that Newton played in it. (Notre Dame Philosophical Reviews, 2016)

Tremendous things are there achieved by using that proto-calculus – 'you showed that even what is not subject to the received analysis is an open book to you' as Leibniz said in his letter to Newton praising the *Principia* (7 March 1693) – but it is the integral calculus we see there, not the differential form.

There is in Part II the so-called 'fluxions lemma' (Lemma II) where Newton is considered to have staked his claim to co-discovery of the differential calculus. It defines and uses what a mathematician would call small changes – not infinitesimal changes. The lemma gives *no* ratio of small changes, *nor* does it mention infinitesimal ones. The myth created by Newton himself later on in 1712 that he understood and had used differential calculus in composing the *Principia* was the root cause of the confusion. The book would be vastly easier to read were such the case.

So how were 'centripetal' force computations performed in the *Principia*, if F=Ma was not in fact being used? An answer for the modern reader has to be, with great difficulty, and by use of a geometrical model. For example, in Proposition VI of Book I, centripetal force in elliptical motion is said to vary inversely as the 'solid' $(SP)^2(QT)^2/QR$ where SP is the distance of the point from the force-centre and the other lengths are geometric constructs. Professor Brackenridge has named this exceedingly obscure concept, the 'dynamics ratio' and claimed that it was 'the key for the solutions to the set of problems attacked in Propositions 7-13 of the *Principia*' concerning forces involved in orbital motion.[20] That may be so, but whether anyone since then was able to understand such a concept, may be doubted.[21] Such a construct tends to reinforce the view that it was only after Pierre Varignon and others transcribed the dynamics (Leibniz' term) of the *Principia* from geometrical into fluxional terms, that it could be, in any general sense, understood.

After completing the *Principia*, Newton did then rework a few of the propositions into fluxional terms. Around 1691 we find him composing what Cohen refers to as 'an apparently unique example of fluxions applied to the Second Law'.[22] In an unpublished manuscript he wrote:

> 'If a body ascends or descends on a line y, its speed will be ẏ and the gravity ÿ. For the fluxion of the height is the body's speed and the fluxion of the speed is as the body's weight [*velocitatis fluxio est ut corporis gravitas.*].'[23]

This has little to do with the Second Law but pertains to a body moving up or down under gravity. The fluxion of speed is said to be '*ut corporis gravitas*' which means 'as the weight of the body' and does not mean 'as the acceleration due to gravity'. As the fluxion of speed (which the eighteenth century came to call acceleration) is independent of weight for a falling body one can appreciate that this text was not regarded as publishable.

The manuscript from which the above is taken remained unknown for three centuries when Whiteside unearthed it. Newton had two major opportunities to make it public had he deemed it worthwhile: firstly, Wallis asked him for something to put in his *Algebra* which emerged in 1693 (he obliged with some suitable excerpts from a text, this being the first public appearance of the Newtonian method of fluxions); and secondly, when he printed an abridged form of *De Quadratura* as an appendage to his *Optics* in 1704. In neither of these cases was there any hint of the above – suggesting he was not happy with the argument and did not wish to present it. Whiteside depicts Newton at this time of his life as 'caged by its [the *Principia*'s] very brilliance and originality, unable to transcend its mental confines', as he returned to the quiet backwater of Cambridge from the excitement of London politics, for the last year or two of his academic existence.[24] The above quotation evidently signifies a mere half-formed possibility never actualised.[25]

Let's take one further example of a mythic differential equation, albeit in a quite different realm. Sir William Dampier wrote, à propos of the development of the fluxions method:

> 'An equation which contains differential coefficients is called a differential equation. That Newton was acquainted with the principle [of differential equations] is shown by the fact that he calculated a table giving the refraction of a ray of light passing through the atmosphere by a method equivalent to forming the differential equation to the path of the ray.'[26]

Newton's use of calculus in this vital astronomical problem, to compute the refraction suffered by a ray of light entering the earth's atmosphere, was indeed significant, and would have been even more so had he made it public. Flamsteed, the Astronomer Royal, was sent a table of atmospheric refractions thus calculated, which varied with time of year as air temperature affected its degree of refraction. He had the fairly baffling task of evaluating whether they were any better than his own *ad hoc* tables. Such issues were involved as, how high was the sky? No fluxion or differential was involved in its computation: Whiteside has described the integral equations used.[27]

Of the pioneering work by Sir W. C. Dampier, *A History of Science*, Bernard Cohen wrote, 'A whole generation of scientists and students of the history of science has been introduced to the panorama of scientific development' through its pages (in a Postscript to the fourth edition, 1966). Normally one would hardly expect an historian of science to confuse an integral and a differential equation, however in this area it is quite normal. Glittering illusions swirl endlessly around the myths, the grand myths by which the students are edified, while the equations penned by the historic figure lurk unpublished or did until recently.

The Force of Gravity

'More extensive investigations', wrote Morris Kline in *Mathematics in Western Culture,* 'showed Newton that the precise formula for the force of attraction between *any* two bodies is given by the formula:

$$F=kMm/r^2$$

where F is the force of attraction, M and m are the masses of the two bodies, r is the distance between them, and k is the same for all bodies.'[28]

Here we have yet another historic equation which the maestro never composed, and which no-one in his lifetime had even heard of, laid at his feet. Textbooks the world over have agreed upon such.[29] Just supposing he had not accepted his job at the Mint, or had accepted it briefly for the recoinage operation and then returned to his Alma Mater at Trinity (as De Morgan complained that he should have done), then quite possibly he might have come up with such a formula as a convenient summary of a major argument in the *Principia* – but he didn't. In 1715, Newton wrote to a correspondent that 'It is now above 20 years since I left off mathematics.'[30] The occasional flash of the old fire may have emerged as when answering Bernoulli's challenge problem, and with great effort he did improve his lunar theory for the next edition of the *Principia,* but otherwise his interest in mathematics subsided as he came to preside simultaneously over the Mint and the Royal Society.

The above-quoted formula uses *M* for gravitational mass which would have been a radically new concept. Scientists ('natural philosophers') of the day were just about getting used to multiplying *M* by *v* to get momentum, and even then, they were calling that 'motion' or 'quantity of motion'. The above formula for the force of gravity may seem self-evident to the modern reader, but to go from inertial to gravitational mass (as we would nowadays say) and moreover to use the same symbol for the two is quite a long journey. Once the stroke of genius has forged the new link, it then becomes the common sense of all. This we saw with Euler's brilliant generalisation F=Ma. After that it becomes hardly possible to comprehend how physics appeared before it existed, and years of training are required to enter the antique mind-set.

With his profound mathematical intuition, we find Newton managing to perform a computation involving a ratio somewhat resembling the above formula, in his section on the tides in Part III of the *Principia.*[31] The relative gravity pull of the Moon and the Earth upon the sea are being compared. The distances of the centres of the two orbs from the surface of the sea are in the ratio of 60:1. He has demonstrated that – as Hooke had earlier suggested – the gravity pull of the Earth acts as if from its centre, and the Moon is 60 earth-radii away. The two masses are in the ratio 40:1 he has concluded. Thus the relative pulls of earth and moon will be directly as the masses and inversely as the squares of the distances. That is the law of gravity, is it not? Here we have that very rare thing, a pleasantly simple computation in the *Principia*, an easy exercise of cancelling two ratios – at least for the modern reader, who has the formula.

The relative pull of Earth:Moon should be 40×60^2 from the above formula, or 1:144000, but the answer Newton gave give in the *Principia* was '1 to 2871400', which errs by a factor of 20.[32] This was unchanged in the 3rd edition, i.e. no-one pointed out the error. We're merely observing that computations which seem straightforward to us now, were not so before the formula had been developed.[33]

An Enduring Myth: 'Newton's Method of Approximation'

A method of approximate solution to equations, probably the most widely used one today, was developed by John Simpson in 1740. Its origin has strangely migrated back in time as if through a time-warp, becoming attributed to Newton's *De Analysis* of 1669.[34] It used an iterative or repetitive technique, nowadays found in millions of computer programs, and involves differentiating the function.[*]:

Its attribution to Newton has been an organic part of the deceptive logic, whereby the invention of the differential calculus was attributed to him.

To follow the steps of this curious historical transposition, we have to examine three methods of solving equations by approximation: that used in Newton's *De Analysi,* that of Joseph Raphson published in 1690 and finally that published by Simpson.

What is today known as 'Newton's method of approximation' is *iterative,* that is to say it uses the fundamental equation repetitively, re-inserting at each stage the more accurate solution; and it employs a differential expression. Neither of these characteristics applies to the method of approximate solution developed by Newton in *De Analysi,* which also appeared in his unpublished *De methodis fluxionum et serierum inftnitorum.*[35] The method of approximation published by Joseph Raphson in his *Analysis aequationum universalis* of 1690 was iterative and was the first such method to be iterative – but, it was *not* expressed in fluxional terms.

The method used by Newton was expounded in John Wallis' 1686 *Algebra,* a book composed in English – unusual for the time – and concerned to champion the rights of English mathematicians. Wallis felt they were being unfairly neglected, and that continental mathematicians had been claiming undue credit. The technique used by Newton which Wallis described did *not* use calculus and was a modification

---

[*] If $x = \alpha$ is an approximate root of the equation $f(x) = 0$, then a better approximation will be $\alpha - f(\alpha)/f'(\alpha)$, where $f'(x)$ is the derivative of the function.

of traditional approximate-solution methods.[36] At each step it generated a *new* equation. If we suppose a first approximate solution is two, then let a more exact solution be 2 + y, and putting that back into the original equation instead of x the unknown will give us a new and different equation. We repeat the process, to seek for a more exact solution. His method took only the first-order terms in a binomial expansion, i.e., it ignored all powers of y. This was a subject with which his *De Analysi* was much concerned.*

Obviously it didn't employ the fluxional calculus: after all, no-one had yet invented it, had they?

A different method was later described by Raphson, and this was *iterative*. The successive approximations to the answer were fed back into the *same* mathematical function. There was no need to work out a new equation for each stage as in the method of Newton. This new method was first presented in 1690, entitled *Analysis aequationum universalis* and it naturally enough made no reference to the method Newton had earlier described. Edmond Halley reported to the Royal Society, that Raphson had invented a 'Method of solving all Sorts of Equations 'and that he had desired of him an equation of the fifth power to be proposed to him, 'to which he return'd an Answer true to seven figures in much less time than it could have been effected by the Known methods of Vieta'.[37] The published tract had a preface referring to Newton, among several other mathematicians, in which Raphson declared that his own method was somewhat similar ('aliquid simile') to Newton's earlier account,[38] but he removed that preface when publishing his method as a book in 1697. He referred to Viete as the ancestor of his method but also alluded to the English mathematicians Harriot and Oughtred. An Appendix alluded to Newton's binomial theorem.

Raphson presented his method as follows. Taking as an example the equation ba - aaa = c (we would nowadays write that as ba - a³ = c) where a is the variable, let an approximate solution be 'g'. Then, if a more accurate solution is g+x,

$$x = (c+ggg-bg) / (b-3gg)$$

The quotient expression was obtained by a two-step procedure. One substituted (g+x) for a, then expanded the power terms to give a larger equation; a straightforward binomial expansion. The second step was to extract the terms in x; the terms which multiplied x in this example were (b-3gg), and these became the quotient. Iterating this procedure, Raphson explained, would give any desired level of accuracy.

---

* Taking the cubic equation x³-2x-5 = 0, as the example given in De analysi, he started with the approximate solution of 2. Let the exact solution be 2+p, where p is small, and substitute 2+p into the equation in place of x. This generates a new cubic equation, namely p³+6p²+10p = 1. As p is small, its powers are ignored, yielding the approximate solution 10p = 1 or p = 0.1. Next, 0.1+q is inserted in place of p to form another new equation, and so on. This is continued to achieve any desired level of accuracy.

Raphson's method sounds odd today, because once the calculus technique was established, such *ad hoc* rules could be forgotten. Nowadays, it is invariably viewed in calculus terms – in the above case, the derivative of (a^3 - ba + c) is ($3a^2$ - b): dividing the original function by its derivative, and substituting the approximate solution g to obtain the increment x, gives the improved answer. But for Raphson, no such general concept appeared to be available. His book contained many pages of recipes showing how for each specific algebraic expression one could obtain the required quotient; for example, the quotient for gggg was 4ggg. However, *no general proofs* of these recipes were provided.

Even after De l'Hôpital's classic *Analyse d'infiniments petits* was published in 1696, and rapidly became *the* textbook on the new Leibnizian differential and integral calculus, Raphson republished his method without alteration. As testimony to the British lack of awareness of the new differential or fluxional procedures in the 1690s, this situation could have been referred to by Raphson in his *History of Fluxions* published in 1715 – but that would have greatly undermined the staunchly pro-British tenor of its argument.

Newton's fluxional method first appeared in John Wallis's 1693 *Opera Mathematica*;[39] it described an implicit differentiation method which used *time-based fluxions* (such as ż and ẏ) embedded in the equation, which would not have been any use here. Over this period Raphson evidently saw nothing to make him recast his method into a fluxional format for the second edition of his *History of Fluxions*. After all, new ideas take a while to catch on.

Raphson did allude to the fluxional method in his *Mathematical Dictionary* of 1702, citing Wallis's *Opera* text of 1693 (which Newton had sent to him). His account was polemical, relating to the storm of controversy then gathering: Newton's fluxional method, Raphson wrote rather outrageously, 'passes there [Germany] and in France, under the name of Leibniz's differential calculus'. That account made no allusion to methods of approximate solution for equations.

In the nineteenth-century his method became known as the 'Newton-Raphson method' as Newton's method ceased to be used. Nowadays, mathematicians calmly refer to the Raphson method as 'Newton's method of approximation.' Given the very biased account of the *History of Fluxions* which Raphson composed in 1715, in which calculus appears invented by the English and merely copied by the continentals, one is tempted to say that this treatment was perfect justice.

Thomas Simpson was a well-known British mathematician of the eighteenth century, author of e.g. 'Simpson's rule' for obtaining the area under a curve. Writing in 1740, he described *A new Method for the Solution of Equations*,[40] making no reference to any predecessors, and affirming that 'as it is more general than any hitherto given, it cannot but be of considerable use'. It was indeed. His fine opening words were, 'Take the Fluxion of the given Equation...' Fluxions were taken in the manner that Newton described to Wallis, which left x and ẏ terms on each side of the equation. Dividing though by left what would nowadays be called the derivative of the function on the right-hand side, and $\dot{y}$ /(what we'd call dy/dx) on the left. In this manner, he applied fluxions to the approximation method.

In the nineteenth century, the method came to be described in terms of the Leibnizian calculus, being called the 'Newton-Raphson method'.[41] An appreciation of Joseph Raphson discussed the historically perceived difference between the two methods, concluding, 'it is actually Raphson's simpler (and therefore superior) method, not Newton's, that lurks inside millions of modern computer programs'.[42] In support of this argument, it presented the familiar claim that Raphson's method involved 'calculation of the first derivative', but the historical record hardly supports such a viewpoint. The method of approximation lurking inside millions of computer programs is rather that of Simpson.

Boyer's *History of Mathematics* (1968) affirmed that 'Newton's Method' for the approximate solution of equations could be found in *De analysi*,[43] citing its modern formulation in terms of a derivative f'(x). A marginally more accurate version has appeared in *Makers of Mathematics* by Stuart Hollingdale (1989), which correctly described the method of approximation given in *De analysi*, but then blithely asserted, 'Newton also devised an iterative method ... first published in its original form by Joseph Raphson in 1690'.[44]

How did all this confusion arise?

The seeds of lasting confusion were sown by Wallis in his *Opera* of 1693: he received in August 1692 historic letters from Newton, now lost,[45] containing the recipe for what would nowadays be called implicit differentiation in fluxional terms of an equation, using the newly-invented dot notation;[46] he published that method without acknowledging a contemporary source, alleging that the method was present in Newton's letters of the 1670s sent to Leibniz, which was far from being the case.[47] That act needs to be seen within the context of the controversy then beginning over the genesis of the new calculus methods. To quote Whiteside, 'The letters to Wallis in 1692... [were] the first significant announcement to the world at large of the power of Newton's fluxional method'.[48]

Modern scholarship has located the fairly limited extent to which Newton did compose differential equations, in the early 1690s.[49] These were reformulations of dynamical issues from his *Principia* and did not include methods of approximate solution of equations. Only at the tercentenary of these events were myth and fact disentangled, by my article on the subject.[50] Disputes over the birth of calculus have led mathematicians to locate such achievements at a too-early period. The myth we have surveyed is a legacy from that dispute.

It was unequivocally the method of approximation invented by Thomas Simpson that Joseph Fourier restated using a derivative notation, and which has somehow come to gravitate within a Newtonian orbit. We have to conclude that neither Raphson, Halley nor anyone else prior to Simpson applied fluxions to an iterative approximation technique. I found no source which credited Simpson as being an inventor of the method.

School Myths

A hypothesis which Newton considered but finally decided not to accept seems to have been the source for what came to be called the 'law of viscosity' – until recently, learnt by every physics student. The turgid Book II of the *Principia* was much concerned with vortex motion, and whether this could account for the motion of the planets. Was there a huge vortex in our solar system as Descartes had proposed? Did some planets have vortices of their own which carried their moons round? Could he, Newton, establish that Kepler's third law would *not* hold in a vortex system? That was the supreme issue with which Book II grappled. While pondering these issues, the hypothesis was considered that 'the resistance to fluid motion could be proportional to the velocity with which the parts of the fluid were separated from one another'. After various consequences have been deduced from this hypothesis, the author finally advises *against* accepting it:

> 'And though, for the sake of demonstration, I proposed, at the beginning of this Section, an Hypothesis that the resistance is proportional to the velocity, nevertheless, it is in truth probable that the resistance is in a less ratio than that of velocity...'

A man who can consider a hypothesis, decide not to accept it and yet have a law named after him in consequence – not to mention liquids, Newtonian liquids! – is clearly in a different category from other mortals. Laws involving differential equations especially have tended to gravitate towards his name. After Laplace called him the 'legislator of the Universe' this perhaps seemed only natural, indeed polite. The above discussion of viscosity for example *could be interpreted* in terms of the velocity gradient dv/dy, even though such is hardly present in the text,[51] where, as throughout the *Principia*, we find no differential calculus, but merely an integral calculus (Chapter Eight). We have seen a number of cases where, by a kind of natural gravitational attraction, the historical image of Newton has drawn towards itself – somewhat as the planet Jupiter has captured asteroids from out of the asteroid belt until they have ended up as moons orbiting around Jupiter – achievements appropriate for its demi-god form, in the discoveries of others.

Chapter 5

The Hollow World Of Edmond Halley

'The concave arches may in several places shine with such a substance as invests the surface of the Sun,' explained a 36-year-old Edmund Halley to the Royal Society. To what was he referring? Had his recent descents in a diving bell affected him, or had he perhaps been listening to sailors' tales? In 1689, he had published his paper on *A Method of Walking Under Water*. But now, in 1692, his mind was on profounder matters, in fact a new theory about the Earth, which occupied his mind for several decades,[1] to the embarrassment of his biographers.[2]

Halley had funded the printing of the *Principia*, had been the midwife for its birth, had heralded its arrival to the Royal Society, and now was presenting a deduction of his own which followed therefrom. Some years later, he deduced the periodic return of the 1682 comet which bears his name, but this was not as is often claimed the first inference to have been drawn from that august tome. The *Principia* had concluded that the moon was denser than our earth in the ratio of about 9 to 5 and Halley reasoned therefrom that the Earth was hollow.

An Ultra-Dense Moon

The *Principia* had concluded that the Earth-Moon mass ratio was about 1 to 26 (Book 3, Proposition 37, Corollary 4) so that their densities were as 5:9. The true ratio is 1:81 so the error here is a factor of three.[3] This, the most significant error in the *Principia,* echoes through Book III in computations given to 7 or 8 figure accuracy. It left an ultra-dense moon circling our earth, to the bafflement of subsequent geologists and astronomers. In the mid-eighteenth century, the French astronomer d'Alembert proposed a realistic mass ratio of 1:80, but this did not gain acceptance.[4] Writing in 1855, Lord Brougham, in a detailed analysis of Newton's lunar theory, said, 'It is now known that the true mass is about 1/49th that of the Earth.'[5] This is true greatness, that even a man's errors roll down the centuries. The error was not rectified until the latter half of the nineteenth century. In 1873, a correct figure of 1/81.4 was finally determined by Proctor.

124

THE HOLLOW WORLD OF EDMOND HALLEY

There was no rational basis available to Sir Isaac for computing the Moon's density, because nothing revolves around it. Its orbital characteristics in circling the Earth are fairly independent of its mass – i.e., for any density of a Moon in that position it would orbit in much the same manner. And so he developed an argument which was a fantastic tightrope-walk of assumptions whereby an apparently firm conclusion was reached concerning lunar mass derived from Bristol tidal data. That no-one questioned this when Halley propounded his theory is testimony to the book's unreadability, to its presence in their midst as Mystery, revered yet inscrutable. Its author never felt moved to visit the seaside to inspect or ponder upon the motion of the tides and their monthly changes, whereon his theory of lunar mass rested.

The twice-daily peak of the tides he had accounted for, as one of the epochal achievements of Book III, but could he achieve a converse argument? The Spring and Neap tides twice a month, at syzygy (Full and New Moons) and at the two quarters, result from the addition and subtraction of vectors of the solar and lunar gravity fields. Could he infer from these to the relative densities of the Sun and Moon? If he had indeed rightly computed the Sun's density (he had, as it happened) could he then infer mean lunar density, by way of the tides?

A problem here was that the Sun and Moon play on the tides as the inverse *cube* of their distance, not as the inverse square, which law wasn't demonstrated until the mid-eighteenth century, in France. By any computation, Sir Isaac would have realised that the gravity pull of the Sun on the Earth must be several hundred times greater than that of the Moon. Equally evident was that the tides were pulled more by the Moon than by the Sun. The two luminaries have tidal pull-ratios of about 5 to 2. Therefore, a high tide will tend to appear at lunar zenith or not far from it but will not often occur at noon when the Sun is overhead. Long chains of mathematical deduction flowed back and forth through the Newtonian brain, and incredibly the inverse cube law of tidal attraction was formulated:

'But the force of the moon to move the sea varies inversely as the cube of its distance from the earth,'[6]

with a similar statement for solar gravity. Thereby, Newton was able to explain what is otherwise baffling, that the Moon pulls on the tides more strongly than does the Sun, an argument which would have baffled his contemporaries. He seldom receives credit for this rather intuitive discovery of the inverse cube law.

L=4.4815S was the *Principia*'s outrageously precise estimate of the ratio of solar to lunar tidal pull – from rough tidal data of the Bristol Channel (2nd and 3rd editions). The true ratio is about half that.

Inside the Hollow Earth

Returning to Edmund Halley's bold new theory, its basis was simplicity itself:

> 'Sir Isaac Newton has demonstrated the Moon to be more solid than
> our Earth, as 9 to 5; why may we not then suppose Four Ninths of our
> globe to be Cavity?'

Not one of his audience could have been capable of following the 'demonstration' to which he referred, as it hinged upon an inverse cube law which had neither been heard of hitherto nor explained in the *Principia*; but they did not query the assertion, as far as we are informed.

The Earth was, Halley explained, a mere shell of some 500 miles thick, containing within itself a second, hitherto unheard-of concentric globe. The latter did not bang around against the inside shell as one might surmise, but rather was held in the middle of the hollow shell by the force of gravity. Halley was confident that his audience would see the necessity of this if only they rightly viewed the law of gravity:

> … should these globes be adjusted once to the same common centre,
> the Gravity of the parts of the Concave would press towards the centre
> of the inner Ball... It follows that the Nucleus being once fixt in the
> common centre, must always here remain.'[7]

As all nature teemed with life, opined Edmond Halley, as the planets too were doubtless inhabited, so also this under-world would surely also be occupied. 'I have adventured to make these Subterranean orbs capable of being inhabited,' he added, in words for which science fiction writers of futurity would be grateful.[8] For that purpose, the luminiferous 'substance as invests the surface of the Sun' was interfused with the upper atmosphere of those caverns. He conceded to his perhaps startled audience that he was here using a 'final cause', though Bacon had advised somewhat against their use, in asserting that the luminosity was for the convenience of those denizens of his under-world.

But might not the seas all leak away, once an earthquake opened up a crack beneath the sea, leading to a flooding of the lower regions? Halley had an answer; within the ground there existed 'Saline and Vitriolick Particles as may contribute to petrification', and any water leaking down would soon find its path blocked by these petrifying particles.

His theory could account for why the Earth had, as he firmly believed, *four* magnetic poles. As early as 1683, when but a youthful Clerk to the Royal Society, which meant sitting at the end of the table and not being allowed to wear a wig – yet with a mantle of glory from his having mapped the stars in the southern sky, with the accolade of 'The Southern Tycho' from the Astronomer Royal – he had formed his theory of Earth's four magnetic poles.[9] From an intensive study of global compass variations he had come to realise that two southern magnetic poles lay in the 'Southern ocean', while the northern poles were in the Bering Strait and Spizbergen.

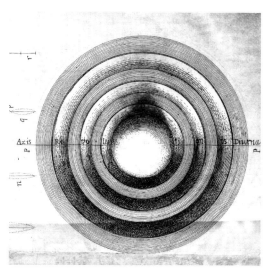

Edmond Halley's diagram of the concentric shells of Earth

He had not then been able to comprehend how this could be but at last the *Principia* had given him the key. There existed he realised a slight differential rotation between the inner sphere and the outer shell of the Earth, enough to generate a slow motion of four poles about the surface of the Earth, with each sphere having one pair of magnetic poles. By an interference effect, a sort of differential drive, his four magnetic poles would wander slowly about the Earth's surface, a result of the hidden motion of a sphere below the hollow earth.

Another phenomenon was accounted for by Halley's new theory, concerning the viscosity of interplanetary space. To appreciate the subtlety of this issue – which explained how the very clockwork of the universe was winding down – one has to review the circumstances whereby Halley failed in his bid for the Savilian Chair in astronomy at Oxford; he was rumoured to believe that the universe might be older than 4004 B. C.

A Moon Left Behind?

In 1691, the Savilian chair at Oxford fell vacant, a chair under the joint control of the Archbishop of Canterbury and the Bishop of Worcester, both of whom were much concerned about the advancing threat of atheism, beneath the guise of natural philosophy. It had reached the ears of the Bishop of Worcester that, 'Halley was a skeptick, and a banterer of religion, and he scrupled to be concerned, till his chaplain, Mr Bentley, should talk with him about it, which he did.'[10] According to William Whiston, when Richard Bentley spoke to Halley, 'He was so sincere in his infidelity that he would not so much as pretend to believe the Christian religion, tho' he thereby was likely to lose the professorship, which he did accordingly, and it was then given to Dr Gregory.'[11] Gregory was scarcely noted for his piety, and was accused of drunkenness and sloth in teaching, and there is the story of the Scotsman who, on hearing that Halley had come unstuck with the bishop, immediately packed his bag and travelled to London, 'to meet a man with less religion than Gregory'.

As this issue is rather central to Halley's dire rift with Flamsteed, a man who did not jest with his religion, one more witness may be cited. The philosopher Bishop Berkeley was informed by Addison of a deathbed conversation of a mutual friend, Dr Garth. Dr Garth had refused the sacraments, and with his last words to Addison was said to have confessed that 'I have good reason not to believe these trifles, since my friend Dr Halley... Has assured me that the doctrines of Christianity are incomprehensible and the religion itself an imposture'.[12]

After failing to acquire the Savilian post despite being highly competent for the job, Halley wrote in alarm to his friend Abraham Hill, '... There being a caveat entered against me, till I can shew that I am not guilty of asserting the eternity of the world.' Could he perhaps demonstrate that the world was running down, and so would not last forever? His first step was to write to Flamsteed asking whether Saturn's period was less than it had been a century or so ago. Flamsteed replied that its orbit period was unchanged from a thousand years ago, as far as he could tell.[13]

Undeterred, Halley continued to explore the necessary running down of the cosmic clockwork. (The reader wondering what this has to do with a hollow Earth must be patient; it will appear in due course) The subtle point was, he eventually grasped, that if the Moon's orbit were to diminish, then its speed must increase. Moving through the viscous fluid of interplanetary space, the Moon gradually slowed down – or did it speed up? – so that eclipse times in antiquity would therefore be different from expected. He had in 1691 read a paper on Julius Caesar invading Britain with an eclipse recorded, thereby deducing when the invasion occurred, so here he was on familiar ground.

The earliest timed eclipses he could find came from a middle Eastern astronomer Al-Battani of the tenth century.[14] In 1691, Halley had read a paper to the Royal Society on how the Moon was gradually being pulled nearer and nearer to Earth as gravity increased, due to comets impacting on the Earth as Newton had explained to him, whereby the mass of Earth increased;* and because the Moon was being drawn nearer, partly by the friction of space, its orbit period was decreasing through history. In fact, the reverse is the case, and the Moon is gradually decelerating as it moves ever further from Earth, but the discovery is known as 'secular acceleration' in honour of Halley's discovery. Al-Battani's data showed, Halley argued, that the

---

* On October 24 1694, Halley read to the Royal Society that Newton had said that there was 'reason to conclude that the bulk of the Earth did grow and increase... by the perpetual Accession of new Particles,' which would induce 'an Acceleration of the Moons motion, she being at this time attracted by a stronger Vis Centripeta than in Remote Ages.' The *Principia* had suggested that it was from comets' tails that the increase in terrestrial mass must come, thereby producing the lunar acceleration.

eclipse times were an hour or so earlier than they should have been and claimed that this proved his case.*

In the 1692 paper, Halley gave one further argument in favour of a hollow Earth. As Earth, accompanied by its Moon, sojourned through space, they were slowed down by the drag of space. This deceleration he showed, flexing his mathematical muscles, would be proportional to the cross-sectional areas of the two orbs (radius^2) but inversely as masses (radius^3), which meant that, if they were both of the same density, but being of very different sizes, the Moon would soon become left behind! In order that this should not transpire (another final cause), Earth had been designed as hollow:

> 'the cavity I assign to the Earth may well serve to adjust its weight to the Moon. For otherwise the Earth would leave the Moon behind it and she become another primary planet.'

With this poignant image, of Luna left behind, his argument concluded. The paper was a popular one, reprinted several times in abridged versions of the Philosophical Transactions. In an article on 'Edmund Halley and early geophysics', Colin Ronan observed of the above theory that 'In its final form the theory was widely accepted'.[15]

The presentation must one feels have been a memorable occasion. We are told that Halley possessed:

> 'the qualifications necessary to obtain him the love of his equals. In the first place, he loved them. Naturally of an ardent and glowing temper, he appeared animated in their presence with a generous warmth which the pleasure alone of seeing them seemed to inspire.'(*Biographica Brittannica* 1757)

That was praise indeed.

The Pink Amidst Icebergs

Halley was thrust into a new phase of his versatile life when, failing to gain the post of mathematics lecturer, and not at all liking the post of Warden of the Mint at Chester which Newton had procured for him, he was requested by the Admiralty

---

* The discovery of secular acceleration is credited to Edmund Halley, this being a very slow decrease in lunar orbit period which is measured per century. Secular acceleration is the 'apparent speeding up of the Moon in its orbit' (Patrick Moore, Guide to the Moon, 1976). The Moon is moving away from the Earth, due to a tidal friction effect: it loses kinetic energy causing its orbit period to increase. In the mid-nineteenth century the true character of the phenomenon was understood, as being due to the deceleration of the Earth's rotation rate, whereby the Moon's orbit period appears to be shortening.

to explore the Atlantic Ocean. The Royal Society were probably instrumental in procuring this post for him, just as they had earlier voted that he should be sent to St Helena to map the stars of the southern sky, and then agreed that he be sent to Amsterdam to meet Hevelius, to patch up a row which had erupted due to Hooke claiming rather too publicly that his new telescope apparatus was more accurate than Hevelius' naked-eye astronomy. The ship was a 'pink', a vessel of Dutch design with three sails and able to navigate in shallow waters. The purpose of the mission was to determine more exactly the magnetic declination variations around the ocean for the aid of sailors.

As if that were not sufficient for an aspiring mathematician, to whom it had surely never occurred that he would command a ship, the Admiralty instructions added, 'If the season of the year permit, you are to stand soe farr into the South, Till you discover the Coast of Terra Incognita.' He became Captain Halley, the phrase Flamsteed always used in referring to him, and set forth from the Pool of London in his Pink Paramour in 1698. Twenty years ago, he had sailed to St Helena as a passenger, and now the crew were not long in apprehending their captain's lack of experience. He reached the west coast of Brazil before he was driven to arrest one of the officers. Some years before, Edward Harrison had published a small volume on how to measure longitude at sea. This was an issue of the greatest moment where opinions differed as to whether a clock, the Moon or Jupiter should be employed, and Halley had judged doubtless quite rightly that the book was not up to much. This was one matter where Halley did know what he was talking about, and he had been one of a group of experts asked to comment on the Harrison book. If there was one thing Halley could have done very well without, it was Edward Harrison as second-in-command on his maiden voyage. The whole voyage had to be aborted because of this row.

A second was planned and undertaken. In 1699 he reached the deep south where his little Pink, a mere fifty feet long, navigated amongst icebergs, and saw penguins and sharks, and he and his crew were mistaken for pirates off the coast of Brazil. On the eastern coast of Brazil, he attempted to determine longitude by an occultation of one of Jupiter's satellites, but was frustrated by cloud cover, and then determined it to within nearly 1° accuracy using a conjunction of the Moon with the bright star Aldebaran, the Bull's Eye.

Through all these voyages, as he checked up on the magnetic declination maps, we can picture Halley as pondering his great theory, of how the subterranean spheres revolved. Perhaps there were six or more magnetic poles and not merely four as he had said, which would mean that there were more concentric shells below the Earth, each with their own two magnetic poles?

Later in life, Halley expounded once again his theory of the hollow spheres of Earth. In 1716, he, and most of North-West Europe, witnessed a dazzling *aurora borealis* display and as the Astronomer Royal he was expected to comment. It was

Halley at 80, holding a diagram of what he views as his most important contribution to science, his hollow-earth theory, omitted by his biographers. Used with permission from the Royal Society.

caused by a luminous substance inside the Earth, he explained, which was emerging through a fissure in the North Pole. This would 'transude through and penetrate the Cortex of our Earth', and then spread about glowing as the *aurora borealis*. Newton had shown the Earth to be a flattened sphere, with the shell thinnest at the poles, which explained why the luminous vapour would only 'transude' at the North Pole.[16]

How Halley would have liked to hear the real reason, viz that the 22-year heart-beat of the Sun had started up again! The so-called 'Maunder minimum' ended

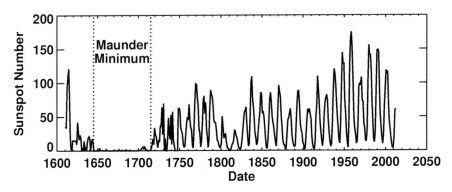

Maunder Minimum from sunspot numbers, 1645-1715.

around 1715 as sunspots started to reappear on the solar surface: the 'little ice age' had come to an end.[17]

It is not easy to conjecture how a small satellite could have ended up with a far higher density than its parent planet; and hard to see how any conclusion other than the hollow earth theory of Edmund Halley could be drawn once the initial premise was granted: and, in the eighteenth century, it must have been hard not to do so. Nearly two centuries after Newton first performed his outrageously misguided computations deriving an extra-dense Moon from English seaside tidal data, Lord Brougham as we have seen took the mass of the Moon to be 1/49th that of Earth. This figure was hardly any different, and still gave it a far higher mean density than the Earth.

In the 1860s, the true and strangely low density of the Moon was eventually ascertained by determining the position of the baricentre – the converse of the method used by Newton – by the astronomers Stone, Leverrier and Newcomb. The reverse problem was then perceived, and we find the British astronomer H.P. Wilkins surmising in 1954 that the moon might perhaps be hollow with large caverns to account for its low density,[18] and H.G. Wells composed a hollow-Moon story.

Chapter 6

The Crushing Of Hooke

'It is sufficient to say that Hooke was almost, if not quite, the most prolific inventive genius that ever lived and that at least one of his books, the *Micrographia*, is among the most important books ever published in the history of science.'[1]

Sir Geoffrey Keynes

The entire Royal Society turned out for Hooke's funeral, but a generation later not even the place of his grave was known. The introduction of *Early Science in Oxford* by Gunther (1920-45) – the opus where Hooke's collected works such as they survive may be found – cited a prodigious list of instruments and apparatus which Hooke contributed to the Royal Society, and concluded, 'Not one of these now remains'.[2] Gunther feared that even the existing papers of Hooke were in danger of perishing, as 'the original papers in archives of the Royal Society are not well arranged, and are undergoing deterioration with age and the dirt of London'. He regretted that he had not been able to obtain permission from them for access to Hooke's diagrams, to illustrate his compendium; and deplored such an 'obstacle to an endeavour to do belated justice to the memory of a member of my own University, and to rescue his manuscripts before they share the fate of his instruments'.

The *Life of Robert Hooke* by his eighteenth-century biographer Waller has a section on 'His Character' which begins, 'As to his person he was but despicable, being very crooked...' In conclusion it discussed 'all his Failures' and how 'humanum est errare.' From a posthumous biographer, who could ask for more? The only portrait of Hooke, which was reckoned to be one of the two finest in the Royal Society's possession, the other being that of Robert Boyle, was after his death lost,[3] so one cannot well assess the veracity of Waller's statement. The portrait seems to have been discarded in 1710 when Newton moved the Society from Gresham College to Crane Court, by Fleet Street.

THE DARK SIDE OF ISAAC NEWTON

We lack even the titles of most of Hooke's papers for the years between his correspondence with Newton 1679/80 and the appearance of the *Principia*. Thomas Hearne the diarist reported the London gossip:

> 'I was told last night by Mr Whiteside, and I suppose 'tis what others think and say also, that Sir Isaac Newton took his famous Book call'd *Principia Mathematica,* another edition whereof is just come out, from Hints given him by the late Dr Hooke (many of whose papers cannot now be found)...'[4]

One lecture Hooke gave to the Royal Society called 'the line of the falling body' was on the subject of his 9 December 1679 letter to Newton about his theory of gravity. Hooke's copy of that letter was itself classified by his eighteenth-century biographer Waller as a 'discourse' and then mislaid, only to turn up and be published in 1952, enabling the present thesis to be composed. To quote Patterson:

> 'Waller does not mention the fact that it was a letter, nor in any way reveal its connection with Newton – in fact Waller throughout his memoir is curiously silent on the subjects of Hooke's gravitation theory and of Sir Isaac Newton, whom he mentions only once.'

Waller dedicated his collection of Hooke's papers to Newton, Hooke's arch-enemy.

Newton waited until Hooke had died before publishing his treatise on optics, a fact normally adduced to show just how much this sensitive person had suffered from the latter's carping tongue. An alternative view would be based upon Gunther's observation that it was 'certainly hardly fair to Hooke's memory that the coloured diffraction bands discovered by him should be everywhere known as "Newton's rings."'[5] *Optics* did not acknowledge who had discovered the phenomenon.

Hooke is always described pejoratively in the histories of science – as remarkably vain, as grasping and boastful, as confused and incompetent in mathematics. He could certainly be tactless, and sometimes exaggerated, and no doubt as Aubrey said he was forgetful. He was the victim of an act of plagiarism unparalleled in scientific history, and was personally crushed thereby. Prior to that, he seems to have been a sociable and extrovert character, who did much to bring the Royal Society together, and was busy designing London in the years when Newton was being led about the Sophic garden by Neptune with his trident. Margaret Epinasse in her biography of Hooke well described him as 'irascible, generous, brilliant, simple'.*

---

* Hooke's private diary, published in 1940, was plainly was not intended for public view as it recorded such matters as the times he made love to his mistress, eg: 'Nell , slept not well,' 'Played with Nell - . Hurt small of Back' (for 1672). Other comments were such as 'noyse in head' and 'Strange dreames.'

Hooke has been described as 'perhaps the most brilliant and versatile artist of the later seventeenth century'.[6] The onetime President of the Royal Society Samuel Pepys wrote in his diary in 1665 of 'Hooke, who is the most, and promises the least, of any man in the world that ever I saw'.[*]

John Evelyn recorded in his diary how in the year 1665, while the plague was raging at its worst, he saw the genius of British invention:

> 'The 7th, I returned home, calling at Wodcot and Durdans by the way, where I found Dr Wilkins, Sir William Petty and Mr Hooke contriving chariots, new rigs for ships, a wheel for one to run races in, and other mechanical inventions: and perhaps, for parts and ingenuity, three such persons were not to be found elsewhere in Europe.'

As a matter of habit, science histories have spoken derisively of Hooke's character. Again we quote Gunther that 'no adequate attempt has been made to do justice to one of the most inventive geniuses the world has ever seen'. In the 1670s, he was criticised for not giving enough attention to the Royal Society because of his work in reconstructing London.[7] One may consider that, were his character as the historians assert -vain, grasping, quarrelsome and so forth[**] – he would hardly have had the effect of bringing together so distinguished a group of persons. No doubt his brain teemed with too many projects, but the main continuous thread from 1664 to 1687 in his work appears as his developing theory of universal gravitation.

On observing 'the rise and fall of Robert Hooke' one cannot but feel that he followed an unlucky star and that his genius was almost nullified by self-destructive elements in his character. Before his death he had accumulated a case containing a solid eight thousand pounds in wealth. He kept declaring he was going to leave it to the Royal Society but never made a will, and the huge fortune passed to a quite illiterate relative. Had he made such a bequest it would have done much to ensure a favourable memory, at a time when the Society was acutely short of funds.

'The Virtuoso' by the poet laureate Shadwell of 1676 was a most successful play, and effectively terminated Hooke's interest in the theatre. For indeed, he was

---

* On March 1, 1665 Pepys heard Hooke lecture about the late comet, 'among other things, proving very probably that this is the very same Comet that appeared before in the year 1618 and that in such a time probably it will appear again.' No record of this is found in the Society's journal, so we only know this from Samuel Pepys diary, which led Andrade to conclude 'Oldenburg does, in general, seem to have done his best to discredit Hooke's work.' (Andrade p.470)

** It is pointed out by F. Centore in 'Robert Hooke's Contributions to Mechanics' 1970 that such negative views came from persons who knew him only in later years, whereas the sympathetic account of him by his contemporary John Aubrey describes the younger man.

its hero, as the learned and prolific inventor Sir Nicholas Gimcrack. It was a searing satire, expressing the public's horror equally at the teeming microbial life in London water revealed by Hooke's microscope and at the vivisection experiments performed by the Society. (The latter Hooke was ordered to perform, try though he might to excuse himself.) 'Damned dogs. Vindica me Deus. People almost pointed,' his diary recalls, after his visit to the play. Incautious remarks of his about flying machines, or alchemic processes, appeared centre stage. Worse, allegations of sexual misconduct had got about, and were the climax of Sir Nicholas' eventual downfall.

Such a play does at least show the Royal Society achieving renown. 'Who has not heard of the Society, if he is in any way drawn to an interest in true learning...?' wrote Leibniz in his first letter to Oldenburg in 1670. As its curator and man-about-town, frequenter of coffee-houses – still something of an innovation, and which had a quite major social function – and whose short, hunchback figure was ever to be seen bobbing in and out of Tompion the watchmaker's and assorted artisan shops in London town – Hooke formed a natural target for satire. Of Sir Nicholas we are told at the start:

> 'Trust me, he is the finest speculative Gentleman in the whole World
> & in his Cogitations the most severe Animal alive [and are shown]
> His Laboratory, a spacious Room, where all his Instruments and fine
> Knacks are.'

In this play the public were shown a strange new type of person, an inventor who was not aspiring to natural magic, who had no Faust-like aspirations towards the supernatural, upon whose walls no astrological charts were drawn, but who espoused the mechanical philosophy. To be sure, Shadwell's play sought to deride Sir Nicholas' allusions to Rosicrucianism, and indeed Hooke had once tried to form a Rosicrucian club with Aubrey. He was always trying to form clubs. The play made effective use of Sir Nicholas' habit of claiming to have done somewhat more than could credibly be attributed to one person.

Hooke seems to have been mainly responsible for the cohesion of he Royal Society of London, in its first decade or so. 'Of him only is it recorded' – quoting Gunther again – 'that on certain occasions owing to his absence or unpreparedness there could be no meeting. He was more than a star-turn: he was the pivotal factor.'[8] *

---

* 'There can be no doubt that Hooke was the one man who did most to shape the form of the new Society and to maintain its active existence. Without his weekly experiments and prolific work the society could scarcely have survived, or at least, would have developed in a quite different way. It is scarcely an exaggeration to say that he was historically, the creator of the Royal Society.' *The Diary of Robert Hooke* 1968 Ed. W. W. Robinson and W. Adams, p XX.

This was in part because he was expected to make experimental demonstrations work for other speakers, which might otherwise not have been up to much.

Aubrey's Friend

We now quote extensively from John Aubrey's *Brief Lives* potted biography of Hooke, chiefly because this present work is the sole published account of the great events to concur with that of Aubrey.

At the age of 13, young Robert journeyed up to London alone, from the Isle of Wight where he was born and grew up and where his father had been the curate. His father had died suddenly bequeathing him the sum of £100 with the condition, that he should use it to become apprentice to a painter, as he had shown some talent in that direction. The painter liked him well enough, but the young lad soon had other ideas. Let Aubrey continue:

> 'thought he, why cannot I doe this by my selfe and keepe my hundred pounds? He went to Mr Busby's the Schoolemaster of Westminster, at whose howse he was; and he made very much of him. With him he lodged his hundred pounds. There he learned to play 20 lessons on the organ. He there in one weeke's time made himself master of the first VI books of *Euclid*, to the Admiration of Mr Busby. At Schoole here he was very mechanicall, and (amongst other things) he invented thirty several wayes of Flying.'

One notes that this was within a decade of the young Newton at Cambridge designing his anti-gravity turbine... But, to continue:

> 'Anno Domini 1658 he was sent to Christ Church in Oxford, where he had a Chorister's place (in those days when the Church Musique was putt-downe) which was a pretty good maintenance... He was there Assistant to Dr Thomas Willis in his chymistry; who afterwards recommended him to the Hon'ble Robert Boyle, Esquire, to be usefull to him in his Chymicall operations. Ano Domini 1662 Mr Robert Boyle recommended Mr Robert Hooke to be Curatorof the Experiments of the Royal Society, wherein he did an admirable good worke to the Commonwealth of Learning, in recommending the fittest person in the world to them.

> 'Anno domini 1666 the great Conflagration of London happened, and then he was chosen one of the two Surveyors of the Citie of

London; by which he hath gott a great Estate. He built Bedlam, the Physicians' College, Montague-house, the Piller on fish-street hill, and Theatre there; and he is much made use of in Designing Buildings.

'He is but of midling stature, something crooked, pale faced, and his face but little belowe, but his head is lardge; his eie full and popping, and not quick; a grey eie. He haz a delicate head of haire, browne, and of an excellent moist curle. He is and ever was very moderate in dyet, etc.

'As he is of prodigious inventive head, so is a person of great vertue and goodness. Now when I have sayd his Inventive faculty is so great, you cannot imagine his Memory to be excellent, for they are like two bucketts, as one goes up, the other goes downe. He is certainly the greatest Mechanick this day in the World.

''Twas Mr Robert Hooke that invented the Pendulum-Watches, so much more usefull than the other Watches. He hath invented an Engine for the speedie working of Division, etc., or for the speedie and immediate finding out the Divisor.

'Before I leave this Towne, I will gett of him a Catalogue of what he hath wrote; and as much of his inventions as I can. But they are many hundreds; he believes not fewer than a thousand. 'Tis such a hard matter to get people to doe themselves right.

'Mr Robert Hooke did in Anno 1670, write a Discourse, called, An Attempt to prove the Motion of the Earth, which he then read to the Royal Society; wherein he haz delivered the Theorie of explaining the coelestial motions mechanically: his words are these: I shall explaine a systeme of the world, differing in many particulars from any yet known, answering in all things to the common rules of mechanicall motions. This depends upon 3 suppositions; first, that all coelestiall bodys whatsoever have an attractive or gravitating power towards their own centres, whereby they attract not only their own parts, and keep them from flying from them, as we may observe the Earth to doe, but that they doe also attract all the other coelestiall bodys that are within the sphere of their activity, and consequently that not only the Sun and Moon have an influence upon the body and motion of the Earth, and the Earth upon them, but that Mercury also, Venus, Mars, Saturne and Jupiter, by their attractive powers have a considerable influence upon its motion, as, in the same manner, the corresponding attractive power of the Earth hath a considerable influence upon every one of their motions also. The second supposition is this, that all bodys whatsoever, that are putt into direct and simple motion will soe continue to move forwards in a straight line, till they are by some other effectuall powers deflected and bent into a motion describing a circle, ellipsis, or some other uncompounded curve line. The third supposition is, that these attractive powers are soe much the more powerfull in operating, by how much nearer the body wrought upon is to their own centres.

'About 9 or 10 years ago, Mr Hooke writt to Mr Isaac Newton, of Trinity College, Cambridge, to make a Demonstration of this theory, not telling him, at first, the proportion of the gravity to the distance, now what was the curv'd line that was thereby mede. Mr Newton, in his answer to the letter, did express that he had not thought of it; and in his first attempts about it, he calculated the Curve by supposing the attraction to be the same at all distances: upon which, Mr Hooke sent, in his next letter, the whole of his hypothesis, *scil.* that the gravitation was reciprocall to the square of the distance: which is the whole coelestiall theory, concerning which Mr Newton haz made a demonstration, not at all owning he receiv'd the first Intimation of it from Mr Hooke. Likewise Mr Newton haz in the same Booke printed some other Theories and experiments of Mr Hooke's, without acknowledgeing from whom he had them.

'This is the greatest Discovery in Nature that ever was since the World's Creation. It never was so much as hinted by any man before. I wish he had writt plainer, and afforded a little more paper.[9]

Aubrey sometimes resided at Hooke's Gresham College premises. Generations must have dismissed Aubrey's account as a mere story before the key letter in question was finally discovered and made public in 1952. Even then, it is only in the post-Whiteside era, and that is since 1970, that an assessment of the soundness of Aubrey's account has become possible.

'A mind so active, so fertile'

'No one has ever devoted a book to [the] life and achievements', of 'probably the most inventive man who ever lived, and one of the ablest experimenters ...' observed

Dr E. N. Andrade, in an address to the Royal Society in 1940. Things have changed now, with the tercentenary of his passing, and the greatest of English inventors is now well acknowledged.[10] It is doubtless true that in most cases, the flow of inventions from Hooke's teeming brain were insufficiently developed to establish his priority claims – as no lack of commentators have pointed out. The flow of invention commenced around 1658 when he constructed the air-pump for Boyle and also tried out various designs for flying, abandoned in the end because 'the Muscles of a Man's Body were not sufficient to do anything considerable of that kind'.

After such, comments Andrade:

> 'we are to be confronted with the difficulty of coping with the stream of inventions, notions, brilliant suggestions, accurate observations, daring speculations and prophetic conjectures that poured from Hooke's fertile brain and contriving hands. It will be impossible to mention them all; to classify them will be difficult; in many cases, in view of the scanty record, it will be hard to decide exactly what was done. Practically everything, however, will bear witness to a truly extraordinary inventiveness and a truly modern outlook. Sometimes Hooke is wrong, but he is wrong in a strictly scientific and not a medieval way. Very often the ideas he tumbled out in such profusion were taken by others; sometimes his findings were reached quite independently by others, which Hooke found hard to believe. At every stage we are witnessing the workings of a mind so active, so fertile in experiments, so interrupted in every hour, at every endeavour, by the inrush of new concepts, new projects, that it is hard to disentangle his doings.'

When Hooke invented the modern spring-controlled balance wheel by 1665, the clocks available tended to be out of time by at least a quarter of an hour per day. The king took a keen interest in this invention, and in his Whitehall abode collected many enamelled clocks and watches, which ticked and chimed away in dis-unison, in his special room together with rare jewels and crystal vases, models of ships and large maps – the nearest he came to an interest in the mechanical philosophy. The hunchback Hooke presented a watch to the Merry Monarch.

One of his demonstrations to the Royal society comprised what are today known as 'Newton's cradle' or 'Newton's balls' – several metal balls which hanging in a line, such that when one was pulled and released, the three of them together kept swinging. It was used to illustrate how momentum or 'motion' was conserved. This was the one bit of Hooke's apparatus that remained when the Royal Society moved its premises to Crane Court off Fleet Street, all the rest being lost. The experiment ended up in Newton's *Principia* with no acknowledgement and three pages of Latin text.[11]

THE CRUSHING OF HOOKE

'To turn the pages of Birch's *History of the Royal Society*, which is a record, sometimes a very detailed record, of the meetings, week by week, from 1660 to 1687, is to convince oneself that Hooke's experiments and theoretical ideas, and the discussions which they provoked, were the main agent that held the Society together,' concluded Andrade. Friction came from Oldenburg: '

> I have no doubt that Oldenburg, who hated Hooke – in my opinion as the man who dominated the Royal Society meetings where he wished to shine as the administrator on whom all depended – did all he could to make trouble between the two men [Newton and Hooke]..
> Newton wrote to Oldenburg "Pray present my services to Mr Hooke, for I suppose there is nothing but misapprehension in what lately happened," but it is unlikely that Oldenburg ever conveyed the complement; he was concerned to keep up the dispute.'

When Oldenburg died in 1677, Hooke 'was unanimously asked to be secretary', suggesting he was not such an unpopular character as the generations of Newtonian history-writers have made out. Two years later, the *Philosophical Transactions* ceased to appear and then Hooke was asked by the council to publish a scientific sheet mainly concerned with what was being done abroad. Called the *Philosophical Collections*, it ran from 1679 to 1682.

As an example of Hooke's mechanical wizardry, we note the Royal Society's comments upon his sound experiments:

> 'He showed an experiment for making musical and other sounds by the help of teeth of brass wheels, which teeth were made of equal bigness for musical sounds, but unequal for vocal sounds.'(Birch, IV, p96)

This was Savart's wheel, discovered in 1820, but with an additional refinement. Other experiments involved the formation of Chladni figures using flour as the powder: 'it being manifest', says the account, 'by this experiment, that as every different stroke makes a different sound, so the making of a different impression upon the flour gives it as many several motions.' The flour responded to the different modes of vibration for each note. Samuel Pepys, President, paid a visit and then noted in his diary:

> 'Discoursed with Mr Hooke about the nature of sounds, and he did make me understand the nature of musicall sounds made of strings, mighty prettily; and told me that having come to a certain number of vibrations proper to make any tone, he is able to tell how many

strokes a fly makes with her wings, those flies that hum in their flying, by the note that it answers to in musique, during their flying. That, I suppose, is a little too much refined; but his discourse in general of sound was mighty fine.'

The *Micrographia* described how sound travelled much faster through wires over long distances, and its author seems to have considered this as a possible method of communication.

By way of contrast, the *Principia* pondered the nature of sound from a hugely different viewpoint, of an abstract theory. It hypothesised as to how oscillating particles gave a longitudinal waveform and derived a speed of sound differing from observed values by 20 per cent, then covered this up by what Westfall has called a 'fudge factor.' To quote from Westfall's perceptive analysis:

> '... The deception in this case was patent enough that no one beyond Newton's most devoted followers was taken in. Any number of things were wrong with the demonstration... Nothing short of deliberate fraud... The compulsion behind the pretence to precision...'[12]

The *Principia* and the *Micrographia* formed polar opposites; the latter was *enjoyed by* the intelligentsia of the day, it was the first popular science best-seller. Pepys declared that it was 'the most ingenious book that I read in my life', while the former in contrast appeared as a paragon of inscrutability, meriting the supposed comment from an anonymous Cambridge student, as Sir Isaac passed by: 'there goes a man that writt a book that neither he nor anyone else understands'.

Comparing these differing approaches to science, the engineer David Hanby concluded:

> 'The achievements of Robert Hooke appeal to me in the same way as those of Leonardo da Vinci. Both men had a profound understanding of the world and did not mind getting their hands dirty. It seems a shame that in the world of learning the abstruse and inductive philosophies should be placed on a pedestal to the detriment of the creative and practical subjects. This has not only resulted in our forgetting our inheritance from Robert Hooke, but it has also diverted many talented people away from the challenges and rewards of creative design and manufacture.'[13]

Hooke 'was on good terms with most of the first-class intellects of the time', explained Andrade:

'he dined with Evelyn and stayed for weeks at his house, was invited by Sydenham (who liked Oldenburg as little as Hooke did) to stay with him for six weeks, was on intimate terms with Christopher Wren [there is an entry of his buying a hobby horse for Wren's son], was very friendly with John Aubrey, who wrote of him in the highest terms, and was constantly in the company of Haak, Abraham Hill, Daniel Whistler and others. Busby, his schoolmaster kept up friendship with him all his life; in 1679 Hooke designed a church for him. As for Tompion, the famous clockmaker, he occasionally enters him as "a slug", "a rascall", but they worked together for years, and, as supreme craftsman and supreme inventor, no doubt knew one another's worth – lost their tempers with one another and met next time as if nothing had happened... It is clear [from his *Diary* edited by Robinson and Adams] that Hooke was, anyhow for the years that it covers, a sociable and free-spending man, a frequenter of coffee houses who smoked and drank with his friends. He also entertained them with wine at his lodgings... An entry like "Drunk. Promised to pay whatever I signed to be paid" shows his usual directness, but is hard to reconcile with the miserable recluse that he is painted as by ill-wishers. He also drank tea, which cost 25 shillings a pound, at a time when a shilling was a purchasing sum. It is quite possible that Hooke was a man who did not mind spending freely on himself and his friends but disliked wasting money or being cheated... He spent large sums on books.'

The study of the heavens was transformed by the use of telescopic sights and micrometer screw gauge. To quote Andrade, 'Anyone who contrasts Hooke's instrument with those of Hevelius will see a difference of kind; one is completely modern in spirit, with a careful discussion of the limits of accuracy and of experimental error, the other is a much improved version of the instruments of the ancients.' (p.456) Telescopic sights and eyepiece micrometers were invented in Lancashire in the 1640s by William Gascoigne, then transmitted via Oxford astronomers such as Christopher Wren to Hooke at Gresham College in the 1650s.[14] The design of the Greenwich apparatus, which was the finest in the world, derived from such designs of Hooke.

Today Hooke is remembered merely for a dull little law of elementary physics, that the extension of a spring is proportional to its load (*ut tensio sic vis* as he phrased it); yet even here fate has bound him together with his arch-enemy, as the schoolchildren of today apprehend his law using a spring balance calibrated in newtons. When in 1678 he announced the principle (in 'Lectures de potentia Restitutiva') he also affirmed that any vibration in which the restoring force was proportional to the displacement must be isochronous. In the previous decade he had grappled with the principle of how to design a watch-spring of regular period, and this insight derived from that experience; yet this context within which he came to discover his law has been ignored and forgotten. London's Monument designed by Hooke,[15] with its inscription declaring it to have been designed by Wren, forms a fitting symbol for the way England has treated its greatest inventor.[*]

Rebuilding London

> 'Methinks already, from this Chymic flame,
> I see a city of more precious mold.'
>
> > Dryden, 'Annus Mirabilis', on the rebuilding
> > of London after the fire.

---

[*] Another character assassination was published by Dr Stephen Shapin in 'Robert Hooke, New Studies' 1989 Edited by M. Hunter and S. Schaffer. The volume as a whole is moderately commendable, as it should be for the price, well demonstrating that 'no single scholar can now do justice to all his [Hooke's] activities.'(p.6) 'Spies and traitors were lurking everywhere in Hooke's world' Mr Shapin informs the reader, in his thoroughly paranoid account. Two examples of Shapin's 'scholarship' may be cited.

    'Leibniz accounted Hooke's illegitimate claims to priority 'unworthy of his own estimate of himself, unworthy of his nation, and unworthy of the Royal Society,''affirmed Mr Shapin. Startled, we turn to the letter in question by Leibniz to Oldenburg, in the year 1673. It pertained to Leibniz' new calculator, able to multiply and divide as well as add and subtract, which had so much impressed the Royal Society that it led to its inventor being elected as a Fellow, but which alas was not entirely completed and fully operational when its inventor then came to the shores of England as an ambassador of Louis XIV. Hooke had been fascinated by the machine, had been allowed to see it with its back removed, but not to take it to pieces. He then demonstrated his automatic calculator to the Royal Society in 1674. What Leibniz actually said in his letter was,

> 'I am certain that the very famous Hooke will not bring confusion to another's invention, for I think he is so generous and cautious that he will rather improve his own inventions (of which he has no lack) than demand possession of that which has been publicly proposed already by someone else.'

Then, to further underline his concern, he added that if perchance Hooke were to claim such a priority, this would be unworthy of him, etc. The statement cited by Shapin was actually made in the conditional tense, and the opinion of Leibniz on Hooke was very much the opposite of that claimed by Shapin. No 'illegitimate claims to priority' had been made, in Leibniz' opinion.

    'When Hooke entertained friends in his room, he observed the consumption of claret with the carefree generosity of an Edinburgh accountant,' sneered Shapin. A reference was given to the Hooke diaries. Turning to the page in question, we find no more than that a Mons. Pappin came to visit, and 'Gave him 1 bottle of claret.' Why the Frenchman received a bottle of claret we are not informed, but the event simply has no conection with Mr Shapin's version. Aubrey's opinion that his friend was 'a person of great vertue and goodness' was dismissed by Shapin as 'improbable.' John Aubrey's character sketches of Stuart England have been much admired down the centuries, and will one hopes continue to command a greater respect that the view of Mr Shapin.

THE CRUSHING OF HOOKE

After the Fire of London, Christopher Wren submitted a plan for its reconstruction, grandiose and sublime but quite impractical. A more mundane blueprint was submitted by Robert Hooke, as a result of which he was appointed Surveyor and one of the three Commissioners for rebuilding London, by the City Corporation. There was to quote Aubrey 'a wonderful consumility of phansey' between Wren and Hooke, so that it was difficult to say exactly who designed what, in their extensive partnership which has been so effectively blotted out of the history books. We are never likely to know the extent to which Hooke assisted Wren in designing the dome of St Paul's for example.[16]

Robert Hooke's reputation in architecture disappeared when Wren's son composed Wren's biography *Parentalia* in 1750, attributing Hooke's works to Wren. Evelyn recorded in his diary for 11 May 1676, 'Went to see Mr Montague's new palace near Bloomsbury, built by Mr Hooke of our Society, after the French manner'. At the beginning of the eighteenth century, it became the British Museum. Hatton's *New View of London* of 1708 extolled it as 'an extraordinary noble and beautiful Palace', though did not go quite so far as to name its architect. It was demolished in the mid-nineteenth century to make way for the neoclassical edifice which now stands. Nor have 'The splendour of Ragley and the brilliance and charm of the Physician's Theatre' (Espinase p.105) survived to display their designer's skill. Yet, so well was the building of the Royal College of Physicians regarded, that a French guide of the period recommended that tourists pay someone threepence to be shown around.

In the 1690s, with his health deteriorating, his elder brother John having committed suicide and his beloved niece Grace having died of tuberculosis, and the main discovery of his life having been snatched from under his nose, Hooke's attacks of melancholy worsened.[17] Then, his teeming brain immersed itself in the subject of geology, resuscitating his early childhood memories of playing with sea-shells on the Isle of Wight where he grew up, and he formulated theories too far in advance of his time so they were destined to be forgotten.

As Hooke was the first to describe the cellular basis of life, in his microscopic examination of cork, and was the first to use the word, 'cell' in its biological sense, so too was he the first to observe the Red Spot of Jupiter. He noted that the star *α Arietis* consisted of two stars 8 seconds apart, one of the earliest records of a double star, was probably the first to proposed a periodic orbit for a comet, that of 1664, and was one of the first to note the period of Mars' rotation at 24 hours (Huygens had discovered it some years earlier, but Hooke didn't know that). He described the life-cycle of the gnat, his 'truly frightening' pictures of these little creatures becoming famous, and developed the oil-immersion principle for improving the microscope image. He lived when science was called 'natural philosophy' implying a more universal range of interest before that new kind of man, the specialist, took over. Today a character who studied chemistry and used a telescope would be a mere figure of fun. It is for this reason that the characters of this early period, touched as they all were with the realisation that something vast was taking place in their time, something more far-reaching than any of them could fully comprehend, remain of enduring fascination.

Chapter 7

The Intractable Moon

At last we learn wherefore the silver moon
Once seemed to travel with unequal steps,
As if she scorned to suit her pace to numbers -
Till now made clear to no astronomer...
Explained too are the forces of the deep,
How roaming Cynthia bestirs the tides...

Halley, ode to the *Principia*

Prelude

In the seventeenth-century, ships wound their way to the East Indies without very much idea as to where they were once land disappeared; they were indeed, as we still say today, 'at sea'. All the wealth being garnered from third-world exploitation – chocolate, African gold, Indian rosewood – came to Europe by ship. Many a cargo of silver, sugar or hardwood had been navigated across wide oceans only to be dashed to pieces against the rocks of Land's End. Indeed, it was said of sailors that, 'Of so many, so few grow to gray hairs'.[1] 'Finding the longitude' entered the vernacular as signifying a goal impossible of achievement yet endlessly sought, foiling all endeavours. No greater scientific challenge existed, and various European powers had offered great prizes for the solution of longitude. King Charles, whose royal budget did not permit him such an option, appointed a Royal Commission to look into the matter.

The British fleet was shipwrecked on the Scilly Isles in 1707 when it was supposed to be proceeding up the Channel, highlighting this most pressing of scientific problems. The Greenwich Observatory was set up for this very purpose. If only the astronomers could manage to predict the moon's position, then all longitude measurements could simply be derived from it, given that a fairly rudimentary measure of time was available.

Studying the moon's motion was the odds-on favoured method for resolving the supreme theoretical challenge of that era; finding the longitude at sea. The trouble was, to work such longitude computation one required a theory which could predict the moon's position within two or three minutes of arc. That was the minimum accuracy required to be of use for such a purpose. Such accuracy remained unattained by any almanack prior to the late eighteenth-century.[2]

The Royal Society received in 1669 an anonymous letter giving some useful data on forthcoming eclipses and other celestial events. Its secretary, Oldenburg, soon guessed the source, and Flamsteed received an appreciative letter of reply. Thus, his reputation came to blossom. The king was much intrigued by some glass barometer tubes he made, for the young Flamsteed provided some instructions whereby weather changes could be predicted by their use. Robert Boyle had said this could be done in a general sort of way, but this guide was more detailed, or so Flamsteed averred. It was Jonas Moore who brought these new devices to the monarch's attention. Some tidal tables he prepared also impressed the king. Like other key characters in our story, he combined a manual skill for invention with a deep discernment of theory. The King decided that Flamsteed should receive an honorary M.A. from Jesus College, Cambridge.

The *Opera Posthuma* of Jeremiah Horrocks was published in 1673 by the mathematician John Collins, where the extent of Flamsteed's contribution was evident from the fact that he was the only living author referred to on its title-page. He there gave a more detailed explanation of the Horrocks lunar tables and became the authority on Horrocks' peculiar improvement on the obscure 'evection' inequality[3] of the Moon's motion, whereby its future position could be predicted to within ten or twenty minutes of arc. Years later, he computed therefrom the best-ever moon tables, in his 1680 *Doctrine of the Sphere*.

A Royal Observatory was to be set up in pursuit of this tempting chimera, and Flamsteed was in 1675 appointed the King's Observator, which title later became, 'Astronomer Royal' – a proud moment. It seems to have been the first occasion in the annals of history when an astronomer employed by a monarch was not expected to cast horoscopes. He was not employed to give royal advice by prognosticating from the heavens, nor even to interpret eclipses, but merely to re-chart the heavens more accurately, for the benefit of the navy. He did cast a horoscope for the Observatory when it was opened, but beside it he derisively inscribed (in Latin), 'Friends, can you help laughing?' But, without the glamour of prognostications from the heavens, would he be able to retain a monarch's interest, could he sustain his salary?

It was hardly his fault that the goal he was given was unattainable and his life-work devoid of success as far as the aim of ascertaining longitude was concerned. His approach towards mapping the moon's erratic path was one of three main approaches taken in this period. Flamsteed used the Horroxian scheme which he tried to improve – Isaac Newton did much the same, but rather better, and claimed that he was deducing these inequalities from his theory of gravity; while Edmond Halley consistently believed that the best approach was to follow a complete Saros cycle.

THE INTRACTABLE MOON

The setting up of the Observatory was the third major contribution of the Merry Monarch to the establishment of the scientific enterprise. The first was the granting of a royal charter to the Royal Society in 1662, and the second was the adjustment of the terms of the Cambridge Lucasian professorship so that it no longer necessitated taking holy orders; whereby a certain occupant was not thrown out in 1676. In the year 1675 the zero longitude by royal decree had been made to pass through Greenwich, through the new Observatory which Christopher Wren had designed in the royal park – which must have mollified Flamsteed somewhat for his having to purchase most of the astronomical equipment himself from his own resources plus his salary. Greenwich was selected as being a suitable distance from the smoke and grime of London. Two centuries later, this line became internationally accepted as the single meridian line for all nations.

The new Astronomer Royal entered his job at a period of revolution, when the telescope, the pendulum clock and the micrometer screw gauge gave the possibility of making measurements of unprecedented accuracy. No one else had used a telescope in a systematic manner before Flamsteed for celestial measurements. The heliocentric theory as Kepler had framed it posed a new challenge to astronomers. Other observatories at Paris with Cassini and Leyden where Hevelius worked were far better funded, being provided both with assistants and with equipment, neither of which were supplied at Greenwich.

How could one person entering an empty building possibly contemplate so vast an endeavour? As Flamsteed looked in amused disbelief at the horoscope he had drawn up for the inauguration, did shadows of a tragic future to come cross his mind? Did he himself ever believe that longitude at sea would be attainable by such means, and if not then what security had he? All he produced for King George, consort to Queen Anne, was an improved table of the tides, which was definitely not of great royal interest. Or, perhaps some inkling that this empty building in the Royal Park was to become the most celebrated observatory in all the world dawned upon him.

The moon's motion was the one issue that gave Newton a headache – as Edmond Halley was informed, when he would now and then urge Newton to re-open his study of the subject. With the benefit of hindsight, we can see that the problem with which Newton was grappling, and which he regarded as more difficult than any other problem in the *Principia*, was not so much difficult as impossible. The moon's unique path is three-dimensional and can only be loosely approximated by models based on ellipses drawn upon plane surfaces. Its path interweaves between earth and sun, always being attracted twice as strongly by the sun as by the earth. This is indeed a curious position for what is supposed to be a satellite to find itself in, but there it lies and some apprehension of this is a prerequisite for understanding the difficulties with which astronomers in the seventeenth century had to grapple. The moon's motion is a three-body problem, and only the two-body problem is amenable to analytical mathematics. If one body moves round another, in orbit, then its path can be described mathematically by the three laws of Kepler, for planetary motion. Kepler realised that these did not apply to the moon and had made no serious attempt to do so.

Prior to Newton's endeavour, the young Jeremiah Horrocks had devised what came to be regarded by for example Flamsteed, the Astronomer Royal, as the best model to describe the moon's orbit: it imagined an orbit resembling a wobbly rubber band whose 'eccentricity' varied and where the rotation of the 'apse line' – the line joining the apogee and the perigee positions – changed direction periodically and where earth was positioned somewhere near one focus of the ellipse, perhaps on a little wheel attached to one focus! But it worked...

The long and bitter struggle between Flamsteed, Britain's only professional astronomer, and Newton, is seen nowadays as a fruitful conflict between theoretical and empirical approaches, a blending of what Whiteside called, 'The twin strands of the mathematical-cum-theoretical and the observational-cum-practical which intertwine down the ages', and which he found were 'aptly personified' in these two contrasting characters.[4] In some ways, one can compare the collaboration with that between Tycho Brahe and Kepler, where the latter remarked that one could not come near Tycho Brahe without exposing oneself to the gravest of insults. Alas, the twenty tempestuous months which those two spent together at Benatek castle near Prague seem rather pleasant by comparison. But, while it is common to place the onus of blame upon one or both of these two melancholic characters, Newton and Flamsteed, both of whom grew up as motherless children, we shall in addition seek a celestial cause, in the intractability of the great issue over which they collaborated, namely the motion of the moon.

To what extent was Newton's lunar theory inferred from his gravity theory? The question remains to this day quite enigmatic.[5] After long endeavour, Newton finally came out with his terse 'Theory of the Moon' in 1702, his most popular treatise in the early eighteenth century which was continually reprinted. It gave seven equations for predicting the moon's motion, four of which he had invented, but these did not look as if they had any discernible connection with a theory of gravity. It didn't win any prize for determining longitude at sea – that wasn't claimed until the chronometer was invented in the mid-eighteenth century.

Charles II's favourite mistress, the Duchess of Portsmouth – more or less contemporaneous with Nell Gwyn – advised him that a Frenchman by the name of Le Sieur de Pierre had the solution to the much-desired goal of finding longitude at sea. She did not add that she was sharing her favours with him at the time. The French had presented Louise de Querouaille to the king to console him when his sister the Duchess of Orleans died – to the annoyance of Nell Gwynn – and she became the Duchess of Portsmouth, and the royal favourite. In 1674, le Sieur de Pierre was summoned to the royal presence.[6]

Le Sieur de Pierre proceeded to expound his view that ships would be able to ascertain their longitude by charting the moon's position against the stars of the night sky. He boldly asserted that, if only he were given two lunar sightings, with their times as well as their latitudes, then he would be able to compute the *longitudes* of the places from which they had been taken. Flamsteed, then 28 years old, was a member of the Royal Commission through the recommendation of Jonas More – along with Christopher Wren and the ubiquitous Hooke – and he was requested to supply such data. He came up with a couple of observations supposedly made at European observatories a few years earlier. The Frenchman was supposed to work out the location of these observatories.

The Frenchman, when shown these observations, indignantly called them 'feigned' and 'obscured', and in such a huff walked off the stage of history; we lack further information about him. The historian Eric Forbes combed over the records and discovered that Flamsteed had indeed made the two sightings in question, but at his home town of Derby. The trigonometry whereby the young astronomer had then computed what he supposed the observations would have been, had they been taken at the European cities, was not quite as faultless as he had supposed. In other words, or so Forbes concluded, the Frenchman was fairly justified in claiming that the data were unusable. Unperturbed, the Commission drew from this episode the doubtless correct conclusion that, as Flamsteed had said at the start, the Moon's path was too erratic to be usable for such a method.[*]

The king was taken aback to hear about the unreliability of the star-charts which his navy had to employ, being a keen sailor himself. For a maritime nation, he decided, this was not tolerable. A promiscuous royal mistress, a fiddled computation - and, presto! Greenwich was launched on its historic course.[7]

A North-country talent

'A free, affable and Humble man, not at all conceited or dogmatical.'
Thomas Molyneux to William Molyneux,
in 1683, describing Flamsteed[8]

---

[*] The Frenchman's theory - which was not new - worked on a 'two-clock' basis: the moon's position against the stars, as it revolved once per twenty seven days, would give a 'universal time' measurement. Local time was then found using a pocket watch, corrected by sunrise and sunset. The difference between the two gave the longitude, fifteen degrees for each hour of difference between the two times. The method led to an error of one degree in longitude, or some fifty miles at the latitude of Britain, for an error of two minutes in the Moon's position. For comparison, tables based on Tycho Brahe's lunar data were likely to be out by as much as 20 minutes.

THE DARK SIDE OF ISAAC NEWTON

John Flamsteed grew up in Derby, at the same latitude as Grantham where Newton was born. His introduction to astronomy came chiefly through a remarkable constellation of north-country astronomers, who lived and worked before the civil war was unleashed. Around what are now the cities of Manchester, Leeds and Preston, the remarkable but little-extolled dawn of British astronomy took place, by courtesy of the Venus, the Evening Star. We digress briefly to describe this.

At Westminster Abbey, Newton's bust stares balefully down the aisles to a monument at the far end, in memory of the young Jeremiah Horrocks. The latter was widely romanticised in the nineteenth-century as having founded the tradition of British astronomy: 'the pride and boast of British astronomy' as William Herschel called him. He alone in all the world had computed the motion of Venus well enough to realise that it was due to pass in front of the Sun.

Jeremiah Horrocks lived but for 22 years. He published no papers, but left a few stanzas of poetry, describing his delight at being the first to witness Venus passing in front of the Sun, and a notebook with his lunar theory written out. Arguably the first convert in England to the use of Kepler's tables, he improved upon them and found an error in the Venus' latitude prediction, whereby he realised that a solar transit was due. His act is commemorated in paintings and stained glass windows, in the company of elaborate scientific instruments that he never possessed, 'and probably never even saw'.[9]

The historic Venus-transit took place in 1639. Horrocks nearly missed it, on account of 'being called away on business of the highest importance which for these ornamental pursuits could not with propriety by neglected' a reference to his work as a priest's assistant: he was then a mere twenty years of age. He had notified his friend William Crabtree of the impending event, explaining that it would not happen again for another 120 years. Crabtree's telescope projected the solar disc onto a screen, but clouds obscured the image. Shortly before sunset the clouds parted, with Crabtree almost too excited to be able to perform the necessary observations – or, that was Horrocks' story; 'rap't in contemplation he stood, motionless, scarce trusting his senses, through excess of joy'. But afterwards he pulled himself together and was able to recall the position of Venus – and, more important, its size, against the sun.[*]

The size of Venus turned out to be far smaller than its appearance in the night sky, appearing as a mere speck against the sun's disc. What is called the 'solar

---

[*] The *Principia* took a dim view of Crabtree's accuracy, averring that his measurement was much too small: 'Venus appeared to Mr. Crabtrie only 1' 3"; to Horrox but 1' 12'; though by the mensurations of Hewelcke and Huygens without the sun's disc, it ought to have been seen at least 1' 24'.' (*The System of the World,* section 16) In fact, Crabtree's value was the most accurate of those cited in the *Principia.* The apparent angular size of Venus at a solar transit cannot exceed 1' 6'.

parallax' was thereby determined, which gave the key to the scale of the solar system. The young Horrocks' opinion of this value was vastly superior to previous estimates, and meant that the astronomers in this north-country circle were the only ones to enjoy an approximate conception of the scale of the solar system.*

It was all *seven times larger* than Kepler had supposed.

The other major innovation accomplished by the young cleric Horrocks was a scheme for determining the Moon's motion, which was used and developed by Flamsteed. Horrock's method remained, with slight modifications, the most accurate method of determining lunar motion throughout the seventeenth century. Indeed, its use was spread right across Europe in the first half of the eighteenth century – in the form that Newton gave to it.

William Gascoigne measured the angular size of Moon, and how it varied through the monthly and yearly cycles, using an ingenious micrometer gauge fixed to his telescope. These were, as Flamsteed recollected in his *Historia Coelestis* Preface, the first measurements of the solar and lunar diameters, the variation of which indicate the orbits involved. Gascoigne fell in the Civil War, but Richard Towneley of Lancaster inherited his manuscripts and instruments, and somewhat improved upon the latter. The young John Flamsteed was heir to these powerful developments, both in the theory and in the practice of astronomy, becoming the first working scientist to apply their inventions. We know very little about these north-country astronomers beyond what Flamsteed preserved by transcriptions from Towneley.

In 1672, Flamsteed paid a visit to Towneley, who was an antiquarian, a scholar and patron of learning, the man probably responsible for bringing together the group of north-country astronomers. Flamsteed had come on his father's business. The two of them observed Mars and determined its position against the stars, whence a solar parallax value was derived. Flamsteed published in the *Philosophical Transactions* his first letter, giving what has been called his 'astonishingly close approximation to the value of the solar parallax,'[10] a value of 10'. It involved Mars-against-the-stars measurements of arcseconds precision. The micrometer gauge used for this historic measurement was constructed by one of Mr Towneley's tenants in accordance with a description of Gascoigne's original model, as described in a letter he wrote

---

* Solar parallax can conveniently be defined as half the angular size of the earth as seen from the sun. Tycho Brahe determined every other astronomical constant anew except for the solar parallax, retaining the ancient value of 3 minutes of arc. As the sun appears as 30' of arc in the sky, a 3' solar parallax would mean that the sun was a mere 15'/3' or five times larger in diameter than the earth, the view accepted by astronomers before Kepler. Its rapid change thereafter shows the proper scale of the solar system dawning upon the human race. Kepler took a smaller value, of 1.' Horrocks placed it at 14-15', and then Hevelius, living a generation after Horrocks, gave it a value of 40'. Hevelius was familiar with the latter's work, as it was he who first published Horrock's tract on the Venus transit, but evidently he could not accept so drastic an enlargement of the solar system

to Crabtree. Towneley presented this device, which incorporated some improvements of his own, to the mathematician Jonas Moore, who in turn gave it to Flamsteed during his first visit to London in 1671.

In France, Cassini was also scrutinising Mars at this period of its closest approach and gained a fairly comparable solar parallax measure quite independently. Cassini was funded by Louis XIV, 'Le Roi Soleil', and so could do the job properly. A French team had sailed to South America where it took synchronous sightings of Mars-against-the-stars, later compared with those of the Paris Academy. From the difference in 'parallax' of Mars, its distance was determined. Cassini derived a remarkable value of the sun's distance of eighty-seven million miles, which approximated the correct figure of ninety-three million miles. Flamsteed's result however was achieved without any synchronised team at the other end of the world with whom to compare his measurements.

We have built up the background of the young astronomer in some detail, chiefly because his character normally gets destroyed in histories of these matters.[11] David Brewster's verdict – 'an astronomer without principle, and a divine without charity' is hardly improved upon by several more recent histories one could mention. His virtues – what Baily called 'his piety, his honesty, integrity and his independent spirit' – we shall see tested to the limits of endurance. The Preface to his life-work, his *Historia Coelestis Britannica*, was first published in 1982 in a tolerably complete form, and no earlier.

It is due to the Victorian astronomer Francis Baily that we have access at all to the relevant material. He discovered in the early nineteenth-century a pile of old papers mouldering on the shelves at Greenwich, and from these he was able to reconstruct a near-obliterated life, of the Reverend John Flamsteed. He published the papers, causing deep consternation of Victorian England and a severe threat to his own reputation. Were it not for Francis Baily, Britain's first Astronomer Royal would be in much the same boat as Robert Hooke, for Isaac Newton had the unique capability of not merely marring the lives of the giants upon whose shoulders he stood, but of obliterating their reputations as well.

A talent from the North-country came and effectively initiated the tradition of British astronomy. Few are the Flamsteed experts, indeed only two have really existed, Baily and Forbes. The onward-rolling tercentenary celebrations gave birth to the publication of his complete correspondence.

The King's Observator began his employment in 1675, at the Tower of London, resolved to investigate the moons of Jupiter. His telescope was erected from the turret of the White Tower, but he was there disturbed by the ravens; or, that it the story told by the wardens of the Tower. A few months later he moved on to Greenwich, where Hooke and Wren were seeing to the construction of a brand-new Observatory.

Sir Jonas Moore, the Surveyor and General of Ordnance of War Machines in England under Charles II, donated a fine iron sextant to Greenwich, seven feet in radius, with telescopic sights and a new method of screw gradation; Hooke had a hand in its design, and the heavy iron-work was done by the smiths in the Tower of London. Several of the instruments used at Greenwich were designed by Hooke, who in a 1674 publication had claimed that a 40-fold improvement in accuracy could be obtained by using a telescope with cross-wires together with a pendulum clock – a gross exaggeration, which so upset the Dutch astronomer Hevelius that Halley had to be sent over to patch up relationships. Fourteen years after his appointment, as the King's Observator in 1675, Flamsteed finally came to possess the essential instruments required for his mighty task, a task he himself likened to the building of St Paul's.

The time at Greenwich was kept by two large grandfather clocks, also donated by Sir Thomas More, and specially made for the purpose. Flamsteed used them to time the daily transits of Sirius, to establish the daily 'isochronal' rotation of the Earth upon its axis. There was no temperature compensation to the pendulums – on a warm day they just went more slowly! He acquired a third pendulum clock and adjusted it to the *sidereal* day, a few minutes shorter than the solar day, so that it measured star-time.

As well as the first systematic use of the new instruments, Greenwich's fame grew from the working procedures developed, involving error detection methods and instrument tests to evaluate accuracy. Flamsteed concluded that the obliquity of the ecliptic was 23°29'00", a lower value than previous astronomers had derived, but still out by two minutes. It required a more accurate theory of atmospheric refraction before those two minutes of error could be vanquished. The accurate determination of the zodiac stars was especially vital as the basis for all his planetary and lunar measurements. Locating the equinoctial points, the sun's position against the zodiac at the equinoxes, was no easy matter. He found them by measuring the sun's angle to Venus in the evening sky, and then taking Venus' position against the stars at night. He showed the annual rate of precession from them, i.e. the motion of the earth's pole, never before achieved by an astronomer from his own data. He found the precession of the equinoxes to be 1° per 72½ years. His values for the period of Jupiter's four discovered satellites were used in the *Principia.* He determined the seasonal variations in the size of the solar disc, which showed the shape of the Earth's orbit. His 'equation of the natural days' demonstrated the uniform rotation of the earth upon its axis. Once these basics had been fixed, he could set about cataloguing the motion of the moon and planets, compiling tables for public use.

Greenwich became the foremost observational astronomy centre in Europe, not least because Hevelius' observatory was destroyed by fire in 1679, just as he was setting about publishing his 35 years of data. The two astronomers were on cordial and respectful terms, patching up somewhat the rows which had developed from Flamsteed asserting (at the close of his 1672 letter to the Society's journal) that Hevelius' naked-eye observations were not going to improve greatly upon Brahe's observations taken at the turn of the previous century. Hooke weighed in, and even despite Halley's tactful lying about the extreme accuracy of Hevelius' methods, to within 10" of arc he averred,[12] the quarrel greatly upset the Dutch astronomer.

The keen eyesight of Hevelius seemed able to resolve down to about half a minute of arc. Not for nothing had he formed the new 'Lynx' constellation as a tribute to his own eyesight! The normal human eye had a resolving power of about one minute of arc, as Robert Hooke had pointed out. The astronomers of the time did not appreciate that they were working at a level of accuracy where the stars were no longer absolutely fixed but moved with respect to one another. Tycho Brahe's star-positions were in fact slightly different from those of Hevelius and Flamsteed. A year after starting his job, Flamsteed agreed to enter into a contest with lynx-eyed Hevelius, whereby they were both to measure eight zodiacal stars with respect to each other. It was found that their results generally agreed within half a minute.[*]

Two years later, Flamsteed was startled when he received an advance copy of Hevelius' *Machina Coelestis* in 1678, and discovered that the Dutchman's stellar positions commonly differed from his by less than 20" of arc.[13]

'Seen, Greenwich, from thy lovely heights, declare
How just, how beauteous the refractive law.'
James Thomson, 'To the Memory of Newton' 1727.

Not until 1689 did Flamsteed acquire the proper instrument he required for taking his astronomical measurements. After the death of his father in 1688, he had sufficient funding to order its construction. It was called a mural quadrant and was fixed to a wall facing south so that his telescope could be swung up and down in a vertical plane. As the nineteenth-century astronomer Baily remarked:

'From this moment [September, 1689, when the instrument was first used] every thing which Flamsteed did, every observation that he made, assumed a tangible and a permanent form, and was available

---

[*] each case, their present positions were adjusted according to their 'proper motions' to give their positions when these three observed them. The results were: Tycho Brahe: 34", Hevelius: 27". Flamsteed: 18".

Tycho Brahe Hevelius Flamsteed
   34"   27"   18"

These were relative angles measured between fixed stars around the ecliptic. This does give us an interesting measure of the accuracy attained by the several experts. 'J. Hevelius and his catalogue of Stars,' 1971, Chicago Press Brigham Young p.47. (The figures quoted are as standard deviations of the eight measurements of stellar angles, after correcting for proper motion). Working with positional astronomer Bernard Yallop at the RGO in Cambridge, shortly before it was closed down, he and I ascertained that RA & Dec stellar positions in Flamsteed's *Historia Coelestis* were within five arcseconds.

to some useful purpose: his preceding observations being only subsidiary, and dependent on results to be afterwards deduced from some fixed instrument of this kind, which he had long sought for. It was from this point only that the Observatory could be considered as complete; and from this period we must date the commencement of his valuable and fundamental observations.'[14]

Using this instrument, his telescope scanned a narrow, vertical slice of the night sky. As the heavens appeared to revolve, the stars would swing one by one into view. 'Declination' was measured by the vertical angle of the telescope and 'Right Ascension' by sidereal time. The latter was measured by one of the Observatory's grandfather clocks, which swung to a two-second beat. From the minutes and seconds of their time, Flamsteed's method derived stellar position to within minutes and seconds of arc.[15]

A thousand stars had been seen and recorded in the night skies, from Hipparchus to Kepler. Ptolemy had described 1028 stars and Tycho Brahe a thousand, of which three quarters were accurately placed. Then, Hevelius' eagle eye managed to catalogue one and a half thousand stars. Applying a telescope to the heavens caused their number to grow without limit. Flamsteed's *Atlas Coelestis* finally contained almost three thousand stars, while Bode's *Uranographia* of 1801 contained seventeen thousand.

In 1691, a letter with some sage advice was received by Flamsteed from Newton. 'In my opinion it will be better to publish those [positions] of the first 6 magnitude [stars] observed by others and afterwards by way of appendix to publish the new ones observed by yourself alone,' it said, expressing the hope that it would not be long before the catalogue of fixed stars was published. If only he, Flamsteed, could first print an account of some such limited number of zodiac stars known to tradition, then his skill in positioning them could be appreciated. One may regret that he ignored this advice.

'The subtle gentleman'[16] pays a visit

The letter cordially explained that Newton had hoped to be able to pay a visit to Greenwich with the mathematician David Gregory, but had in the event been unable to come and so had sent on Gregory to see Flamsteed, as he felt they ought to meet. Flamsteed's reply of 24 February 1692 claimed with undue optimism that it should take him another year or two to complete the task of listing all the fixed stars, adding that he had 150 Moon positions at meridian, from his newly-operational mural quadrant.

In another letter of 1693, Flamsteed tells Newton that he now has 2200 fixed stars observed and 30 maps of the constellations drawn. These maps of the constellations

– destined to become the best-known of star-atlases and used Europe-wide through the next century – employed a new method of projection, 'in which the appearance to the naked eye is less distorted than by any projection I have yet seen,' to quote their author's description.[*]

His star-maps are all of the 1690 epoch.[17] This means that they were exactly true for the year 1690. Stars have to move away from the positions assigned to them by mapmakers at a rate of 1° over 72 years, owing to the reference-framework involved, so gradually a map of a given epoch becomes obsolete, a fact not without relevance to Flamsteed's supposed reticence to publish his work, which will be considered later.

A year later, a fateful pact was established with a letter by Newton to Flamsteed dated 7 October 1694, alleging with a startling optimism that an accuracy of 2 or 3 minutes should be achievable for the Moon's position. This was a week after a rare visit of his to Greenwich on the first of September, to discuss a new edition of the *Principia*, when he was shown a list of 'about fifty positions of the Moon reduced to a synopsis', and their deviation from the predictions in tables. The Astronomer Royal had by that time observed it over a whole Saros cycle of eighteen years, and so was in an excellent position to assess its major irregularities. On the inside of the back cover of Flamsteed's leather *Diarium Observationum* Newton had inscribed a promise, a memento of his visit. 'Sept 1.1694. Received then of Mr flamsteed two sheets MS of the places of the Moon observed & calculated for years 89 90 & part of 91 wch I promise not to communicate without his consent.' He managed to keep it, for a while.

Flamsteed later noted in his biography that, 'In the year 1694, I rectified the solar theory,[**] and laid the foundation of the rectification of the fixed stars' (Baily, p745). This was relevant to Newton's visit to Greenwich in 1694, for the astronomer did not want his data to be made public till he had finalised his co-ordinate system. His list of lunar positions plus errors (i.e. their deviations from lunar positions given in current tables) was, in Baily's view, the stimulus for a new assault on the problem of lunar motion.

---

[*] This is known as the 'Samson-Flamsteed' method of projection. The latter could have invented it independently, but it is thought probable that he at some stage saw a Sampson-style map and decided to use that method.

[**] The old-fashioned term 'Solar theory' referred to the motion of the earth around the sun, but viewed as the apparent motion of the sun around the zodiac. There were two principal inequalities, one due to the small eccentricity of the earth's orbit, called solar parallax, the other due to earth's monthly wobble in space as it moves around the earth-moon baricentre. Failing properly to reckon with these would mean that all planetary tables would have the earth's rhythms of motion ('solar theory') wrongly incorporated into the motions of the other planets. This was then the case, as has been well shown by Owen Gingerich's computer analysis of such tables of the period. For example, in the Jupiter positions as given in Vincent Wing's tables in the 1650's and '60s, some 10' of error which was about half of the total (in zodiacal longitude) was of a 1-year period, while the other half of the error in his tables was of a 12-year periodicity. (Gingerich and Welther, p. Xiv) Thus 'solar theory' ie the earth's rhythms of motion, monthly and yearly, was the essential basis for constructing planetary tables.

When Halley got to hear that Newton had acquired new, high-quality observations from Greenwich, he was eager to see them, and was annoyed to learn that this wasn't allowed! Newton merely disclosed to Halley (his letter assured Flamsteed) that the observations revealed a 'quadrature parallax' of 8-10', but no more. He expressed the hope that Halley and Flamsteed would patch up their differences and that, whatever the problem was, 'I hope it will end in friendship'. This letter shows tact! It was embarrassing for Newton that the two people to whom he was most obliged should have somehow become estranged.

Flamsteed's reply on 29 October 1694 tells how he has had a long chat with Halley in London about the moon, and that the latter would like to understand how Newton plots the motion of apogee and the altering of its eccentricity. The letter related how Halley had also explained to Flamsteed his theory of how the mean motion of the moon was swifter in centuries gone by than at present – what came to be called 'secular acceleration', one of Halley's three great discoveries in astronomy for which he is now remembered.[18] We need not enter into the arcane mathematics whereby these three minds grappled with the irregularities of the moon's motion. Our concern here is merely to show how Flamsteed was being quite civil with his younger colleague. It seems indeed that he found Halley's broad, hearty, shiver-me-timbers manners hard to cope with, being a somewhat reserved and fastidious character himself. Loose comments which Halley made in taverns doubtless without malice intended seem to have reached the ears of Flamsteed in somewhat altered form as if he could do Flamsteed's job a deal better, or perchance desired the job himself. In later years, Flamsteed said of Halley that he 'talks, swears and drinks brandy like a sea-captain'.

'Apogee in ye summer signs'

A long correspondence of nineteen letters from Newton now began where lunar data was sent from Greenwich to Cambridge. In November of that year, an urgent request came for lunar data when 'apogee is in ye summer signs', by which the mathematician could locate some inequality concerning the lunar nodes; in particular, for apogee in 'ye sun's opposition in midwinter', the only time for many years.[19] The letter also announced that some of the observations from 1690 were 'faulty.' The astronomer indignantly replied that most of the positions queried were correct, and went on to refer to Horrocks' theory, 'which it was my good fortune to meet with and usher into ye light'. Would Newton please let him know 'when you have delivered what corrections or additions are to be made to that theory' – a provocative and presumptuous remark, since Horrocks' theory was unrelated to the theory of gravity. Flamsteed's headaches were playing up at this time, and he was in no position to spend long and freezing nights to gain these vital Moon positions, however important the winter's full moon might be. His salary covered no heating bills. He also flared up somewhat over an offer by Newton to pay cash for the lunar observations. Especially in later life, it was a habit of Newton's simply to offer cash in a way that could annoy people who imagined they were in some sort of relationship with him. Making a great mistake, the King's Observator stood on his dignity and affirmed that he had a sufficient income – when in fact he was having to waste much time and energy giving tuition lessons and doing lengthy computations himself because the government never offered to pay for any assistants, let alone for the purchase and maintenance of his equipment.

'I would set the Moon's theory right this winter,' wrote Newton, with a bold optimism. It was he declared a work of 'about 3 or 4 months' – adding, 'when I have done it once, I would have done with it forever,' revealing the mental strain involved. 'If you can but have a little patience with me till I have satisfied myself about these things, and make the theory fit to be communicated without danger of error, I do intend *you* shall be the *first* man to whom I shall communicate it.' Twice he promised in writing not to give the data to others, and now a third promise likewise destined to be shattered rather shockingly was made.

On 17 November, Newton explained that 'being at a stand about ye Moons theory', he has turned to constructing a table of atmospheric refraction instead, a thing which the astronomer would certainly be eager to receive. A couple of months later, he added considerately, 'I was desirous to complete it that I might have something to present you with for the paines you have taken for me about your observations.' An optimistic letter followed in February of 1695, where he diplomatically revealed the great endeavour, the mirage on the horizon:

'For all the world knows that I make no observations my self & therefor I must of necessity acknowledge their Author: And if I do not make a handsome acknowledgement, they will reckon me an ungrateful clown. And for my part I am of the opinion that for your Observations to come abroad thus with a Theory wch you ushered into the world & wch by their means has been made exact would be much more for their advantage & your reputation then to keep them private till you die or publish them wthout such a Theory to recommend them. For such a Theory will be a demonstration of their exactness & make you readily acknowledged the Exactest Observer that has hitherto appeared in the world.'

Otherwise, he would have to wait for someone else who

'...by perfecting the Theory of the Moon shall discover your Observations to be exacter then the rest. But when that shall be God knows: I fear not in your lifetime if I should die before tis done. For I find this Theory so very intricate & the Theory of Gravity so necessary to it, that I am satisfied it will never be perfected but by somebody who understands the Theory of gravity as well or better then I do. But whether you will publish them or not may be considered hereafter. I only assure you at present that, without your consent, I will neither publish them nor communicate them to anybody whilst you live, nor after your death without an honourable acknowledgement of their author.'

It was an offer Flamsteed couldn't refuse. It was the biggest mistake he ever made. The siren song, the delusive promise, could not be resisted. Its consequences were to shatter his reputation in his lifetime and blight it with calumny for centuries to come. He would have been far better off just collecting together all his lunar data – when he had it, when time was on his side, and submitting it to the Society's journal, the *Philosophical Transactions,* together with his rules ('equations') based on the Horrocks model of which he was the acknowledged authority. Instead, he sent it to another to use, and maybe pass on to a third. In later years, he explained his motive. 'I designed indeed to save myself some labour by putting the Moon into his hands' (10.5.1707, Lowthorp, quoted in Baily).

So, Flamsteed set about extracting and tabulating yet more lunar observations from his notebooks. His biography recalled, 'All the year 1695 I had lost in sickness and furnishing Mr I.N. with the moon's places in order to restore her theory' (Baily, p.745).

The above-quoted letter by Newton was the *last* to display a confidence that his gravity theory would conquer what Whiteside called 'this Everest of the major irregularities in the moon's smooth, stationary orbit'. After it, his confidence seems abruptly to have evaporated. Drafts of a second edition of the *Principia* were now being composed, and Whiteside who has studied all of the draft manuscripts of the mid-1690s involved, commented:[20]

'In this flurry of rough calculations and hurried drafts to increasingly futile purpose, it is easy to see Newton's mounting frustration at not being able to contrive the precise mathematical theory of the moon which 10 years before he had seemed to be on the brink of achieving. Never again in his later years, despite his continuing show of assurance in the power of his mathematical expertise to permit him to do so, did he make more than a desultory try to reach that pinnacle of elementary dynamical argument. For the rest, he was content ostentatiously to travel the well-trodden foothills where the equations to the moon's motion which he chose to isolate were presented with the vaguest of loose quantitative dynamical justifications...'[21]

For over two decades the relationship between these two had been candid and trustful. To quote Baily, 'throughout the whole of this correspondence, there is a kindly feeling and a mutual disposition to assist each other' (p.194). 'Mr Newton's approbation is more to me than the cry of all the ignorant in ye world' Flamsteed wrote to a colleague in February 1695. The correspondence had been a model of collaboration between mathematical theorist and practical observer. The first edition of the *Principia* had handsomely acknowledged Flamsteed's vital input. The winter drew to a close and a letter in April merely said, that the Moon had now been let alone for a while. On 29 June the blow fell, with a shrill letter threatening Flamsteed with blame for the ruin of the whole lunar section of the *Principia,** because he was not sending enough lunar data. The letter claimed that Newton was 'about to lose all the time and paines I have hitherto taken' on the Moon and his refraction table and exploded with, 'I want not your calculations but your observations only'. Gossip lethal to the astronomer's reputation began to circulate amongst influential people such as Richard Bentley, to the effect that Flamsteed was withholding vital data out of mere perversity. His headaches had assuredly delayed replies, but what could warrant such an outburst? On the back of this astounding letter, Flamsteed totted up the 243 observations he had *already* sent; was that not enough? No one had hitherto ever had so many lunar positions from which to deduce a theory.

'These and almost all your communications will be useless to me unless you can propose some practicable way or other of supplying me wth Observations...' the letter seethed. Were the two-hundred odd lunar sightings he had sent 'almost useless'? And what right had anyone to speak to him in this manner? A calm but hurt reply explained, factually as ever, that right ascension values came from sidereal time measurements across the meridian, and that the mathematician might find it inconvenient to be given positions of the Moon as time measurements: and, instrument errors had to be allowed for.

Concluding the letter of reply, Flamsteed wrote, 'What one friend may Justly expect from another you shall ever command from Yours J. F.' but the pleasant amity of earlier days was gone forever. Rumours had now sprung abroad, with Richard

---

* 134 In the view of D. T. Whiteside, the outburst of frustration derived in part from Flamsteed adding his own correction for refraction to all the data, however as Newton had exact details of this correction it would have been easy enough for him to subtract it out had he so wished. But further, Whiteside claimed that the problem lay in Flamsteed applying corrections 'according to his own theory of the sun's apparent motion (with its further somewhat shaky parameters of terrestrial eccentricity and solar horizontal parallax).' Leaving aside the question as to whether Flamsteed's estimate of 'terrestrial eccentricity' was 'somewhat shaky,' as he had spent most of the previous year grappling therewith, a theory of the Sun's motion (in modern terms, the Earth's motion) is without relevance to lunar sighting against the stars of the night sky: it is used for planetary motion computations, because these too orbit the Sun, but hardly for the moon: the corrections there applied, were likely to have been merely instrument errors and refraction corrections.

Bentley complaining that the new edition of the *Principia* would have to come out without the lunar section due to his withholding, a slander which has persisted to this day. At the top of another yet more furious letter from Newton in July of 1695, claiming that Flamsteed should appreciate that he was highly indebted to him for such things as a table of refractions he had prepared - and in truth, he had spent a month or two on it, and sent it to Flamsteed, though the latter had his doubts whether it was any good - Flamsteed wrote 'hasty artificiall unkind arrogant letter', but what could he do? If he broke off communication, then these rumours would no doubt appear as true. He gathered together as much more lunar data as he could extract from his notes, another 50 or so observations, and sent them off, but was the recipient any longer interested in the problem?

The new gossip travelled around the coffeehouses of London, as well as those of the continent. 'Flamsteed withheld his observations of the moon from Newton,' Leibniz wrote to Roemer in 1706. 'On that account they say he has as yet been unable to complete his work on the lunar motion.'[22] In 1816, the *Biographie Universelle* stated, under the life of Flamsteed, that:

> 'the public were very desirous of seeing his observations printed; but that, from the character of Flamsteed, this desire was a reason why they should not expect it from him: and the English Government was obliged to use its authority, by directing Halley to supply that which the author would not give.'[23]

David Brewster, in 1855, described how his hero, serene in mind and noble in intention:

> 'resumed the study of lunar and planetary theories ... but the difficulty which he experienced in getting the necessary observations from the Astronomer Royal, interfered with his investigations, and contributed more than any other cause to prevent him from bringing them to a close.'[24]

Myth has here triumphed over historical truth, and the situation has endured even after Baily's *Account* of 1835 had decisively and in great detail refuted the charge. Brewster dismissed Baily's opus as a 'system of calumny and misrepresentation unexampled in the history of science' (p. xii). Brewster had no intention of permitting the fine, marble image of his subject to be tarnished by a pile of old papers at Greenwich. Francis Baily was a distinguished Victorian astronomer who had his reputation rocked but not ruined by the book, published by the Admiralty. The distinguished astrophysicist, the late Stephen Hawkins gave a thumbnail sketch of Flamsteed, 'who had earlier provided Newton with much needed data for the *Principia*, but was now withholding information that Newton wanted.'[25] Even Patrick Moore, from whom one might have expected a charitable account of the genesis of the Royal Observatory, reaffirmed the traditional dog-in-a-manger attitude image of its first occupant, as holding on to his data and not wishing to part with it:

> 'Trouble began when Newton asked for his observational data, and Flamsteed said bluntly that he was not ready to provide them. The quarrel was patched up for a while...'[26]

The long-established trust between the two broke down, as the endeavour to describe the moon's orbit by gravity theory fell apart. Climbing back from his nervous collapse, Newton had tried to resolve the one great issue beyond the first edition of the *Principia* – despite Halley's ode intimating otherwise. The onus of blame for failure was now shifted onto the person who had supplied the data. Newton's decision to move from Cambridge to the Mint in London was then being finalised. It may well have been the case, as Whiteside has suggested, that his perceived failure with the moon was in part the stimulus, in the spring of 1696, for his abandoning a safe, ivory-tower job in académe for the fumes and bustle of the Metropolis.[27]

The correspondence having terminated, Flamsteed heard nothing of a four-page document which Newton forwarded a few years later to David Gregory, published by the latter under the title, *Theory of the Moon's Motion* in 1702, as part of an astronomical treatise. Gregory had held a mathematics chair at Edinburgh university, where his lectures constituted the first university presentation of the new physics, but by this time had moved to Oxford where he was the Savilian mathematics professor. In this text were seven 'equations' which described the irregularities of lunar motion around the zodiac; seven being, presumably, the magic number. In a preface, Gregory claimed that by these rules an accuracy of two or three minutes could be attained. Four of the equations were new, without any explanation as to how they had been deduced, or indeed whether they were linked to the theory of gravity. In the view of the astronomer Baily, the major equations were applied in a similar manner as Flamsteed had for many years used, but some small and rather dubious ones had been added (p.692).[28] The 'equations' were as we would now say sine functions of varying amplitude fluctuating with the lunar month, from the largest of 35 minutes down to the smallest of merely two minutes of arc. To use Flamsteed's expression, would the heavens allow such equations? The astronomer Clairaut in France made substantial advances on the subject some decades later but was fairly critical of these Newtonian equations. William Whiston, who succeeded Newton in the Lucasian chair, remarked of one of these equations, that he had no idea why causes 'which are so unlike', should be conjoined as had there been done with the Sun and Moon apogee motions, and suspected that 'this equation was rather deduced from Mr Flamsteed's observations than from Sir Isaac Newton's own argumentation'.

The news that something had resulted from the grand collaboration first came to the notice of Flamsteed when he received a copy of the published work. No acknowledgement was found therein as to who had supplied data. He recalled the solemn promises, 'I do intend you shall be the first man to whom I will communicate it' had been written, ' [or if not] They will reccon me an ungrateful clown...' The new century dawned leaving Flamsteed in a position of weakness, with no powerful allies, nothing substantial published for two decades, and now mocked at and unacknowledged by his former colleague to whom he had supplied so much.

Newton had informed Gregory that the lunar data used for his *Theory of the Moon* came from Halley![29] Gregory preserved notes of his conversations with Newton, from which we quote:

> 'Newton often told me, but especially in December 1698, that these tables [Flamsteed's lunar ones] were first made and computed by Edmond Halley, and communicated to Flamsteed, and published by him without the knowledge of Halley, and that this theft was the origin of the eternal quarrels between Halley and Flamsteed. Newton said he had seen the handwriting of Halley.'[30]

Halley could have refuted this rumour had he so wished, as the measurements he had made with his sextant could hardly compare with those using the precise space-time co-ordinate system of the vertical mural arc plus pendulum clocks in use at the Royal Observatory. Only persons ignorant of the principles of astronomy could credit such a tale. When Flamsteed heard this story, he merely commented, 'Mr Halley's [tables] could be of no use to him [ie, Newton], because he used the tychonic places of the fixed stars to rectifie & state the Moons by.'[31] Brewster cites this discovery, as showing the Astronomer Royal caught in the very act of forgery.[32] What it rather showed was the readiness with which the mind of David Gregory could be manipulated by his hero, and turned against a fellow-member of the Royal Society.

Next, Flamsteed was informed both by Gregory and Halley that there was no need for him to make any further lunar observations, because a theory accurate to *two or three minutes* in longitude had been achieved, based on the new theory of gravity. Flamsteed set to and compared some predicted lunar values, which he computed from the new opus, with his observations. His verdict was:

> 'But when I compared the moon's places, calculated from them, with her places deduced from the observations, I found that those

numbers which were said to agree with the observations within two or three minutes, would seldom come so near, but often differed 8,9, or 10 minutes.'

And that was at the full and new moon positions, where the predictions were supposed to be most accurate. Gregory and Halley had no basis of observational data for making their claim,[33] that a two or three minute accuracy had been achieved.

'The Glory of the Work'

Much of the great star-catalogue was approaching completion by 1702. As he told Sharp in that year, a thousand pounds would be needed to publish it all, chiefly on account of the large constellation-plates which required engraving. He continued to eke out his £90 per annum salary by giving tuition. Twelve large volumes of manuscripts piled up, each computation therein checked two or three times by separate persons, a memory of years of throbbing headaches.

The terms of his employment had specified, to quote the Royal mandate of March 1674:

> 'Whereas, we have appointed our trusty & well-beloved Flamsteed, Master of Arts, our astronomical observator, forthwith to apply himself with the most exact care & diligence to rectifying the tables of the motions of the heavens, and the places of the fixed stars, so as to find out the so much-desired longitude of places for the perfecting of the art of navigation.'

The tables of the motions of the heavens had been rectified, and the places of the fixed stars, but the goal, of improving the art of navigation, the purpose of it all, to map the moon's motion, to comprehend its errant path with equations and predict it in tables, had by no means been accomplished. Inferior though the Italian Cassini at the Paris observatory might be in the exactitude of his measurements, yet seamen used his tables. The only British ones which might be used, in the latter half of the seventeenth century, were in essence astrological, i.e., designed for astrologers. Otherwise, the British ephemeris tradition ground to a halt with the passing away of astronomers/astrologers such as Vincent Wing and Thomas Streete and was not to be recommenced until the great nautical almanacs appeared in the later eighteenth century.

The astronomer's anguish at not receiving any acknowledgement from Newton for all his lunar data, of not even being permitted to state publicly that he had spent so much time in generating the data for his second edition of the *Principia* (as he had planned to state in Wallis's *Opera Omnia*, until rebuked by Newton and forced to drop the plan), needs to be seen in terms of this failure. In retrospect, he would have been far better off just publishing his lunar data himself with an explanation of such equations derived from Horrocks' method as he used himself: at least the public would then have been able to appreciate the endeavour, if not the success.

The new century dawned with the astronomer having harvested a rich crop of observations but lacking the means of publishing them. Headaches without end had been his reward for attempting to cope with too many different factors, with the entire motion of the heavens, which was more than one person could manage in a lifetime. His reward for such hubris, of overreaching the terms of his employment, was to be the mutilation and more or less ruin of his great life-work in the hands of his erstwhile close colleagues, now in the new century destined to become his arch-enemies. Had he published when he had wished to, in the early 1700s, he would then have enjoyed a wide correspondence throughout Europe with men of letters about his star-maps and the peerless astronomical methods developed at Greenwich.

In 1701 Flamsteed wrote to the ageing Wallis, still holder of the Savilian astronomy chair at Oxford, saying 'I will draw ye Mapps of ye Constellations this Summer and perhaps Engrave the Plates too'. These constellation-maps used his new projection method but did not require the accuracy for the star-positions in minutes and seconds as would be given in the catalogue. He was ready to do them any time, if only he could find the cash to produce them. In 1703, he employed a skilled artist to prepare the twelve constellations, each map having about twice as many stars on it as those of Bayer or Hevelius.

Following the death of his arch-enemy Hooke, Isaac Newton became the president of the Royal Society in 1704, when he soon developed a new interest in the Observatory. Meeting Flamsteed now and then in London, he would inquire as to how the star-catalogue was coming on, to which the reply was always the same, that its progress was hindered by lack of assistance, 'But this I could not get him to take notice of,' recalled the Flamsteed memoirs. (Baily, p. 73) A friend then informed Prince George of Denmark, husband to the future Queen Anne, who expressed an interest in having the work printed. As the Lord High Admiral, he was naturally interested in such a matter. Coming to visit Greenwich in April 1704, Newton was shown the constellation maps drawn up, 'the glory of the work', as Flamsteed described them to Sharp, (4.5.04, Baily p. 216) as well as the half-finished catalogue. Replied the President, would Flamsteed entrust these documents to his hands so that they could be recommended to the Prince?

After the treachery of former years, this smelt like a trap. The president was now like an extinct volcano as far as his scientific work was concerned, maturing into the imperial despot of the Royal Society who was, to quote William Whiston '… of the most fearful, cautious, suspicious temper that ever I knew ... he could not, in his old age, bear such contradiction.'[34] (Whiston was then holding the Lucasian mathematics chair at Cambridge as Newton's successor). Beholding these glorious star maps, the President sensed danger. Here was a moment of success of his chief English rival coming up, the one person in the country who understood the Moon's orbit well enough to critique what he had published on the subject. Why, astronomers all over Europe would be listening to him if ever these saw the light of day.

Declining the kind offer, Flamsteed explained his behaviour in the Preface to his *Historia* (suppressed and not published until 1982):

> 'I had formerly tried his temper, and always found him insidious, ambitious, and excessively covetous of praise, and impatient of contradiction ... I considered that if I granted what he desired, I should put myself wholly into his power, or be at his mercy, who might spoil all that came into his hands, or put me to unnecessary trouble and vexation about my own labours: and all the while pretend that he did it to amend faults, where none were but were unavoidable, or easy to be corrected, and therefore excusable.' (p.163)

Following the visit, he drew up in 1704 a summary of his *Historia Coelestis Brittanica,* which turned out to be rather long; 500 pages just for Volume I, which could be printed immediately, 630 pages for Volume II, and a further 1450 pages for Volume III – though this with all the fixed-star positions was not quite ready. It was certainly comprehensive; too comprehensive, perhaps? This summary 'chiefly urged that the maps of the constellations should be first of all set upon: that, being carried on apart, they might be finished by the time the observations were printed off.' This was sound psychology, for the Prince would certainly be pleased with these new maps of the heavens, would see how they would redound to the glory of the English nation and would be used by navigators the world over. This would motivate the less glamorous task of publishing the positions of three thousand stars, numbered and grouped per constellation after years of collating the data. There was a further motivation for publishing the plates first, namely that as already mentioned they had been plotted for the epoch 1690: as these maps were not in the event published until 1725, they were by then all half a degree out, as the stars move 1° per 72 years away from such a celestial reference grid. The artist who had then drawn the first twelve plates was ready to proceed with the rest, had the cash been available.

The summary was forwarded to the Royal Society where it was read out, approved, and forwarded to the Prince, who agreed to cover the expenses. A Committee was set up, which seemed to have two clear priorities: to prevent the publication of the plates; and prevent Flamsteed being paid the cash needed to employ assistants for completing the *Catalogue*. Of this group, Flamsteed wrote, 'But, who they were, when they waited on him,[the Prince] and how they made their recommendation, I was never informed: nor did they vouchsafe to consult me about it, or take me along with them.' (p.162) This stage of the proceedings is reminiscent of the clandestine group which assembled the *Commercium Epistolicum* under the supervision of the President to blight the reputation of another long-serving Fellow of the Royal Society, Gottfried von Leibniz.

An august group bearing a letter from Prince George's secretary arrived at Flamsteed's doorstep, in December of 1704, desirous of checking through his life-work: these were, Sir Christopher Wren – then mainly occupied with the construction of St Paul's, who Flamsteed always maintained was the one honourable person he had to deal with; Dr David Gregory the mathematician; Dr Arbuthnot the Queen's physician; a Mr Roberts; and Newton. After doing this, the group drew up a budget for printing the *Historia Coelestis Brittanica*, amounting to £863. This budget turned out to lack any reference to the design or engraving the plates of the constellations. Flamsteed commented, 'this was likely to be the heaviest part of the charge, and the observations could not be understood without them. I had further proposed them to be the first taken care of and begun.'(p.163) The ordering of the stars by constellations in his atlas required images of the constellations to which they must refer; mere printed volumes of stars, where half of them would be traditional and half brand new, all ordered together, would be hard to follow by anyone.[35] None of the supervisory group were astronomers, except for Christopher Wren, who had been one forty years before.

A sum of £180 was allocated, to employ two men as calculators to finish the work, but this never arrived at Greenwich. To quote Allan Chapman,

'It is a curious fact that in the face of the growing complaint from Newton and the *Historia* Referees, no one either enquired into the adequacy of Flamsteed's resources, or did anything when their deficiencies were pointed out. Flamsteed's official assistance ended with the payment of a nominal salary, and the whole preparation, reduction, checking and transcribing of the manuscript observations had to be performed by assistants paid out of his own pocket. In fact, the inadequacy of the small team of assistants that he could afford to pay was pointed out as a regular reason for delay. As early as 1706, informed Newton that he had been forced to lay off a 'calculator' and an amanuensis, and could not afford to take them on again until he was remitted an outstanding £125 from the Referees. Six weeks later he was sent £50, but it was not until April 1708 that the full £125 was reimbursed and, by then, he had a new pile of bills and wage claims to meet.'[36]

As Master of the Mint, Newton then enjoyed a quite considerable income, which was a fraction of the total amount of money minted for the nation over a year.

The spring of 1705 found Flamsteed 'almost incandescent with excitement',[37] as he visited London each week, hoping that some form of his work was at last emerging in print. The previous October he had written to a friend that 'The Providence of God that has conducted my work hitherto seemed now designing to perfect it', because Prince George 'will be at the charge of the Impression'.[38] As it happened, a force mightier even than Providence barred his way, in the form of the ageing President, who knew better than he how his life-work was to emerge.

A letter of his dated 2 November 1705 to Newton enthuses about the magnificent new star-charts he was drawing up, of Orion, Ophiucus, Aquarius, and Pisces and how he had made a translation of the relevant sections of Ptolemy from the Greek into Latin! This was vitally important, as the star-charts of his day had sunk into deep confusion and only a re-evaluation of the forms of the constellations as given by Ptolemy could sort them out, whereby one could compare one's own star-charts with those of antiquity. Flamsteed's star-maps formed part of a tradition which began with the German Bayer's *Uranometria* of 1603, the first great star-atlas, and ended with Bode's *Uranographia* of 1801. A major problem arose because Bayer's opus, in common with Hevelius' star-atlas published posthumously in 1690, had the human constellation images all back to front, presented as their rear views. In the starry images of the Dutchman Hevelius, the human posterior was a persistent motif: Aquarius, Orion, Virgo, Ophiucus the serpent-bearer, Hercules, Bootes, Cepheus – all had their backs turned to the viewer! This meant, as Flamsteed pointed out, that they had also suffered a left-right reversal, making it hard to sort out where the stars described by Ptolemy were meant to be. Hevelius had followed a tradition extending through the seventeenth century, from Durer to Bayer and sundry other middle-European star-maps, whereby the figures had their backs turned. This was either, Flamsteed surmised, due to a mistranslation of the Greek text, or because of a rather strange view that one was looking at the sphere of the universe from the outside in a star-map... Whatever it was, Flamsteed was having no truck with it. Boldly, the astronomer turned the star-images the right way round. There survive from antiquity no maps of Ptolemy's images. With the aid of his Greek translation of Ptolemy, Flamsteed rescued the tradition.

Chaos was threatening to break out in the heavens. An astronomer of the day was hardly worth much unless he had designed some new constellation. As astronomers cluttered up the heavens with new constellation images, chiefly mechanical inventions, the night skies came to resemble a Victorian drawing-room where every cranny of space was occupied. Thus Halley, while in the South Atlantic island of St Helena, diplomatically conceived 'Charles' Oak' ('*Robur Carolinum*'), in memory of the oak tree in which the king had hidden during the Civil War while Parliamentarians searched for him. This earned Halley an honorary M.A.

from the king but had the problem that a classical constellation already covered that patch of the southern sky, namely Argo. Halley's oak tree was stuck like some ghostly apparition in front of it! It remained on star-maps for about a century then faded away. Fortunately, the Astronomer Royal was a match for the situation. Unfortunately, the President lacked any interest in the matter – despite his touching tale of the Centaur and the Argonauts which he was soon to develop for Princess Caroline.

Anguish in the years of Flamsteed's old age is recalled by his letters to his trusty friend and assistant Sharp:

> '... he [Newton] thrust himself into ye businesse purposely to be revenged on me because I found the fault... however I take no notice of this but carry on as if I thought he onely wanted better information & take care to oblige him with enough of it' (p.463 Baily).
>
> 'Sir Is carrys himself very cunningly... (12.8.1706) I have not received a farthing from him (who has drawn the Prince's mony into his hands & forced himself into my business).' (12.10.1706).

> 'S. I. N. takes particular care I shall not receive a farthing for all my expenses' (9.12.06).

> 'S. I. N. plays all the tricks he can to keep me from receiving one penny towards the reimbursement of this expense... for the Truth is he is designed by what I can collect absolutely to hinder the publication of this work' (20.1.1707).

Sir Isaac's knighthood in 1705 seems not to have impressed the astronomer!

A leading Whig bookseller, Churchill, was commissioned as an 'undertaker' for the enterprise of publication, and Newton ensured that he obtained far more of the Prince's beneficence than ever went to Greenwich. As Churchill cast about for a publisher, he formed the ideal intermediary for generating administrative and bureaucratic delay.

The committee of referees further required possession of Flamsteed's manuscripts of which he had no copy. Clearly it was vital that these should come into Sir Isaac's hands, and not merely pass between the author and the printer. In November 1705, an agreement was drawn up defining the conditions for publishing four hundred editions, one item of which stated, that the referees must have access to the raw data 'with a promise... To return the same to the said John Flamsteed in a reasonable time'. It also specified that the author had the right to inspect every first proof copy before it was sent off, that Churchill would be obliged to reprint every mistaken page, and that the author would 'speedily and diligently collate' the material so that no stop would be put to the press. The King's treasurer would give £250 to the author for employing an assistant and servants, half of which was to be paid when Volume I was delivered. Various copies exist of the agreement, none of which are signed, yet it is assumed that some agreement was struck.

The nub of this agreement was some years later expressed in a letter by Newton addressed to Flamsteed, in no uncertain terms:

> 'You know that the Prince had appointed five gentlemen to examine what was fit to be printed at his Highness expence, & to take care that the same should be printed. Their order was only to print what they judged proper for the Princes honour & you undertook under your hand & seal to supply them therewith, & thereupon your observations were put to the press.' (letter of 1711, Correspondence, V, p.102.)

The *Historia's* author, not competent to evaluate what should be printed, was expected merely to supply manuscripts to a committee, of which he had not approved, so that they could decide. The referees disagreed with the author's view on the sequence in which the volumes were to be published. The first sheet was printed on 16 May 1706. Flamsteed was highly dissatisfied with both the accuracy and the pace of printing, with a mere sheet or so appearing per week. The press continued at its 'glacial pace', to quote Westfall, all through the next year, with none of the Prince's cash being released for the employment of calculators (p.665). Finally, after endless disagreements, the project foundered with the Prince's death in 1709.

For what reason did Newton do this? His Committee of Referees when it originally met the Prince told him, 'This set of observations we Repute the fullest & Completest that has ever yet Been made: and as it tends to the perfection of Astronomy & Navigation: so if it should be Lost, the Loss would be irreparable.' (Correspondence, IV, p436) A fortnight later, the Prince was elected to join the Royal Society. These were major steps, for which some motive is required. There was no need for more lunar data, because such endeavours had terminated in the previous decade. Westfall provides no evidence that any further lunar endeavours were attempted, but merely assumes this.

When the Second Edition of the *Principia* came to be composed, its illustrious author scratched out Flamsteed's name from fifteen different places, even from the Jupiter moon observations which had started him off: from just about everywhere except the 1680 comet observations, which he could not really delete.

An alternative view would be that Newton's goal in this entire episode was well achieved, that his endeavours met with success and not with failure. Manuel's biography found that the Preface to the *Historia's* account of events 'betrayed classical symptoms of paranoia'. This was in reference to statements like:

'For, *honest* Sir Isaac Newton (to use his own words) would have 'all things in his own power', to spoil or sink them; that he might force me to second his designs and applaud him, which no honest man would nor could; and, God be thanked, I lay under no necessity of doing.'

The question of whether such constituted the 'symptoms of classical paranoia' or a realistic assessment of events, is the one which we must now address.

A mace on the table

Through the year 1707, the printing of the *Historia Coelestis* crept along at a snail's pace. We have an amusing glimpse of the two ageing melancholics irritating each other, as they inspected the process. Flamsteed, who had just had to lay off his one calculator for want of funds, was aware by then that the Master of the Mint had received the Prince's money for the printing of the *Historia* and was holding on to it, except for sums he gave ostentatiously to Churchill, considerably more than Greenwich ever received:

> 'In the meantime Sir Isaac Newton sometimes stopt the press without assigning a reason for it, or any occasion given by me: but upon my complaint at the first, and afterwards, without any solicitation of mine at all, let it go on again. I happened once to visit the press when he was there, and took the opportunity to show him how ill the compositor had placed the types of the figures, and how much awry to the lines to which they belonged. He put his head a little nearer to the paper, but not near enough to see the fault (for he is very near sighted) and making a slighting motion with his hand said, 'Methinks they are well enough.' This encouraged the printer in his carelessness: the sheet was printed off, and the fault was not mended; and caused me to be more watchful over the printer. For now, it was plain to me that the referee, as he called himself, was not displeased with the faults he committed; and the undertaker never concerned himself about them.'[39]

The Referees threatened to exclude the astronomer from checking the manuscripts at the printer's, in 1708, 'another Corrector [would] be employed' if he didn't take care, he was informed on 13 July 1708. Commented the Editor of Newton's Correspondence, 'It is not easy to find an excuse for the tone of this resolution, ...[for] at no time had he [Flamsteed] shown any unwillingness to do so [inspect the proofs]'. At times the astronomer would sink into self-pity about the injustice of events, and bemoan his fate in his diary:

> ''Tis very hard, 'tis extremely unjust, that all imaginable care should be taken to secure a certain profit to a bookseller, and his partners, out of my pains, and none taken to secure me the re-imbursement of my large expenses in carrying on my work above 30 years.'[40]

but he could rise above this and show an indomitable spirit, even though bent double by gout, withstanding the Presidential ire as no-one else ever managed to do. Faith in his Deity gave him the assurance that his work would not be destroyed, even when the threats made against him extended as far as withdrawal of instruments and his person from the Observatory.

In the year 1710, the Observatory was placed under the supervision of the Royal Society. The Referees were appointed as 'Visitors and Directors' of the Observatory, to quote from the Royal Society's Journal Book. The source of the warrant is unknown, but it remained in force until quite recently. The undertones of suspicion and mistrust in such an appointment were quite evident. In or around that same year, the custom began at the Royal Society of placing a mace on the table, at such times as the President was in the chair. 'Orders of the Council' were read out which included no talking amongst members while meetings were in progress, all remarks having to be addressed through the President, and that only two secretaries should sit at the high table with him. Distinguished foreign visitors were sometimes permitted to sit also at this high table.

The next year, an 'order' arrived at Greenwich from the Royal Society, that the eclipses of that year be properly observed! It was signed by the secretaries Sloane & Mead (15.5.11, Corr. V p.130). The astronomer then came to understand that the printing had at last commenced in earnest, and that an abridged version of his work was emerging – produced and edited by Edmond Halley.

In October 1711, something called the 'Council' of the Royal Society, required of Flamsteed 'to know from him if his instruments were in order, and fit to carry on the necessary celestial observations,' and it summoned him to appear at the Royal Society's premises. He attended, despite the tone of this request; indeed, it reveals the weakness of his position that he did attend a summons couched in such terms, considering that not one item of his present equipment had been provided or maintained by the Royal Society. He arrived at the new Fleet Street residence and was greeted at the entrance by Halley (according to the version of events he told Sharp). Many were the times when those two had been inseparable in the early days of the setting up of the Observatory, but now a different climate obtained:

'Dr Halley met me as I entered, and would have had me drink a dish of coffee with him. I refused: went straight up to the house: my man helped me up the stairs, where I found Sir I. Newton, Dr Sloane, and Dr Mead. These three were all the Committee that I found there: and the two last, I well knew, were the assertors of the first, in all cases, right or wrong.

'After a little pause, Sir I. Newton began; and told me that the Committee desired to know what repairs I wanted, or what instruments in the Observatory? I answered that my repairs were always made by the Office of the Ordnance: that I had applied myself to them; but the season of the year not being fit, it was thought best to forbear them till February next, when I doubted not they would be taken care of. As for the instruments, they were all my own; being either given to me absolutely by Sir Jonas Moore, or made and paid for out of my own pocket. This he well knows, though he dissembles it. He answered, 'As good have no Observatory as no instruments.' I gave him, hereupon, an account of Sir Jonas Moore's donation, in the presence of Mr Colwall and Mr Hanway his son-in-law: how he soon after died, and a controversy about his gift arising betwixt his son Sir Jonas, and myself, we had a hearing before the Board of the Office; whereat Mr Colwall and Mr Hanway both attested what I affirmed, that the instruments, books, goods &c. were given me by Sir Jonas More. Whereupon he seemed much moved; and repeated what he had said before, 'As good have no Observatory as no instruments;' asked Dr Mead if it were not so, who assented. I proceeded from this to tell Sir Isaac (who was fired) that I thought it the business of their Society to encourage my labours, and not to make me uneasy for them. He asked Dr Sloane what I said: who answered, that I said something about encouragement. Whereupon I told him that a frontespiece was engraved for my works, and the Prince's picture (without any notice given to me of it), to present to the Queen: [evidently, news of Halley's forthcoming 'pirate' edition of his work had reached him] and that thereby I was *robbed of the fruits of my labours*: that I had expended above £2000 in instruments and assistance. At this, the impetuous man grew outrageous; and said, 'We are, then, robbers of your labours?' I answered, I was sorry that they owned themselves to be so. After which, all he said was in a rage: he called me many hard names; puppy was the most innocent of them. I told him only that I had all imaginable deference and respect for Her Majesty's order, for the honour of the nation, &c. (nay, to the President himself), to use me so. At last, he charged me, with great violence (and repeated it), not to remove any instruments out of the Observatory: for I had told him before that, if I was turned out of the Observatory, I would carry away the sextant with me. I only desired him to keep his temper, restrain his passion, and thanked him as oft as he gave me ill names: and, looking for the door, told him God had blessed all my endeavours hitherto, and that he would protect me for the future...'[41]

Flamsteed reported the meeting to Sharp as 'another contest' with Sir Isaac, who had 'formed a plot to make my instruments theirs', adding, 'I had resolved beforehand his knavish talk should not move me' (22.12.11). The account does indeed sound like an attempt to divest the ageing astronomer of his position.[*]

Briefly we pass over the publication by Edmond Halley of his version of the British star-catalogue in 1712, after negotiations had collapsed; 'the thief's transcript' as Flamsteed called it. For Halley, morality was a kind of light baggage. Halley's preface to this opus explained breezily how he had had been obliged to correct many errors in the manuscript he had received, and then characterised the total output of the Astronomer Royal as 'nothing': after working as Astronomer Royal for 30 years it averred, 'still nothing had yet emerged from the Observatory to justify all the equipment and expense, so that he seemed, so far, only to have worked for himself...' The preface did admire Flamsteed's talents and achievements, but yet referred to the 'excessive number of mistakes' in the work.

---

* Testimony in support of Flamsteed's viewpoint comes from Abraham Sharp, a man who was as Baily said versed in all aspects of practical astronomy. He was also a respected mathematician who had computed π very accurately; Halley had corresponded with him over this issue, so Sharp was by no means unfamiliar with the persons involved. In March of 1710, that is over a year prior to the above-related incident, he wrote to Flamsteed declaring that it was:

> but too apparent, he [Newton] has a design if possible to get you turned over into his hands, that he may have you at command and impose what trouble he thinks fit upon you, which no doubt if his designs be accomplished will not be a little. I am apt to imagine he is carrying on a design to make you sit uneasy in the Observatory and if possible to forsake it, that he may substitute some other whom possibly he may have in view for the place. But I hope all his malicious contrivances will be prevented, though I am much concerned to find that he has so much influence at Court. 'Tis not to be doubted he has calumniated and misrepresented yourself and the management of the business committed to your interest, and magnified his own better abilities, but I hope none of his undermining acts will have effect. (Life and Correspondence of Abraham Sharp, Ed. W. Cudworth, 1889, letter of March 10th.)

Halley's opus he everred had 'mutilated and corrupted' and 'garbled' the stolen documents on which it was based. It was Baily's opinion that, had the astronomer been allowed to be the judge of the sequence of publication, 'The whole would then have been finished in much less time than this single volume of Halley's.' (ibid, p. Xlii)

With the demise also of Charles Montagu, or Lord Halifax as he became known, the 'great courtier' of Newton's in 1715, the tables were finally turned. The Lord Chamberlain signed a warrant made out to Newton, plus the other referees and Churchill, requesting them to deliver to the Observatory every copy of the *Historia* which they had printed. They sent back a reply, saying that their authority over the work had ended with the Queen's death! However, next year Flamsteed obtained and burnt the whole lot; a kind of triumph, though rather late in the day. He first tore out from these volumes the sections of which he approved, and from these formed the first volume of his *Historia Coelestis Brittanica.*

Prior to this dismal sacrifice, as years of frustrated endeavour went up in smoke, Flamsteed relates how Edmond Halley ('the impudent editor') turned up at Greenwich with his wife, son and daughters, plus a neighbouring clergyman to boot, perhaps to keep the peace should it need keeping. One assumes Mrs Flamsteed was also present, of whom we know very little. Quoting from the suppressed Preface to the *Historia,*:

> 'He offered to burn his catalogue (so he called his corrupted and spoiled copy of mine, of which I had now a correct and enlarged edition in the press, and the second sheet printing off) if I would print mine. I am apt to think he knew it was so, and was endeavouring to prevent it.'[42]

Perhaps the two families had a pleasant tea-party in the June sunshine, as Britain's two foremost astronomers debated who should immolate the newly-printed British star-catalogue. A large amount of Halley's correspondence has gone missing, so we don't have his version of events.[43]

Ultimately, the Reverend John Flamsteed's last phase of life was sublime and not tragic, even though he was doubled up with gout from the long, freezing nights. His opponents did succeed in forcing his life-work out of his hands, and yet he believed that what he had harvested would not be destroyed. He found serenity in mapping the skies. The years of racking headaches whereby his 50,000 observations had been harvested were largely past. He ordered the stars in each constellation, developing Bayer's scheme of six magnitudes.

A decade after the astronomer's death, the star-atlas finally emerged, with its novel method of projection, its double as many stars as previously mapped, its restitution of the classical star-images to their pristine glory, and its unmatched accuracy. It 'brought honour to the whole British nation' declared the *Acta Eruditorum* in a review. It was an atlas 'which satisfied the needs of astronomers generally for almost a century'.[44] But, where was the lunar theory, which had been a primary purpose of his employment? It was only published in Paris some decades later,[*] which has to be more skulduggery by Edmond Halley, after he gained access to the Greenwich manuscripts. There is a whole story of how Newton's lunar theory came to be adopted on the Continent which we don't need to go into.[**]

At the end of the eighteenth century, adaptations of the British star-catalogue were still appearing in France, in 1776 and 1795, prized as the best available. Its space allotted to southern-hemisphere stars was scant, perhaps not wishing to give undue coverage to those mapped by his erstwhile friend and colleague, on the South Atlantic island St Helena.

When Edmund Halley finally inherited the Observatory, he converted the quadrant and sextant rooms into pigeon-houses and commenced a lawsuit against Mrs Flamsteed endeavouring to wrest from her the instruments which had formerly belonged to her husband, which was perhaps the stimulus for their disappearance. He lost the case,[45] she lost the instruments, and only two grandfather clocks now remain, one of which resides at Greenwich.[46]

---

[*] An account of how Pierre Le Monnier came to publish Flamsteed's lunar theory in 1746 would be an undue digression. Suffice to say that what was there published gave 'Newton's sevenfold lunar heory in its most accurate form:' NK, *Newton's Forgotten Lunar Theory* 2000, p.211.

[**] Flamsteed's assistant James Hodgson inherited the manuscripts, and in a Foreword to a 1749 publication deplored the fact of their having been given to Le Monnier: F. Baily 1837, (ref. 26) p.704. For a discussion of how these excellent lunar tables published in 1746 came from the Astronomer Royal, see NK Ibid, pp.211-4: In its preface, 'Lemonnier here appears as knowing more about Flamsteed's ... labours than ever did the British, in a manner of one announcing a scoop who is not at liberty to disclose his source,' p.213.

Chapter 8

The Duel With Leibniz

The Calculus Dispute: A chronology

1669	Newton's *De Analysi* sent to Wallis.
1672	Newton writes 'tangent letter'
1673	Leibniz visits England
Oct 1675	Leibniz's discovery of differential calculus
Jun 1676	Newton's 'first letter' to Leibniz (binomial theorem)
Oct 1676	Leibniz visits England and is shown *De Analysi* by Collins
Nov 1676	Newton's 'second letter' to Leibniz
Jun 1677	Newton's second letter delivered to Leibniz
Jun 1677	Leibniz's reply, contains first statement of his method
1682	Leibniz publishes his $\pi/4$ series
1684	First calculus paper published by Leibniz
1685	1st edition of Wallis' *Algebra*, no calculus in it
1687	Newton's *Principia* published
1689	Leibniz publishes *Tentamen*, treating planetary motion by calculus
1693	Wallis published 2nd edition. Algebra, with polemical foreword
1696	First text-book on calculus published, by L'Hôpital
1697	Newton solves challenge problem from Bernoulli
1699	Leibniz called a 'second inventor' by Fatio de Duillier
1704	Newton's *De Quadratura* published as appendix to *Optics*
1712	Royal Society's report on the priority dispute published
1716	Leibniz dies.

179

THE DARK SIDE OF ISAAC NEWTON

'Priority of discovery has always been based on priority of publication, or at least on documentary evidence dated in the presence of a witness.'

More, p581

'We are to conceive them as the just nascent principles of finite magnitudes'

Principia, Book II, Lemma II.

What in retrospect we call the birth of calculus was then experienced as a gradual transition from geometrical to algebraic modes of reasoning, within the newly-developing realm of infinitesimal problems. These were being hotly pursued simultaneously in France, Italy and England. Calculus 'sealed the victory of algebra over geometry' in the latter half of the century, to quote J.W. Field. The two professors at the newly-created mathematics posts at Oxford and Cambridge were John Wallis and Isaac Barrow, and they developed respectively the integration and differentiation procedures. These were cast in a geometrical mould and as such rather specific to individual curves. In his *Arithmetica Infinitorum* of 1656, Wallis wrote, of areas and volumes, 'the surface is a book of threads, the solid is a book of leaves'.[1]

Integration developed from the method of 'quadrature', as differentiation evolved out of the method of tangents. The latter involved constructing a tangent to a curve at a given position, and the former's name derived from the problem, as to how a square could be constructed made of the same area as a circle. As the hare could never overtake Achilles in Zeno's paradox, so could the Greek mathematicians not achieve the summing of an infinite series.

If the question is asked, 'Who invented the calculus?' then that at least has a simple answer; Johann Kepler invented it. He first devised and publish an integral calculus method involving the summing of an infinite series. In 1615, he published a monograph entitled, *Solid Geometry of Wine Barrels*. He wondered, *how much wine had he got*, in his cellar? He visualised the casks as composed of an infinite number of concentric discs, each of a knowable area, and by summing them he was able to determine the volume per cask. He later applied a similar method in demonstrating his second law, that planets sweep out equal areas in equal times. The first application of calculus in the *Principia* is to Kepler's area law using a not dissimilar technique. In 1690, the name *integration* was given to such operations, by the Swiss Johann Bernoulli, the illustrious disciple of Gottfried von Leibniz.

Suppose we ask the question, 'When was it realised that integration and differentiation were converse operations?' Whoever it was who perceived this reciprocal property might well be called a discoverer of calculus, or at least a major chunk of it. Distressingly, no simple reply seems available. To quote from the *History of Mathematics* by Howard Eves:

'In spite of tenuous evidence pointing elsewhere, Barrow is generally credited as the first to realise in full generality that differentiation and integration are inverse operations. This capital discovery is the so-called fundamental theorem of the calculus and appears to be stated and proved in Barrow's *Lectiones*.' p330.

Isaac Barrow published his *Lectiones* in1669, the year he resigned from his Cambridge Lucasian chair to let Newton take it, having failed to persuade the latter to publish his *De Analysi* with them. The publication bankrupted the publishers as sales were less than expected. Did anyone notice this startling new theorem? Not according to Whiteside:

'It remains bluntly factual that no one in the mid-17th century seems to have seen in even the very general BARROW theorem more than a subtle theorem on the relation of properties of two curves. Only many years later, in the first priority disputes over the new calculus, do we find some acknowledgement of the generality of BARROW's work.'[2]

If a present-day mathematician were shown the relevant historical documents and asked as to when what was recognisably the calculus technique first appeared, so as to include the differential as well as integral calculus, then the choice would tend to be the letter of Leibniz to Oldenburg the Secretary of the Royal Society of London, in June 1677. It has been said that this letter 'marks an epoch in pure mathematics'.[3] It described the reciprocal nature of the two operations, differentiation and integration, and the Leibnizian notation of dy and dx, which gained acceptance from then onwards. This letter was a reply to Isaac Newton, expressing deep gratitude for the latter communicating his insights on infinite series expansions and conveying his discovery by way of reply.

Amongst the archives of Hanover are to be found the precious pages on which Leibniz's notions of calculus first appeared, as a part of his quest for a universal symbolic language. They are dated the 25-29 October 1675.[4] It had dawned upon him while pondering the significance of a theorem by Pascal published two decades earlier. The symbol dx is to be found in these very first jottings, then on the 29th he first used the modern integral sign, as a long letter S signifying Summa (sum). But, not until 1684 did he first publish his method, entitled *A new method for maxima and minima as well as tangents, which is impeded neither by fractional nor by irrational quantities, and a remarkable type of calculus for this*. It showed that 'We can find maxima and minima as well as tangents... To any given equation we can write its differential equation.... we can always obtain the value of dx:dy, the ratio of dx to dy.' Points of inflexion on a curve were found from the changing sign of the differential. A follow-up article of his in the *Acta Eruditorum* gave a rule for differentiating a product, d(uv)=udv +vdu.[5] But his style was said to be rather cryptic, and bewildered many readers. The maths professor at the University of Basel, Johannes Bernoulli, viewed it as 'more of an enigma than an explanation'.

The next year in a book review, Leibniz published his rules for integral calculus, introducing the symbol '∫', and writing the all-important ∫ydx. The two Bernoulli brothers absorbed the meaning of these articles and ensured the growth of Leibniz' new method on the Continent. In France, the Marquis de L'Hôpital hired Johann Bernoulli to teach him the new technique, and then wrote his textbook in 1695.

Who found pi?

The term 'quadrature' was the predecessor of integration. A method of squaring the circle, involving an infinite series, would nowadays be understood as a formula for the value of π; but, this term was not used until 1706, nor generally accepted till much later. Instead, such formulae were described as methods of 'quadrature' – the same term as was used for what later became integration. This is somewhat confusing to the modern ear, because, though in both cases an infinite number of terms are to be summed, the methods are entirely different: for the infinite series only, the last term is infinitely small (if one may so express it), while all the terms summed in an integral (∫ydx in Leibnizian notation) are infinitesimal. Deep confusion persisted concerning the relation between such infinite series and methods of integration, certainly exacerbated by the *Commercium Epistolicum* report.

In 1673, Leibniz discovered the formula:

$$\pi/4 = 1 - 1/3 + 1/5 - 1/7 \ldots$$

Leibniz had been fortunate enough to be receiving mathematics lessons from the illustrious Huygens, in Paris, which he visited as part of a diplomatic mission to try and prevent Louis XIV from invading Germany (he failed), and after a year's instruction, both he and Huygens stood amazed at the beauty and simplicity of this series. As Leibniz put it in his enthusiastic letter to Oldenburg, 'And so the problem of squaring the circle has now been transferred from geometry to the arithmetic of infinities', adding boldly – and correctly – 'This has now been done by me for the first time.' (6.10.1674). By combining pairs of terms, he obtained the faster-converging series $\pi/8 = 1/1.3 + 1/5.7 + 1/9.11 +$ which he described as the area of a circle circumscribing a square of sides half a unit.[6]

After thousands of years, had the dream of mathematicians been realised? Oldenburg cautioned him in reply, that 'Gregory (a Scottish mathematician) is on the point of proving in writing that this accuracy is unattainable' and Leibniz explained by way of reply that such accuracy would indeed be unattainable for any finite series, but, being infinite, it was exact. Naturally, the English cannot endure the thought of Leibniz being the first to discover this series and so textbooks refer to it as the 'Gregory-Leibniz' series. Three years earlier, James Gregory had discovered an infinite series for the tangent function, from which he could readily have derived such a series of π ... but he didn't.

In the great controversy in the next century, attempts were made to deprive Leibniz not only of his credit for the calculus, but also for this exquisite series, bracketing them together (as we have explained) under the generic term, 'quadrature'. With these preliminaries, we turn now to the question of three historic letters sent to Oldenburg, and what they contained.

Newton responds

One assumes that Newton read the 1684 treatise, sometime in 1685. He showed no sign of it. As with the Leibniz letter to him of 1676, he simply did not respond, just as he ceased to respond to John Collins' entreaties for more mathematics following in the steps of *De Analysi*. We now know, from unearthed early notes, that in the 1660s he had explored this whole area in depth, with a process somewhat resembling what he was in the 1690s to call, 'fluxions.' So, why was he now remaining silent about it? Collins was informed that he was finding mathematics 'at least dry if not somewhat barren'. Of *De Analysi*, Collins was informed that its author wished he had not even imparted as much as he had. 'Hence these tears,' writes Professor A.R. Hall, in his comprehensive account of the whole bitter controversy.[7] The hammer-blows of inspiration were diverting Newton to quite other directions, in colour theory, as well as his 'esoteric' interests of theology and alchemy. Later on, his magnum opus was cast in a geometrical mould and contained integral but not differential calculus.

Commentators on the *Principia* never seem to digest the implications of the geometrical mould in which it was cast. They almost always claim that the 'fundamental theorem of classical mechanics' as it is often called, F=Ma or F= d(mv)/dt is present therein which is simply not the case, as Leonhardt Euler had not yet conceived it. They normally accept the comfortable illusion that Newton had employed his dot-notation, which he developed in 1691, before writing his *Principia*, and up until recently swallowed the story that the propositions were first worked out in fluxional form before being re-cast into their inscrutable geometric mould. These misconceptions do not just make historical evaluation difficult, they prevent it altogether. One is left with a traditional, demi-god image which simply glosses the whole subject of how differential methods developed in Britain.

An historical analogy may help. Thomas Edison invented the filament lamp, and then commenced a lawsuit against Joseph Swan in Northamptonshire who was also claiming to have invented such a lamp. The two ended up forming the Edison-Swan company to retail the new invention. The latter was historically first, but the former had a far greater effect in making the lamp known. If Swan had decided after inventing the new lamp that after all it was not much use, its filament kept breaking, and the old gas lamp was much safer; but then, after so deciding to forget it, he had been roused by hearing of Edison publicising his new invention and had come forth to claim credit – who then would one call its inventor?

If a man makes extensive private studies which he leaves unpublished, and what he does publish is of a rather different tenor, then a cautious attitude is required for any inferences based on the unpublished material. The reams Newton wrote on alchemy may possibly have aided the *De natura acidorum* manuscript which he gave out in 1692, or the chemical notes in his *Optics* queries, but what finally emerged into the light of day was generally speaking chemical rather than alchemical. Thus, *The Foundations of Newton's Alchemy* by B.J. Dobbs (1975) has been criticised by Whiteside for too readily supposing that its subject believed what he was in fact merely transcribing.[8] Newton may have thundered against the Trinity in the privacy of his own study, but in public he defended the Anglican religion against Catholicism and was thereby elected for parliament. Anyone perusing the mass of unpublished Newtonian manuscripts should not permit themselves the simplifying assumption that its author believed all of it but was merely too diffident or whatever to say it in public. A chasm existed between the private and public selves, with strict limits to what the public figure would affirm. In mathematics, the classical certainty of demonstration might be undermined by introducing infinitely small or 'just nascent' quantities. Unpublished studies interest the biographer – but a history of calculus should confine itself to what has been brought into the public domain.

A case in point is the *De Analysi* manuscript, composed in 1669 to secure priority of discovery for the infinite series he was working on, but which Newton refused to have published and later said to John Collins that he regretted showing to anyone. A method of finding the slope of tangents was there briefly described, amounting to what would nowadays be called differentiating from first principles, but it did involve dividing both sides of an equation by zero. (See Appendix 3) The small increment involved was equated to zero – '0 to be zero' – *after* both sides had been divided thereby. Intuition may have told Newton that this was a fine new method, but as a mathematics lecturer he may not have wished for a reputation of one who was liable to divide both sides of an equation by zero. This is mere surmise, but the fact is that he could not be prevailed upon to let this manuscript be printed.

In the mid-1660s, gates of infinity opened up before the young Newton, and quite new expansions had become accessible for him, such as that for $\sin \theta$, and also the binomial theorem,[*] the fullness of which became evident to him by 1675. The white heat of discovery is evident in these youthful excursions, now published in full by Whiteside. In the letters which Newton composed in the 1670s, he drew upon these youthful insights of a decade earlier. Newton wrote two in particular to Oldenburg, that invaluable German secretary of the Royal Society who maintained so comprehensive a correspondence with European scientists, to be forwarded to Leibniz. Such mention as may be made of what later became calculus is there indissolubly linked to these infinite series expansions, which are their prime concern.

The Three Letters of 1672 and 1676

'... In which Letter the Method of *Fluxions* was sufficiently describ'd to any intelligent Person', affirmed the Royal Society in its official verdict on the controversy in 1712, as the crux of its entire argument: it was referring to a letter of 10 December, 1672.[9] To quote Augustus de Morgan, 'How far this celebrated letter deserves the character here given of it is one question; whether Leibniz actually received it, is another. Comparatively little notice was taken of either...'[10] But then, the Royal Society's Committee was rather short of time. Leibniz probably received some years later a summary of the letter written by Oldenburg describing results, but no method.

There were two other key letters of 13 June 1676 and 24 Oct 1676, concerning which that same report affirmed, 'By Mr Newton's two letters, it is certain that he had then (or rather above five years before) found out the Reduction of Problems to fluxional equations...' and '... Which puts it past all dispute that he had invented the Method of Fluxions before that time' (i.e., 24 October 1676). These two letters were received by Leibniz, and greatly valued by him. They were in the later storm of controversy referred to as the 'first letter' and the 'second letter.'

Newton's October letter (17 pages of it) starts off by praising Leibniz's insight into series:

> 'Leibniz method of obtaining convergent series is certainly extremely elegant, and would sufficiently display the writer's genius even if he should write nothing else. But there are other things scattered

---

[*] The binomial theorem to expand eg $(1 + a)^n$ where a is small, had been explained by Pascal, it is simple algebra. But for negative indices eg $(1 + a)^{-1}$ things are quite different, and its value can only be expressed using an infinite series, as $1 + x + x^2 + x^3 +$ etc. That's the equation for a hyperbola. Integrating that gives us log (1+a) which Newton found in 1665 could be expressed as $x - x^2/2 + x^3/3 -$ etc. That gives the 'area under a hyperbola' which Newon then found to 52 figures. These infinite series expansions were very successfully muddled up with differentials or fluxions during the calulus dispute.

through his letter most worthy of his reputation which also arouse in us the highest hopes in him.'

Of this second letter, Leibniz wrote to Oldenburg, that it was 'a truly excellent letter... I am enormously pleased that he has described the path by which he arrived at some of his very elegant theorems'. Thus, a London-Paris correspondence on the vital mathematical issues of the day was sparked essentially by the favourable impression which the young Leibniz made when he first visited the Royal Society in 1674, as a part of a diplomatic mission which sent him across the Channel. He stepped onto England's shore with two things; an automatic calculator, and his new series for the quadrature of the circle. Pascal's calculator could only add and subtract, but his could multiply and divide as well. When Robert Hooke saw the device, he evinced a string desire to take it completely to pieces, than which it is hard to imagine higher praise. On the strength of this, the 28-year-old Leibniz had been elected a Fellow of the Society. On his second visit in 1676, John Collins met him and wrote to a friend, 'I perceive him to have outtopped our mathematicians as the moon's brightness dims that of a star.' But then later on, brooding suspicion hatched the notion that these visits were but to steal the insights of the British mathematicians and dress them up as his own!

A.R. Hall, in his thorough survey of the whole controversy, *Philosophers at War*, has followed in harrowing detail its whole unfolding, and a few quotes therefrom may be helpful. Of the calculus in the first letter, 'only results (with explanatory examples) were conveyed without demonstrations' (p.95). Of Leibniz's reply to the first letter, 'There was, in fact, a good deal more basic calculus in this letter of June 1677 than Newton was to make public in his *Principia* lemma or anywhere else before 1704.' On the 'second letter': 'The second letter contained many mathematical treasures, but not the concept of a fluxion, nor one example of an expression involving fluxions' (p.95).

Much later on, when acrimony was embittering the glory of the discovery, Leibniz wrote of these letters to the Abbé Conti that:

> 'There was not the least trace or shadow of the calculus of differences or fluxions in all those ancient letters of Newton that I have seen, except in the one he wrote on 24th October 1676, where he spoke of the matter only enigmatically; and the solution of that enigma, which he gave ten years later, did say something, but not as much as one might have expected.' [11]

How true! Entirely opposite interpretations thus appear of the same letters, by the sender and recipient, the former finding it 'past all dispute' that something was substantially contained therein, while the latter found not 'the least trace or shadow' thereof!

THE DUEL WITH LEIBNIZ

An early method of finding 'tangents' was published in January 1673 by the British mathematician Sluse.* A month before that, the 'tangent letter' of Newton to Oldenburg of December 1672 described this method – which was a precursor to the method of calculus – and averred that it was his.**

As De Morgan observed, it unequivocally was Sluse's method there described.[12] One cannot say it contains the method of differentiating. Sluse had developed it a year earlier, and the aim of Newton's 'tangent letter' seems to have been to secure a priority claim before Sluse printed his method, as he did the year after. Newton later tried to imply that Sluse had derived it from his work, which was not the case. Leibniz had indeed seen the method, from Sluse's published presentation of it, and he used it as a sometimes convenient method for finding tangent equations.

Newton's letter of 24 October 24 1676 adds, 'Nobody, if he possessed my basis, could draw tangents any other way, unless he were deliberately wandering from the straight path,' and he was here referring to the Sluse tangent method described in his earlier 'tangent letter'. Its author was affirming rather categorically that the method he has earlier described is the best way of finding a tangent to a curve. He did not, we are invited to conclude, have a superior method tucked away.

The letter describes some difficult integrations, such as the area under a parabola, which is doubtless impressive but is not a fluxion. Also, it enclosed the anagram *6a2cd13e2f7i3l9n4o4q2r4s9t12vx.* In the heights of paranoia to which early eighteenth-century debate ascended, a *History of Fluxions* by Raphson (1715) claimed that Leibniz had deciphered this anagram and thereby learnt the method. Its meaning was revealed to be, 'given any equation involving fluent quantities, to find the fluxions, and vice versa' - according to the 'fluxions' Lemma in the *Principia*'s Book II where it was disclosed.

---

* Sluse, R., Phil Trans, 'A Method of drawing tangents to all Geometrical Curves.' 7: 5143-7. His method, derived from that of a Mr Hudde, was characterised by Whiteside as 'complex' and 'cumbrous:' Whiteside, 'Patterns of Mathematical Thought in the later 17th century,' *AHES* 1960 1:359.

** To find the tangent to an equation (Newton wrote) such as: $x^3 - 2x^2y + bx^2 - b^2x + by^2 - y^3 = 0$,

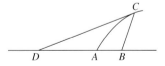

its terms were multiplied first by the powers of y in each term, and then by the powers of x, to give two expressions. Dividing the first expression by the second gives 'the length of BD, to whose end D the tangent CD must be drawn.' (Diagram) So BD= $(-2x^2y + 2by^2 - 3y^3) / (3x^2 - 4xy + 2bx - b^2)$ For the parabola $y = \sqrt{(az)}$, where a is a constant term, its 'quadrature' (the area under it) was given as $2/3. \sqrt{a}\, z^{3/2}$.

An anagram was a respectable method of securing a priority claim, for example Huygens encoded his discovery of the rings of Saturn as also did Galileo for his discovery of the moons of Jupiter. But, did this anagram say enough? Would it go beyond for example what Isaac Barrow had discovered in 1670? Was it not more a statement of the problem than its solution? The two letters do not really contain any trace of fluxions and their determinations of areas under a curve do not evidently use infinitesimal summation methods as later came to be called, integration.

The Editor of Volume I of the *Correspondence* would seem to agree with the Royal Society's verdict in 1712 that in the 1672 letter, the method of fluxions was 'sufficiently described to any intelligent person', for he says of the Sluse method there given for finding a tangent, 'the method is that of a first-order partial differential of a polynomial $\varphi(x, y)$'. Had such been present, it would indeed have settled the matter. Westfall, in his *Never at Rest* repeatedly affirms that the seeds of mistrust and suspicion were sown initially by Leibniz failing to acknowledge Newton's work in his initial calculus publication. 'As we have seen, the storm that burst in 1711 had been gathering for many years, indeed from the moment in 1684 when Leibniz chose to publish his calculus without mentioning what he knew of Newton's progress along similar lines', (p742) or, 'Nothing could vindicate Leibniz from the charge on which so much of the dispute hinged, that he failed to mention the correspondence of 1676 when he first published' (p776). The reader is invited to evaluate whether there was any such obligation, and if so, what could have been acknowledged. Leibniz did not reach his breakthrough by pondering the series expansions Newton had shown him,[13] nor did he 'square the circle' via the equations of Gregory, as the English felt he should have done, but by a different method. There might have been less controversy had he made these acknowledgements, but that he was obliged to do so is far from self-evident.

Integration has less of a general method than differentiation and remains to this day more of an art; one has to find the integral by trying methods until one works. The differential technique by contrast is more or less automatic, and here bears comparison to Leibniz's new calculating engine, or his search for a universal symbolic logic, which would give an automatic procedure for evaluating certain truths. What could have been acknowledged, was that certain difficult integrals had been achieved by the English maestro. It is hard to think what else could or should have been acknowledged, by way of supporting Westfall's position. To quote Hall again, 'Leibniz had it fixed in his mind, all his life, that Newton's great expertise was in the manipulation of series - nothing else.'(Ibid, p.66).

In 1685, John Craig who lived in Cambridge wrote *The Method of Determining the quadratures of figures*.[14] His testimony gives us a vital insight into that period between the first fluxions paper of 1684, and the magisterial emergence of the *Principia* three years later. Craig acknowledged the kindness of Mr Newton in permitting him to leaf through his unpublished manuscripts. Of the Leibniz article he said:

> 'For to this difficulty the outstanding geometer G.W. Leibniz has furnished the best of remedies. For that very famous person shows a neat way of finding tangents even though irrational terms are as deeply involved as possible in the equation expressing the nature of the curve, without removing the irrationals.'

Newton read through Craig's manuscript and even supplied some pro-Leibniz ammunition against a rival. He offered some suggestions of integration methods by converging series. To quote Hall again:

> 'Thus, by silent implication, Craig's evidence also testifies to Newton's having no feelings of criticism towards Leibniz in 1685 or any desire to proclaim to the world that he had been the first to discover a general process of differentiation...'(p.80)

Craig's attempt to interest his fellow-countrymen in the Leibnizian calculus proved futile. The only sequel to his initial opus was his own second edition years later, in 1693. No mention was made of the subject by Wallis, the Oxford mathematics lecturer, in his *Algebra* of 1685. In his second edition Craig added:

> 'In order not to seem to assign too much to myself or to detract from others, I freely acknowledge that the differential calculus of Leibniz has given me so much assistance in discovering these things that without it I could hardly have pursued the subject with the facility I desired; how greatly the very celebrated discoveror of it has advanced the solid and sublime art of geometry by this one most noble discovery cannot be unknown to the most skilled geometers of this age, and this treatise now follow-ing will sufficiently indicate how remarkeable its usefulness has been in dicovering the quadratures of figures.'[15]

For the Marquis de l'Hôpital in France, composing his calculus textbook in 1695, Craig's was the only English text to which he could refer.

Fluxions in the *Principia*

De l'Hôpital was one of the few persons competent to read the *Principia*. On being shown a copy, the story went, 'he cried out, "Good God what a fund of knowledge there is in that book!" he then asked the Doctor every particular about Sir Isaac even to the colour of his hair, said does he eat & drink & sleep, is he like other men?'[16] His conclusion was, that the author of this opus 'had also found something having a semblance to (or, 'resembling') the differential calculus'.* which is as fair a statement as any. The 'fluxions lemma' in Book II of the *Principia* disclosed the meaning of the anagram of 1676 and asserted that its author was in possession of a method similar in essence to that of Leibniz's differentials. It was widely understood to be a statement of co-discovery, and when it was deleted from the second edition, in the heat of the controversy, Leibniz was very upset.

The *Principia* defined *momenta* as 'only just-born finite magnitudes' (*jamjam nascentia finitarum magnitudinem*) with the essential paradox that *'Momenta, quam primum finitae sunt magnitudinis, desinunt esse momenta'* (as soon as they reached a finite magnitude, they would cease to be moments). The term 'fluxion' was *not used* in the *Principia*, being first introduced in the 1693 Wallis opus, despite which the above-quoted section in its Book II has misleadingly come to be called 'the fluxions lemma.'[17] This has caused so much confusion, especially in Rupert Hall's book on the subject. It is the first edition of 1687 that here matters, not what was added to later editions, when a retrospective priority claim was being cooked up.

We now discover what is to be said in support of the anagram code as a claim to equal and independent discovery. The 'just nascent principles of finite magnitudes'

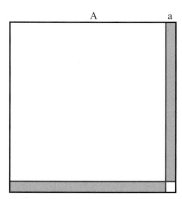

---

* The preface to *Analyse des Infiniments Petits* of 1696 acknowledged, 'He [Mr Leibniz] began where Dr Barrow and others left off. His Calculus has carried him into countries hitherto unknown; and he had made Discoveries by it astonishing the greatest Mathematicians in Europe ... The Messieurs Bernoulli were the first who perceived the Beauty of the Method; and have carried it to such a length, as by its means to surmount Difficulties that were before thought insuperable... 'I must here in justice own (as Mr Leibniz himself has done, in Journal des Scavans for August, 1694) that the learned Sir Isaac Newton likewise discovered something like the Calculus Differentialis, as appears by his excellent *Principia*, published first in the Year 1687 which almost wholly depends on the Use of the said Calculus. But the method of Mr Leibniz's is much more easy and expeditious, on account of the Notation he uses, not to mention the wonderful assistance it affords on many occasions.' (Translation from *The History of Mathematics, a reader* ed., J.Fauvel and J.Gray, 1987 p.442)

are here called 'moments'. Thus, a square of length A whose sides increase by a small amount a, so they become of length (A + a), has a small area increase of approximately 2aA, see figure.[18] That small increase is therefore the 'moment' of A^2. For the general expression x^n, where 'a' is the small increase in the value of the variable x, its 'moment' is given in the *Principia* as nax^{n-1}.[19] This is a binomial expansion process – not the differential calculus!

Let us turn now to an illusory account of this brief section in the *Principia*, which describes like an optical illusion, what is *not* therein present. Quoting from Hall's book, widely regarded as the definitive work on the subject:

'We can see (as Newton explains) that the moments of any number of related quantities are proportional to their fluxions, because... The sum of the added or subtracted moments will be proportional to the rate of change, that is to the fluxion of each quantity.' (p.32)

The word 'fluxions' only appears in the Second Edition. There is *no mathematical treatment of rate of change in this lemma.* It simply is not present. There are small changes, but no infinitesimal ones. For a sound, correct evaluation we go back to Augustus De Morgan: '... In the *Principia*, Newton still gave nothing more than the most general description of it [the method of fluxions] and avoided its direct use entirely' (op. cit., p.26). British scientists have loyally believed what the Royal Society came out with in 1712, more or less as an official and collective opinion, and this has conditioned them to see a certain thought-structure, where it was simply not present.

In the next decade, a definition emerged of fluxions as the rate of change of a variable, and a moment as the product of a fluxion by a small interval of time. Just as the Second Law, the 'fundamental equation of classical dynamics' as it is called, has no rate of change concept in any edition of the Principia, neither has the so-called fluxions lemma any concept of a fluxion, as it later came to be understood (de Morgan, p.89).

A big question-mark hung over such a 'moment' concept as a just-nascent increment, or indefinitely small increment as it was also to be called. Would it not undermine the rigour of mathematics to have it existing alone, and not as a ratio? The ratio dy/dx has a fixed value as the slope of a curve, and the smaller the separate differentials become, the nearer to its limit-value does it become. However, having an indefinitely small moment, <u>not</u> expressed as a ratio, could mean that its value is indeterminate. The path lay wide open for Bishop Berkeley's damaging critique of the whole notion:

'Now as our Sense is strained and puzzled with the perception of Objects extremely minute, even so the Imagination, which faculty derives from Sense, is very much strained and puzzled to frame clear Ideas of the least Particles of time, or the least Increments generated therein; and much more so to comprehend the Moments, or those Increments of the flowing Quantities in *statu nascendi*, in their very first origin or beginning to exist...'[20]

One could escape from this dilemma by having the moments remaining of a finite magnitude, but this would be some way from a claim to have discovered the calculus.

In later years, Leibniz stated that 'it was evident from the *Principia* that Newton had not known the differential calculus in 1687, because he had avoided its use in circumstances which demanded it'. He then added, (growing himself a little paranoid) that Newton had waited so long before publishing anything on the method to wait for the deaths of Huygens and Wallis, who would have functioned as independent judges.[21] There certainly is a sense in which the Royal Society's President triumphed by outliving his rivals.

In the text of the *Principia,* as Whiteside sagely remarked, 'the geometrical limit-increment of a variable line-segment plays a fundamental role.'[22] Small changes of geometrical magnitudes are continually taking place. This is a *geometrical prototype* of calculus; he was able to use it, though it was not a method which others could adopt. There is one celebrated theorem in Book II concerning how a projectile moves when the air-resistance varies with its speed; this would nowadays be solved using a differential equation, but is it there so solved?[23]

The Invention of Fluxions

To the invention of fluxions by Newton, a clear date can be assigned; 17 September 1692. (Corr. III, p.222) On this date the method was first communicated to another person, namely John Wallis, then preparing his second edition of *Algebra*, which appeared in print the next year. We there find a clear operational definition of fluxions, given for the first time, together with a negation of the confusing 'moments' concept given in the *Principia*:

'For although Flowing quantities & their fluxions may at first sight seem difficult to Conceive (new things being somewhat difficult to conceive), yet he thinks [Wallis wrote] ye Notion of them will soon become more easy, than is that of Moments or parts Infinitely little...'

In this way, Wallis paraphrased a couple of letters (now lost) which he received from Newton. The method as described had two stages. First, each term was multiplied by the power of its variable (the 'flowing quantities'), and then secondly one power of each variable was changed into a fluxion. So for the equation y=x³, one obtains ẏ =3x². That was the method. At this stage it has resolved the problem of infinitesimal quantities, by dealing only with ratios thereof. It does this by regarding every algebraic term as a 'fluent', i.e. as varying with time. Some algebraic functions do vary with time, but others do not. This 1692 method did *not* give any gradient formula,[24] and nor did it have in its notation any connection with the converse process of integration. It gave a recipe for what would nowadays be called implicit differentiation and did so using for the first time the dotted notation for fluxions – the English equivalent of the dy/dx notation which was developing on the Continent. The seeds of lasting confusion were sown by Wallis claiming in a Preface to this second edition that the method he had so described was extracted merely from the old letters of 1676 – which was far from being the case – and failing to acknowledge the personal assistance of Newton in giving to him the method in recent letters. Newton had (so Whiteside discovered) invented this notation only late in the previous year, 1691. Wallis was the Savilian mathematics lecturer of Oxford and so a man of some reputation.

The hidden hand of Newton here penned its first-ever public definition of a fluxion and described the celebrated dot notation. By way of preface, Wallis made the polemical claim that the differential calculus had sprung from early fluxion manuscripts. Wallis candidly acknowledged his ignorance of the relevant publications after Leibniz wrote to point them out to him, and they struck up a long correspondence subsequently. Leibniz found in Wallis' preface, 'an amusing affectation of attributing everything to his own nation' (writing to Thomas Burnet). To quote Wallis, 'By fluxions he understands the swiftness of their [the fluents] increase or decrease...' How to apply this method was described *a decade later* in *De Quadratura Curvarum.*

Leibniz struck up a friendly correspondence with Wallis, and some years later wrote a letter to him with the request that it be relayed to Newton (whose address at the Mint he may not have had) proposing that they should both be regarded as co-inventors of the calculus:

'I did not only observe, after the publication of his book [the *Principia*], that the most profound Newton's method of fluxions was cognate to my differential calculus, but have also proclaimed the same in the *Acta Eridutorum* and advised others of it. I judged this [avowal] to conform to my honest nature no less than to his merits. And so I generally call it by the common name of infinitesimal analysis which is [a name] broader in scope than the quadrature method.' (Wallis conveyed the message verbatim to Newton July 1, 1697).

At any time during the controversy this letter could have been produced to show Leibniz's stated – and fairly generous – opinion of two equal and independent discoveries. The same opinion he expressed in the *Acta*, namely:

'... But that he was occupied with a calculus so similar to the differential calculus, was not known to me until the appearance of the first of a two part work by Wallis... Neither of us is indebted, for the geometrical discoveries made in common by us both, to any light kindled by the other, but to his own meditations.' (*Responsio* to Fatio de Duller).

Though over the years he may have made one or two careless statements, Leibniz's overall and formally stated policy was that two independent but equal inventions deserved equal credit. This admittedly did suffer alteration after 1712, with the bitter blow of the Royal Society's verdict, but not before. We need not be concerned with all the incidents of aggravation, which reflected a changed climate after the deaths of Collins and Oldenburg, who had maintained such excellent communication between scientists of the warring nation-states of Europe. There was now Wallis, known for the way he had offended almost every foreign mathematician with whom he came in contact, battling for British rights. There was Fatio de Duller, who fired the opening salvos of the dispute, and ended up in the stocks at Charing Cross because he functioned as the secretary of a religious sect which irritated the authorities. There was John Keill, whom Leibniz described as a 'bumpkin' and refused to correspond with, endeavouring to the last to believe that he did not speak for Newton though probably he did. These developments we shall glide over.

The years between the emergence of the *Principia* and of De l'Hôpital's *Analyse des infiniments petits* on calculus are critical as far as any English claim to independent discovery of the differential calculus is concerned. After 1696, any English mathematician could just copy out De l'Hôpital's principles, transposing them from the differential to the fluxional notation - indeed they did so, according to De Morgan.

De Morgan composed, in the nineteenth-century, popular introductions to the methods of calculus, and he understood this matter as well as anyone. He wrote:

'The fact is, that as to everything elementary that was published with demonstrations under the name of fluxions, up to the year 1704 [when Newton himself first published anything under that name] the method of fluxions was nothing but the differential calculus with the notation changed... No one ventured to print an elementary treatise in England until the seed had grown into a strong plant under the care of Leibniz, the Bernoullis, and so on. When de l'Hôpital in 1696, published at Paris a treatise so systematic, and so much resembling one of modern times, that it might be used even now, he could find nothing English to quote, except a slight treatise of Craig on quadratures, published in 1693... Our countrymen began to write upon fluxions [after 1696]. Some writings are so advanced that they do not define their terms: from these therefore we cannot tell whether $\dot{x}$ means the velocity with which x changes, or an infinitely small increment of x... Such were Dr Cheyne's tract on fluents (1703) and De Moivre's answer to it (1704)... And the only elementary writers, Harris and Hayes, are strictly writers on the differential calculus, as opposed to fluxions, in everything but using $\dot{x}$ instead of dx.' (Ibid, p.90).

This is a valuable summary of fin de siècle British writing on the subject, presenting a case for suspecting writings subsequent to de l'Hôpital's opus. If any case exists for a British origin or genesis of differential calculus, then it needs to be established prior to that date.

In France, the Newtonian inverse-square gravity law suffered a sea- change, upon crossing the channel. It became understood in terms of the new calculus but translated into the physics of vortices which remained alive and well.

The French priest Pierre Varignon at the age of forty set himself to master and teach these new methods, setting out the whole of the science of mechanics up to that time, including Newton's work, in the new language of calculus. Arguably this is the only real sense in which the *Principia* has ever been understood. As E.J. Aiton explained:

'It is unlikely that Varignon devoted much attention to Newton's proofs, for he never discussed them in his own work. Whenever Newton's results were cited, it was always to show how easily they followed from Varignon's general theory. To describe Varignon's work as a translation of Newtonian propositions into the language of the differential calculus would certainly be misleading. Rather do we see in Varignon's work the rediscovery of Newtonian propositions as corollaries of a general analytical theory of central forces.'[25]

Varignon derived the results velocity=ds/dt and acceleration=dv/dt, results of epochal significance which have passed unnoticed by English science historians.

Four Steps in the Birth of Fluxions

We have now alluded to several basic steps in the emergence of fluxions. Before reaching the last phase, which was the rewriting of history – only now in our own time beginning to be untangled – it may be as well to recapitulate.

- The letters which Newton sent to the royal Society in 1677 revealed the general binomial theorem, major new series expansions, the use of negative indices and important new integration techniques ('the method of quadrature'). These do help with certain aspects of the method but are not that method itself.
- In 1687, the *Principia* defined a moment as a small increment, showed a general algebraic procedure for extracting these, and claimed co-discovery of Leibniz' method. It referred back to the letter of June 23, 1676 saying that it showed how, 'in the case of any given series, it could ascertain the quadratures of curves from which they proceed, as well as volumes and centres of gravity of bodies described by these curves.' This was no doubt the case, but these methods are integrals, and integration was discovered long before its converse. The Principia here decoded the anagram, but did *not* explain its meaning.
- The dot notation is first used and fluxions defined, in Wallis' *Algebra*. This first public announcement was coupled with the pretence that the method had been extracted from letters of 16 years ago. The question as regards how to use the fluxions eg for finding maxima and minima was left for the reader.
- 'De Quadratura' of 1704: Writing under his own name, the sketch given briefly in Wallis' opus is now consolidated into a usable method. How to apply fluxions to different kinds of equations was explained, and so for the first time is the converse nature of the two operations, fluxions and quadrature. This date is surely the proper birth for the method of fluxions, which was to do so much to restrict British mathematics for the next century and a half.

As an example of the method of integration ('quadrature') given in 'De Quadratura', we may cite:

If the line of a curve is $y = dx^{n-1}$ then the area under it will be $t = d/nx^n$

where 'd' does *not* refer to the differential.[26] This method has *no link* with the method of fluxions in its notation. It was the genius and simplicity of Leibniz' method that by 1686 he was writing $\int ydx$ for 'quadrature', where 'dx' was the *same* symbol as was used in the converse, differential method.

Bernoulli's Challenge

Johann Bernoulli posed a challenge problem in the June 1696 issue of *Acta Eruditorum,* designed to sort out which mathematicians in Europe had mastery of the 'golden equations' as he called them, of the new calculus. He was confident that no-one could solve his challenge, concerning changing rate of motion along a curve, without them. Very simply, the challenge was:

> 'Given two points A and B in a vertical plane, what is the curve traced out by a point acted on only by gravity, which starts at A and reaches B in the shortest time?'

The six-month deadline elapsed with no English response, so Leibniz persuaded him to extend it. Bernoulli posted a copy to Newton, in January 1697. After all, there had been rumours that Newton was in possession of the new calculus, and should not this resolve the matter?

The distinguished mathematicians John Wallis in Oxford, David Gregory in Scotland and Pierre Varignon in Paris had all struggled in vain, and admitted defeat.[27] Only four answers were finally received – from Leibniz, De l'Hôpital, Bernoulli's brother Jacob, and Newton.

We quote the view of Pierre Rémond de Montfort, concerning Newton's solution: 'One finds in 1697 a solution by Newton of the problem of the quickest path of descent, but in a way that has no analysis so that no-one knows how he did it'[28] – i.e., there was no analysis and no-one knows what route he took! The *purpose* of that challenge question was to show how the new calculus was required to find a curve, to ascertain which mathematicians in Europe were in possession of its 'golden theorems' (to quote Bernoulli) capable of demonstrating these things. Newton sent off on 30 January a two-sentence solution,[*] which *presupposed* that the catenary curve was to be used, indeed it was little more than the joining up of two points using a catenary; then a month later a slightly fuller version was published in the *Phil Trans.*[29] The question of the path of quickest descent of a falling body was highly pertinent to Newton's work. Bernoulli's May 1697 published solution[30] *demonstrated* that a cycloid curve resulted from such a path of quickest descent – whereas Newton's had merely submitted an 'undemonstrated construction of its cycloidal curve,' to quote Whiteside.[31] It was no mystery that a cycloid was the curve traced out by the edge of a rolling wheel.[32] There was a second problem also to be solved in this challenge and Newton's

---

[*] Catherine Barton recalled – thirty years later - how Newton solved the problem: receiving it that day at Jermyn Street on coming home from the Mint, he stayed up till 4 am to do it. Her testimony was given to her husband John Conduit (notebook, Kings College Camb. manuscript, Whitside MP Vol. 8, p.73).

solutions to both were purely geometrical – he *did not use* any 'fluxions' to solve them. A consequence of his not having utilized the calculus, in de Montfort's view, was that one could *not follow* what Newton had done.

Whiteside conjectured that Newton had actually used his maximum/minimum infinitesimal method on this problem (MP 8:6, n.12), but had not shown it. What right had he to make that conjecture?[33] A Newtonian text using fluxions to demonstrate this matter did appear, but only in March 1700. That was a year *after* Fatio Duillier had published a book on the subject[34] and *three years* after the Leibnizian solutions were being debated in German and French journals – and even that Newtonian text remained unpublished![35]

What eventually appears as a Newtonian solution demonstrating that the curve was a cycloid emerged though discussions with David Gregory *after* Newton has sent off his response to the challenge problem (thereby rescuing England's mathematical reputation) and as a kind of echo of the solutions given in *Acta Eruditorum*. This ended up years later in Hayes' *Fluxions* of 1704 as a worked example – with no acknowledgement of its Continental origin! Nothing could be more pertinent to gravity theory than this problem of a path of descent, a challenge problem emerging from what Leibniz had named 'dynamics' that was transforming mathematics in Europe.[36] This analysis of the challenge problem has reinforced our claim, that Newton *did not ever use* his 'fluxional' methods in any public context – he preferred to use methods that were geometric.[*]

Fin de Siecle textbooks

Do books on the new calculus published at the end of the seventeenth century show a British invention? Is some Newtonian method 'working' in these books – or, do they rather appear as being a mere echo of what had developed on the Continent?

There is an important sequence of British publications over the nine-year period 1695-1704 which utilised the new Newtonian concept of 'moments' as small changes, while labelling them as fluxions.[37] Thus, in 1702, John Harris wrote, 'These infinitely small Increments or Decrements, our Incomparable Mr Newton, calls very properly by this name of fluxions,' and likewise in 1704, Charles Hayes wrote, 'the infinitely little Increment or Decrement is call'd the fluxion.'[38] Likewise in 1711, John Hayes' *Lexicon Technicum* had a twelve page section on fluxions which

---

[*] *The Calculus Wars: Newton, Leibniz and the greatest Mathematical Clash of all Time* (Jason Bardi, 2006) has a chapter on the Bernoulli challenge, but no word about the form of solution which anyone came up with - or even what calculus has to do with a cycloid. What, one wonders, is the point of such a math-free book? It is a second history of the calculus dispute (following that of Hall, 1980) composed for readers who do not wish to be troubled by mathematics.

started with such a definition: 'the fluxion of a quantity is its Increase or Decrease infinitely small.' *For none of them* does a fluxion signify a rate of change (dx/dt in differential form) or a line-gradient value. They remain as little quantities, little enough that squares and higher powers can be ignored.

Here is a diagram from the 'first British textbook on the new calculus' by John Harris in 1702.[39] A ratio between the two sides of the small triangle gives the gradient of the tangent. As the triangle grows smaller and smaller, the value of that gradient assumes a limiting value. An ordinary school math teacher,

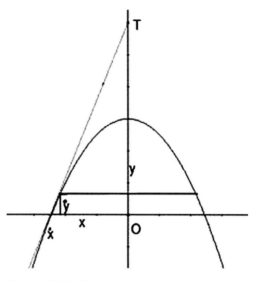

Harris 1702 diagram, copying de l'Hôpital's textbook without acknowledgement, showing how to find the gradient of a curve, but using the British dot-notation.

asked if the differential method was described in this book, would probably reply 'yes.' To have a grasp of this method means to apprehend that as these two sides grow smaller and smaller, their ratio does not change.

Hayes' 1704 textbook used the same format as de l'Hôpital had done for finding the tangent to a curve, just putting ẋ instead of dx, i.e. he gave the gradient of his parabola-tangent as ẋ / ẏ, a ratio between two infinitesimal increments (p.18). That was (I found) the first British textbook on the subject[40] which *expressed the gradient* of a curve – eight years after the concept had been defined with luminous clarity in France. British books at the turn of the century appear as being years behind their continental rivals. I suggest that they fail to show evidence of an indigenous or independent source for the new calculus, but rather indicate more of a copycat process.

Newton's *De Quadrature* of 1704 did not find the gradient of any curves, nor the equation of a tangent, and it certainly did not find maxima and minima of curves. It was basically a work (as its title implied) concerned with integration.[41] I suggest that Newton *did not ever publish* a method of finding the gradient of a curve by calculus (See Appendix 3). What he did do, as we've seen earlier, was to show in a letter to Leibniz how to find the gradient of a curve using the Sluse method – which was a pre-calculus procedure. The Hayes textbook in that same year of 1704 was the first British publication to show how to find the gradient of a curve – *twenty years* after Leibniz had done so.[42]

'A mind neither fair nor honest'

Nobody paid Newton more glorious, golden complements than did Baron von Leibniz. Conversing with the Queen of Prussia, at the royal palace in Berlin while having dinner in the year 1701:

> 'Leibniz said that taking Mathematics from the beginning of the world to the time of Sr I., what he had done was much the better half - & added that he had consulted all the learned in Europe upon some difficult point without having any satisfaction & that when he wrote to Sr I. he sent him answer by first post to do so & so & then he would find it out.'[43]

By this time Leibniz was a Baron because of his archival research for the Hanover family, and was also President of the Berlin Academy of Sciences. He conceived and planned the Berlin Academy of Sciences, the first institution of its kind in Northern Europe, and it was established in 1700 with him as its first President. Eminent in history, law, philosophy, religion, mathematics and theoretical mechanics, he shone as Europe's foremost intellectual. It remained his formally stated opinion, right up until the bitter climax, that there were two separate and independent discoverers:

> 'I, too and my friends have on several occasions made obvious our belief that the illustrious discoverer of fluxions arrived by his own efforts at basic principles similar to out own. Nor do I lay less claim to the rights of a discoverer... Thus I throw myself on your sense of justice...'

This was his appeal to the Royal society of London in 1712, of which he was then its most distinguished foreign member, against unjust voices (as he saw them) within the Society claiming he had filched his discoveries from another. All he was asking it for was a politic, minimal affirmation that the two methods though similar had been discovered independently. He asked for justice. To quote the recent Lucasian Professor of Mathematics at Cambridge, astrophysicist and Fellow of the Royal Society, the late Stephen Hawkins:

> 'As the row grew, Leibniz made the mistake of appealing to the Royal Society to resolve the dispute.'[44]

As our tale grinds on towards its grim finale, in 1711 we find the 69-year-old President informing the Royal Society of 'a Beginning to the present Controversy': this had been he said a review in the *Acta Eruditorum* by Leibniz of his 1704 publication, *Optics.* That had contained a Newtonian tract *De Quadratura*, and this first public statement of the method of fluxions written by its author contained the claim that he had developed the method forty years earlier in the mid-1660s.[45] Clearly this was a somewhat provocative remark, and the review in the *Acta* said, by way of elucidation, 'Instead of the Leibnizian differences, Mr Newton employs, and has always employed, fluxions, which are very much the same as....' The President declared that this implied a derogative sense, that 'employs, and has always employed' meant, somehow, that he was a mere second inventor. This, the Royal Society was informed, 'gave a Beginning to the present Controversy'. In 1716, Leibniz wrote to the Abbé Conti that such an interpretation was 'the malicious interpretation of a man who seeks a guard.' The words he used, '*adhibet, semperque adhibit,*' had no other meaning he insisted. A continental historian Rosenberger viewed Leibniz's statement as an 'impolitic and foolish act' but one which could not possibly be construed as a deliberate attack. A further sentence of the review compared the two methods to two mathematicians of the time, one of whom was better than the other, which was indeed a foolish thing to do. Eight years later this straw was used by the Royal Society's President for the setting up of an inquiry, if one can call it that.*

'On 6 March 1712', to quote Westfall:

> 'the Royal Society appointed a committee to inspect the letters and papers relating to the matter: Arbuthnot, Hill, Halley, Jones, Machin, and Burnett, to which they later added Robartes, DeMoivre, Aston, Taylor, and Frederick Bonet, the minister in London of the King of Prussia. Newton liked to refer to this committee as "numerous and skilful and composed of Gentlemen of several nations..." Rather it was a coven of his own partisans to which Herr Bonet, to his undying shame, allowed himself to be coopted to provide some minimal veneer of impartiality. The veneer was so minimal, in fact, that the published report did not name the committee, whose membership remained concealed in the society's records until the nineteenth century.

---

* 'The Commercium Epistolicum... was Newton's historicist answer to Leibniz' claim to the first discovery of th new infinitesimal analysis,' claimed Rupert Hall (*Isaac Newton Adventurer in Thought*, 1992, p.313), quite wrongly; adding that it 'contained no falsehoods that Leibniz was ever able to demonstrate.' That is a rather sophistical remark in that no-one can demonstrate or prove a negative: but Leibniz did explain that the infinite series expansions with which the C.E. was concerned, were not about the differential method; and that the early letters he recieved from Newton had not contained what had there been alleged. One is taken aback that so grave a scholar as Rupert Hall should have made such claims.

'Neither Herr Bonet nor the others found the task difficult. Newton had already done the spadework in a year of intensive investigation. The full advantage of Jones's lucky recovery of Collins' papers now emerged. Together with Oldenberg's correspondence in the records of the society, Collins' papers provided the factual foundation of the report which did not need to call upon Newton's own papers at all. Leibniz later complained - with full justice - that the committee conducted a judicial proceeding without informing him of the fact or of allowing him to present evidence. The committee did not call upon Newton to present evidence either. It did not need to. Newton carried out the investigation, arranged its evidence, and wrote the report, which explains why the commitee was able to submit the report, which presumed to survey the whole history of the calculus, on 24 April, a full month and a half after its appointment. The final three members had been appointed on 17 April, one week earlier. The procedure may explain why the committee did not sign the report, but Newton's creatures were too tame to balk at not submitting it. Of his own central participation there can be no doubt.' (Westfall p725).

One may admire the power which Newton evidently enjoyed, that he could thus manipulate the Royal Society and corrupt the integrity of its proceedings without inviting criticism. In the next century, Brewster in his two-volume biography reprinted the *Commercium Epistolicum* and simply endorsed it, as if it were an impartial investigation. It became widely accepted as a just account in France and England in the eighteenth century. Surely this was the all-time nadir of scientific morality, to which not even Edison's treatment of Nicola Tesla during the AC-DC battle over the electrification of America can compare. To quote More, 'The President, the Committee and the Fellows of the Royal Society are to be condemned for a reckless and disgraceful exhibition of injustice against one of the oldest and most illustrious members.'[46] As the corporate ethos of the Society was rotted by a fabric of deception and misrepresentation, as the oldest and longest-time foreign member of the Royal Society was stabbed in the back, did members protest?

Newton's behaviour has finally ended up where it deserves, in 'Betrayers of the Truth', a book on fraud in science:

'Newton's willingness to resort to sleight of hand is evident in more than just falsification of data.[47] He used his position as President of the Royal Society, England's premier scientific club, to wage his battle with Leibniz over who first invented calculus. What was shameful about Newton's behaviour was the hypocrisy with which he paid lip service to fair procedure but followed the very opposite course. It would be an iniquitous judge 'who would admit anyone as a witness into his own cause' announced the preface of a Royal Society Report of 1712 which examined the question of priority in calculus. Ostensibly the work of a committee of impartial scientists, the report was a complete vindication of Newton's claim and even accused Leibniz of plagiary. In fact the whole report, sanctimonious preface included, had been written by Newton himself.'[48]

The President – Fellow of Trinity, Knight, Master of the Mint, twice Member of Parliament, and Justice of the Peace – rewrote history. The main burden of this *Commercium* has already been examined, that a series of three letters was credited with a meaning absent therefrom. The first of these letters does show a method of finding tangents, and a later letter asserts it to be the best method, but it is the method of Sluse and as such but a precursor of the differential method. The Committee asserted that this very letter, which in their minds had the method of fluxions 'sufficiently described to any intelligent person' was sent to Leibniz, when they had evidence before them in Collins' notes that no copy thereof had been sent, but only a summary by Collins. The report denied categorically that Leibniz had developed any method of calculus prior to receiving these letters.

Next the report shifted back to the mode of composition of the *Principia*, affirming, in what Hall called 'a famous and delusive passage,' (p.229) that:

> By the help of the new analysis Mr Newton found out most of the propositions in his *Principia Philosophiae*; but because the Ancients for making things certain admitted nothing into geometry before it was demonstrated synthetically, that the system of the heavens might be founded upon good geometry. And this makes it now difficult for unskilful men to see the analysis by which those propositions were found out.'

A use had at last been found for the opaque nature of the book's format – persons who could not perceive its fluxional infrastructure were now 'unskilful'. By this hoax, two centuries of science historians were thrown off the scent, their judgements largely worthless. 'The system of the heavens' had to be founded upon 'good geometry'.

It was only the exhaustive researches of Whiteside which finally dispelled the so-tenacious myth:[49]

'Be ever wary of accepting uncritically at face value Newton's retrospective assessments of the nature and sequence of his scientific achievement... As Newton himself never forgot (though he tried cleverly to conceal it by various sly turns of phrase from his contemporaries) the standard dot-notation for fluxions was invented by him only in mid-December 1691... There are no extant autograph manuscripts of Newton's preceding the Principia in time which could conceivably buttress the conjecture that he first worked the proofs in that book by fluxions before remoulding them in traditional form. Nor in all the many thousands of such sheets relating to the composition and revision of the Principia is there any trace of a suggestion that such papers ever did exist.'*

As to why the Royal Society needed such depth of deception over the genesis of calculus, then coming to be apprehended as the most significant development in mathematics since the Arabs discovered zero – the answer here suggested is, that they could by no means find a valid claim for an English seed or source for the new technique. There was simply nothing that had grown from any English source.

'An affront to all grave and good men' was Leibniz's comment upon the *Commercium Epistolicum,* in a letter to Johann Bernoulli.[50] 'A mind neither fair nor honest' was his judgement in 1713 on the man he had hitherto admired above all others, but now had to realise was his arch-enemy: he said that in a statement replying to the Royal Society's judgement (the *'Charta Volans',* see Hall p.200) that his position henceforth was that Newton's earlier work in mathematics was *not* the calculus, but was rather concerned with 'advancing geometry synthetically or directly by infinitely small quantities'. As he said, 'It was evident from the *Principia* that Newton had not known the true Calculus of Differences in 1687, because he had avoided its use in circumstances which demanded it.'[51] His reply to the *Commercium Epistolicum* was entitled *Historia et Origo Calculi Differentialis* (unmentioned in Hall's opus) but this remained unpublished until 1846. In this, he said of the Royal Society's report:

> 'they have said very little about the calculus; instead, every other page is made up of what they call infinite series. Such things were first given as discoveries by Nicholas Mercator of Holstein, who first obtained them by the process of division, and Newton gave the more general form by extraction of roots. This is certainly a useful discovery... But it has nothing at all to do with the differential calculus.'[52]

Standard historical accounts tend to affirm that the early series expansions by Newton were somehow a basis for the discovery of the differential calculus.

---

* One would have thought and hoped that such a judgement would be fairly final, however the erudite Mr Guicciardini has been arguing against this view, i.e. for an unpublished 'fluxional' method having been used, in: *Isaac Newton on Mathematical Certainty and Method*, 2011, Chapter10.

By such logic, Leibniz continued, 'with as much justice [one] could assign the geometry of Descartes to Apollonius'. He recalled how he came by his inspiration for the new calculus 'by which the imagination is freed from a perpetual reference to diagrams'. That is such an important phrase and has to be central to any definition of calculus.[53]

Did Leibniz lie, as did the others? By way of comparison, we refer to the behaviour of Johann Bernoulli, first scion of the most eminent mathematical family that has ever existed, promoter and developer of the Leibnizian calculus and a pillar of support for Leibniz personally when under attack. After his colleague's death in 1716, Bernoulli then brazenly denied that he had written any of the letters in support of Leibniz and, 'rising to yet greater heights of mendacity' as Manuel phrased it, claimed he had always been on Newton's side – and asked Newton for a portrait! He didn't get it. The worst Leibniz did by way of mendacity was to publish tracts anonymously and then deny that he was the author thereof, in which he was not unique. Both protagonists were seeking a posture of detachment which they could not emotionally attain, because of the cosmic, all-embracing nature of their disagreement, and they strove to attain such a posture by publishing anonymously and referring to themselves in the third person. It would be harsh to call this procedure, which was fairly transparent to most people, dishonesty.

The dispute had wide-ranging philosophical ramifications. The view of Carolyn Merchant, in *The Death of Nature* (1982, p283) was as follows. Leibniz stressed that there was a life and perception animating all things and criticised the new philosophy for 'maintaining the inertness and deadness of things'. For Leibniz, the world of substance was really organic, with every being in the universe, from living animals down to the simple monad, alive and composed of living parts. 'Thus there is nothing fallow, sterile or dead in the universe,' he wrote. 'All matter,' he said, 'must be full of animated, or at least living, substances.' He could never reconcile himself with the atoms-and-the-void philosophy emanating from England. He coined the word 'dynamics', which concept was for him part of a large system of things. His philosophy was a dynamic vitalism, representing a last gasp of vitalistic thinking before the advent of the mechanical, corpuscular philosophy which swept all before it in the eighteenth century.

A King from Hanover

The debate reverberated across Europe, so that as Manuel remarked, those who could not understand the calculus could at least enjoy the exchange of insults, until a startling development occurred. It had been in the pipeline ever since 1701, when an Act of Settlement made the Hanoverian dynasty the next in line for the British throne. The Elector of Hanover was the grandson of James I, and his son Georg Ludwig was thereby placed in the line of succession to become George I of England. Leibniz had been employed for years in polishing up the pedigree of this Hanoverian dynasty, by extensive correspondence and library research, and had been made a baron in reward. He secured electoral status for Hanover in the Holy Roman Empire, and undertook religious, legal and political reform at the Hapsburg court in Vienna, where he served as imperial privy councillor. He had been tutor to princess Caroline. Hanover was a pocket of Protestantism within the atrophying Holy Roman Empire, and Elector Georg Ludwig agreed to forsake his princedom to become George I of England. The calculus dispute raged within, and was embittered by, the context of a dynastic change from Stuart to Hanover.

The base for Leibniz's existence was drawn from under his feet. He tried to persuade his sovereign to take him along, but the broadside from the Royal Society made this unfeasible. His letters to Caroline, his former pupil and now Princess of Wales, reveal desperation at his increasingly isolated and unsatisfactory position at Hanover, and his frustration at being unable to secure an official position at the English court. He had been the court philosopher. What sweet revenge for Newton that Caroline should end up chatting with him as her court philosopher, or its nearest equivalent, that he could refer to her in print as 'a particular friend', and produce a 'Chronology' of ancient history at her royal command.

Events must have severely strained Leibniz's adherence to his philosophic maxim that this world was 'the best of all possible worlds' which he came out with in 1710.[54] He died in poverty and isolation, with no-one but his servant at the grave. One Ker chanced to arrive on the day of his death, and declared that he saw 'a funeral more like [that of] a highwayman than of one who had been the ornament of his country'. As if Fate was at his beck and call, the ageing Royal Society's President had moved from an intellectual disagreement, over the Deity and also calculus, to a move which devastated the last years of Germany's leading intellectual, the father of German philosophy. Opined More (p.577):

> 'It is an extraordinary fact, that, from the time of Newton to the present day, nearly everyone, who has treated the subject, has either accused Leibniz of plagiarism, or has, when defending him, left his reputation to some extent tarnished.'

Turning to Bertrand Russell's *History of Western Philosophy* (1962) by way of testing this observation, we there gather that Leibniz was 'one of the supreme intellects of all time' but that alas 'as a human being he was not admirable', because he was 'wholly destitute of the higher philosophic virtues'.

'Second Inventors'

'There is enough glory in the discovery for both of you,' Pierre Varignon wrote to Leibniz, which was the latter's view entirely. The Royal Society report came to reject this view with its stern edict, 'Second inventors have no right'. If there existed a second inventor, then two sources of the new method of calculus would be seen to flow and mingle together. The reader has now been exposed to fairly careful scrutiny of the historical record and may agree that it has rather failed to show this. What it does show is that in the eighteenth century, the illusory *Commercium Epistolicum* version of events came to be widely accepted (when there was no idea who had composed it, merely that it was a Royal Society statement). In 1740, for example, the Comte de Buffon published in France his *Method of Fluxions and Infinite Series* which fully endorsed its claims.

In 1718, writing to Brook Taylor, Pierre Rémond de Montfort took issue with Taylor's avowal that 'I always took Sir Isaac Newton, not only for the Inventor, but also for the greatest Master of it' and that he knew neither of other inventors nor improvers. Montfort insisted that this was 'an error of fact:'

'I shall not examine here the rights of Mssrs Newton and Leibniz to the first invention of the differential and integral calculus. I shall report to you when you would like the details of the reflections that a long and serious examination have furnished me, and I hope you will not be unhappy with them. I want only to have you note that it is untenable to say that Leibniz and the brothers Bernoulli are not the true and almost unique promoters of these calculi. Here is my opinion; you may be the judge of it. It is they and they alone who have taught us the rules of differentiating and integrating, the manner of finding by these calculi the tangents of curves, their turning points and points of inflection, their greatest and their least ordinates, evolutes, caustics of reflection and refraction, quadratures of curves, centres of gravity, centres of oscillation, and of percussion, problems of inverse method of tangents such as this for example (which lent so much admiration to Mr Huygens in 1693): *to find the curve of* which the tangent is to the part intercepted on the axis in a given ratio. It was they who first expressed mechanical curves by means of equations, who taught us to separate the variables in differential equations, to reduce their dimension, and to construct them by means of logarithms, or by means of rectification of curves when that is possible; and who by pretty and numerous applications of these calculi to the most difficult problems of mechanics, such as those of the catenary, the sail, the elastic, the curve of quickest descent, the paracentric, have put us and our successors on the path to the most profound discoveries. Those are facts not to be contradicted. To convince oneself of them it suffices to open the journals of Leibniz [i. e., the *Acta Eruditorum*].'

This letter Westfall describes as 'a breath of fresh air in a miasma of deceit and hypocrisy' but adds that it 'did not alter the controversy in the least'(p.785). We leave perforce unexamined the state of Edmund Halley's conscience, Halley being the co-ordinator of that clandestine group of mathematicians of 'many different nations', chiefly Scottish, Welsh and English. At that time Halley occupied the Savilian chair of astronomy at Oxford. This was one of the two most unethical actions of his life.

The question is often asked, as to whether the two protagonists discovered the same thing? Here the answer must surely be in the negative, and for the reason already given, that the method of fluxions always gave a time-derivative of the variables in an equation, while the differential method gives the rate of change of one variable with respect to another. A further answer to this question could be based on a mature evaluation of the difference given by Sir Isaac himself. *His* method, he claimed, could be used with any symbolism, whereas:

'Mr Leibniz confines his Method to the symbols dx and dy, so that if you take away his symbols you take away the characteristic of his method.'[55]

One must concur with this view; take away dx and dy, and could one perform calculus? It is precisely in this automatic character of the two operations that the invention consists, which saves having to go through the whole operation from first principles every time. Yet at times the Royal Society viewed the two inventions as one and the same; for example, there was a long, anonymous *Account of the Commercium Epistolicum* which filled an entire issue of the *Philosophical Transactions* in 1715, (though its authorship was never in doubt) which concerned, its title proclaimed, *the Right of Invention of the Method of Fluxions, by some call'd the Differential Method.* For 'some', read 'Europe.'

It had been Leibniz's youthful ambition to create a universal logic, which would lead of necessity to correct conclusions merely by virtue of the symbols used. His differential calculus was this. As with his calculating engine, one just turned the handle...

Summing up the case, Professor Hall concluded

'One may feel, perhaps, that Leibniz was less greathearted than Alfred Russell Wallace who, having certainly known nothing of

Darwin's speculations and notebooks, nevertheless accepted the Linnean Society's actions in 1858 in good part.; (p.257)

One is taken aback by such a comparison. Darwin, on receiving Wallace's note, did within a couple of weeks express his astonishment at receiving a theory in essence identical to his own. Newton, on receiving Leibniz' letter, expressed no interest let alone astonishment to anyone and only came forward with a comparable method sixteen years later; and then only in a hidden manner, penning words in a book written by another. If Charles Darwin had said nothing on receiving Wallace's theory, but sixteen years later had placed a similar theory in another's book, referring to himself in the third person – would anyone then speak of co-discovery? It requires to say the least the eye of faith to perceive Professor Hall's comparison.

DISCUSSION

Salviati, Sagredo and Simplicius sit in the Royal Society library.

<u>Salviati:</u> To start at the beginning, Leibniz came to understand his method of calculus only *after* receiving Newton's letter to him of June 1676 – that was the view of David Gregory on the matter, a sensible and well-informed character. Leibniz may possibly have developed his symbolic language of calculus in the previous year; but, before he received that letter, what he wrote about for example finding the gradient of a curve did fail to impress the English mathematicians. In 1677, Leibniz came to understand his calculus rules, when he composed his letter to the Royal Society on the subject.

<u>Sagredo:</u> The synchrony is curious, I admit, but you will surely not suggest that Newton's letter of June 1676 contained anything about the method of fluxions?[56] It was all about infinite series. But, supposing for the sake of argument we accept the absurd verdict which the Royal Society circulated around Europe: that in Newton's letter of December 1672, 'the method of fluxions was sufficiently described to any intelligent person.' It added similarly categorical statements about his two further letters of 1677. These letters were public knowledge as they were owned by the Royal Society. In that case, the question should have been: why did Wallis's *Algebra* of 1685 contain no hint of the new method? After all, Wallis was keen to promote any new British developments in mathematics, as he believed that the continental mathematicians were getting away with too much credit. His book did well describe the contents of Newton's two letters of 1677, as containing important new series expansions and it admired his notation for expressing powers, such as $2^{1/2}$ to represent the square root of two, which was quite an innovation. Lastly, it described his method

for solving equations by approximation, but that was all. Wallis had a special interest in the arithmetic of infinities, concerning infinitely small quantities, and had a new method been in the air, he would certainly have heard about it. This shows the great hypocrisy of 'perfidious Albion' in claiming, decades later, that some early letters contained material which they patently did not.

Later, in 1686, both the integral sign and the differential 'dy' notation were described by Leibniz in the *Acta Eruditorum*. This, together with his previous article two years earlier, laid down the mathematical basis of the differential method and its relation to the opposite process, which they called 'quadrature'. These articles of Leibniz didn't clarify the notion of infinitesimal quantities, which more philosophical issue was resolved by the time of de l'Hôpital's calculus textbook in 1695. The decade between those two events we should see as the birth-period of the calculus.

Simplicius: It occurs to me that the *Arithmetica Universalis* came from Newton's lecture notes deposited in his college library, during the decade before he composed the *Principia*. William Whiston undertook to publish these notes and one gathers that Newton had little time to revise them beforehand. Had he been working on his fluxional method in that period, prior to Leibniz' articles appearing, then such a work should reveal this and establish his priority claim. After all, his early lecture notes well showed his development of the colour theory which he published in 1672. The book *Arithmetica Universalis* had a great influence in the eighteenth-century. Why, here it is on the shelf.

Salviati: Our author has sadly underestimated Newton's great invention of the calculus in the mid-1660's, as if he had only developed the method decades later! Why, there is a wealth of manuscripts from this early period which scholars have pored over, and they leave no room for doubt. Only a brief mention was heard of the masterly *De Analysi*, and hardly any appreciation of how fluxion methods were used in the great *Principia*.

Sagredo: What *are* you suggesting?

Salviati: Why, this was the clear, collective opinion of the Royal Society, expressed in 1713. I will read from their report:

> 'And in his [Newton's] *Principia Philosophica*, where he frequently considers... Points whose velocities increase or decrease, the velocities are the first fluxions, and their increase the second.... The increase or decrease of the velocities ... is the second fluxion of the quantity and therefore he had not then forgotten the method of second fluxions.'[57]

You see, the increase of velocity or acceleration is the second fluxion or differential of motion. I cannot accept our author's assertion that Newton never viewed acceleration as the fluxion of velocity. Why, that is what Newtonian science is all about.

Simplicius: Quite so! It is plain that Sir Isaac must have done calculations using acceleration because how else can gravity be calculated? And that's what he discovered, wasn't it?

Sagredo: Hush, keep your voices down. Textbooks nowadays concede that fluxions were not used in the *Principia*. Mind you, they usually add that no doubt its illustrious author could have used them had he so wished, but that mysteriously he chose not to, instead using a cumbersome geometrical method that no-one could understand. On the other hand, they tend to agree with Salviati, or rather with his quotation from the anonymous author who occupied a complete issue of the 'Philosophical Transactions' with a 50-page tirade on the matter: that the 'second fluxion' of a distance signified the 'increase or decrease of the velocities', or what we would call acceleration, and that such calculations were used by Newton. But was this really so?

The *Principia* is all about motion in time of bodies attracted by a central force. My answer to Simplicius' rather vital question is as follows: had this theme been treated using anything resembling fluxional methods, ie the differential calculus, then we today would be able to understand that book. It would not be a tome sealed with seven seals as it is for us. In fact, there is not a single fluxion in the *Principia*, nor anything resembling it, in any edition. If you wish to argue that the fluxional method had been developed and was viable prior to that date, then you are obliged to explain why it was not so used in the master-work. That wouldn't be easy.

Simplicius: Hmm, this is rather strange. This copy of the *Arithmetica Universalis* - a work which enjoyed a much greater popularity in its time than either the *Principia* or *Optics*, though nowadays rather forgotten – contains no hint of fluxions. It seems to have a rather traditional view that geometry and algebra should be kept in separate compartments. Here, I'll read it:

> 'Equations are expressions of arithmetical computation, and properly
> have no place in geometry... The Ancients so assiduously distinguished
> them one from another that they never introduced arithmetical terms
> into geometry... And the moderns, by confounding both' - he means
> geometry and computation - 'have lost the simplicity in which all the
> elegancy of geometry consists.'[58]

That sounds to me like someone arguing *against* fluxions; which were after all a means of tackling geometrical problems by making equations out of them. I certainly wouldn't have guessed that the author of this book had just stumbled across the biggest mathematical discovery since the Arabs invented zero. I am perplexed.

Day Two

<u>Salviati</u>: I think that a clear definition of fluxions was given in the *Principia*. In the first edition, the Fluxions lemma of Book Two defined 'just nascent principles' or 'moments'. I'll read it:

> 'Moments, as soon as they are of finite magnitude, cease to be moments. To be given finite bounds is in some measure contradictory to their continuous increase or decrease.'

I find that a rather imaginative first attempt to explain the infinitesimal concept in his fluxions.

<u>Simplicius</u>: That definition isn't about rate of change; fluxions as rate of change didn't appear *publicly* in any equations by Newton prior to 1704. Our author is claiming – though I find it hard to believe - that the most elementary aspects of differential calculus, namely the gradients of curves and how to find maxima and minima, were not published in any British text prior to 1704. If that was so, I am puzzled as to how they could claim priority for its invention.

Our author further strains my credulity, by claiming that a mathematical description of acceleration did not appear until the end of the seventeenth century by a French disciple of Leibniz called Varignon. I seem to recall that Galileo defined 'uniform acceleration' as motion where, he used to say, the distance an object moves over successive intervals of time is as the sequence of odd numbers. That was how he phrased it.

<u>Salviati</u>: I'd be doubtful about the Varignon text. David Gregory said of the treatise to which you refer: 'In the History and Journales of the French Royal Academie for the year 1700, M. Varignon has a long treatise concerning *vis centripeta,* filled with a great number of Blunders.'[59] That's all he said! Gregory lived in Oxford and so had John Wallis to discuss matters with. Between them they must have had a fair idea of what was going on.

The drift of our argument seems to be that the *Principia* contained definitions of moments or fluxions, but did not use them mathematically. I can see some sense in this point of view. To give an example: the *Principia's* Book Two has that celebrated theorem which demonstrated the shape of a boat prow offering minimum resistance to water[60] – a brilliant application of the calculus of variations. I gather that much the same equations were used in this century to design the contour of space rockets.

Now, the *Principia's* demonstration of this theorem was geometrical and had no fluxions, whereas when Newton was asked by Gregory to explain this theorem to him in 1694, he did so using his fluxional method.[61]

Sagredo: I like the idea of Gregory, a supreme mathematician, being unable to comprehend that theorem until it was rephrased for him in fluxional terms. Let's recall that the year 1694 was also the year when Newton sent a theory of atmospheric refraction to Flamsteed based upon an integral calculus. It seems that the astronomer didn't think a great deal of it, but it is of much theoretical interest. Evidently Newton was deeply immersed in the matter. Incidentally, dare I suggest that the boat theorem was the sole instance in his scientific career of his making a proposal of practical utility, of which Francis Bacon would have approved?

If we are going to use that phrase 'fluxions lemma', let us be aware that such a title was only conferred afterwards upon that section of the *Principia*, while attempts were being made to imply that it contained such a method. That section had a definition of small increments which it called moments or fluxions, and by such small increases it meant magnitudes whose squares and higher powers could be ignored. I wouldn't personally call that a definition of infinitesimal changes, though no lack of commentators have done so.

Day Three

Salviati: Let us recall another sublime discovery of the great mathematician, his method of approximation for solving equations, nowadays learnt by every mathematics student. These days there is a greatly increased interest in Newton's method of solving equations, as computers use its iterative technique to converge upon solutions, for any equation whatsoever! The invention of this Newton-Raphson method (as some old books used to call it) clearly refutes Sagredo's outrageous claim that the British could not use the calculus until they learnt about it from France. That seems to be his viewpoint.

Simplicius: Quite so. As a mathematics teacher, I have taught 'Newton's method of approximation' for many years. It shows the deep grasp of differential calculus by its illustrious inventor. I congratulate Salviati on introducing this important new argument. All we need to do now is ascertain when he first invented it.

Sagredo: We can agree that a perusal of this fine British invention will give us insight into the development of differential calculus. I only wish that historians would take more notice of what it has to teach us about the development of calculus in England. Let us start with this first edition of Wallis' *Algebra*, to which we have already referred, where the first public account of the method of approximation used by Newton appeared. As you can see, it lacks any trace of fluxions.

Raphson published his rather different approximation method for solving equations in 1690. Unlike Newton's, his was an *iterative* method. Raphson there used nothing resembling a formula for differentiation, even though nowadays his method – miscalled Newton's method – is always described using such. Instead, Raphson wrote out long lists of what we would now call differentials. Thus, for the expression aaaa, the rule was to divide by 4aaa, for aaa, one had to divide by 3aa, and so forth. Even in this second edition which he brought out in 1697, we can see that he did not so much as mention fluxions or differentials.[62] What should we make of that?

Simplicius: I am shocked by your claim that Newton was not the inventor of this method. Why, here are a whole row of mathematics history textbooks and I challenge you to find a single one which will agree with you on this matter! I am also perplexed by your assertion that Raphson did not describe his method using fluxions. After all, he composed *A History of Fluxions* in the early eighteenth-century so was an expert on the matter. It would have been much to his advantage to use a fluxion or differential, saving him having to write out his method in terms of long lists for all the different types of equation. After all, a public account of the method of fluxions had been given a couple of years earlier, in the second edition of Wallis' *Algebra*, he should have used that.

Sagredo: Here again, our author's account of the unfolding of fluxions as a step-by-step process is particularly helpful. What appeared in 1693, as the shy debut of fluxions on the English stage, was a method of implicit differentiation for time-dependent functions. For the *Principia's* author, rates of change in time were what mattered. It described for example how a^4 became $4a^3\dot{a}$. That was hardly a recipe for finding the gradient of a curve. Could Raphson have used that? The so-called Raphson-Newton method requires differentials and is not concerned with time-functions. The publication of Raphson's treatise is striking evidence of how the English had not cottoned on to the new idea of calculus even by the mid-'90s.

Simplicius: What puzzles me is why these mathematicians kept getting ordained. Both John Wallis at Oxford and Isaac Barrow at Cambridge took holy orders and served as chaplains to the King, the latter after resigning his Lucasian chair. There were also Cheyne, Whiston and Samuel Clarke. Clarke composed the first notes on Newtonian mechanics that came to be used by Cambridge undergraduates, then later on conducted the grand theological debate with Leibniz. This ecclesiastical connection is hard to fathom. But, it is time for us to go now.

(They exit, passing a glass cabinet containing the reflecting telescope donated to the Royal Society by Newton, his death mask and a lock of his hair.)

Chapter 9

'Restorer Of Solid Philosophy'

Synthesis

> '... Those memorable eighteen months which it cost him to produce
> the great work that has immortalised his name.'
>
> Cajori[1]

Towards the end of his life, Sir Isaac recollected that 'I wrote [the book] in 17 or 18 months, beginning in the end of December 1684 & sending it to ye R. Society in May 1686' (to Varignon in 1719). This timescale has often been quoted, as indicating the superhuman power of the creative process involved. As his British biographer Sullivan remarked, it was beyond mortal ability to comprehend how such a thing could have been accomplished in a mere eighteen months, but we merely had to accept that it was so.[2]

His biographer Michael White alluded to 'a 550-page treatise that had taken just eighteen months to complete'[3] – no, it was only 316 pages, and took some two-and-a-half years to compose. Even Rupert Hall has this first edition as a book of '510 dense Latin pages.'[4] One gains the impression that people hardly peruse the First Edition, which is much the most interesting.

The composition of this magisterial opus began in the Autumn of 1684. Initially, it was merely *De Motu*, 'concerning motion' that Newton was composing, but this swelled progressively until it became the *Principia's* Book I. The first volume of the *Philosophica Naturalis Principia Mathematica* was delivered to Edmond Halley in April of 1686, and the second and third volumes followed in March of the next year. There was thus a composition period of two and a half years. The first two volumes of the *Principia* were completed in that 18-month period.[5]

There is really only one authentic guide to how the mighty creative process unfolded, and that is the correspondence he shared with Flamsteed at Greenwich, as he continually required information from him. At the end of the year 1684, as the Thames froze over and England lay in the grip of one of its iciest winters,

215

Flamsteed wrote to Cambridge in reply to a request for information concerning the satellites of Jupiter, saying that their orbital radii were 'as exactly in sesquialterate proportions to their periods as it is possible for our senses to determine', adding that the data he was enclosing had been corrected for 'Roemer's equation of light', a small adjustment for the varying time it took light to travel from Jupiter according to how near it was to the Earth. Part III of the *Principia* begins with a demonstration of how the satellites of Jupiter show the three laws of Kepler. The verifying of these laws in our solar system was fraught with difficulties, because the inferring of planetary orbits around the Sun starting with their observed tracks across the night sky was far from easy. But, thanks to the ultra-accurate new observations from Greenwich, one could now observe directly the elliptical orbits of moons as they whirled around their parent planet Jupiter and perceive the laws directly in their motions. A table compared the Flamsteed data to that of Cassini at the Paris observatory for these Jovial moon-periods and radii, proudly displaying the superior accuracy of the British data.

It was odd, Flamsteed added, that these moons so well adhered to the Kepler laws whereas our Moon didn't. Part III of the *Principia* would gesture towards an explanation of this intractable issue. A swift reply from Newton excitedly requested more information on the Jovial satellites if available, and did he have any on the moons of Saturn? He did, as it happened. Newton was also having certain problems with the retardation of Saturn's orbit at its conjunction with Jupiter (the mutual gravity pull affects their orbits as they come together), a phenomenon which was first observed by Horrocks. The two correspondents wished each other a happy new year.

In January 1685 Newton wrote to Greenwich saying, 'Your information about ye error of Kepler's tables for Jupiter and Saturn has eased me of several scruples.' There had been a problem in that Kepler's data for Saturn's relative orbit-radius was slightly too small. Flamsteed had heard of the *De Motu* received by the Royal Society the previous year, surmising that some great endeavour was going on, and was glad to be of assistance; indeed, he was excited at the prospect, having studied Newton's earlier theory of colours and the reflecting telescope with great admiration. But surely, Flamsteed wrote, Newton could not really believe that Saturn and Jupiter could affect each other's motion across such an immensity of space? The reply came on 12 January, that he had an approach of 'diminishing their virtue in a duplicate proportion to their distance...'. That was the first public communication of his belief, in a certain property of the universe to become indelibly associated with his name!

Let's place this correspondence in its historic context:

August 1684 –	Halley visits Newton
December '84	*de Motu* draft given to the Royal Society, explaining central forces and the inverse-square law

December '84   Flamsteed's letter affirms that Kepler's 3rd law
                    applies to the satellites of Jupiter.
Spring '85   First volume of the *Principia* is ready.

In the Spring of 1685, when King Charles died, Newton derived his grand theorem which opened the way to Book Three of the *Principia,* which demonstrated that the gravity pull from a planet acted as if from its centre. By a three-dimensional summation of all the different particles of matter comprising the sphere of the Earth, he showed how they pulled on for example an apple, demonstrating (by a process later to be called integration) that all their masses acted as if from one point, their centre. As this atomistic mode of viewing the sphere of the earth dawned upon him, he spoke of it to no-one, but perhaps marked out the theorem with a stick in the fresh gravel of the Trinity gardens, which the other dons walked around so as not to disturb. He took a great pride in this theorem, choosing to be portrayed in later life with his *Principia* open at its page. During the Victorian bicentenary celebrations of the *Principia*, this theorem was extolled as:

> The great event that stands out by itself in this memorable period
> [1684-6], and forms a dividing point in the history of this wonderful
> work... No sooner had Newton proved this superb theorem... than all
> the mechanism of the universe lay spread before him.'[6]

Not until this had been demonstrated was there a sound basis for performing the Moon-apple computation.

The Flamsteed correspondence resumes in September 1685, with a request by Newton for observations on the 1680 comet, because he now wished to compute its orbit. He conceded Flamsteed's earlier claim (which he had earlier denied) that the 'two comets' espied a fortnight apart had indeed been one and the same. Also, could he send the tidal data he had, preferably indicating the relative heights of spring and neap tides? The tidal information duly arrived, giving times of the high tides and a reply expressed regret that they did not contain measurements of tidal height! That was not the concern of the King's Observator.

Flamsteed was asked to oblige with fixed star co-ordinates against which the path of the great 1680 comet had passed. It would be a few years before that could be available, he replied, 'it will be two or three years ere I can hope to settle ye aequinoctial points accurately amongst the fixed stars'. Years of solar observations were required for Flamsteed to be able to determine these equinoctial points, from which the obliquity of the ecliptic could be calibrated, from which the celestial co-ordinates of the fixed stars could then be accurately derived; however in the meantime he would try to get some reasonably accurate co-ordinates for the stars in the foot of the constellation Perseus as had been requested.

This star-data was sent in celestial latitude and longitude, which was the old method as used by Kepler and Hevelius where longitude measure follows the ecliptic: later, all Flamsteed's data was to be expressed in Right Ascension and Declination, as was outlined in 'De Sphaera' by Flamsteed in 1680 and which astronomers have used ever since. His letter concludes, 'Sr I shall ever be willing to serve you & if you please to lay any commands upon me they shall always be faithfully and readily discharged.'

A year rolled by, then in September 1686 Flamsteed received a letter from his mathematical colleague concerning Cassini's observation that Jupiter was flattened at the poles, adding cryptically, 'If this were certain it would conduce much to ye stating ye reason of ye praecession of ye Equinox.'(3.9.1686) Flamsteed definitely confirmed this observation – newly revealed by telescope observation – but made no attempt to inquire what was going on. Jupiter appeared as more oblate than the other planets, and this could be related to its faster rate of rotation, could it not? Some titanic logic process was occurring: no astronomer in history had ever accounted for the motion of the earth's axis, i.e. the precession of the equinoxes.

The slowing of clocks at the equator was the start of the argument, suggesting that there was a bulge around the equator, confirmed by the oblate shape of Jupiter, but then what? If the pull of the Sun was used to account for the rotation of the plane of the lunar orbit around the earth in 19 years, could not a similar pull by the Sun and Moon somehow pull on the bulge around the equator? Cosmetic computations purported to show how their gravity pulls could cause the gyration of Earth's axis, once in twenty-six thousand years. This awesome estimate was carried out in September 1686, which gives one some idea of the timescale involved. A few months earlier, when he fumed to Halley that the entire Part III might be suppressed because of Hooke's pretensions, he was then in the very midst of its composition.

The very first mechanical image in the *Principia* is that of circular inertia; two globes revolve around each other, held together by a string.[7] They point to the mystery of absolute space, that the tension in that string measures the rotation rate of the globes – sidereally against the stars. This rotation rate measures the centri*petal* force – the new term invented by Newton for a bucket on a string, or for the Moon round the earth. It is introduced in the *Principia's* Preface as part of a theological argument, concerning absolute space. The previous decade, the converse concept had been first defined, centrifugal force, by Christian Huygens.

Instead of Descartes' plenum of vortices, a 'mechanistic' explanation, Newton substituted attraction across a void. Instead of 'feigning hypotheses for explaining all things mechanically' as had Descartes, he introduced the void with its consequence of action at a distance, while periodically denying that he was doing any such thing. He said (to Bentley) that to suppose gravitation could operate across a vacuum without matter 'is to me so great an absurdity that I believe no man who has in philosophical matters a competent faculty of thinking can ever fall into it'. Yet for all practical purposes this was what he had done.

There may have been an ether-hypothesis for gravitation in the back of his mind, but he realised that he had to keep it out of the *Principia,*; after all was not the meaning of the entire turgid Book II that no fluid medium exerting friction could exist in outer space? This treatise periodically reminds the reader that it does not aim to give the causes of things, but merely to describe them mathematically. This is perhaps the meaning of its disturbing affirmation made at the start, that the principles of philosophy are not philosophical but mathematical.

Jupiter sustains a key argument of the *Principia*, namely the precession of the equinoxes. The question had been raised as to why pendulum clocks run slower at the equator. Was it, as Hooke had argued, because of a bulge at the equator? Telescope observations of Jupiter by Cassini revealed a huge bulge in its equator, and a very fast rotation rate. These sections are adjacent in the Principia, and from them follows on the grandiose deduction as to the precession of the equinoxes, never before grasped: from the slowing of clocks at the equator to the motion of the world-axis.

There is little more that can be gathered about the process of the *Principia's* composition, at least from the correspondence. It is evident that the whole tone of this phase of the correspondence between the mathematician and the astronomer was amicable, building on their mutual respect derived from their comet correspondence of 1680/81. There is no hint of the dire arm-twisting which appeared in the next decade.

A theoretical mechanics forged the link between heaven and earth. A new universe gleamed, rational to the core. The mighty new synthesis, inscrutable to ordinary folk, was (I suggest) eight-dimensional. The major themes welded together were:

* One physics for earth and sky (DESCARTES), in opposition to Aristotle's notion that the sublunary realm was different in kind from that above.*
* A moving Earth (COPERNICUS), in opposition to the 'common sense' stationary-earth theories of Brahe and Ptolemy.
* The laws of planetary motion (KEPLER), rejecting the Greek notion held eg by Galileo that circular motion was perfect and therefore followed by the heavens.

---

* Descartes had devised a full universe, which Newton had to empty out, to introduce centric forces. Descartes had given a purely qualitative scheme of things: any mathematics of vortices was hardly practical. In principle the scheme may have been quantitative but in practice his vortices had the effect of hiding the mathematical problems. He *may* have been the first to realise that circular motion was non-inertial and accelerated, but could not mathematically describe the accelerating force. 'My physics is nothing but geometry,' he admitted.

219

* An inverse square law of gravity (HOOKE), in contrast with the traditional notion that levity applied to Air and Fire, and gravity only to Earth and Water.
* The void (BOYLE), as the medium the planets moved through, in opposition to the vortices of Descartes, and the Aristotelian notion that 'Nature abhors a vacuum'.
* The Concept of impetus (BURIDAN), developed into the notion of straight-line inertial motion by Descartes and Hooke, to account for why the planets kept in their motions.
* GALILEO's treatment of free fall, showing acceletation.
* An infinitesimal calculus (BARROW, LEIBNIZ) for dealing with motion by which both the parabola of free-fall and the ellipse of a planetary orbit could be subsumed under one law.

A Dynasty Ends

England in the mid-1680s was cold.* The winter of 1683/4 was such that Pepys was asked to write a memoir about the special cold for the Royal Society. It described how the sea froze two miles out from land such that not a ship could come or go, how oxen were roasted on the Thames, chamber-pots froze under beds and inkwells turned solid by the fireside. Coaches, carts and horses were driven across the Thames, and a trade developed for plates struck to commemorate its freezing over, as no-one could recall such a winter. Trees split asunder 'as if lightning-struck' and cattle perished and froze solid, Evelyn's diary recalled. In London, one could hardly see across the street or even scarcely breathe because of the choking fumes from all the coal fires.

After the cold came a summer of drought. For 2 July, Evelyn's diary noted, 'such a drought still continued as never was in my memorie ... the leaves dropping from trees as in Autumn'. The Thames again froze over in the next winter – 'so sharp weather and so long and cruel a frost' Evelyn recorded (1 January 1685), though it was not quite so bad as the previous year. Another summer of drought followed. 'Not any raine for many months,' his diary recorded for May, and then in June, 'The exceeding drowth still continues. Such two winters and summers I had never known,' he added. Then towards the end of June, some rain came.

February of that year saw the death of Charles Stuart, the most popular of all English monarchs. That same year saw a huge majority of Britons turn solidly against

---

* The cause - little did they suspect - lay in an afflicted Sun: from 1645 to 1715 sunspots disappeared from the Sun, the so-called 'Maunder Minimum' period, consisting of three 22-year solar cycles. It was this which lead to the 'little ice age' of the period. The 1680 Gresham lectures found a baffled Astronomer Royal wondering, where had all the recently-discovered sunspots gone to? In 1684 he reporting the occasional single sunspot to the Royal Society, as an object of great rarity.

the Crown, as disaster struck with his successor trying to impose Catholicism on the land. It was the swan-song of absolute monarchy. In February 1687, Newton wrote to members of Trinity College, that, 'If his Majesty be advisd to require a Matter wch cannot be done by Law, no Man can suffer for neglect of it,'[8] urging that his university oppose king James' attempt to impose Catholicism. It is doubtful whether those words had been true hitherto, but they became true very soon after with the Glorious Revolution.

The transition from Stuart to Hanover was climactic and irrevocable, as the old meaning of monarchy departed forever. Charles II had 'touched' some hundred thousand people to heal them, and in the last year of his reign, people were even killed in the crush to enter the palace for treatment of 'the King's evil' as it was called. Queen Anne 'touched' only one person, Samuel Johnson, but without success. Such a practice could no longer make sense.

William of Orange had no royal blood but had risen in Dutch politics through the third Anglo-Dutch war of 1672, when he heroically let in the sea as his great ancestor had done, and thereby repelled the British and French invaders. The year in which the *Principia* rolled off the press saw him as then the most popular Protestant hero in Europe, having married, the 14-year old niece Mary of Charles II. He sent an envoy to London, to inquire about whether Britons wanted a new monarch!

April 1688 saw the Declaration of Rights whereby the monarch was deprived of the power to suspend the law of the land. To quote from Christopher Hill, on the new Deist philosophy, 'God was no longer an absolute monarch. He was bound by his own laws, which were those of reason.'[9] In November 1688, Louis XIV declared war against the Dutch, and Germany.

In January 1689, Newton and several other MPs dined with William, a week before the latter was offered the crown of England as the consort of Queen Mary. William of Orange took the English crown to finance his wars against Louis XIV. Of him it was said, 'William's life was warmed by hate rather than love ... a passionate fire ever glowed within him. Everything – wealth, health and happiness – was subordinated to his desire to destroy the menacing power of the French monarchy,' and when he died, it was 'in a unique odour of unpopularity'.

At the dawn of the eighteenth century, the sole university where Newtonian science was taught was Edinburgh, by David Gregory. William Whiston, who succeeded Newton in the Lucasian chair at Cambridge in 1701, referred enviously to Gregory's position, adding 'while we at Cambridge, poor wretches, were ignominiously studying the fictitious hypotheses of the Cartesian'.[10] Not until 1710 did a textbook appear on the new Newtonian physics, written by Samuel Clarke, a Cambridge Fellow, for use by students. It was a traditional textbook on Descartes' physics, but Clarke composed extensive footnotes on a Newtonian note refuting the main text. The main Cartesian physics textbook continued to be used by Cambridge students until at least 1730.[11]

Ingratitude

As the sombre opening chord of some huge symphony, Book III opens with the motion of Jupiter's four observed satellites, and how they demonstrate the 3rd law of Johannes Kepler. This is thanks to the author's having received precise new observations from the most accurate astronomer in the world. In later editions, he deleted all acknowledgement thereto, as by temperament he could not bear to acknowledge the giants upon whose shoulders he stood. The Jupiter-moon orbits could be observed directly as ellipses and timed unequivocally, whereas ascertaining that the planetary orbits were likewise elliptical was very much more difficult. No-one knew well the Sun's distance and a rough notion of the size of the solar system was only then coming into focus. Nowhere does the *Principia* use absolute distances; its solar system distances are given as relative to the astronomical unit, viz. Earth's distance from the Sun, and the moon's distance from Earth is given in terms of Earth-radii.

Books I and II were theoretical and in a sense 'just' mathematical, but now with the opening of Book III the titanic implications of using Kepler's 3rd law in a context never suspected by him, viz. the four Galilean moons of Jupiter, becomes evident. We are here at the core meaning of 'universe' which means (in Latin) 'turning as one.' The little moons – no longer called the Medician stars but not yet named as Io, Europa, Ganymede and Callisto – are faithfully expressing the 3/2 power law, turning together.

Satellitum tempora periodica.

1d. 18h. 28′$\frac{3}{5}$.   3d. 13h. 17′$\frac{9}{10}$.   7d. 3h. 59′$\frac{3}{5}$.   16d. 18h. 5′$\frac{1}{5}$.

Distantiæ Satellitum à centro Jovis.

Ex Observationibus	1.	2	3	4	
Cassini	5.	8.	13.	23.	
Borelli	5$\frac{2}{3}$.	8$\frac{2}{3}$.	14.	24$\frac{2}{3}$.	
Tounlei *per Micromet.*	5,51.	8,78.	13,47.	24,72.	Semidiam.
Flamstedii *per Microm.*	5,31.	8,85.	13,98.	24,23.	Jovis.
Flamst. *per Eclips. Satel.*	5,578.	8,876.	14,159.	24,903.	
Ex temporibus periodicis.	5,578.	8,878.	14,168.	24,968.	

It was surely the appropriate place for Book III to start, being what astronomers call, a 'one-body problem.' Further on, Newton will grapple with the two-body problem in which the Sun as well as all the planets move around their combined centre of mass: Jupiter pulls on the Sun as well as vice-versa. But, such effects can here be ignored because Jupiter is so huge in comparison to its tiny moons. Also their nearly circular orbits make their orbit-radii easy to compute (in relation to Jupiter's size), so Kepler's first and second laws are not relevant.

The two giants preceding Newton had been Galileo and Kepler. The former found what he called the four *stella Medici* i.e moons of Jupiter - here used to test the 3rd law of Kepler as published in his *Harmonices Mundi* of 1618. The whole context within which Kepler presented his great discovery – the world-harmony, the music of the heavens, the world-soul, etc – is dismissed, and instead the matter is re-formulated in terms of weight, inertia and gravity. Wrenched away from the context he gave to it, Kepler's 3rd law became the cornerstone of the new, mechanical philosophy, his name unmentioned. No longer did angels or intelligences draw the planets round, but only gravity.

The table shows how the closest moon Io orbits at between five and six Jupiter-radii away from its parent planet. All measurements here are relative distances, the agreement here being *exact* to one part per thousand. That is a lot closer than anyone could obtain for the planetary distances – the notion of achieving and working to such precision was an entirely new thing. That could never be achieved for Newton's 'Moon-test' as we'll see: bound with various approximations, it could not go beyond 1 per cent accuracy.

Luna cannot be plural in the *Principia*, any more than it could for Galileo. Galileo could not discover the 'moons of Jupiter' (contrary to most accounts of the subject) because Luna was a proper noun, like Mars: no-one could add an 'e' onto it. What he found, were the four 'stella Medici'. Newton here uses the same word 'planetae' as did Galileo – for what *we* call moons.

Flamsteed was properly acknowledged in the First Edition, both for the high-precision data and for having suggested the idea. As the Table indicates, only the data supplied by Richard Towneley (a North-country astronomer) might be as accurate as that of Flamsteed.

Years later in the 3rd edition, when Flamsteed was dead and gone, all mention of him was deleted. This is the man who *first assured him* that these moons adhered to that Kepler law. That was his reward for all his hard work, guiding Newton in the right direction over the 1680 comet, supplying high-precision data of the moons of Jupiter, plus the most accurate ever lunar data, etc. While composing his *Principia*, Flamsteed

The four 'Galilean' moons of Jupiter, showing their size in relation to parent planet.

223

Phenomenon 1. *Lines drawn from the satellites of Jupiter to its centre sweep out equal areas in equal times, and the periods of revolution of the satellites, measured against the background of the fixed stars, are proportional to their distances from the centre, raised to the power three over two.*

This is confirmed by astronomical observations. The orbits of these satellites do not differ observably from circles centred on Jupiter, and they move round in these circles at constant speeds. Astronomers agree that the periods are indeed proportional to the radii raised to the power three over two, and this can be seen clearly from the following table:

The periods of the satellites of Jupiter.

$1^d.18^h.27'.34''. \quad 3^d.13^h.13'.42''. \quad 7^d.3^h.42'.36''. \quad 16^d.16^h.32'.9''.$

Distances of the satellites from the centre of Jupiter, as multiples of the radius of Jupiter.

By observation	1	2	3	4
Borelli	$5\frac{2}{3}$	$8\frac{2}{3}$	14	$24\frac{2}{3}$
Towneley *by microm*	5·52	8·78	13·47	24·72
Cassini *by telescope*	5	8	13	23
Cassini *by eclipse sat.*	$5\frac{2}{3}$	9	$14\frac{23}{60}$	$25\frac{3}{10}$
By period.	5·667	9·017	14·384	25·299

Proposition 1 of Book 3 of the 1627 3rd Edition of the Principia, showing compete erasure of Flamsteed's name.

was the main and almost the only person he had corresponded with. The new data in this 3rd Edition is of course more accurate, by a couple of orders of magnitude, as one would expect after several decades* - but that cannot excuse what is by any standards gross betrayal and treachery.

Newton kept alluding to his work in Book III as 'philosophy' which sounds to us rather strange: it could be more like '*la mechanique celeste*' to use the French term.

'Theology Aside ...'[12]

The style of 'glacial remoteness' rolls implacably on through the *Principia's* five hundred pages, but on occasion a more personal note is struck when its author pays homage to his muse and deity, at its beginning and at the end. The Preface to the first edition commences by discussing the relation of mechanics to geometry,

---

* Sidereal periods for the first two Jovian satellites, Io and Europa, are here exact to within a single second. He has attained six-figure accuracy, these being almost the most accurate values given in this tome; which may help us to appreciate why Book III started off with them. We are reminded of how, for Newton, sidereal periods were absolute, meaning in the Mind of God. Only his lunar-month values, tropical and sidereal, were more exact, by an order of magnitude.

reversing the age-old Platonic ordering: instead of having a demiurge for whom the truths of geometry pre-existed the creation of a world, here a vision of the Divine Artificer is given, for whom geometry is an abstraction from the principles of 'rational mechanics':

> But as artificers do not work with perfect accuracy, it comes to pass that mechanics is so is distinguished from geometry that what is perfectly accurate is called geometrical; what is less so, is called mechanical. However, the errors are not in the art, but in the artificers. He that works with less accuracy is an imperfect mechanic; and if any could work with perfect accuracy, he would be the most perfect mechanic of all, for the description of right lines and circles, upon which geometry is founded, belongs to mechanics... It is the glory of geometry that from those few principles, bought from without, it is able to produce so many things. Therefore geometry is founded in mechanical practice, and is nothing but that part of rational mechanics which accurately proposes and demonstrates the art of measuring.

Briefly the clouds part, to reveal the divine Artificer, subject to no human limitations of inaccuracy, Blake's figure of Urizen measuring the deep. This Preface clearly introduces the opus as a work on geometry.

At the conclusion of the treatise the adoration properly due to this Being is explained:

> 'We know him only by his most wise and excellent contrivances of things, and final causes; we admire him for his perfections; but we reverence and adore him on account of his dominion: for we adore him as his servants...'

The new deity ascends not so much into the sky as into the fabric of space: 'He endures forever, and is everywhere present; and, by existing always and everywhere, he constitutes duration and space.' The notion of a deity whose presence 'constitutes duration and space' was further developed in *Optics* of 1704, where space was said to be the sense-organ or 'sensorium' of the deity, which shocked a lot of people. This was toned down in the next edition to, 'like a sensorium'. Otherwise, how could the deity tell what was going on?

From His vantage-point of absolute space, the Newtonian deity was able to perceive the real and absolute quantities of matter and motion, as opposed to the merely relative measures experienced by human sense. The Preface to the *Principia* stressed this distinction:

'Nor do those less defile the purity of mathematical and philosophical truths, who confound real quantities with their relative and sensible measures.'

It was vital to distinguish real from merely apparent motion, otherwise one would be 'defiling the purity of mathematical and philosophical truth'. The difficulty here lies in discovering the true motions of things, 'because the parts of that immovable space, in which those motions are performed do by no means come under the observation of our senses'. As we are moving about, and so too is the Earth, and so even is the Sun, how can we hope to achieve that ascent from the merely human perception of relative motion to the contemplation of motion in absolute and immovable space as perceived by the deity Himself? Difficult though such a task might be, it was the very *raison d'etre* for this treatise, its author affirmed in the Preface; 'For to this end it was that I composed it.'*

A mere five years after the *Principia's* publication, its author's advice was being sought for a course of theology lectures: the 'Boyle lectures', set up by the will of Robert Boyle, who died in 1691. Like Canute facing the incoming tide, the lecturer had to attempt to stem the tide of unbelief unleashed by the new philosophy. Christopher Hill referred to 'the sort of tolerance, born of indifference, which finally triumphed in 1689.'[13] The first set of these lectures was delivered by Richard Bentley, a cleric who had made strenuous efforts to comprehend the *Principia* and had also corresponded with Newton in preparation for the lectures. 'Sir;' explained Newton in his first letter to Bentley in 1692 (Corr. 3, p.233):

'When I wrote my treatise [i e., the *Principia*] about our Systeme, I had an eye upon such principles as might work wth considering men for the belief of a Deity & nothing can rejoice me more than to find it usefull for that purpose... The same power, whether natural or supernatural, which placed this sun in the centre of the six primary planets, placed Saturn in the centre of the orbs of his five secondary planets, placed Jupiter in the centre of his four secondary planets; and the earth in the centre of the moon's orb; and therefore, had this cause been a blind one without contrivance or design, the sun would have been a body of the same kind with Saturn, Jupiter and the earth; that is, without light or heat. Why there is one body in our system qualified to give light and heat to all the rest, I know no reason, but because the

---

* The cryptic sentence belongs here, 'They do violence to sacred scripture who interpret these words as concerning measured quantities here.' (Proinde vim inferunt Sacris literis quivoces hasce de quantitatibus mensuratis ibi interpetandur). This is in his Scholium where the Definitions are set up. Quite what these have to do with sacred scripture, has remained obscure.

Author of the system thought it convenient: and why there is but one body of this kind, I know no reason, but because one was sufficient to warm and enlighten all the rest.'

The first argument here advanced for the existence of a deity was based on the Sun being bright and hot, and not cold and dark. From this the letter progressed to an argument for design using the nearly circular orbits of the planets. Left to themselves, it was explained, they would have developed far more elliptical orbits, like the comets. It was thanks to the 'Divine arm' that these planetary orbits, excepting those of Mars and Mercury, were almost perfect circles.[14] A further letter explained how the deity also held the stars apart. A few years later, Bentley became Master of the College of the Blessed Trinity at Cambridge, which seems appropriate.

Richard Bentley developed a knack for turning the propositions of the *Principia* into arguments of divinity and expatiated thereon from the pulpit of St Martin's in the Fields in London. His sermons became the first popular exposition of the new physics, passing through five editions in five years. The new physics was first publicly presented and debated in religious terms, by the Church of England.

Bentley's lectures were used to combat the threats of atheism and sedition, because they showed how each station of society had its proper place, just as gravity kept the planets in order. Other eminent Newtonian clerics such as Samuel Clarke and William Whiston in turn gave Boyle Lectures, so that they became 'the most influential and consistently republished lectures ever delivered during the eighteenth century'.[15] 'For God's sake keep Sir Isaac Newton at work, that we may have... His thoughts about God' wrote a colleague of David Gregory's to him.[16] Advice from the new mage was eagerly sought to combat irreligion.

As power shifted, the Church was obliged to alter its attitude towards the Epicurean philosophy of atomism, which it had traditionally loathed. The mechanical philosophy had been adopted by leading luminaries such as Isaac Barrow and Robert Boyle as the base for a broad and tolerant Anglicanism. These moderates were known by the curious name of 'Latitudinarians'. Their views found little favour among the Anglican hierarchy, though they enjoyed a modest esteem amongst London intellectuals. This situation changed abruptly with the Glorious Revolution of 1688, which shook the authority of the Anglican church. 'The effect [of the Glorious Revolution] on the church's morale was close to devastating' commented M.C. Jacob.[17,18] In a nutshell the Anglican church had staunchly backed the Divine Right of Kings and then the king turned out to be Catholic. For the Anglican church to hold itself together, a readjustment suddenly became necessary. The 'Latitudinarians' found themselves propelled to centre stage, as having a suitably cohesive and tolerant philosophy. The Whig politicians looked favourably upon it:

227

> 'Newton's mechanical universe controlled by mathematical laws and rules of right reasoning... Became the natural model for the triumph of the Whig constitution.'[19]

Newton dropped some further hints in his *Optics* concerning the intricate task of the divine Artificer, in readjusting a universe that would otherwise tend to move out of kilter. Such examples could not be prevented from multiplying, and eventually there turned out to be scarcely any limit to such instances of divine providence. George Cheyne, who had enjoyed a brief encounter with the master in his mathematical days, became one of the most esteemed doctors of the time and composed a treatise on 'natural religion' based on Newtonian principles. He there explained how Providence had designed the waters at Bath to enable the English to cope with their weather and diet. Deism spread through the eighteenth-century mind like a new contagion.

Enthusiasm and Apocalypse

In the autumn of 1707, Newton advised the Scottish mathematician David Gregory that 'King Louis shall be made a prisoner in the present war, and shall be kept betwixt an Iron Grate on one side and a Fire on the other'. He was reporting the views of Fatio de Duillier, who had recently returned from France. Newton added to Gregory that 'We shall clearly understand' the meaning of such prophecies only when they came to be fulfilled, but not before.[20] He totally believed these prophecies, as Margaret Jacobs has emphasised – and his general philosophy here was that we are to understand them only after their fulfilment. Gregory betrayed no trace of scepticism in his report of this conversation.

In earlier days Newton and Fatio de Duillier had discussed many issues, from calculus to chemistry. Fatio had published a treatise, on how vines could be grown better by adjusting the angle of the wall on which they grew to maximise sunlight. An early letter from Fatio to Newton had revealed the alchemic secret of the Great Work, concluding with instructions to burn the letter. No one else could get away with writing letters of such a tenor to him. When the two met up again in the new century, Fatio was enjoying his new role of secretary to some French peasant prophets, the 'Camisards'. The two discussed the fate of the Catholic king Louis XIV as the Anti-Christ and whore of Babylon, and how he would soon be defeated and captured, the 'iron grate and fire' motif being symbols from Revelations. The 'Camisard' prophets would fall into trances in the streets of London, which the authorities found rather trying. Their inspired utterances, recorded by Fatio as their secretary, pertained to the imminent downfall of the Roman church and the overthrow of the French king, within the first decade of the eighteenth century. However much Britons might sympathise with such a goal, the promotion of regicide was quite beyond the pale and so members of this sect along with Fatio ended up in the stocks at Charing Cross.

William Whiston took over Newton's Lucasian professorship at Trinity after the latter had moved to London. He gave the Boyle lectures in 1707, but then found himself expelled from Cambridge in 1710 as an outright anti-Trinitarian. His presence was always bad news for Newton, because Whiston knew his secret views on theology and was not prepared to be discreet about the awful heresy. As President of the Royal Society, Newton threatened to resign if Whiston were admitted as a Fellow. It did not help that he had published his prophecy of the Second Coming for 1716, the year of a major solar eclipse, which nourished the apocalyptic tenor of the Camisard prophets.[21]

In 1715 there came a blistering attack on Newtonian theology from Leibniz, in a letter to Princess Caroline, his former pupil at Hanover. He sarcastically noted that:

> 'According to their doctrine, God Almighty wants to wind up his watch from time to time, otherwise it would cease to move. He had not, it seems, sufficient foresight to make it a perpetual motion.'[22]

Princess Caroline passed it on to Samuel Clarke to reply. Clarke was Newton's parish priest at Piccadilly, and no correspondence survives between them since they were neighbours. As a clergyman, Clarke became notorious for his heretical Arian belief. Voltaire recounts the quip that Clarke would be the best man in the Kingdom for the See of Canterbury if only he were a Christian. Clarke never spoke out about his heresy[23] – unlike William Whiston, whose demise became the theme of Goldsmith's comedy 'The Vicar of Bray' – and thereby managed to avoid expulsion from office.

Samuel Clarke was, one hardly need add, assisted by Newton in composing his replies. 'The true glory of God's workmanship,' intoned Clarke, to Princess Caroline, in the heat of his great debate with Leibniz, 'is that nothing is done without His continual government and inspection.' But could a deity be kept on duty in this manner, would not His station grow increasingly vacant with the advance of science? The debate lasted five rounds or ten letters in all, terminating with the death of Leibniz.

The letters which passed between these two were collected and edited by Pierre Desmaiseaux, who was one of an international circle of freethinkers and materialists. He relished the spectacle of the two great philosophers clashing on theological issues. It was his view, and that of others besides, that the Newtonian system could be turned quite away from the deistic context its author had framed. To some, it came to appear as if the Newtonians had 'by their avowal of the new mechanical philosophy as the foundation of natural religion, effectively undermined all religion'.[24] This had indeed been the thrust of Leibniz's letter to Princess Caroline, above-quoted, about how 'natural religion itself, seems to decay [in England] very much,' which placed the blame squarely with the Newtonian natural philosophers.

Heeding the sage advice of Stephen Shapin – 'After two and a half centuries the Newton-Leibniz disputes continue to inflame the passions... Only the very learned (or the very foolish) dare to enter upon this great killing-ground of the history of ideas',[25] we shall refrain from entering further into such deep waters.

In the early eighteenth century, one quarter of all Fellows of the Royal Society were Freemasons, and the proportional overlap between these two societies reached a maximum during the years of Newton's presidency. It would be an understatement to say this was a little-discussed fact. The 'new philosophy' was supposed to have been promoted by the force of the rational intellect, and not by a peculiar handshake. The Great Architect revealed and proclaimed by the *Principia* turned out to be very congenial to the views of Masonry (Although Newton himself was *never* a Freemason). A generally Deist outlook was promoted at its rituals. The Grand Lodge of London established in 1717 was, like the Royal Society, an all-male club. Much the same group of Whigs came to dominate both the Royal Society and the Grand Lodge of London. Ms Jacobs' researches have shown how Freemasonry, a 'uniquely British institution', rapidly spread from London into the provinces and thence into 'almost every European urban centre'.

'The Newtonian and Whig leadership of the Royal Society, whose authority had been enhanced by Newton's own presidency, guided the Grand Lodge in its formative years,'* concluded Ms Jacob.[26] For example, Brook Taylor was a Freemason, and Secretary of the Royal Society in the early eighteenth-century, and his book *Some Reflections relating to the First Principles of General Philosophy* showed his concern to establish a fully rational and coherent natural religion based on Newtonian principles. At the Grand Lodge, aristocrats and bourgeoisie would mingle on an equal footing, and would discuss power, the ladder of social success and the expansion of Masonry through Europe. Soon there were few artisans left in the fashionable London lodges. The celebrated apple myth was first related to the world in 1726 by two eminent Freemasons who were also fellows of the Royal Society; Martin Folkes and George Stukeley.

Over a million words on theology were left by Sir Isaac to posterity, all unpublished. His niece, Catherine Barton, inherited what became known as the

---

* Of the two hundred or so Fellows of the Royal Society in 1725, fifty-nine were masons, i.e. more than one in four. See 'The Royal Society and Early Grand Lodge Freemasonry,' J. R. Clarke, *Ars Quatuor Coronatorum,* 1967, 80, p.111. This fact is totally ignored in for example Michael Hunter's 'History of the Royal Society,' 1989. Membership of Masonic lodges is no longer published, but was then.

Portsmouth Collection of Newton's unpublished papers and requested in her will
that efforts be made to publish its 'Tracts relating to Divinity', but nothing came
of this – she may not have appreciated the magnitude of the theological heresy
contained therein.

Much of his unpublished manuscript material is rather strange:

> 'At the sounding of the fifth Trumpet, the bottomless pit was opened
> with a key to let out a false religion... It continued open till the
> sounding of the seventh trumpet ... So then the seven trumpets and
> seven thunders are but several names of one & the same temple-
> music and are synchronal to the seven vials of wrath, as may appear
> by their being the prophecy of one and the same page of the sealed
> book.'

Rightly or wrongly, these private reflections by the ageing sage have been exposed to
the public gaze by Castillejo. He detected an 'expanding force' irradiating through
them.[27] In such passages one does indeed find number symbolisms, maybe patterns
of three, five, seven and of eight. Castillejo pointed out that the layout of *Optics* had
been structured by such patterns, which may be of interest, but otherwise one may
feel uneasy at perusing texts not evidently intended for public view. Brewster viewed
such texts as being a mode of reverie, as relaxation and unwinding after the day's
hard toil.

Newton was a mortalist, seeing the doctrine of an immortal soul as a corruption
of primitive Christianity. There could be no consciousness after death, nor could
the soul exist without the body. On Judgement Day however, the fortunate 'good'
souls would be resurrected from out of their graves, while the wicked would stay
dead forever. As Iliffe puts it, 'no-one could go anywhere until they were judged...
until they were resurrected the dead could not experience any consciousness'.[28] He
denied evil spirits or personal demons, denied the devil, was rumoured to outright
deny the Incarnation, the Trinity, Transubstantiation, etc and held that Christ was
God by office not by nature:

> 'If there was one greater heresy than denial of the Trinity or the
> immortality of the soul, it was the rejection of the existence of
> the demonic hordes and the archfiend himself. In an age when
> leading members of the Royal Society catalogued case histories of
> witches, demons and ghosts as evidence for the reality of spirits (in
> turn used as pivotal proof for the existence of God), denial of evil
> spirits (as opposed to mere skepticism about particular witchcraft
> cases) was viewed as beyond the pale of Christianity...Those who
> discounted the ontological reality of these malevolent beings did so

against the powerful weight of tradition and the passionate rhetoric of orthodoxy. And yet this is exactly what Newton did.'[29]

'Sometime in the 1680s, Satan for Newton had been transformed from an angel of darkness into a symbol for the spirit of error … Newton began to dismiss the reality of demons beginning in the 1680s.'[30] This was all damnable heresy, and in some respects quite Islamic. Royal Society members would never have let him in through the door had they known the depth of his unbelief. The last Antitrinitarians had been burnt at the stake in 1612, at Smithfield. But times were a-changing, and William Whiston merely lost his post in 1710 after a public denial of the Trinity.[31]

So much did Newton empty out from the universe, from the world that people had thought they lived in. Nearly everything, it turned out, was empty space:

> 'Newton's universe, when stripped of metaphysical considerations, as stripped it would be, is an infinite void of which only an infinitesimal part is occupied by unattached material bodies moving freely through the boundless and bottomless abyss, a colossal machine made up of components whose only attributes are position, extension, and mass.'[32]

There was, it turned out, nothing in the world except small balls:

> 'God in the beginning form'd matter in solid, massy, hard, impenetrable, moveable particles… and these primitive Particles being Solids, are incomparably harder than any porous Bodies compounded of them; even so very hard as never to wear or break in pieces.' (*Optics*, Query 31, 1706)

For the classic statement of this predicament we turn to *The Metaphysical Foundations of Modern Science* by A.E. Burtt, written in 1924:

> 'The cosmic order of masses in motion according to law, is itself the final good. Man exists to know and applaud it; God exists to tend and preserve it. All the manifold divergent zeals and hopes of men are implicitly denied scope and fulfilment; if they cannot be subjected to the aim of theoretical mechanics, their possessors are left no proper God, for them there is no entrance into the kingdom of heaven. We are to become devotees of mathematical science; God, now the chief mechanic of the universe, has become the cosmic conservative...
>
> 'To stake the present existence and activity of God on imperfections in the cosmic engine was to court rapid disaster in

theology...In short, Newton's cherished theology was rapidly peeled off by all the competent hands that could get at him, and the rest of his metaphysical entities and assumptions, shorn of their religious setting, were left to wander naked and unabashed through the premises of subsequent thought, unchallenged by thorough criticism because supposed as eternally based as the positive scientific conquests of the man who first annexed the boundless firmament to the domain of mathematical mechanics. Space, time and mass became regarded as permanent and indestructible constituents of the infinite world-order... The only place left for God was in the bare irreducible fact of intelligible order in things...

'Wherever was taught as truth the universal formula of gravitation, there was also insinuated as a nimbus of surrounding belief that man is but the puny and local spectator, nay irrelevant product of an infinite self-moving engine, which existed eternally before him, enshrining the rigour of mathematical relationships while banishing into impotence all ideal imaginations; an engine which consists of raw masses wandering to no purpose in an undiscoverable time and space, and is in general wholly devoid of any qualities that might spell satisfaction for the major interests of human nature, save solely the central aim of the mathematical physicist.' (pp. 297, 299)

'Through his words blew the chill winds of death for Christianity', opined Richard Westfall, 'for Newton equated Christ with reason and pruned Christianity of all supernatural elements.'[33]

Chapter 10

Jason, The Golden Fleece, And the Turning Of The Zodiac

> 'When the Sphere was first formed, the Solstice was in the fifteenth degree or middle of the Constellation of *Cancer*: then it came into the twelfth, eighth, fourth, and first degree successively.'
>
> Newton, *Chronology,* p.82.

The 'Chronology of the Ancient Kingdoms, Amended' by Isaac Newton was arguably the only book to be reviewed, criticised and dismissed before it had even been published. It came about in this manner. Caroline, Princess of Wales had come to hear of a new system of chronology developed by the illustrious Master of the Mint. The thunder-clouds of the disputes over theology and calculus had passed away with the death of Leibniz, and a new issue now made its appearance at the court. Princess Caroline was advised of this new matter by the Abbé Conti, a French aristocrat who had functioned quite successfully as an intermediary in the calculus dispute, as was witnessed by the fact that Newton was still speaking to him. In the year 1716, Conti advised the Princess that a whole new method for dating the events of antiquity was at hand.

Upon the royal request, an 'Abstract' was drawn up, whereby Newton cast his views on chronology into 'that shape the properest for her perusal'. At this point, we respectfully relate the opinion of Westfall to the reader; that the *Chronology* was a watered-down version of the *Origines*, a polemical and unpublishable opus which Newton composed in the 1680s, concurrently with the *Principia*, which had surveyed how erroneous theologies of antiquity came to develop and diverge from the pure patriarchal religion as Noah received it. Therefore, opined Westfall, upon the royal request, Newton:

> 'had even less desire to hand over to the Princess of Wales a treatise which might have contained assertions heretical enough to secure his instant dismissal from the Mint. Well-schooled as he was in the art of delay, he pleaded that the work was 'imperfect and confus'd...'[1]

The *Chronology* was not so much about theology, but about the dating system to be applied to the events of antiquity, and one is puzzled by the claim that it contained heretical material. Its author's hesitancy would more likely have been due to the speculative nature of the argument. Conti was also given a copy, on the strict promise that he wouldn't show it to anyone, or so Newton later claimed.

The Last Controversy

Returning to France, Conti proudly displayed his new acquisition, which however contained no argument, but only a series of dates. The experts could discern therefrom only a curiously truncated version of the dates of antiquity. Queries by Conti concerning its basis encountered a wall of silence. Finally, a Jesuit chronologer, Father Etienne Souciet, was shown Conti's manuscript, and prepared some learned queries which were forwarded to John Keill, the Oxford astronomer and faithful protégé. Keill obtained in 1720 a verbal reply from Newton and so sent a letter back to Paris. The Parisian cognoscenti were advised that the chronology was a mere abstract of a longer work, that its dating was based on astronomical principles, but that 'he hath not set down the proofs'. In Newton's conversation with Keill, the central nature of the Argonaut expedition in the dating system was for the first time revealed.

Keill's letter, sent to Brook Taylor, former Secretary of the Royal Society then living in Paris,[2] explained tersely how the precession of the equinoxes against the stars of the zodiac was the basis for a radical new chronology system:

> 'According to his best remembrance he (Newton) found that the ancients had recorded that at the time of the Argonauts Chiron had found the equinoctial point to be in the middle or 15th degree of the constellation Aries. In Meton's time it was found to be in the 8th and in Hipparchus' in the 4th degree of the constellations. Hipparchus reckoned the precession to be one degree every seventy-two years and by that means if we compute we shall find the time of the Argonautical expedition to have fallen out at the time Sir Isaac puts it.'[3]

Queries were raised by this laconic and casual recollection from memory whereby the French academies were informed of the complete re-dating of past history. Did the constellation Aries have a 15th degree? The Zodiac with its 360 degrees was not invented prior to the 6th century BC.*

---

* Otto Neugebauer had concluded: .'..hence the change from the older irregular zodiacal constellations to the familiar coordinates of longitude seems to have taken place around 500 BC.' History of Ancient Mathematical Astronomy, II, 1975, p.593.

The astronomer Hipparchus certainly had no such exact idea of precession rate. The 'Abstract' began with calm but outrageous claim that 'there may be errors of 5 or 10 years, and sometimes 20, but not much above'.

Was this to be the carbon-14 of eighteenth-century chronology? Was its venerable author poised to take over chronology as he had done with astronomy, physics and optics? After this astronomical time-key had been released, it gradually became evident as the years ticked by that nothing further was in the pipeline. Jason, the Golden Fleece and the motion of the zodiac hovered adrift in a mid-channel limbo. Princess Caroline treasured her copy of the chronology but Conti, fortunately for our tale, held forth about it over dinners.

A copy of the manuscript finally came into the hands of the French chronologer Nicolas Fréret, the secretary and one of the most distinguished members of the Académie des Inscriptions et Belles-Lettres, and he decided to compose a refutation. To refute an unpublished work was unusual. Apologising for this step, a colleague of his later explained:

> 'At the prospect of a revolution about to change the face or at least the perspective of the historical world it was natural, shall we say it was correct, that M.Fréret should become alarmed and that he should move to the frontier to reconnoiter the terrain.'[4]

A publisher was found who agreed to print the French translation with a refutation by Fréret. The latter's comments were fairly deferential, but he shifted the dating of the Argonaut expedition from 936 BC, where Newton had placed it, back five centuries.

The Presidential ire was again aroused – for the very last time – and the *Philosophical Transactions* contained a rebuttal:

> 'as if any Man could be so foolish as to consent to the publishing of an unseen Translation of his Papers, made by an unknown Person, with a confutation annexed, and unanswered at their first Appearance in Publick.' (July/August 1725)

Fury was directed against Conti, now exposed as the mastermind behind the scheme, who had violated a solemn trust as he had earlier, it was now claimed, conspired to drag him into debate with Leibniz. Conti had intervened in the calculus dispute at the request of the king.[5] A Venetian noble, poet and a man of several distinctions, Conti was a favourite of the English king, and acted as a translator as the king spoke no English. In reply, Conti, insulted before the whole of Europe, managed to maintain a commendable sang-froid. 'I apply myself to learning neither to make a fortune nor to acquire a great name,' he replied. 'I study as I travel, that is to say for my pleasure. I like this study very much but it does not at all agitate me. At bottom

I do not hold it in any greater esteem than the quadrille or hunting. It all comes to the same when one examines the matter dispassionately.'[6]

Father Souciet at this point considered himself absolved of the vow of secrecy and came out with a bulky five-volume refutation of the 20-page 'Abstract', dedicated to Conti. 'But why all this mystery?' Souciet inquired. 'Does Newton want to repeat with some new Leibniz the scene that was enacted over the infinitesimal calculus?' He smugly concluded that 'M. Newton's Chronology cannot stand...he has made an error of about 530 years and... mine on the contrary is correct.' Conduitt was concerned about the effect this would have upon the ageing President's constitution, but the latter seemed little perturbed on reading Souciet's attack, regarding the Jesuit as being simply in error.

The scientific war was now on, and continued intermittently for a century, with theologians, historians, astronomers and amateur scholars all joining in the fray. Hardly had it begun when its principal contender died, buried with honours and pomp never before accorded to a European scientist. It seemed fitting that he should pass away in the midst of an international furore. The celestial theme of the controversy only made it more appropriate. This controversy had the great advantage that people could understand its theme, whereas in the calculus dispute few had fathomed the difference between fluxions and differentials. Edmund Halley composed a refutation of the French attack by Father Souciet.

The full *Chronology* appeared posthumously, in 1728, unfairly dismissed by Westfall as, 'A work of colossal tedium, it excited for a brief time the interest and opposition of the handful able to get excited over the date of the argonauts before it sank into oblivion'. The work is an endless torrent of names, with ten times more male names than female at a rough count. Women are normally only mentioned in a passive capacity, such as being mothers or getting abducted – e.g., '1005 BC Andromeda carried away from Joppa by Perseus'. On very rare occasions they are allowed to do something, for example Ceres, a native of Sicily, introduced a neighbouring province to the practice of sowing corn, in 1030 BC.

Chiron or Cheiron appeared in the *Chronology* as having constructed a map of the heavens for Jason, to aid him in navigating the Argo. Chiron may have been the oldest and wisest of the centaurs, but had he really invented the zodiac? Orpheus and Hercules, Castor and Pollux, manned the *Argo*... This ship, Newton explained, was the first long-boat built by the Greeks, and before that they had only sailed close to the shore:

> 'the Flower of Greece were to sail with Expedition through the deep,
> in a long Ship with Sails, and guide the Ship by the Stars.'

As in a Just-So story, the constellation-pictures were explained: Taurus was the bull which Jason tamed; Aries the Ram was the Golden Fleece; the Centaur was Chiron;

Cygnus the Swan belonged to the mother of one of the Argonauts, and so forth. The 'Abstract' had been prepared after Princess Caroline had asked Newton about what form of education was best for her children, concerning antiquity. Newton never voluntarily published this treatise; he kept polishing it up, and after his death a publisher claimed that an agreement had been made. Much of it seems in the nature of reverie.

The President could have obtained much helpful advice from the Astronomer Royal on these matters, had they been on speaking terms. In his *Historia Coelestis,* Flamsteed reviewed the ancient divisions of the zodiac constellations and the motion of the vernal point in relation to ancient history. He somewhat shared Newton's view concerning the antiquity of Jewish astronomical skills, concerning the creation of the world in 4004 BC as Archbishop Ussher had declared in 1630, and of how the first epoch of the world ended with the Flood at around 2348 BC.

Flamsteed did not concur with the compression of time adopted in the *Chronology*, where, for example, the capture of Troy is placed at 904 BC, though ancient writers had placed it at 1200 BC. Solomon's temple Newton placed in the eleventh century BC, and believed that what he called 'the First Memory of Things in Europe' could not be older than the Hebrew culture. In contrast, the oldest astronomical observations known to Flamsteed were those made by the Babylonians, which he dated at 2233 BC. The Preface to his life's work, the *Historia Coelestis Brittanica* quoted the Greek source Porphry:

> 'the Babilonians had observations of the Heavens wrote upon pillars of brick that were 1903 years older than the taking of Babilon by Alaxander the Great.'

Flamsteed's vision of past history thus extended twice as far as did Newton's. The date of 2233 BC was, the Preface explained 'following the Hebrew method of counting time, in the 1771st year of the world'. Flamsteed thus used a dating system based upon the world having begun in 4004 BC. Space may have expanded but time had not; it remained comfortably bound by 4004 BC. This general view of educated persons in the seventeenth century could be disagreed with only at a cost of suspected atheism as Halley discovered when he found himself rejected for the Savilian mathematics post at Oxford because of his belief that the world would just keep going, like clockwork...

A Centaur invents the Zodiac

The solstices (days and nights of maximum or minimum length) and the equinoxes (days and nights of equal length) are events in time which form a cross in space and rotate slowly against the fixed stars. Sir Isaac was the first person to fathom why this motion occurred, by means of the Moon's pull on the bulge of the Earth's equator, generating a rotation once per 26,000 years or one degree per 72 years, or 50' per annum; it is therefore not unexpected that he should come up with a novel application thereof.

He was one of the first to employ the accurate figure of 1° per 72 years, in the *Principia*, as previous astronomers such as Kepler and Brahe had employed a figure of 1° per 70 years, the latter figure having been endorsed by Flamsteed in his 'Gresham Lectures' of 1680.[7] The idea that astronomical events could give a dating to history was straightforward

Farnese globe of second century AD, note Equinoctial Colure at the boundary between Aries and Pisces, where Claudius Ptolemy put it.

enough, as certain eclipse times given by ancient historians had already been used to check ancient chronology.

Newton was using what is referred to as the 'Greek sphere' zodiac, where the terms 'sign' and 'constellation' were synonymous, i.e. the Chaldean perception, where all the star-constellations on the ecliptic were the same 30° in length. The discovery of Chaldean tablets at the turn of the twentieth century revealed that this fixed-star zodiac was the oldest of zodiacs, which had originated in Chaldea whence it spread to Egypt and Greece, and that it largely vanished from Europe when the Arabs took up the moving Ptolemaic zodiac system in about the fifth century A.D. These Chaldean tablets recording the original zodiac, on which Newton's historical computations were in a sense based, are now in the British museum. They give the modern reader a distinct advantage over the eighteenth-century protagonists, who were highly unclear as to where divisions of the celestial firmament had been placed by the astronomers of antiquity.[*]

No star-maps have come down from antiquity. We have only the 'Farnese globe'. Ptolemy's *Almagest* described and identified the

---

* It is through the researches of Otto Neugebaeur and others that the astronomical sphere of the ancient Greeks is now viewed as in essence identical with that of the Chaldeans. Peter Huber ('Ueber den Nullpunkt der Babylonischen Ekliptic' Centaurus, 1958, V, p192-208) analysed Babylonian star catalogues and gave a definition of the Babylonian zodiac in relation to the fixed stars for the year 100 BC The four first magnitude stars Aldebaran, Regulus, Spica and Antares were the chief reference stars for this zodiac system. Greek astronomers refer to Aldebaran as 15° Taurus, this being its position in the Chaldean zodiac, demonstrating that the Greek sphere was identical to the Chaldean.

stars as if he had pictures of the constellations in front of him, and Flamsteed taught himself Greek to become able to construct authentic star-maps from Ptolemy's comments.[8] Flamsteed reckoned his star-positions from the year 1689, so that became the epoch-date from which Newton's chronological computations were performed. Newton borrowed, or rather stole, Flamsteed's star-manuscripts for about ten years, 1705-15, and, and hung on to them to help get a focus on the star-precession argument, on which his chronological dating of history depended.[9]

The Sun at the Vernal Equinox would have stood at zero degrees Aries, of the original star-zodiac, at somewhere around A.D. 220;[10] then, as it takes 21 centuries to move through a sign, it will have stood at 15° Aries at around 900 BC. With that as a general indication, let us look at the computation which Sir Isaac performed:

'939 BC. The ship Argo is built...Chiron, who was born in the golden Age, forms the Constellations for the use of the Argonauts; and places the Solstitial and Equinoctial Points in the fifteenth degrees or middles of the Constellations of Cancer, chelae, Capricorn, and Aries. Meton in the year Nabonassar 316, observed the Summer solstice in the eighth degree of Cancer, and therefore the Solstice had then gone back seven degrees. It goes back one degree in about seventy two years, and seven degrees in about 504 years. Count these years back from the year Nabonassar 316, and they will place the Argonautic expedition about 936 years before Christ.'

The year 'Nabonassar 316' is equivalent to 432 BC. The calculation here performed is $432 + 7 \times 72 = 936$ years.

The old Greek references to the vernal point's position are hazy, and the argument hinges on characters like Meton and Eudoxus of whose works little survives. When Hipparchus in the second century BC came to estimate the precession of the equinoxes, he plainly would have used any data from Eudoxus had it been available. All he did use – as Edmund Halley pointed out, when he was asked to comment on the debate, as Astronomer Royal – were observations by Timocharis, who lived less than 200 years before his time; and from which, Hipparchus could only estimate the vernal point's motion as 1° in 100 years.[11]

The startling fact arises that the date computed by Sir Isaac (936 BC) differs by less than one degree of precession from the actual date when the vernal point would have stood in that position (c. 860-900 BC) – had the zodiac then existed. He did in a very real sense intuit the framework for the original zodiac framework.

JASON, THE GOLDEN FLEECE, AND THE TURNING

Newton's basis for ascribing the 8° position to Meton in the fifth century BC was a Latin source, Columella:

> 'Meton and Euctemon, in order to publish the Lunar Cycle of nineteen years, observed the Summer Solstice in the year Nabonassar 316, the year before the Peloponnesian war began, and Columella tells us that they placed it in the eighth degree of Cancer...'[12]

Columella was writing in the first century A.D., and so a question arises as to how far he can be relied upon for events six centuries earlier. Newton found a reference in Hipparchus, that the astronomer Eudoxus in the fourth century BC:

> 'drew the Colure of the Solstices through...the middle of Cancer...and through the middle of Capricorn; and that he drew the Equinoctial Colure through...the middle of Chelae [Libra], and through...the back of Aries.'[13]

Eudoxus had not ascertained this himself, it was argued, but had merely transcribed it from the zodiac of the Argonauts, because as precession hadn't been discovered there was no reason for Eudoxus to suppose it had moved.[*]

There is a kind of flaw in the argument, that if the Zodiac had been created *such that* the Colures were at 15° of the signs, they would have stayed there. After all, what could have made them move? But they do move in Newton's *Chronology,* as indeed they did in the ancient world, however unclear this may have been. They in fact moved *because* the culture which invented the zodiac did *not* define it in terms of the equinoxes or solstices. By Ptolemy's time in the second century AD, the equinoxes had arrived, as Newton observed, 'in the beginning of the signes,' as shown on the Farnese globe:

---

[*] An early 30-day 12-month solar calendar had put the equinoxes on the 15th days of first and 7th month of the year, and the solstices on the 15th days of the 4th and 10th months of the year. While discussing this schematic solar calendar, Hunger and Pingree commented: 'This positioning of the colures on the 15th continued into early Greek astronomy, when Eudoxus, using zodiacal signs instead of months, set the equinoxes in the middle of Aries and of Libra..' (Hunger & David Pingree, *Astral Sciences in Mesopotamia*, Leiden 1999, p.66; see also Robert Powell, *History of the Zodiac*, 2007, p.66.) 'In [Thales'] youth the Equinoxes were passing out of the 12th into ye 11th degrees of ye signes or Asterisms of Aries & Chelae & his observations might place them in ye 12th degrees. Meton & Euctemon observed the solstice anno J. Per 4282 at wch time the cardinal points were passing out of the 9th into the 8th degrees of the signes. And Columella saith that Meton placed them in the 8th degrees. Afterwards Hipparchus finding the equinoxes nearer the beginning of the signes concluded that they had a motion backwards in respect of the fixed stars, & at length Ptolemy found them in the beginning of the signes.' Manuscript quoted in Manuel, op. cit., pp.75-6: New College Oxford Manuscript III fol. 169

241

'In 1689, the Colurus Aequinoctiam...did then cut the ecliptic in Taurus 6° 44'; by this reckoning the Equinox in the end of the year 1689 was gone back 36° 44'.'[14]

Taurus? The modern reader is somewhat perplexed here. Let's look at the figure for Newton's starting-point, in the tenth century BC, when as he says the solstices would have gone through fifteen degrees of Cancer/Capricorn, and the equinoxes likewise though the centres of Aries/Libra. We agree with Newton that *if* the Zodiac had been invented then, that is where these would have been. He then informs us, correctly, that they slowly moved over the centuries until in Ptolemy's time they were at zero degrees of these signs. This is a 'backwards' motion so that the 'vernal point' (what Newton is calling the 'Equinoctial Colure') will then start moving through Pisces. To have it instead enter Taurus imposes a strain upon our cognitive faculties.

John Flamsteed was then composing his *Historia Coelestis Britannica* and had a substantial section on just these kind of computations, where 1689 was his modern epoch-date. It may be a help to see how he did the stellar calculations of precession – which Newton probably perused, without acknowledgement. In 1689, the star Spica stood at 19°13' of Libra, and if Timocharis made his observation in 295 BC, then precession over 1984 years would put it at 21°58' of Virgo. That is a clockwise motion on the figure here shown. Hipparchus quoted Timocharis on some star-positions especially Spica as his evidence for precession: Flamsteed is checking over these ancient values.

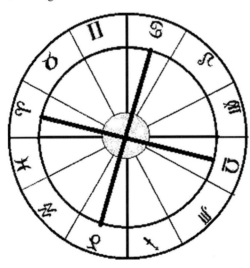

How Newton imagined the four 'coulures' (solstices and equinoxes), originally positioned at midpoints of the (star-zodiac) signs.

Newton's angle of 36° 44' corresponds to 2627 years of history he computed, which was the interval between 1689 and his date when he imagined the zodiac to have been formed. He found, at 6° Leo 'the new longitude of the old *Colurus Solstitiorum* passing through these stars' which is quite an obscure concept. He quoted ancient writers on its motion through their star-zodiac, but his calculations were of star-positions against the tropical zodiac: where the colure (equinox) must always remain at 0° Aries.

JASON, THE GOLDEN FLEECE, AND THE TURNING

Debate

Britain's Astronomer Royal at the time of Anglo-French controversy on the subject, Edmond Halley, was expected to comment concerning Newton's chronological endeavour. Newton had passed away in the previous year. Halley remarked to the effect that, when Hipparchus in the second century BC had estimated the precession of the equinoxes, he would surely have used any data from Eudoxus had it been available, whereas he only used observations by Timocharis, who lived less than 200 years before his time; and from which, Hipparchus estimated the vernal point's motion as 1° in 100 years. Timocharis 'very coarse' measurements were all Hipparchus had to use, Halley explained, whereas Eudoxus, as quoted by Hipparchus, had merely implied that the Colure passed over the back of Aries.[15]

The French critics of Newton's Chronology, Nicholas Fréret and Etienne Souciet, both accepted the dating whereby a Centaur made the zodiac in the tenth century BC, which Halley found rather surprising. The 'Coulure of the Vernal Equinox' had indeed been positioned thus through the back of the Aries constellation, Halley agreed, but as to whether the zodiac was then formed, he wisely refrain from comment. Recomputing Sir Isaac's 36° precessional motion over a period of 2624 years, Halley commented upon the precession of the star v-Arietis (Bayer nomenclature) in the middle of the back of the Aries constellation, as having moved that far in twenty-six centuries.

Halley, like others who joined the debate, made no comment about any zodiac of the stars and thus gave no hint as to what might be the thirty degrees of Aries, with respect to which the ancient astronomers had gauged their different positions of the Vernal point. What Halley wrote was sound but gave little basis for a calibration of ancient chronology which had been the point of the operation.

Father Souciet, apprehending that a sidereal reference was required for Newton's argument, used the only one he knew about, namely that which Copernicus had used, whereby all stellar longitudes were measured from *prima Arietis*. Copernicus, while discussing whether the Earth or Sun had moved, had used that stellar reference. But, would a debate concerning this really help evaluate ancient chronology?

The 'first star of Aries' was 'Mesartim', which Bayer had classified as 'α Arietis'.*

---

* When Halley published his version of Flamsteed's *Historia* in 1712, he used the new Bayer nomenclature in which the main stars of the Aries constellation were given Greek letter names according to their brightness: Alpha-Aries the brightest star is in the brow of the Ram, see figure 3 for Flamsteed's star-map and Table which gives their latitudes and longitudes in Flamsteed's epoch. Thus the star which Ptolemy called 'Prima Arietis' was designated by Bayer as gamma-Arietis because of its brightness. It was called 'Prima Arietis' because as it rose in the sky, it was the first star of Aries one comes across. Thus the old, Arabic names of Hamal for Alpha-Aries and Mesartim for Gamma-Aries were discarded.

Image of Newton 's tomb at Westminster Abbey.

In his reply to Nicholas Fréret, who had published a refutation of the 'Abstract of Chronology', Newton thundered in the Royal Society's *Proceedings*:

'I follow Eudoxus, and, by doing so, place the Equinoctial Colure [ie, the vernal point] about 7° 36' from the first star of Aries. But the Observator [ie, Fréret, who had published his critique anonymously]

244

represents that I place it fifteen degrees from the first star of Aries, and thence deduces that I should have made the Argonautic Expedition 532 Years earlier than I do.'[16]

The star-catalogue of Copernicus[17] took Mesartim to be the 'prime fiducial', i.e. the star from whose position all other stellar positions on the ecliptic were to be measured, in celestial longitude. It is the fixed star on the zodiac nearest to 0° Aries. Fréret had (Powell plausibly has argued) mistakenly supposed that Newton was using the same principle as Copernicus, in* which 15° could be interpreted as 15° east of Mesartim, which is another 7° further East. But that would add on another five centuries to the dating.

At the end of his life, when his interests are mainly ancient history and bible studies, Newton is discussing the vernal point's position - the line where the celestial equator intersects the ecliptic - against the stars for the year (or so) when his mighty *Principia* emerged; how shocked he would have been to learn that he was accurate to one degree within the reference-system of the Babylonians – regarded as a most degenerate culture in his *Chronology.*

Today, one can still make out the 'colure' on the sphere above Newton's tomb at Westminster Abbey, passing over the back of Aries.[18]

In the deep midwinter, near the midnight hour, there rises, far to the South, the large constellation *Argo*, and, following it, *Centaurus,* and, strangely jammed in between these two, a keen eye can detect the constellation *Robur Carolinum,* 'Charles' Oak', depicting an English oak-tree; whereby hangs a curious tale...

---

* 'Newton identified 15° Aries to be in the centre of the constellation of Aries, 7° 36' east of Mesartim (gamma Arietis), the first start of Aries...Freret wrongly assumed that Newton was using the same principle as Copernicus, in which 15° Aries could be interpreted as 15° east of Mesartim.' Robert Powell, *History of the Zodiac* 2007, p.199.

Chapter 11

Gold, Wealth and Empire[1]

In 1707 Great Britain was formed, under the Act of Union, with one coinage established for all of Scotland and England. In the following year, James Thornhill started to paint the magnificent interior of the Painted Hall at Greenwich. That 'Hospital' at Greenwich was designed by Sir Christopher Wren and Nicholas Hawksmoor. On its ceiling today, newly-renovated, we can still admire glorious images of Queen Anne, the last of the Stuart monarchs. Much of the ceiling design concerns great sailing vessels and war-victories.

The Act of Settlement obtained its royal assent in 1701 and named the Electress Sophia of Hanover, the mother of George I, and her descendants as heirs to the British throne. When Anne died in 1714, leaving no heir, that Act of Settlement established that the ever-unpopular George I became the new monarch, Sophia having also died. He had come over from Hanover with his family and could speak no English. Thornhill, working on the giant mural, had to adjust his plans, and designed on the West Wall an attempt to legitimise the new royal dynasty. Leibniz had been its court philosopher in Hanover and was rather brutally left behind owing to the bitter calculus dispute ongoing. He died very soon after, in 1716.

In 1717 Britain adopted the gold standard for its currency, and the first gold sovereigns were minted, which continued to be currency until 1932. As Master of the Mint, it was Newton's business to guarantee that their gold was precisely twenty-two carats. Originally worth one pound sterling, they today sell for some £250.

As Newton supervised that recoinage, the *gravitas* of his presence at the Mint helped to make it all work, a tricky exercise in credibility as well as being the beginning of modern fiat currency. Paper money was first issued in 1695 the year after the Bank of England was established. He was Master of the Mint for 28 years, from 1699 to his death in 1727. He established a bimetallic standard which had the effect of prioritising gold coins over silver: 'England adopted *a de facto* gold standard in 1717 after the master of the mint, Sir Isaac Newton, overvalued the guinea in terms of silver.'[2] The quarter-guinea made of gold started to be machine-produced in 1718.

The Enigma of Newtonian Absence

In great splendour the West Wall depicted the new royal family, together with various mythic figures who were there to bestow good fortune.

Four astronomers adorn the main ceiling: Copernicus; Tycho Brahe; Galileo and Flamsteed. But – where is Newton, the most celebrated of living Englishmen? He had well served his country, becoming *the* court philosopher to the new, Hanoverian monarchy. He was the sage of the era, as well as being Master of the Mint, Justice of the Peace, President of the Royal Society and knighted by Queen Anne for his services to the country during the great recoinage.

Surely his figure could not have been omitted from the grand design? Guide-books to the majestic panorama of the West Wall omit mention of him.

Its cleaning and restoration completed in 2013 has enabled a new approach to this enigma. The new Hanoverian dynasty was trying to legitimise itself before the eyes of England. Members of the new royal family appear in the foreground of the picture, absent George's wife Sophie locked away in a German castle: his

The West wall of the Royal Naval College's Painted Hall, at Greenwich.

son George is to the right, and his disdain for his father has been well shown by Thornhill. His son's charming wife Caroline the Princes of Wales enjoys a central position in the mural, above the globe in the centre.

This mural is endeavouring to confer a degree of divine approval upon a constitutional monarchy. Although Queen Anne had died in 1714, here we see her resurrected, very much at the centre of things.

Some Newtonian geometrical diagrams appear on the main hall's ceiling; is Newton present merely 'by way of metaphorical references' as some have argued?[3] We surely agree that Greenwich naval hospital is a monument to Sir Isaac Newton's 'scientific and broader cultural impact on his time' in term of its depiction of space, etc., but venture to disagree with their conclusion that 'conspicuous by his absence, Newton is paid the singular hour of being present in the form of a tribute to his monumental work'.[4] Nor can we agree with Buchwald and Feingold, that a corner of the Greenwich Great Hall ceiling depicts 'Tycho, Kepler and Newton'[5] – it is Copernicus who is there depicted, along with the other astronomers, not Newton.

A key to this story was given in a paper 'Newton's alchemical work and the creation of economic value' read to the American Chemical Society in 2006. It derived from a study of Newtonian alchemical manuscripts in Cambridge and Jerusalem and is very much at the centre of this chapter's meaning. Only a brief summary of this talk remains, from which we quote – recalling that Newton presented his *Chronology of the Ancient Kingdoms* to Princess Caroline, in 1717:

Newton portrait by Thornhill.

Newton's extensive work on universal history (which presents human history as a coherent unit governed by certain immutable principles) provides an essential setting for linking his work on alchemy and his work heading England's mint in the 1690s .. It is not at all farfetched to think of history as a kind of alchemical process that looks to the creation of value and wealth.[6]

Its author Ken Knoespel added that, in the early eighteenth century, Newton became 'the symbol of the stability of the British economy at this time … I believe that Newton thought by improving the English economic system, he was going to contribute to the ongoing transformation of England into God's kingdom on Earth.' That is helpful as we decrypt this great mural, created during that most optimistic phase of British history, the 'Age of Enlightenment.'

A Time of Optimism, and Virgil's Prophecy

Along the top of the Great Hall in bold capitals there runs a line from Virgil's 4th-Ecologue prophecy, 'IAM NOVA PROGENIES COELO...': 'Now once more there descends from heaven…':

'Now the Virgin returns, and Saturn's reign begins;
A new generation is sent down from high heaven.
Only, chaste Lucina, favour the child at his birth,
by whom, first of all, the iron age will end
and a golden race arise in all the world.
Now your Apollo reigns.'

In this passage (of c.42 BC) Virgil speaks of a boy to be born who will be the ancestor of a new golden race. Use of this text, long taken as a prophecy of the birth of Christ, was certainly audacious, but to what could Thornhill be alluding? Not, surely, to the fat, chocolate-loving king who spoke no English?

The Painted Hall has been described as 'the most Italianate and ambitious of any of Thornhill's decorations.' Michelangelo's Sistine Chapel image of Adam and God with their fingers touching finds an echo in the way Hermes and the central unidentified goddess ('Lucina,' from the Vigil quote) point their fingers at each other. This majestic room at Greenwich seems to be Britain's answer to the Sistine Chapel. On three occasions had Thornhill painted portraits of Newton, so could he have been omitted from this grand masterpiece? His Newton-portrait of 1710 now hangs in Trinity College where Newton lived and studied.

The child-Newton figure

One cherub is here distinguished from the others. His wings glimmer only faintly and we see his head and a shoulder. He peers out from between Saturn and Astreae, whose return, in Virgil, signifies the start of the new Golden era. He is more pensive than other cherubs, though with a hint of a sweet smile. A comparison with Thornhill's portrait of Newton shows an identical profile, the upper half of both faces showing clear similarities. Unlike Thornhill's other cherubs this one is greying at the temples, an odd feature for an angelic being. Newton had gone prematurely grey at thirty. This cherub is situated directly beneath the copy of the *Principia* shown on the edge of the ceiling. Has Thornhill 'cherubised' his portrait of Newton portraying him as the golden Apollo child from Virgil?

Through an audacious use of Virgil's prophecy, we affirm, he has cast Newton as the miraculous child, renewer of the age. He was, after all, born on Christmas day. The god Saturn gazes intently down upon him. It is appropriate that he should be adjacent to the Saturn's cornucopia of gold, if indeed he had just put British currency onto a gold standard. The abundance of gold coins are here shown, minted after 1717.

The cleaning of the West Wall has enabled its gold and bronze-ochre hues to gleam forth once more, and many details have become newly-visible. Vertically above this Newton-cherub in the picture is the letter 'P' in Virgil's text, above which cherubs hold open Newton's *Principia*, next to a globe. One can read the name 'Newton' in this book, and some geometrical figures. The presence of this book may only have been noted after the cleaning.[7] This Newtonian text is held by cherubs directly above the letters 'PR' of the Virgil text – possibly alluding to its title.

Thornhill designed the West Wall with human figures standing on the ground on a carpet, while immortals recline above them on a cloud: the sole exception here being the Newton-child, who resides under the wing of Saturn, next to the cascading gold.

Close-up of cherub with cornucopia of gold coins.

On the ceiling, cherubs read the *Principia*, with a globe to help them.

Saturn as *Chronos* holds his scythe. Thornhill and his contemporaries would have seen Newton's achievement concerning the laws of motion of the planets, as *saturnine* in this respect, by bringing order to the world and explaining the great cycles of heaven. Hermes in the top-right hand corner of the picture, patron of alchemists, also points towards Newton, whose alchemical works would not have been unknown to Thornhill. Mythic themes of a returning golden age are here woven together.

Obliquity of Earth's Tilt

The mural has a straight line passing through it joining the pointing finger of Hermes' left hand at the top, with the extended hand of the seated figure, who might be Virgil's figure of 'Lucina:'[8] supervising the dawning of the hopefully-returning Golden Age. From there this diagonal line passes through the left eye of the Newton-child, through the cascading gold, along the back of Prosperity who carries a second cornucopia of food, and finally intersects the bottom left-hand corner of the whole picture, taking that as framed by the pillar on the left. At the top right it touches the bottom left corner of the letter 'N,' where the letters 'NI' could be here alluding to Newton. At the bottom of the picture it just touches the index finger of Prosperity's left hand, which holds the cornucopia: so there are three different key figures who have a pointing index finger of their left hand right on this huge diagonal line.

The angle of that diagonal we measure as being 23 ½°. By comparing various photographs this seems a reasonable estimate of the angle as seen from the middle of the Great Hall.[9] That angle had a Newtonian meaning, alluding to Newton's framing of the 'System of the World,' to the seasons and how the world turns: it is the tilt of Earth's axis with respect to the ecliptic. No-one before Newton had ever succeeded in explaining the precessional motion of the equinoxes.

Ancient sources such as Ovid had the seasons begin once the Golden Age ends, before which there was a perpetual summer. Thus, the Earth's axial tilt here depicted is part of Thornhill's Golden Age story.

That diagonal line passed through two cornucopias, the first from which the gold coins cascade in great plenty and the second below it symbolising abundance and prosperity. The latter is here associated with the arts of peace, as the grandchildren of King George gather around it. The gentle arts of peace co-exist – in Thornhill's optimistic vision – with a list of triumphant naval battles held by an angel on the far-right of the picture. The latest naval victory here listed is the Battle of Sicily in 1718 against Spain, which helps to date the mural. From the upper beginning of that straight line, viz. the bottom-left corner of the letter 'N' a vertical line falls though the centre of the tower of the newly-constructed St Paul's. Continuing down it passes though the centre of gravity of the son George, who would later become George II. The newly-rebuilt St Paul's was a fine symbol of the glory and optimism to which Thornhill was here giving expression.

The sceptre held by King George has its axis pass through the globe's centre, while his royal robe covers the top of the globe, expressing transatlantic empire, and his children play beneath it. Various lines in the mural point towards this central globe.

Thornhill himself stands in the bottom-right corner of the picture, his left hand pointing to a compass-square for measuring angles, hinting at some important angle to be measured. A globe in the lower foreground on which the Monarch rests displays a great circle tilted at 23 ½ degrees to its Equator – which has now become clearly visible after the cleaning, and it cuts the Gold Coast of Africa. Why should such a meridian line have been inscribed upon a globe? Above the circle of the Equator we see the Tropic of Cancer, tilted at 23½° of latitude, and the hitherto little-noticed diagonal circle passes between these two. Guinea, to the South of the Gold Coast, has the newly-formed Greenwich zero longitude line passing through it. Guinea had been the source of British gold, after which the new guinea coin was named, and is here framed by a triangle of three great circles: the Equator; John Flamsteed's newly-defined zero-longitude; plus the tilted great circle which Thornhill has placed on his globe, intersecting the coast of Africa.

The iconic figure of Newton in the eighteenth century interlinked science and religion, as British imperial power became associated with Newtonianism. The West Wall tableau weaves an image of British optimism, as trade and empire expanded, despite fortunes lost with the collapse of the South Sea Bubble.

The painting's 'golden' theme is thereby endorsed, as too is the diagonal line right through the painting linking the several figures of Hermes, Lucinia, the child-Newton and Prosperity, at Earth's obliquity angle. Thornhill has thus created a golden link between his heavenly and earthly realms, with a terrestrial globe highlighting the Gold Coast, especially New Guinea, more than any other landmass, relating this to the golden wealth that is cascading from Saturn's cornucopia: an ingenious fabric of meaning which holds Thornhill's mural together, in the light of Virgil's prophecy.

Newton's *Chronology of the Ancient Kingdoms, Amended* claimed that the precession of the equinoxes could measure out historical time: the tilt-angle of the Earth, as expressed in this picture – its precessional motion newly-explained by Newton's *Principia* - was the primary basis of its narrative. It featured mythic-archetypal characters such as Jason and the Argonauts, Medusa, the Golden fleece etc. As Court philosopher of the new Georgian dynasty, while it was being painted he was involved in this mythic-history study: which may help us to appreciate, why Thornhill has depicted him surrounded by legendary beings - and cast Newton himself in terms of the Virgil prophecy.

Newton and George I both died in 1727, the year in which the painting was completed.

Appendices

Core of the Apple Myth * The Circle Squared * *De analysi* * The Moon-test * Newton's Headache * Dicing with Death * Halley Muses

1. Core of the apple myth

In the Autumn of 1665 Newton 'lost his groats' in taking the BA exam, i.e. did badly. As John Conduitt recalled in his memoirs:

> 'He stood to be a Scholar of the House & D[r] Barrow examined him in Euclid which he knew so little of, that D[r] Barrow conceived a very indifferent opinion of him.'[1] *

He therefore might not then have expected to be able to return in 1666 to Trinity and apply for a fellowship. Biographies gloss over this vital point and treat the plague years as merely an interval between his studies at Cambridge as if he naturally expected to return, though only a farmer's son. We surmise that conversations he had with Humphrey Babington during the plague years were here significant. Babington was some sort of relative though the historical record is here rather vague.

In the plague years of 1665-6, Newton resided just a few miles away from his family home in Grantham, with his uncle and Trinity College senior Humphrey Babington in the village of Boothby.[2] Or as Rupert Hall explained:

> 'it was certainly at Babington's rectory at Boothby Pagnell (another village close by) that Isaac Newton, in the autumn of 1665, evaluated a hyperbolic area to "two and fifty figures." The computation survives to this day.'[3]

In the year 1665, we picture the 23-year old Newton sitting in front of a coal fire with Babington, the latter holding a sheet on which Newton has just computed the area under a hyperbola to 52 decimal places. Newton may have gone up to Cambridge as Babington's 'sizar' which means a general dogsbody, who copied out sermons, etc which could account

---

* William Stukeley recalled, 'I have heard it as a tradition, while I was at Cambridge, that when Sir Isaac stood for a Batchelor of Arts degree, he was put to a second posing, or lost his groats, as they term it, which is look'd upon as disgraceful.' *Memoirs of Sir Isaac Newton's Life,* 1752. Nine groats were deposited upon standing for a degree, and returned if a satisfactory pass was obtained: see discussion by Alan Ferguson, online.

Newton's apple tree at Grantham? Probably not.

for why this shy young man has retired to his home. Did the conversation go somewhat as follows?

> 'Isaac, you are a bright lad, but shouldn't you be thinking about getting a proper job? You didn't do too well in your Batchelor's degree, and earlier when examined by Dr Barrow about Euclid you were fairly clueless. Why don't you settle down and marry that nice Miss Storey, to whom you were engaged when you entered Cambridge? You could become a parish priest.'

I suggest it was a very personal judgement that Babington made, while gazing into the eyes of this shy young man, that accounts for his return to Cambridge in 1666, applying at Trinity College to become a Fellow.

The apple myth took form (around the time of Newton's death) as having taken place a few miles due west of this location, at the family farm house in Woolsthorpe Manor. As John Conduit wrote in his 1726 notes: in the summer of 1666, '[Newton] first thought of his system of gravitation which he hit upon by observing an apple fall from a tree'. A picture was drawn of it in 1820 by the Rev. Charles Turner, showing its position with respect to the manor house. It was the only apple tree growing in the garden, so it had to be the one. This was visited by David Brewster in 1830. It blew down in a storm and then re-rooted, and is still growing today. Over 350 years old, it still provides a good crop of apples every summer. The story gave rise to a market in selling logs from an old apple tree near that Woolsthorpe farm house, one of which now resides in the RAS library. Even Westfall re-tells the story as having happened at that Woolsthorpe farm.[4] The current English Heritage site does here require to be readjusted.

2. The circle squared

> 'The controversies that raged over Arithmetical Problems reached such a pitch of emotion... when Hobbes thought that he had squared the circle and Dr Wallis knew he had not...
>
> Aubrey, *Brief Lives* 1987, p.18.

When he was a youth, John Aubrey recalled, all accounts were done in Roman numerals. He lived to see a new world open up, as Arabic numerals with their zero come to be accepted. A passion for mathematics developed during the Stuart Century, recalled by John Aubrey:

> 'Edmund Gunter who, with his Booke of the Quadrant, Sector and Crosse-staffe did open men's understandings and made young men in love with that Studie. Before, the Mathematicall Sciences were lock't up in the Greeke and Latin tongues and there lay untouchd, kept safe in some libraries. After Mr Gunther published his books, these Sciences sprang up amain, more and more to that height it is at now.' (1690)

William Oughtred invented the multiplication sign, which, he said, 'came into my head, as if infused by Divine Genius.'[5] Soldiers, sailors, courtiers, clerics, all devoted themselves to this intoxicating study. Controversies raged over recondite riddles.

In *The Virtuoso* by Thomas Shadwell, a popular play of the mid-1670s which satirised the Royal Society, attempts 'to square the circle' were derided as a typically useless and impossible endeavour with which that Society occupied itself. And yet, that was the very moment in history when the millennia-old endeavour to square the circle[6] was finally accomplished: that is, to find a square which has the same area as a given circle, was resolved. Who did it? The answer to such a question is hardly any simpler than the question as to who invented calculus. The intense polemics which the question generated form a valuable analogy alongside the calculus controversy.

The old term 'quadrature' developed into what we now call integration, but retained its old meaning of squaring the circle, and the two issues remained seamlessly joined through the great calculus controversy. The Royal Society's judgement on the calculus dispute *Commercium Epistolicum* did one-sidedly debate the matter. To the modern reader there appears rather little connection between a series giving the value of π (as we would now describe a recipe for squaring the circle) and the method of calculus, whether differential or integral, as the two subjects have long since split asunder.

Similar ideas were impinging on three different minds, in Edinburgh, Paris and Cambridge. That notion was that the area of a circle could be defined by no finite ratio, but only by an infinite series. If one asks the question, 'Who first accomplished this in a tolerably public manner, and claimed that he had done it, viz squared the circle by an infinite series?' then the answer is; Leibniz, in Paris, in the year 1673. Furthermore, Leibniz had a proof for what he had done so that its veracity could be checked. Even so, he declined to disclose his discovery to the English for some years, telling them only that he had squared the circle but not what his series actually was, which damaged his priority claim in later years.

APPENDICES

If one asks the simpler question, who first managed to square the circle, then an answer could be; Newton, in the year 1670, in his letter that was sent to James Gregory (*Correspondence*, I, p28).[*]

Gregory, the most brilliant of Scottish mathematicians, could for a while make no sense of the strange formula sent to him. It was without proof, nor was it given as a circle-squaring recipe, but rather as a formula for part of the area of a circle, as contained between two parallel lines one of which was the diameter.

At much the same time, his *De analysi* gave a slightly different infinite-series expansion for finding an arc of a circle. He never published any of these infinite-series, in his math treatises: *Principia* of 1687, *Arithmetica Universalis* of 1707 (composed in the 1680s) , *De Quadratura* of 1704 (composed in the 1690s) – not until the eighteenth century, when he was around seventy years old and his creative labours quite finished, did he look about for how to take credit for these earlier, youthful insights. No-one in the seventeenth century ever said or averred that Leibniz's series could be derived from or was an expression of that earlier derived by Gregory.

James Gregory was sending some ingenious series of his own to Oldenburg, the Royal Society's secretary, which did somewhat resemble the one later developed by Leibniz for squaring the circle. They were presented as series for the trigonometrical ratios, of sine and tangent. Were they anticipations of Leibniz' series? This was indeed what the *Commercium Epistolicum* averred, and no lack of commentators have repeated the claim. It is hardly our business to try and read the mind of a historical character for what they meant but did not say.

From the book *A History of Pi* by Petr Beckmann, a Czech mathematician, we might expect an impartial account of the matter. Who was it who first resolved this riddle of the ages, which tormented so many brains in vain down the centuries? Who first determined exactly the ratio between the radius and circumference of a circle, and showed that no finite number could ever contain this ratio, whereas an infinite series could do so?

Beckmann's answer was unambiguous. 'For a giant like Newton, the calculation of π was chicken feed.' (p.140) In the plague year of 1666, we are told, that sage computed it to 16 decimal places, and we are shown the series expansion whereby he did it. Almost as an afterthought, Beckmann informed his readers that this was not made public until 1736, when the Newtonian 'Method of Fluxions and Infinite Series' appeared posthumously. He appeared unperturbed by a seventy-year gap between an alleged discovery and its publication. That opus never even had a name in Newton's lifetime, nor do we hear of anyone alluding to it: it's a collection of unpublished notes, of indeterminate date. In later life, Newton recollected that, in the winter of 1664/5, 'I found out first an infinite series for squaring the circle & then

---

[*] Newton approached the problem by integrating $\sqrt{(R^2 - x^2)}$ where R is the radius. The binomial expansion, which he announced to the world in 1676, may have been his means for performing the integration. The opaque formula sent to Gregory in March 1670 gave the area of a strip of the circle as $2RB - B^3/3R + B^5/20R^3 - B^7/56R^5$, where B is an x-value. Putting B=R would thus give half the area of a circle. The *Commercium Epistolicum* later asserted that Gregory had learnt of his calculus method by this formula from Newton ('James Gregory Tercentenary,' Ed H. W. Turnbull, 1939, p.89). In December of 1670, Gregory wrote back to Collins, saying that he had understood Newton's series, and added some extra terms. A year earlier Newton's manuscript *De analysi* gave an infinite series for finding the length of an arc of a circle, which in 1676 he sent to Leibniz.

another infinite series for squaring the Hyperbola soon after.'[7] The first two bulky volumes of the *Math Papers* published by Tom Whiteside, covering this period, have I suggest failed to confirm that: the circle-squaring activity is not found prior to the *De Analysi* text.

Some years later, in response to Leibniz sending him his series for the circle perimeter, Newton's letter of October 1676 computed π correctly to 15 places, rightly pointing out that Leibniz' series converged too slowly to be of any practical use.[8] That is the first time in which Newton comes out with a circle-squaring formula and shows some confidence in it. Historians, starting with John Wallis in his *Algebra* of 1685, have used that series from Newton's letter to Leibniz to give him credit – while simultaneously wresting it from Leibniz by alluding to the 'Gregory-Leibniz series.'

In his old age, Leibniz conceded that his youthful claim of priority in respect of squaring the circle was unwarranted: 'as afterwards it became known it had been worked out by Mr Gregory' he wrote of the circle quadrature by infinite series.[9] While such modesty is becoming, that canny Scotsman had written in 1671 no more than

$$\text{arcus} = t - t^3/3r^2 + t^5/5r^4 - \dots$$

where t is the tangent and r is radius. Putting t = r would thus give a 45° triangle, viz. $\pi/4 =$ 1 - 1/3 + 1/5 -. ... In inquiring as to why Gregory did *not* do this, as has appeared sufficiently baffling that many have surmised that he must have been well aware of it but merely did not trouble to pen so obvious a corollary, one should consider that the concept of π did not then exist, and so the radian measure of angle required for such a substitution could less readily have been performed. The concept of such a ratio being exactly defined only by an infinite series is not the sort of thing that occurs to the ordinary mind. James Gregory was appointed to the first Chair of Mathematics at the University of Edinburgh in 1674, but as he then became blind and died suddenly the year after, he may have had little leisure time to consider the matter.

Gregory had earlier composed a treatise explaining why circle quadrature was an impossibility (*Vera Circuli et Hyperbola Quadratura,* 1667). Huygens published quite an indignant review objecting to this view; he then gave a copy of the book to Leibniz when the latter came to join him in Paris. It was through wrestling with the *wrong logic* of Gregory's text that he was finally able to attain his famous series.[10]

In the year 1705 a corresponence took place between Edmond Halley, then Secretary of the Royal Society, and Abraham Sharp. Sharp had submitted to the *Philosophical Transactions* a value of π correct to 71 decimals, twice as many as anyone had hitherto found. He had employed for this purpose the tangent-series devised by James Gregory some years earlier and he was the first to apply that tangent-series to such a purpose.[*]

In this correspondence, Halley referred to 'Mr Leibniz' famous series 1/1 - 1/3 + 1/5 - 1/7 + 1/9 & as equal to the area of a quadrant.' The sum of this 'famous series' was $\pi/4$ as we would now say, or one-quarter of the area of a circle as Halley phrased it (of unit radius).

Halley in his letter referred to Leibniz's series as converging to such a value, and gave no intimation that anyone else, for example Gregory, had also propounded such a series.

---

[*] This is nowadays expressed as arctanx = $\int 1/(1+x^2)dx$, ie Gregory found a series for the angle whose tangent is x. Sharp in 1699 employed this Gregory formula to derive the series for 30°, making the series sum to $\pi/6$ instead of $\pi/4$, so that it converged a lot faster. He seems to have been the first to use the Gregory tangent formula for obtaining a value of π, further suggesting that such an application was less evident than modern historians tend to assume.

APPENDICES

This correspondence was some years prior to the Royal Society's report, *Commercium Epistolicum*, which attempted to wrest from Leibniz the glory of his achievement.

Even after the death of Leibniz, Newton battled on, and in 1718 asserted that Leibniz had taken Gregory's series and 'printed it as his own'[11] without acknowledgement. 'He should not have concealed his having received it from London, & much less should he have concealed his knowledge that Gregory had invented it before him,' the letter continued, indignantly. Some felt that such continued blackening of his opponent's name in a 'war beyond death' was inappropriate. Recent analysis of Leibniz' methods have shown that his means of arriving at the π-series did not use the Gregory formula.[12]

3. *De Analysi*

In 1672, the *Philosophical Transactions* published the tangent method of the Oxford Mathematician John Wallis, adjacent, as it happened, to the article reporting Newton's new reflecting telescope, and so Wallis's tangent diagrams have been immortalised by bearing in their midst an image of the new telescope. It is of interest to compare this tangent method with that 'briefly exposed' (in Whiteside's phrase) in the *De Analysi* of a few years earlier:[13] transcribed carefully by Collins but hardly yet shown to anyone, and certainly not to Wallis.

They are similar. Both methods entail a small increment of the variable term which is later set to zero. To refresh the memory of readers for whom these things may have been learnt some while ago, take a parabola, this being the first case which Wallis took, and let the variable x increase to $(x + a)$. Then $y = x^2$ so $(y + b) = (x + a)^2 = x^2 + 2ax + a^2$ subtracting the original equation gives $b = 2ax + a^2$ where a and b are small increments. Dividing through by a gives $b/a = 2x + a$.

The trick was, to recognise b/a as the slope of the tangent, while ignoring the term 'a' as being equal to zero, or however one phrased it, so that the slope was equal to 2x. For more complex expressions, this method would give other terms multiplied by 'a' which would also vanish. The slope term b/a is what Leibniz and Bernoulli would later express as dy/dx.

To quote from Wallis' account:

> 'Next, which is the heart of the method, move D to V, making *a=0*, so that all terms multiplied by *a* will vanish.'['Tandem (qui methodi nucleus est) posito D in V (quo fit a=0, adeoque evanescant ipsius multipla omnia)...]'

DV represented an increment in the variable term in Wallis' diagram, so 'position D in V' meant decreasing that length to zero! 'a' was the increment term for Wallis, so 'fit a=0' was the same language as was found in the *De Analysi*, for that tricky stage of the operation. The Newtonian document is a little more algebraic, that of Wallis more geometrical, and in consequence the former makes it more brazenly apparent that both sides of an equation have been divided through by zero, but otherwise they are the same methods.

Students of mathematics learn at an early age, that dividing by zero is not a good idea, and Newton was after all *the* mathematics lecturer at Cambridge.

As experts diverge on this matter, it is only fair to present the reader with a sample of their comments thereon:

L.T. More (1935): 'There is much difference of opinion as to whether this work [*De Analysi*] contained anything on fluxions or the calculus. Newton's partisans hold that it did, and that an able mathematician could have worked out his secret from it. Brewster, who was sufficiently biased, is doubtful, but such critics as De Morgan, Professor Child and the continental mathematicians, hold that it did not; the methods employed are merely a correlation of what he has learned from Descartes, Wallis and Barrow, combined with his original methods of infinite series and their reversion. In the true sense of the word, he could not differentiate, except as we now say, from first principles' (p.188).

C. Boyer (The Concepts of Calculus, 1949): *De Analysi* 'did not explicitly make use of the fluxionary notation or idea.'(p.191)

C. Boyer (A History of Mathematics, 1968): *De Analysi* 'is of great significance also as the first systematic account of Newton's chief mathematical discovery – the calculus' (p. 433, 1985 edn).

R.S. Westfall (1980): 'however briefly, *De Analysi* did indicate the full extent and power of the fluxional method' (p.205).

A.R. Hall (1984): '*On Analysis* is not overtly concerned with fluxions at all, but as its title states[14] with the method of series' (p.187).

'Let Newton Be!' (1988): 'In *De Analysi*, Newton may be claimed finally to have 'invented the calculus', in the sense of recognising and using the inverse natures of differentiation and integration, and of formalising the rules involved' (p.73).

One of these quotes is here endorsed, and that is the judicious, well-balanced verdict of Louis T. More. After Leibniz died, it dawned upon Newton that his protagonist had perused this document in his second, 1676, visit to England. That realisation did much to stimulate the 'war beyond death' of the continuing calculus controversy. In happier days, the text of *De Analysi*, as a study in infinite series, helped to procure for its young author the post of Lucasian lecturer.

A jury of school mathematics teachers could here be consulted, as regards to what extent the differential method, or the method of calculus, was present in a specific ancient text. In my experience, science historians normally proceed by re-phrasing what Newton did in Leibnizian calculus terms, and then using what they have done to give him credit for 'inventing calculus'. One could begin by asking a school math teacher the question, 'What is the first, most simple sign that someone can do calculus?' to which a reply might be, the ability to find the gradient of a curve, to find its tangent and then to find its maxima and minima. We next ask the question, 'Did Newton ever do any of these things?' in a published text. We are not asking, 'Could he do these things?' – where we would no doubt be taken into some unpublished manuscript. We recall our definition of invention, as being a public act. We are asking, *Did he ever publish a method for doing them?* Clearly if the world reckons he invented or co-invented calculus, then we must expect a positive answer to this question.

A method of finding tangents was given by Newton to Leibniz in 1673, and we have ascertained that that was the 'cumbersome' and soon-to-be-forgotten Sluse method, a *pre-calculus* procedure. No such method was given in the *Principia* or in Wallis's 1693 exposition of the Newtonian method. As regards *De Quadratura,* one could here bear in mind the above-quoted comment by More, 'In the true sense of the word, he could not differentiate, except as we now say, from first principles'. By 'from first principles' would here be meant, that the diagram with small changes going on has to be *constructed* – such as

APPENDICES

Determination of tangents in *De Quadratura*:

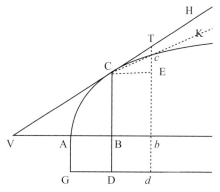

'Draw the straight line *Cc* and produce it to *K*. Let the ordinate *bc* go back into its former place *BC* and, as the points *c* and *C* come together, the straight line *CK* will coincide with the tangent *CH*, and so the vanishingly small triangle *CEc* will as it attains its last form end up akin to the triangle *CET* and its vanishing sides *CE*, *Ec* and *Cc* will ultimately be to one another as the sides *CE*, *ET* and *CT* of the other triangle *CET*: in this proportion in consequence are the fluxions of the lines *AB*, *BC* and *AC*. If the points *C* and *c* are at any small distance apart from each other, the straight line *CK* will be a small distance away from the tangent *CH*: in order that the line *CK* shall coincide with the tangent *CH* and so the last ratios of the lines *CE*, *Ec* and *Cc* be discovered, the points *C* and *c* must come together and entirely coincide. The most minute errors are not in mathematical matters to be scorned.'

one finds on every other page of *The Principia*. The following is I suggest the nearest which *De Quadratura* gets to explaining the matter[15]:

That learned scholar Niccolo Guicciardini has described this geometrical contruction as: 'Newton justifies the basic formula for the subtangent VB = y $\dot{x}$ / $\dot{y}$, that was widely employed in *de Methodis* in terms of limits.'[16] Returning to the original text we confirm that no such expression as $\dot{x}$ / $\dot{y}$ is present, as neither was it present in the manuscript *De Methodis* (published in 1736). Newton as we have seen *did not ever use this expression*, for the gradient of a curve or anything else – it was first used in 1704 in Charles Hayes' textbook. Readers of Prof. Guiccardini's book are going to be misled into believing that Newton here had some 'basic formula for the subtangent.' That formula may exist in his mind, as a convenient or modern way of interpreting what this geometrical construction is about, but it is absent from the historical text.[17] We remind ourselves of how Leibniz defined the calculus which he had invented, as a process 'whereby the mind is freed from a perpetual reference to diagrams.'

Returning to *De Analysi*, which was published in 1711, it may be of interest to see how the *Commercium Epistolicum* published one year later, alluded to it. This was the Royal Society's *official judgement* over the calculus dispute. It quoted various bits of the manuscript, and at one point it remarked: 'Note this well. Here is described the method of operating by fluents and their moments. These moments were afterwards called difference by Mr Leibniz: and so came the name of differential method.' That is a statement made by Newton himself, as regards the one point in *De analysi* where in his view the 'differential method' may be found, by way of endorsing his priority claim. We eagerly turn to this section, or rather to the English translation provided by Whiteside:

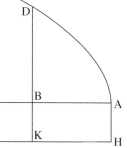

Let HAD be any curve and AHKB a rectangle whose side AH or BK is unity. And consider that the straight line DBK describes the areas ABD and AK as it moves uniformly away

From De Analysi,
Whiteside's translation.

261

from AH; that BK is the moment by which AK(x) gradually increases and
BD(y) that by which ABD does so; and that, when given continuously the
moment of BD, you can by the foregoing rules investigate the area ABD
described by it or compare it with AK(x) described with a unit moment.[18, 19]

That is all. Would our notional math-teacher jury agree with the Royal Society, that
here the differential method has been described? That is unlikely, because this text merely
describes how an area will increase if one of its sides is moved. If that is the best that
seventy-year old author of the *Commercium Epistolicum* could come up with, taken from his
youthful *de Analysi,* then the case is indeed weak.

4. The Moon-test

Retracing the steps of the historic computation which three centuries ago linked earth and
sky in the new science of mechanics, commonly called the 'Moon-test,' we are startled that
they contain no concept of acceleration. So often have we read this, indeed the 'Moon-test' is
more or less always described in such terms, *as if* it involved what became in the next century
called 'g,' the acceleration due to gravity.

We here challenge a recent publication which has endeavoured to contest the view put
forward by Westfall, that Newton fiddled his Moon-test calculation: it mistakenly sought to
show that 'Newton is innocent of Westfall's main accusation of data-fudging in the Moon-
test.'[20] This famous Newton calculation compared the distance of the lunar orbit radius, with
our distance from the centre of the Earth. In order to work, it needed to locate the Earth-
Moon centre of gravity, because the Moon revolves around it; wherein lies the error, the
unavoidably large error, that Newton could not remove.

The First Edition gave the computation in glorious, pristine simplicity - as it
occurred to its illustrious author early in the year 1685[21]. It came near the beginning
of the *Principia's* Book III, the 'System of the World' as Proposition IV, Theorem IV. It
wonderfully used a factor of 60 in two different contexts, which conveniently cancelled
out: the lunar orbit radius as approximately 60 Earth-radii, and a ratio of 60 discerned
between the rates of fall of Moon and apple so to speak: This has been well described
by Dana Densmore, as:

> 'perhaps the most thrilling demonstration in the Principia... Pause to ponder
> the coincidence – or try to explain it! – that gives the same number for the
> moon's fall in a minute from orbit and in a second at the surface.'[22]

As the Moon was continually 'falling' towards Earth at a rate of 16 feet in one *minute*, so
objects on Earth fell 16 feet in one *second* when dropped. The latter is numerically equal to,
as we would say, ½g, where g the acceleration due to gravity is 32 feet per second.[2]

> * In 1684 Jean Picard's calculations for the Earth's size were published
> posthumously, giving one degree at the equator as equivalent to 69½ miles.
> This improved value enabled Newton to form a more accurate estimate
> of the Earth's circumference, as 123,249,600 Paris feet.[23] He has hopped
> up to seven-figure accuracy, however there was no point in carrying his
> computation to more than three figures, because of the ½ to 1% error here
> involved.

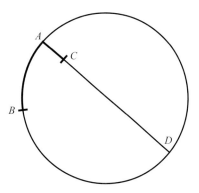

* The Moon's speed in its orbit around the Earth was computed, using the known lunar orbit period of 27 days, 7 hours and 43 minutes, and multiplying the Earth's circumference by 60 to gain the lunar orbit distance.

* Next we asked to imagine, that the Moon is *deprived of its motion,* and instead allowed to fall …. 'it will fall 15 1/12 Paris feet [in one minute]'. This distance of free fall was computed from the Moon's orbit velocity with respect to the Earth, using a 'calculus' given in Book I. Turning back to Proposition IV of Book I, we find the following Huygens-type formula for circular motion. For a body at A in the figure, moving in circular motion under a centripetal force, which would move round the arc AB in unit time, but 'if stopped' would fall in unit time to C, where AD is the diameter of its orbit, then AB²=AC. AD.[24] The mathematically disposed reader will readily verify this equation.

* By the inverse-square law, gravity at the surface of the Earth must be 60² times greater than that holding the Moon in her place. It followed that a body on the Earth's surface must fall 60²x15 1/12 Paris feet in one minute.

* Using Galileo's formula that distance fallen by a body is as the square of the time, in one second the object on Earth would fall 15 1/12 Paris feet.

* That bodies do indeed fall by 15 1/12 Paris feet in one second was confirmed by pendulum experiments. Thus the link was forged, showing how the same force which makes bodies fall, holds the Moon in her orbit.

So, what's the problem? The problem is, that the Moon orbits at 59.6 Earth-radii, around the baricentre, so Newton taking 60 Earth-radii should have given him a difference or an error-value of 0.8%: that is the *limit of accuracy* of his calculation.

This Moon-test in the First Edition of the *Principia* remained unchanged on the grandiose opening pages of Book III through subsequent editions. However, like a disease that could not be resisted, an ostensibly far more accurate computation of the same problem, carried through to *nine* significant figures, burgeoned later on in Book III of the second edition, as a part of its greatly expanded lunar section. Actually, it was *less* accurate than the first version!

The new computation appeared as a mere corollary to Proposition 37. This proposition had conducted the reader along a devious and shaky path, whereby from tidal data of the Bristol channel the relative masses of the Earth and Moon were ascertained and had calmly reached the outrageous conclusion that 'the moon is more dense and earthy than the earth itself.' Its several-fold overestimation of lunar relative mass now formed the basis for a return to the apple-moon calculation, but this time pretending to a shockingly bogus level of accuracy.

Its key value, of the distance the Moon would fall in one minute 'if stopped' had unaccountably diminished, as well as going up to nine-figure accuracy:

> 'The moon therefore,, falling towards the Earth under the action of the force with which it is kept in its orbit, will in the time of one minute describe 14.7706353 feet.'

And that is despite his very different earlier one still remaining, near the start of Book III.

The various analyses of this historic computation: Brougham (1855), Westfall (1973), Densmore (1996) and Harper (2011, over thirty pages)[25] have not really commented, as to why Newton published a second value for his key parameter, to nine-figure accuracy, so very different from his earlier one, nor have they appreciated what it is that gives the limit of accuracy attainable on this computation, viz the baricentre error.

Baricentre error

John Wallis advised Newton in 1695 that:

> 'I understand you are now about adjusting the moon's motions; and, amongst the rest, take notice of that common centre of gravity of the earth and moon as a conjunct body.'[26]

Newton could have written back saying, How am I supposed to do that? His best approach would have been to assume a uniform density of Earth and Moon, but instead he found an estimate of lunar mass so badly wrong that the adjustment created for him a larger error – in the other direction!*

This repeat version of the 'Moon-test' used an estimate of the 'baricentre' position, which is the centre of gravity of the Earth-Moon system, placing it at twice its actual distance from Earth's centre, so Earth revolved each month about a point outside of itself. One could express the problem as follows: because the Moon is quite light, a mere 0.6 that of Earth in its relative density – which they had no means of knowing – any estimate by them of baricentre position was going to be erroneous.

The earlier computation had enjoyed the marvellous simplicity of ignoring all the irregularities of the Moon's motion and viewing its orbit as being in a perfect circle around a motionless centre of mass. That is what astronomers call the 'one body problem' because the motion of only one body is considered in orbit around a stationary centre. When two bodies are more realistically viewed as orbiting a common centre of gravity the equations become more complicated, in the 'two-body problem'.

From various estimates of lunar distance, Thomas Streete's version of 60.4 Earth-radii was selected. Streete was a London almanack maker who had earned a fine commendation from Flamsteed of producing 'our exactest ephemerides'. The modern value for the mean lunar orbit radius is 60.27 Earth-radii, so this was a pretty good

---

* We alas have to rebuke Dana Densmore, in her 'Newton's Principia: The Central Argument' (1996), where she devotes fifteen pages to this computation. She does not have the barycentre position estimate as Newton endeavoured to find it in his 3rd edition. One might expect that in fifteen pages she would convey the basic fact that this computation involves two different centres of gravity: Earth's centre, and a more abstract 'baricentre' for the lunar orbit.

estimate, bearing in mind that the Moon's distance varies by ten percent every month between apogee to perigee.

The 60.4 figure was adjusted by using the greatly mistaken 1:40 mass ratio to give 58.9 Earth-radii as the lunar orbit radius about the baricentre, in error by over one percent. More doubtful adjustments were inserted, and then a computation similar to the above derived the distance which objects should fall in one second as 15 feet, 1 inch, and 1½ lines (a line was one-twelfth of an inch), or 15.11175 feet – close to the correct value of 15.07 Paris feet. An accuracy of a few parts in ten thousand was claimed. One cannot help being awed by the grandiose power and simplicity of this legendary computation, which linked earth to the circling heavens through the same abstract conception of force, and yet even here the deceptive thread is present, seeking to establish what has not indeed been shown. Let us give Westfall the last word here, quoting from his renowned but still-shocking 'Newton and the Fudge Factor':

> 'Not the least part of the *Principia's* persuasiveness was its deliberate pretense to a degree of precision quite beyond its legitimate claim. If the *Principia* established the quantitave pattern of modern science, it equally suggested a less sublime truth -that no one can manipulate the fudge factor quite so effectively as the master mathematician himself.'[27]

In fact, the moon orbits around the Earth-Moon centre of gravity with a mean radius of 59.6 Earth-radii. That is the key figure on which this computation depends. Newton first took a value of sixty, then of 58.9, values erring by around 1%. That is the error inherent in his computation. Science historians have yet to grasp this grasp this simple fact, even though it was described by the writer back in 1991.[28]

The first calculation, performed in the spring of 1685, and residing in Proposition 4 of Book III, was the most brilliant thing he ever accomplished. No human mind had hitherto made that sixty-to-one ratio comparison linking Heaven and Earth. He therefore did not want to remove it in his later editions, even though he had performed an ostensibly far more accurate re-computation. Or, did his fabled mathematical intuition whisper to him, that that was perilously unsound?

5. Newton's headache

The first edition of the *Principia* (1687) contained nothing of any practical use for astronomers. Its celebrated 'Moon-test' was a one-body problem, dealing merely with uniform circular motion around an immobile force-centre. The chief addition to the Second Edition of the *Principia* of 1713 was its extensive new lunar theory. It developed and improved the theory invented by Jeremiah Horrocks. This had used a Kepler-ellipse for the lunar orbit as one might expect, putting the Earth at one focus (Fig 1), and that ellipse revolved once per nine years.

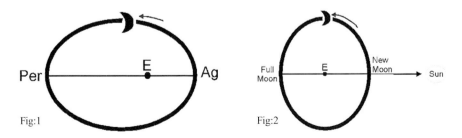

Fig:1   Fig:2

That would have been fine, except that Newton had also developed an 'explanation' for the inequality know as the Variation, as discovered by Tycho Brahe and Kepler. This put the Moon in an elliptical orbit with the Earth at its centre, not at one of the foci (Figure 2). The short axis of this ellipse pointed always towards the Sun, and so it revolved annually in space. Its eccentricity was three times larger than the earlier-mentioned ellipse, of the monthly apogee-perigee orbit. This Variation ellipse allowed Newton to account for why lunar motion was slightly faster at the Full and New positions than at the quarters, and his three-body computations credibly explained why solar gravity would deform a circular orbit in this manner.[29]

Each of these models would have been OK separately, could they really be added together? This mind-wrenching paradox may have been why Newton told Halley that the Moon was the one subject which made his head ache. The 'Variation' inequality was credibly derived from gravity theory in Book III of the *Principia* several propositions earlier that the rest of his lunar theory, as if Newton had more confidence in the former.

In the latter half of the eighteenth century in France, a sceptical tone was expressed by the historian Jean Bailly in his *Histoire de l'Astronomie Moderne*, commenting upon Newton's Horroxian model and its alleged derivation from gravity theory. Around this time lunar theories were being developed on the continent that really were based on gravity theory, using the Leibnizian calculus: 'He (Newton) bequeathed to us a mere semblance, which awaits the real thing to take its place.' This contraption of wheels within wheels with a variable-ellipse orbit like a wobbly rubber band was a mere semblance and could not be a physical cause: '*ce n'est point une cause physique.*'[30]

The lunar theory that Newton published involved several *epicycles*, i.e wheels within wheels, as first introduced by Ptolemy! After being banished from the heavens by Kepler a century ago, Newton brought them back again![31] French astronomers were doubtful about this: 'These centres which roll in circles belong to the ancient astronomy of Ptolemy… These hypotheses can only be mathematical' (Jean Bailly *Histoire,* 1779). An earlier French view here was: 'The most remarkable thing about this tract, nowadays adopted by nearly all lastronomers, and above all by Newton, is that Mr Machin has revived the Epicycles, to explain all the lunar movements and irregularities.'[32] It was remarkable, that British astronomy had revived the old epicycles. (John Machin had composed an exposition of lunar theory, as part of a 1729 *Principia* reprint). But the theory did work, rather well: Newton's text was 'adapted today by almost all Astronomers…'

6. Dicing with Death

It occurred to Samuel Pepys at the Admiralty that a certain wager involving dice could be remunerative; if it were complicated enough that he couldn't calculate the odds, then surely his colleagues at the gaming-table would not be able to, either? A few months before, he had received a strange letter from Newton at Cambridge, in December 1693, with phrases like 'I must withdraw from your acquaintance, and see neither you nor the rest of my friends any more', but it seemed that this could now be put behind. The moody maestro was clearly the person to resolve the problem – after all, the name of Samuel Pepys had been on the title-page of the *Principia*, as he was the Royal Society's President at the time. The science of statistics was just then emerging from the gambling salons of Europe, and it is of interest to look at this early exercise in probability.

Supposing A, B and C each have one throw, Pepys explained in his letter to Newton of February 1694, and they each have 6, 12 and 18 dice respectively. Which is then more likely:

that A will get one or more sixes; that B will get two or more sixes; or that C will get three or more sixes? Newton replied, regretting that he had not been given a problem 'of greater moment'! Pepys confessed, a fortnight later, that he had not fully grasped the force of the argument and he rephrased the question. If instead of the numbers one to six, the dice were branded with the letters A, B, C, D, E and F,

> 'And the Case should then bee this:
> Peter a Criminal Convict being doomed to dye, Paul his Friend prevails for his having ye benefitt of One Throw only for his Life, upon Dice soe prepared; with ye Choice of any one of these Three Chances for it, viz.
> One F, at least upon Six such Dice.
> Two F's at least upon Twelve such Dice.
> or
> Three F's at least upon Eighteen such Dice.
> Question. - Which one of these Chances should Peter in this case choose?'

By this time Newton had realised that Pepys was more concerned with his chances on the gaming table than with probability theory, and so his answer was in the form of how much wager should be placed for each choice for a given stake. Pepys had one last query: did the twelve dice have to be thrown at once or could they be cast as two lots of sixes, and he was assured that it made no difference.

Newton explained that A had the better chance, because 'A has all the chance of sixes... but B and C have not all the chances of theirs. For when B throws a single six or C but one or two they miss of their expectations.' To Pepys' second missive he replied, 'if I were Peter, I would chuse the first,' giving the probability as 31031/46656.

The theory involved in this probability problem involved binomial expansions applied to combinations and permutations as expounded in Jacques Bernoulli's *Ars conjectandi,* the Art of Conjecturing, published in 1713 eight years after his death, that being the earliest substantial volume on the subject of probability. On that theory, the chance of getting at least one six from six throws is the sum of all but the first term in the expansion of $(5/6 + 1/6)^6$, i.e. $1 - (5/6)^6 = 0.665$, while the chance of getting at least two sixes in 12 throws is given by adding all but the first two terms of $(5/6 + 1/6)^{12}$, i.e. $1 – (5/6)^{12} - 12.(5/6)^{11} \times (1/6) = 0.61$. Newton's answers were correct to five-figure accuracy.

Pepys' query might indeed have been a considerate way of helping Newton to recover from whatever it was that had afflicted him, by way of ensuring that the mighty Newtonian brain was still ticking over. He had, after all, much developed the binomial theorem.

7. Halley Muses

'Dr Halley, so I hear, lives in taverns. He is very infirm,' wrote Mr Crosthwait to Abraham Sharp in 1722. At this tail end of his life, Edmond Halley had embarked upon a project he had dreamed of ever since first setting up his sextant in Islington, of taking a whole Saros of the Moon's motion for his observations. So many years ago in Islington, when newly married to Grace Took – described by a contemporary as 'a young lady amiable for the gracefulness of her person and the beauties of her mind' – and with no idea of the dramas due to befall him, he had started its measurement, only to be abruptly interrupted by his father's strange suicide with his body dredged up from the river. Had that not happened, his idyllic life at Islington would have continued, with his charming new wife and the Moon, and he would never have been obliged to move to London to seek his fortune with the celebrated Royal Society for the Improving of Natural Knowledge; when, presumably, there would have been no *Principia*.

As Edmond Halley mulled over his brandy in the taverns of London, memories came back to him – ah, but what memories! Perhaps sailing his little 'frigatt' the Pink by the vast icebergs and whales of the South Atlantic, seeking for 'terra incognita' remained one of his most vivid. Future sailors would be grateful for his mapping of the magnetic field of the Atlantic Ocean with its changing declination. An early memory he liked was his teacher at school saying that, if ever a star was misplaced on the globe, Edmond Halley would be sure to notice it. 'Nearer the gods no mortal may approach,' he had declared, in his hexameter ode to Newton's grand opus – but, after all he had done for Newton, he had not even recommend him for the Savilian mathematics post at Oxford! It became vacant in 1691, but David Gregory obtained the post, Newton having recommended him. Still, Halley had to concede that he was no match for that canny Scot when it came to mathematics, and besides he would have missed his whole adventure in the South Sea had he gained that post. Really, Sir Isaac had been right in his choice. Later on, in 1703 he had obtained the position and, not many people had been captain of a ship then professor of mathematics, that was for sure.

He was never quite as careful in making his observations as the Reverend Flamsteed. It still puzzled him as to why the latter had taken such a dislike to him. Still, he had a substantial grant from the Admiralty to keep him going. Over the years, eighteen in fact, he measured or estimated the celestial longitude of the moon, of the lunar centre, at Greenwich, and did that more exactly than anyone had ever done before, by using and improving the method of his predecessor.

He then calculated what it ought to have been, using his version of Newton's lunar theory. My PhD reconstruction of his version of the Newtonian method is shown in the graph. A mean value has drifted out of kilter by a couple of arcminutes, since the values were given by Newton three decades earlier.[33] Halley logged these into his notebook and subtracted one from the other: that was his 'error' in the theory, shown here. We can see he is getting errors of several minutes of arc which was not bad for the time.

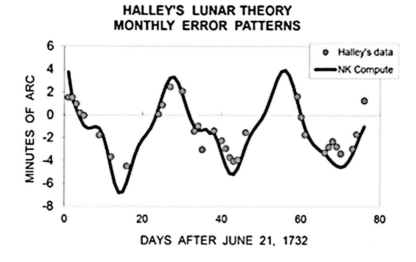

HALLEY'S LUNAR THEORY
MONTHLY ERROR PATTERNS

Halley had on several occasions averred that the Newtonian method only erred by up to two or three arcminutes, and so must have been distressed when in 1733 it started to generate errors up to eight arcminutes, several times the maximum.[34] He faithfully but silently recorded these errors and we have very little comment from anyone concerning what he thought of this, or whether it undermined his will to publish his method.

He believed quite rightly that errors in the method ought to repeat over a Saros cycle and I ascertained that this did work astonishingly well:

My computer-reconstruction of Halley's method, here corrected for the slight drift of mean motion ('TMM' here alludes to Newton's *Theory of the Moon's Motion*, 1702), shows how good Halley's method was. The errors do exactly repeat over a Saros cycle, well enough to win the longitude prize! Nobody knew that of course, Halley being by this time rather secretive and reclusive over what he was doing. As the first astronomer to be overtaken by the pace of progress, his seven-step Newtonian tables published posthumously in 1749 were displaced in the mid-century by improved methods developed on the Continent, in the tables of Euler and Mayer, which used the Leibnizian calculus to derive the lunar inequalities from gravity theory.

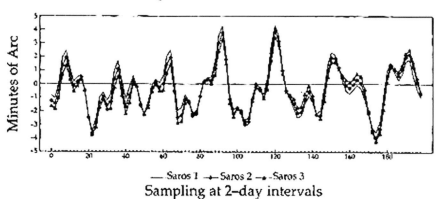

TMM and the Saros
using corrected mean motion

— Saros 1 —•— Saros 2 —•— Saros 3

Sampling at 2–day intervals

THE DARK SIDE OF ISAAC NEWTON

To acknowledge the man without whom this endeavour could not have existed, here are the published works of Tom Whiteside:

1961 Patterns of Mathematical thought in the later 17th Century, Archive for History of exact Sciences 1:179-388: pp 365-384, 'Calculus'.

1961 Newton's Discovery of the general binomial theorem, Mathematical Gazette 45: 175-80.

1962 After the Principia [Review of the corr. Of IN, Vol3], History of Science 1: 96-100.

1962 The Expanding world of Newtonian Research, History of Science 1: 16-29.

1964 Newton's Early Thoughts on Planetary Motion: a Fresh Look, The British Journal for the history of science 2: 117-37.

1964 Isaac Newton: Birth of a Mathematician, Notes and Records of the Royal Society 19: 53-62.

1966 Newton's Marvellous Year: 1666 and all that, Notes and Records of the Royal Society 21: 32-41

1966 Sources and Strengths of Newton's Early mathematical thought,' The Texas Quarterly 10: 69-85.

1970 The Mathematical Principles underlying Newton's Principia Mathematica, Journal for the History of Astronomy 1:116-38.

1970 Before the Principia The maturing of Newton's thoughts on dynamical astronomy 1664-1684, Journal for the History of Astronomy 1: 5-19.

1972 Newton's Mathematical Method, Bulletin of the Institute of Mathematics and its applications 8: 173-8.

1976 Newton's Lunar theory: from High Hope to Disenchantment, Vistas in Astronomy 19: 317-28.

1977 From his claw the Green Lion Newton's Interest in alchemy, (Book Review, The Foundations of Newton's alchemy BJ Dobbs, Isis, 68: 116-121.

1980 Kepler, Newton and Flamsteed on Refraction Through a 'Regular Aire' the Mathematical and the Practical, Centaurus 24: 288-315.

1982 Newton the Mathematician, Z Bechler Ed., contemporary Newton Research Dortrecht 109-27.

1982 Essay Review: Never at rest: a Biography of Isaac Newton, by Richard Westfall Isis 73: 100-106

270

APPENDICES

1989 The Preliminary Manuscripts for IN's 1687 Principia, 1684-5 (Intro), CUP 1989.

1990 The latest on Newton.. Notes and Records of the Royal Society 44: 111-17.

1991 How forceful has a force Proof to Be? Newton's Principia, book I: Corollary to Propositions 11-13: Physis 28: 727-49.

1991 The Prehistory of the Principia from 1664 to 1686, Notes and records of the Royal society 45: 11-61.

I tried to get him to agree to publish these works together, but he was diffident about such matters, declining offers from both OUP and CUP for a 'Whiteside on Newton' volume. Concerning his epic *Mathematical Papers* – fragments of which are now to be found online – each volume has a bio section for the period covered by the volume: one could hardly improve upon the reprinting of these biographical texts.

My published articles on this topic are online, and come up on the first page of Google with two or three keywords:

Newton's lunar theory => My old website at UCL
Newton lunar error => 'Newton's Lunar Mass Error' JBAA 1985
Two Moon-tests => 'Newton's two 'Moon-tests' BJHS 1991
Halley hollow => 'The Hollow world of Edmond Halley' JHA 1992
Newton approximation myth => 'Newton's Method of Approximation an Enduring Myth' BJHS 1992
Venus transit Horrocks => 'William Crabtree's Venus transit observation' IAU 1994
Newton epicycles => 'A Reintroduction of Epicycles: Newton's 1702 Lunar Theory and Halley's Saros Correction' QJRAS 1995 (or, Halley Saros)
Flamsteed lunar => 'Flamsteed's Lunar Data, 1692-95, Sent to Newton,' N.K. & Bernard Yallop, JHA 1995
Halley comet Newton => 'The Path of Halley's comet, and Newton's late apprehension of the law of gravity' Annals of Science 1999 (or, Newton gravity late).
Leibniz birth calculus => 'The Birth of Calculus: Towards a More Leibnizian View' 2012 arxiv.org

Select Bibliography

The Correspondence of Isaac Newton is largely online at the newtonproject.ox.ac.uk, together with sundry theological manuscripts plus various Newton bios, etc, managed by Rob Iliffe at Oxford. There is however no index, for the six million words so far transcribed. The Cambridge University Library has put all its Newton-manuscripts online, in high-res images: the ULC Digital library / Newton Papers. Early issues of the Royal Society's *Phil Trans* journal are online: Royal society / Journals / Phil. Trans. / All contents / Earlier content. For alchemical texts, see 'The Chymistry of Isaac Newton' University of Indiana's website. To consult journal articles, try Google Scholar, or http://adswww.harvard.edu/ (for whole articles, http://adsabs.harvard.edu/abstract_service.html)

AITON, E., *The Vortex Theory of Planetary motions*, London, 1972.

AUBREY, John, ed DICK, O.L, *Aubrey's Brief Lives*, Penguin 1987, first published 1813

BAILY, F. *An Account of the Revd John Flamsteed* 1837.

BECHLER, Z., Ed., *Contemporary Newton Research*, Reidel, 1982,

BECKMANN, P., *A History of* π, 1971

BIRCH, T. *The History of the Royal Society of London,* 1756, vol. IV.

BREWSTER, D., *Memoirs of the life, writings and discoveries of Sir Isaac Newton,* 1885.

BROUGHAM, H. P., and **ROUTH, E. J.,** *Analytical View of Sir Isaac Newton's* Principia, 1855.

CENTORE, F. *Robert Hooke's Contributions to Mechanics a Study in Seventeenth Century Natural Philosophy*, The Hague 1970.

COHEN, I. B., *The Newtonian Revolution, with illustrations of the transformation of scientific ideas,* CUP 1980.

COHEN,I.B., *Intro. to Variorum Principia edition*, HUP 1971.

EINSTEIN, A, *Ideas & Opinions,* NY Crown 1954, 1988.

FAUVAL, J. et. al*., Let Newton Be!, A New Perspective on his life and Works,* 1988

FORBES, E., Ed., *The Gresham Lectures of John Flamsteed*, 1975

GILLESPIE, C.C., *The Edge of Objectivity, an Essay in the History of Scientific Ideas*, 1960

GJERTESEN, D., *The Newton Handbook*, 1986.

GRIBBIN, J. & M., *From the Shadows of a Giant* 2017[1].

GUICCARDIDI, N., *Reading the* Principia, 1999.

GUICCARDINI, N., *Isaac Newton on Mathematical Method and Certainty*, 2009.

GUNTHER, *Early Science in Oxford, Volume 8*, 1931

HALL, A.R., *Philosophers at War,* 1980.

HALL, A.R. & HALL, M.B., *Unpublished Scientific Papers of Isaac Newton, A Selection from the Portsmouth Collection at the University Library, Cambridge*, 1962, CUP.

SELECT BIBLIOGRAPHY

HISCOCK, Ed., *David Gregory, Isaac Newton and their Circle* Oxford 1937.

HERIVEL, J.W., *The Background to Newton's Principia: a Study of Newton's Dynamical researches in the years 1664-84*, 1965, OUP

HOFMANN, J. *Leibniz in Paris, 1672-76, His growth to Mathematical Maturity* 1974.

ILIFFE, Rob *Priest of Nature, the Religious Worlds of Isaac Newton*, 2017.

KLINE, M., *Mathematics in Western Culture* 1954

KUHN, T. *Structure of Scientific Revolutions*, 1970

MANUEL, F., *A Portrait of Isaac Newton* 1968.

MORE, L.T., *Isaac Newton, a Biography* NY 1934, 1962.

SULLIVAN, J.W.N., *Isaac Newton 1642-1727*,1938.

WALLER, BROWN, Eds., *Posthumous Works of Hooke, 1705;* Princeton, 1970.

WESTFALL, R.S., *Never at Rest, A Biography of Isaac Newton*, 1980

WHITESIDE, D.T. *Newton's Mathematical Papers*, Vol. 6, 1975.

WILSON, Curtis: 'The General History of Astronomy,' Vol 2A, 1989, Ch.13, *The Newtonian Achievement in Astronomy.*

The First Edition of Newton's *Principia* is available online at www.gutenberg.org

Notes

Dedication

1. Interview with J.W.N.Sullivan, in *Contemporary Mind, Some modern answers* 1934.

Preface

1. Westfall, Richard *Never at Rest,* 1980, p.154.
2. See Kollerstrom, N and Campion *Galileo's Astrology*, 2003, p.150.
3. Koestler, A. *The Sleepwalkers*, 1968, p. 266
4. Hunter, M., 'Alchemy, Magic and Moralism in the thought of Robert Boyle', *British Journal for the History of Science*, December 1990, pp.387-410.

Chapter 1

1. Westfall,Op. cit., p.72
2. 'Doe you neither lend, nor borrow any things of any Scholler or other' was one of the Trinity rules of conduct. (Westfall, p.76)
3. Humphrey Newton's letter to John Conduit 17.2.1728, online: 'no less as one might suppose, than a 1000 Guineas in it crowded Edgewayes.'
4. Westfall, Op. cit.,, p.194.
5. *Op. cit.* p.193
6. Whiteside, Introduction to Mathematical Papers, Vol. III, p. Xiv
7. 'The downgrading of Christ in Newton's theology…. Makes room for himself as a substitute.' Manuel, *The religion of Isaac Newton* 1974, p.19.
8. *Memoirs of the Life & Writings of Mr William Whiston*, 1749, pp 293-4.
9. More, L. *Isaac Newton, a biography*, p.489.
10. Whiteside, *Math Papers*, Vol. VIII, Intro. p.17.
11. Ibid, p.17.
12. The two Scottish mathematicins David Gregory (1659-1708) and James Gregory (1638-1675), both feature in our story, the former becoming Oxford's mathematics professor in 1691.
13. Ibid, Vol. VIII, p.20.
14. Whiteside, *op. cit.* p.20.
15. Typically misleading is Carl Boyer in 'A History of Mathematics' (1968, reprinted 1980, p.435): 'In 1976 Newton wrote [an]... Account of his calculus, under the title, De Quadratura Curvarum.' This shows the deep confusion endemic to the calculus debate. De Quadratura was composed in the early 1690s using the then brand-new dot or 'pricked letter' fluxion notation. It employed the old concept of 'quadrature,' which was derived from the endeavours of time immemorial to 'square the circle,' and

used the traditional ' ∫ ' notation for what is now called integration (a word proposed in 1690 by Johann Bernoulli) . De Quadratura was designed as a counterblast to the new-fangled Leibnizian ' ∫ ' notation for Sum or 'integral' (see Westfall, p.515).

16. 10 Oct. *Corr*. III p.45.
17. Manuel, F., *A Portrait of Isaac Newton*, p.247.
18. This Lockean term 'sensorium' is used in Newton's 'Optics,' describing how light rays are motions and 'in the Sensorium they are Sensations of those Motions under the Forms of Colours.' The 'Sensorium' was located somewhere in the brain. (1952 edn. of 4th edn,p.125)
19. Nicholl, C., *The Chemical Theatre*, 2004, p.20.
20. Manuel was here rebuked by Rupert Hall: 'This is blood-tub Victorian melodrama rather than biography.' (*Adventurer in Thought*, 1992, p.326) Manuel's view here has also been dismissed as 'almost certainly nonsense,' because there was no record of Newton having been present if and when torture was used: *Newton and the Counterfieters*, Thomas Levernson, 2009, pp.165-6.
21. 'Lord Bacon, ' by Lord Macaulay, in *Miscellaneous Essays* 1837
22. A. de Morgan, *Newton: His Friend: his Niece* 1885.
23. *Corr*. Vol. VI p.225.
24. Gillespie, C., *The Edge of Objectivity*, 1960, p.151.
25. Castillejo, DF.,'*The Expanding Force in Newton's Cosmos* Madrid, 1981, p.95-7.
26. Quoted in Lancaster Brown, P., *Halley's Comet and the* Principia P., 1986 p.30.
27. Conduitt, unpublished memorandum, quoted by Westfall, p.849.
28. Gjertsen, *The Newton Handbook*, p.131.
29. Castillejo op.cit. p.43, from unpublished Conduitt papers.
30. Gouk, Penelope, in *Let Newton Be!* p. 101.
31. The story came from Catharine Conduitt, and Westfall suggests that the sum involved may have been a little less.
32. De Beer, G., and McKie, D., 'Newton's Apple' *Notes & Records of the Royal Society*, 1951, 9, p 46 & 333
33. Westfall found that this sixty-year gap between event and recollection 'does not seriously compromise acceptance of the incident itself.' (p.154)
34. Sagely concluded the two authors, Although we would like to correct the record, we have our doubts that the truth will get in the way of a good story. (Kekulé's dreams: fact or fiction?' Wotiz J.H. and S. Rudofsky, *Chemistry in Britain,* August 1984, p.720-723)
35. McNeil, M., in *Let Newton Be*! 1988, p. 236
36. Hall & Hall, 'Newton's Chemical Experiments' *Archive for History of Exact Sciences*, June 1958, p.32.
37. Sagredo has greatly underestimated the text that Newton came out with in 1702, see Chapter 7, or Kollerstrom, N, *Newton's Forgotten Lunar Theory* 2000.
38. Salviati may have been modelled upon that most learned professor, Rupert Hall, in whose department I worked at Imperial College.

Chapter 2

1. 'Always and forever Newton thought of a shining light ray as a particle.' – Hall, Rupert, in *Adventurer in Thought* 1992 p.356..
2. Flamsteed to Collins, January 1672:
3. Bechler, Z., 'Contemporary Newtonian Research', 1982, Intro., p.8

4. Hook to Oldenburg, Corr I,110-114.

5. Whiteside, D.T., 'Kepler, Newton and Flamsteed on Refraction Through a 'Regular Aire' *Centaurus* 1980 24 p.307.

6. *The Gresham Lectures of John Flamsteed*, Eric Forbes Ed., 1975, p.120.

7. Shapiro, A, 'The Evolving Structure of Newton's Theory of White Light and Colour' *Isis,* 1980, 71, p.211-235.

8. Brewster, D., Memoirs,Vol 1, 1885, p.86

9. Birch, Lecture by Hooke on 11.3.1675 *History of the Royal Society,* Vol III, p.194.

10. 'Anyone who honestly looks at the spectrum cannot see more than six distinctly different colours' G. Biernson 'Why did Newton see indigo in the spectrum?' *American Jnl of Physics* 1972, 40, pp.526-533

11. See, , McGuire & Rattansi 'Newton and the Pipes of Pan', *Notes & Records of the Royal Society*, 1966, p108-143.

12. Castillejo, D., *TheExpanding force in Newton's Cosmos*, 1985, pp.95-7, 102.

13. Gouk, P. *Let Newton Be!* Ed Fauval et. al., 1988, p.119.

14. The theory of light advanced by Christiaan Huygens focussed on its speed (found to an accuracy of 10% by Roemer in 1676), that it travelled in straight lines, and its reflection plus refraction. It mentioned Hooke as one who 'had begun to consider the waves of light.'.

15. Trans. by Crew, H., *The Wave theory of Light* 1900, p.40.

16. Leibniz to Newton, Corr. III, p.258.

17. In his Gresham lectures of 1681 Flamsteed referred to the new design as *potentially* valuable if only a suitable mirror could be constructed (*The Gresham Lectures of John Flamsteed,*,1975 Ed J. Forbes p.140)

18. British Museum manuscripts, MSS Add. 6782-89, 8 volumes. Lohne, J., 'Thomas Hariott' *Centaurus*, 6, no.2)

19. But see 'Robert Hooke as an Astronomer' by Nakajima, H., in *Robert Hooke, Tercentennial Studies,* 2006, 49-62.

20. Andrade, E.N., 'Robert Hooke' by *Proceedings of the Royal. Society.*, 1950,201, p.472.

21. Bechler, Z. 'The disagreeable case of Newton and Achromatic Refraction' *B. J. H. S.*, 1976 8,103.

22. Ibid p 110.

23. Shapiro, A., Newton's 'Achromatic' dispersion law' *Archive for History of Exact Sciences*, 1979/80 21 p.128.

24. Kuhn, T. *Structure of Scientific Revolutions,* 1970, p.67.

25. Westfall, R., *Isis*, 1962, LIII, p. 354.

26. Gouy, M., 'Sur le movement lumineux' 1886, *Journal de Physique*, cited in Sabra, op. cit., p.280

27. Jenkins & White, *Fundamentals of Optics* 1976; quoted in Sepper D.L., *Goethe contra Newton*', 1988.

28. Professor I. A. Sabra was an Egyptian science historian, with a background in Islamic theories of optics.

29. Westfall, R., *Op. cit.*, p.244.

30. *Correspondence*, Vol.. I, p.264.

31. Sabra, 1981, p.244) The Query 29 of Newton's *Optics* (1717) asked: 'Are not the Rays of light small corpuscles emitted from shining substances?' They were 'Bodies of different Sizes' he suggested, with violet the least, so most easily diffracted.

NOTES

Chapter 3

1. Westfall, R.S., *Never at Rest* 1980, p.402
2. But Hooke did endeavour to show how a central field of force would give Kepler's first law of planetary motion. Articles by Mike Nauenberg are here definitive, all online: 'Hooke, Orbital motion and Newton's Principia' Amer Jnl. Phys., 1994, 62, 331-350; 'On Hooke's 1685 Manuscript on Orbital Mechanics,' *Historia Mathematica, 25* 1998, 89-93; and 'Robert Hooke's Seminal Contributions to Orbital Dynamics' *Physics in Perspective* 7, March 2005 4-34.
3. Letter to Hooke, 5 Feb 1675.
4. An English translation of Part III of the *Principia* appeared in 1728 entitled *A Treatise on the System of the World.*
5. Lohne surmised that it was 'more than likely that Hooke suspected or knew this law k/r^2 before summer 1676,' by a combining of Kepler's third law and Huygen's centrifugal force demonstration for circular motion. ('Hooke versus Newton,' Centaurus, 1960, 7, p.13)
6. It is generally agreed (See Westfall, 'Newton's Marvellous Years,' *Isis* 1980 71 p117) that this memory relates to a document dated around 1669 printed in *The Correspondence of Isaac Newton*, Vol I, p 299-300.
7. Letter of 26 April 1676 to Oldenburg.
8. Iliffe Ibid, 65-85.
9. Ibid, 69; Westfall, 349.
10. Cambridge University Library Add. MS. 3973 Westfall Op. cit., 364.
11. *Correspondence*. II, 1960, p.319 sent 24 December, 1680; and p 331, sent January 1681.
12. What he said to Hooke in his letter was, 'And having thus shook hands with Philosophy, & being also at present taken of with other business, I hope it will not be interpreted out of any unkindness to you or ye R. Society that I am backward in engaging myself in these matters.' He added that his affection for philosophy was 'worn out, so that I am almost as little concerned about it as one tradesman was to be about another man's trade or a countryman about learning.'
13. Letter of 28.2.1681 to Flamsteed, *Correspondence*, Vol II, p.340-347.
14. Its perihelion distance was a mere 0.006 AU, so it passed by the Sun at only a small faction of the solar radius away from its surface (Marsden & Williams, *Catalogue of Cometary Orbits*, 1992, p.10).
15. Flamsteed's Preface to his *Historia Coelestis Britannica* was not properly published until 1982, edited by Allan Chapman.
16. Halley's comet is tilted at only 18° to the plane of the ecliptic. Therefore, it would have had to be carried along by any solar vortex that existed, however it was going in the reverse direction to all of the planets. Its perihelion distance was 0.6 AU so it was about Venus' distance away from the Sun at closest approach. The 1680 comet had a much larger tilt of 61°.
17. Hooke's lecture, 'Of Comets and Gravity' given in late 1682, in his *Posthumous Works* (1705 1971): pp.149-185, 167.
18. The brutal murder of Halley's father in March of that year seems to have involved a conspiracy connected with his work at the Tower of London. The Earl of Essex had been killed in mysterious circumstances the previous year, and it seems that Halley's father 'knew too much' about it, and so had to be silenced. The lifelong silence which Halley kept over this matter - he never spoke to anyone about it, that we have record – surely argues in favour of such a view. (Alan Cook, *Edmond Halley, Charting the Heavens and the Seas*,1998, pp.132, 148)

The event interrupted Halley's marital bliss at Highbury, and caused him to have to oversee his late Father's affairs, involving eg collecting rents. It would have been this, we surmise, that led him to visit Cambridge five months later. Over the previous couple of years he had sent comet-data to Newton and they may have previously met in 1682.

19. Nelkon & Parker, *Advanced Physics* 1970, 4th edn., p.44

20. Hall & Hall, Ibid, p328.

21. Cook, 'Edmond Halley', 1998, p.150..

22. The first mention of this calculation anywhere in Newton's writings occurs in one sentence, in a hard-to-date third version of 'De Motu' (late in 1685?) which says: 'My calculations reveal that the centripetal force by which our moon is held in her monthly orbit around the earth is to the force of gravity at the surface of the earth very nearly.' Herivel, 1965, p.302; Westfall, 1980, p.421.

23. Manuel, F., *A Portrait of Isaac Newton*, p318.

24. Letter to Halley of June 20, 1686.

25. Halley letter of May 22, 1686.

26. Halley wrote to Wallis on April 9, 1687, saying 'I have now lately received the last Book of that Treatise (Principia). .. Wherein is shown... How he falls in with Mr Hooke, and makes the earth of the shape of a compressed sphaeroid...'

27. Around 1720, Voltaire wrote: 'In France it is the pressure of the Moon that causes the tides, but in England it is the sea that gravitates towards the Moon; so that when you think that the Moon should make it flood with us, those gentlemen fancy it should ebb, which, very unfortunately, cannot be proved.' (*Lettres Philosophiques,* 1778)

28. Nichols, R. *Diaries of Robert Hooke* 1994 p.197: quoted as a comment made by a dinner-guest at the house of his friend Dr Busby.

29. Whiteside, 'Newton the Mathematician' in *Contemporary Newtonian Research* Ed. Zev Bechler, 109-127, p.124.

30. Letter to Royal Society dated January 25, 1676 *Correspondence* 1, pp.361-365.

31. Manuel, F., *A Portrait of Isaac Newton*, p181.

32. These two ether-gravity theories which Newton propounded in the 1670s have been well described *in The Janus Face of Genius* by BJT Dobbs (1992).

33. That well-known comment appeared in 1713, in the foreword to the *Principia* 2nd Edition.

34. This late date was advocated by Betty Jo Dobbs in *The Janus Face of Genius* (1992, p.148) and endorsed by Bernard Cohen (Isaac Newton *the Principa A New translation* 1999, p.47.);

35. Whiteside, 'Newton's lunar theory: from high hope to disenchantment', *Vistas*, 1976: ULC Add.3965.14, f.613.

36. Hooke's works are published in 'Early Science in Oxford' 1920-45. See Vol 6, p.262 (One may consider the significance of a situation where even the works of Hooke are not published under his own name). The calculation - the first ever involving a theory of gravitation - relates a fractional decrease in the Earth's radius of 1.4×10^{-5} and a corresponding fractional decrease in weight predicted of 1.4×10^{-6}, as if he were assuming the gravity force would be linearly proportional to distance from the Earth's centre.

37. *Diary of Samual Pepys*, Vol. VI, p.209 ff.

38. ECLIPTIC: Plane in which the earth orbits the Sun.

39. This was read to the Royal Society on November 8th and November 15th, 1682, as recorded in Birch's *History of the Royal Society of London*, 1756, vol. IV. The discourse

is recorded in the *Posthumous Works* of Hooke, edited and published by Waller in 1705. (Reprinted 1970, Ed. Professor T. Brown, p.166-185.) Waller was there in the habit of conflating several lectures at a time, delivered by Hooke at short weekly intervals, without dating the separate parts. As Waller was elected FRS in May 1681, he would have been familiar with the lectures then delivered. The chapter entitled, 'A Discourse of the Nature of Comets' was cited by Waller as having been published 'soon after Michelmas' of 1682, and the *Notes and Records of the Royal Society* by Birch record three dates for this comet series having been delivered. The Discourse starts on page 150, then on p.166 the running title changes from 'A Discourse of Comets' to 'Of Comets and Gravity.' The discussion of Hooke's epochally new theory of universal gravitation really begins at the bottom of page 176, over nine pages until it breaks off abruptly on page 185. It is introduced with phrases like, 'These my conceptions (as being, I think, wholly new, and not yet asserted by any person whatsoever)...' His explanation as to why gravity diminished reciprocally as the duplicate of distance occurs on the last page. In his introduction to the 'Nature of Comets' discourse, Waller stated: 'I shall only give some account of what is immediately annext to it, and which indeed the Thread of the Discourse led him to; that is, a short Treatise of Gravity.' Thus it was the logic of the comet lecture which led Hooke on to the theme of universal gravitation, confirmed by a later remark on another occasion (p.202), when he was again discussing gravity, and remarked: 'yet 'tis very evident by many arguments I produced in my lectures about the Comet, that the Power thereof [ie, of gravity] is not limited with so small an extent...' He was there arguing against a popular notion that gravity terminated in the atmosphere and reached no higher. Thus the overall context for that lecture-series wherein he argued extensively about the nature of gravity was 'the Comet,' viz the giant one of 1680.

40. Robert Waller Ed., *the Posthumous Works of Robert Hooke,* 1705, 1971, 'Of Comets and Gravity' 149-185, p185:the, text ends on p.185 with the comment, 'the author here breaks off abruptly'

41. 'Solid orbs' – An allusion to the crystal spheres of the planets conceived as gliding smoothly past each other in the Aristotelian scheme of things. Actually, Ptolemy's orbs had been of an aethereal nature, as likewise they were for the Mediaeval poet Dante.

42. Ibid., p.167.

43. Ibid., p.73.

44. Gunther, *Early Science in Oxford*, VI, p114.

45. Lohne, J., 'Hooke versus Newton', *Centaurus*, VII 1960, p.42.

46. In *Astronomia* Nova Kepler sometimes expressed this law as velocity being inversely proportional to distance, from the ellipse focus. It is in this approximate form that Hooke here quotes it.

47. It would decrease linearly *if* the earth were a body of uniform density. Mathematically, $F \alpha r$ below the surface while $F \alpha 1/r^2$ above the surface.

48. Edmond Halley had journeyed to this island in the South Atlantic in order to survey the stars of the southern hemisphere, a feat for which he was elected a Fellow of the Royal Society in 1678, and which earned him the accolade from Flamsteed of being 'the southern Tycho' (in '*Doctrine of the Sphere*,' 1680).

49. The manuscript is ULC Add. 3965.14, f.613 states, that 'Materiam coelorum fluidam esse [et] circa systematis cosmici secundum cursum Planetyrum gyrare'[roughly] 'The material of the heavens is fluid, and revolves in circles around the planets.'

50. 'Philosophical origins of gentile theology' was commenced in 1683/4 and re-worked later on see Chapter Ten.

51. Naylor, R.H., 'Galileo & the Problem of Free Fall', *Brit. Jnl. Hist. Sci.,* 1974 VII p124.
52. The Correspondence of Isaac Newton, II, pp. 435-441.
53. Huygens, Christian, *Oeuvres Complètes*, Hague 1888 Vol 7, p.325-328.
54. *Principia*, Preface, 1st Edition.
55. These remarks on gravity were however missing from the text of the letter sent to Huygens, on 23 June 1673, and now in the possession of the library of the University of Leiden, published in the *Oevres Completes* of Huygens. It is present however in the 'copy' belonging to the Royal Society and published in Volume I of *Correspondence*.
56. Borelli, G., *Theory of the Medician Stars* G.Borelli, 1666.
57. RECTILINEAR: motion in a straight line.
58. Manuel ibid p.147.
59. R.Westfall, Ibid, p.387.
60. 'Essay Concerning Human Understanding' 1924 edn p7
61. Newton to Halley, 20 June 1686 and 27 July, 446-7: *Correspondence* II pp. 435,446..
62. RS Archives LBC.6.172, dated 23 June, 1673 (*Correspondence*. II 290-295).
63. The Hague copy of Huygens' letter is in the University of Leiden, published in the *Oeuvres Completes* de Christiaan Huygens, Vol. 7 (Hague 1888), 325-8.
64. *The Correspondence of Henry Oldenburg*, II, 1975, 58-69, 68 sent 27 June 1673.
65. Patterson, L.D., 'Hooke's Theory of Gravitation and its influence upon Newton' *Isis* 41 (1950), 32-45, 32.
66. *Correspondence* II 290-295, 290; sent 23 June 1673.
67. Corr I, 290-295 dated 23 June 1673 (RS Archives LBC 6.172); Corr, II, 435-40 sent 20 June, 446-7; sent 27 July 1686, to Halley.
68. Newton's third letter to Halley alluding to this matter claimed that he had 'unexpectedly struck upon a copy of ye letter' of thirteen years ago, to Huygens, adding: 'Tis in ye hand of one Mr John Wickins who was then my chamber fellow … so it is authentic.' (27 July, Corr II p.446) He is assuring Halley that the letter must be authentic, because it is in another's hand. No-one has seen that copy of the letter, ostensibly identical with that now in the Royal Society archives.
69. Ellen Tan Drake, *Restless Genius Robert Hooke and his Earthly Thoughts*, OUP 1996, p33
70. D.T.Whiteside, 'Before the Principia', *JHA* 1970, I, p.11.
71. D.T.Whiteside, 'The Prehistory of the Principia', *Notes and Records of the Royal Society*, 45 (1991), 11-61, 12.
72. D.T.Whiteside, 'Newton's Principia Mathematica', *JHA* 1970.
73. J.Lohne, 'Hooke Versus Newton', *Centaurus,* 7 (1960), 6-52, 36.
74. I.Bernard Cohen, 'The Principia, Universal Gravitation, and the 'Newtonian Style..."' *Contemporary Newton Research,* Ed. Z.Bechler (Dortrecht and London, 1982), 84.
75. Quote from Newton's *System of the World'* Cajori, Volume II 1962 p. 550.
76. Herivel, 1965 p.70; quoted in Cohen, 1980, p.346, note 4.
77. Gregory MS: *Corr*. Vol. 3, pp.331-333; alluded to in Cohen, 1980, p.346, note 5.
78. Moore, P. *The Story of Astronomy*, 1969, p.72.
79. Hall & Hall, *De Gravitatione,* in Hall & Hall 1962, p. 148.
80. Cohen, 1980, p.346, note 5.
81. This was the argument used by Curtis Wilson for denying credit to Hooke for the inverse-square law. (Wilson, 1989, p.239.) The conclusion to Hooke's discussion of comets in *De Cometa* was that the nucleus of a comet was of a like nature to the central parts of the planets, but 'much impaired in its attractive or gravitating power.' (Gunther, 1931, p.231).

NOTES

Chapter 4

1. This evidently was the law to which Einstein was referring: see *Einstein, Ideas and Opinions,* 1954, Chapter on 'The Mechanics of Newton,' p.225.
2. I.Bernard Cohen, *The Newtonian Synthesis*, 1980, p.18.
3. Westfall,R. Op. cit., 1980, p.150.
4. Rosenfield, L. 'Newton and the Law of Gravitation', 1966, *Archive for History of Exact Sciences*, 2, p.367.
5. Westfall, 'Newton & the Fudge Factor', *Science*, 1973, 179, p.754.
6. J.Roche, in *Let Newton Be!* 1988, Ed.J.Fauvel *et. al.*, p.56.
7. I.Bernard Cohen, *The Newtonian Revolution*, 1980, pp.230-240.
8. Gillespie, J.C. *The Edge of Objectivity*,1960, p.503
9. I. Bernard Cohen, *op. cit.*, p.304.
10. Mathematically, the Principia's second law stated that F α Δ (MV), so that its 'impressed force' was what we would call 'impulse,' or change in momentum. Today, students learn the Second Law in its (eighteenth-century) differential form as F α d(MV)/dt, from which F = MA is derived.
11. Beckmann, P., *A History of* π,1971, p.135
12. Not uintil the mid--nineteenth century did a group including Sir John Herschel, Babbage and Augustus de Morgan finally put an end to it.
13. I.Bernard Cohen, 'Newton's Second Law and the Concept of Force in the Principia', in 'Texas Quarterly journal', Autumn 1967 Vol 10 p.128.
14. E.T.Bell, 'Men of Mathematics' , by The Scientific Book club, p.115.
15. Bernard Cohen credits Jacob Hermann for this equation: Hermann 'states Newton's second law for continuous forces in differentials' i.e. in Leibnizian terms: *Phenomena; sive, De Corporum Solidorum et Fluidorum,* Amsterdam, 1716. Cohen, *Newtonian Rev.* 1980, pp.143-5, and *Isaac Newton The Principia* 1999, p.113.
16. E.T.Bell, *Ibid*, p.116.
17. E.J.Aiton, 'The Celestial Mechanics of Leibniz', *Annals of Science*, 1962, 18, p.82 (See also his earlier *Annals of Science* article, 1958, 14, 157-172, 161). Varignon's equations were published in 'des Forces Centrales…' Mémoires de l'Academie des Sciences,1700, 218-37.
18. T.L.Hankins, 'The Reception of Newton's Second Law of Motion in the eighteenth Century', *Archives Internationale d'Histoire des Sciences,* 1967, 20, p.44.
19. In 1752 Euler presented to the Berlin Academy of Sciences a paper on 'The Discovery of a New Principle of Dynamics,' which was that $2M\ d^2x = \pm F\ dt^2$ (The factor of 2 arose from choice of units and the $\pm$ indicated that a vector was involved.) Of this 1752 Euler treatise, the historian Clifford Truesdall wrote: **'These are the famous Newtonian equations, here proposed for the first time as general, explicit equations for mechanical problems of all kinds. The discovery of this principle seems so easy, from the Newtonian ideas, that it has never been attributed to anyone but Newton; such is the universal ignorance of the true history of mechanics.'** ('A programme towards rediscovering the rational mechanics of the Age of Reason,' *Archives for the History of Exact Sciences*, Vol 1, 1960, p.23). Though stated plainly enough, these words have never percolated through to textbook writers.
20. Brackenridge, B., *Annals of Science*, 'Newton's Mature Dynamics: Revolutionary or Reactionary?' 1988, 45, p.451-476.
21. But, See Guiccardini, N. *Reading the Principia,* 1999, 3.4.2,.'Synthetic method of first and last ratios applied to the geometric representation of central force.'

22. Cohen, I.B., *The Newtonian Revolution*, 1980, p.304 n.1. f
23. Ed., Whiteside, *Mathematical Papers* Vol. VII, p.129.
24. Whiteside, D.T., *Mathematical Papers*, Vol VII, intro.
25. Cohen again confirmed this in the Introduction to his 'Variorum' edition of the *Principia* (1971, p.166), where he said that Newton 'did not ever write' a fluxional equation such as F = kmä [a = distance] or F = kmv.' These words have here been accepted as true and final, but there is disagreement here: see Guiccardini, 2009 p.240.
26. Dampier, W.C., *The History of Science and its relation to philosophy and religion* 1929, p.160.
27. Whiteside, D.T., 'Kepler, Newton and Flamsteed on refraction through a 'regular aire' '*Centaurus,* 1980, 24, p.288-315).
28. Kline, M., *Mathematics in Western Culture* 1954.
29. A notable exception here being I Bernard Cohen, *The Newtonian Revolution*, 1980, p.89.
30. *Corr*. Vol VII, 29 Mar.
31. *Principia*, 2nd Ed. 1713, Proposition XXXVI, 'To find the force of the Moon to move the sea' (not in the First Edition).
32. *The Principia*, 3rd Edition: Book III, Propn, 36, Problem 18, Cor. 2.
33. The nearest Newton came to formulating 'a full and explicit statement of the law of universal gravitation' according to Bernard Cohen, was his statement that: 'all bodies universally gravitate towards one another with a force proportional to the product of their masses.' (Propn 7, Ist Edn) *The Newtonian Revolution*, p.89.
34. J. Pepper in *Let Newton Be!* 1988, 63-80: 'Newton made a major breakthrough [in De analysi] by introducing what is now known as the Newton-Raphson method' (p. 73). .
35. Whiteside, *Mathematical Papers II*, pp. 206-47, also 218-19.
36. Wallis, J., *A Treatise of Algebra*, 1685, 338.
37. *Journal Book of the Royal Society of London,* 30 July 1690.
38. Raphson, op. cit. (7), Preface.
39. Wallis, J., *Opera Mathematica*, ii, London, 1693, 391-6.
40. Simpson, T., Essays on … Mathematicks 1740
41. Cajori, F., 'Historical note on the Newton-Raphson method of approximation', *American Mathematical Monthly* (1911), 18, 29-32, on 30.
42. Thomas, D.J., 'Joseph Raphson, F.R.S.', *Notes Rec. Roy. Soc. London* (1990), 44, 151-67, 155.
43. Boyer, C., *A History of Mathematics*, 1968 1980, 449.
44. Hollingdale, S., *Makers of Mathematics*, London, 1989, 179.
45. CorrespondenceIIIpp. 222-8.
46. Whiteside, D.T., 'The mathematical principles underlying Newton's Principia', *JHA*1790, 1, 116-38, on 119.
47. Hall, R., *Philosophers at War,* Cambridge, 1980, 94-6.
48. Whiteside, T. 'Essay review of The Correspondence of Isaac Newton, Vol. III', *History of Science* 1962, 1, 97.
49. Whiteside Op. cit. JHA 1970, p.119.
50. N.Kollerstrom, Newton's Method of Approximation, an Enduring Myth, *B.J.Hist. Sci.*, 1992 25, 234-54.
51. It was suggested by Newton that the frictional force F between layers of a liquid is proportional to A the area and the velocity gradient dv/dy, ie F α A dv/dy This equation is sometimes called Newton's law of viscosity. It is obeyed by 'Newtonian liquids.'' (Source: R. Muncaster, A/Level physics)

NOTES

Chapter 5

1. Halley, E., (1692) *An account of the cause of the change of the variation of the magnetical needle with an hypothesis of the structure of the internal parts of the earth* Phil. Trans. 17. p.563-587.
2. The topic is omitted by both of Halley's biographers: *Edmond Halley, Charting the Heavens and the Seas* by Alan Cook, 1998, and *Edmond Halley Genius in Eclipse* by Colin Ronan, 1998.
3. In the 3rd edition this was revised to 1:39.788, the bogus accuracy here no doubt conveying credibility.
4. Curtis Wilson, *AHES* 1980 p.88, *AHES* 1987, p.242.
5. Brougham, H. P., and Routh, E. J*., Analytical View of Sir Isaac Newton's Principia,* 1855, p.294.
6. *Principia*, 3rd Edition, Book III, Propn 37.
7. Halley, E., op. cit., p.568.
8. Zirkle, C., 'The Theory of Concentric Spheres: Halley, Mather and Symmes' *Isis*, 1947, 37, p.155-1549. Jules Verne's *Journey the the Centre of the Earth* appeared in 1864, and Bulwer Lytton's *The Coming Race* in 1871, both employing a hollow earth.
9. Halley, E., Phil. Trans., 1683, 13, p.208-221.
10. Schaffer, S., 'Halley's atheism and the end of the world', *Notes and records of the Royal Society*, xxxii (1977), 17-40, p. 18.
11. Schaffer, op. cit, p.18
12. Stock, J.,*Life of George Berkeley*, 1776, p.28, cited in Scaffer op. cit.
13. Flamsteed to Sharp, Feb. 11, 1710, in Baily, *An Account of the Rev. John Flamsteed*, 1837.
14. Halley, E., op. cit. 1692, p568.
15. Ronan, C., *Jnl of the RAS*, 1968, 15, p.241
16. Halley, E., Phil. Trans, 1716, 29, 407-428.
17. Not until 1976 was this concept was formulated, by astronomer John Eddy, linking extra-cold weather in Europe and North America with a dormant Sun: the Minimum extended over three twenty-two year cycles or 'heartbeats' of the Sun.
18. Wilkins, H.P. *Our Moon* 1954.

Chapter 6

1. Keynes, Sir Geoffrey, *A Bibliography of Robert Hooke*, 1960, pXI.
2. *Early Science in Oxford* edited by R. Gunther, Vol VI, pXIV., 1930.
3. Margaret Espinasse *Robert Hooke* 1956, p.13. A German visitor Von Offenback visited the Royal Society in 1710, making the comment that the Hooke and Boyle portraits were the two finest.
4. Salter, H.E., Ed., *Remarks & collections of Thomas Hearne*, 9, 1725-8, p.111.
5. Gunther Ibid Vols 6 &7.
6. J. F. West, *The Great Intellectual Revolution*, 1965, p82
7. After the Great Fire of 1666, the advice of the Royal Society was sought and at the age of 31 Hooke was appointed City Surveyor and he made a model for rebuilding the city. Private interests blocked his attempt to realign and widen important thoroughfares.
8. Ibid, Vol VI, pXIV.
9. *Aubrey's Brief Lives* Penguin 1987, edited by O. L. Dick, first published 1813.

10. See *Restless Genius, Robert Hooke and his Earthly Thoughts*, Ellen Tan Drake, OUP 1995; *A More Beautiful City, Robert Hooke and the Rebuilding of London after the Great Fire*' Cooper, M., 2003; *Robert Hooke and the English Renaissance*, Ed Kent & Chapman 2005; *Robert Hooke, tercentennial Studies*, Ed Cooper & Hunter, 2006; *Out of the Shadow of a Giant: Hooke, Halley and the Birth of British Science* by John and Mary Gribbin, 2017.

11. Thomas Birch, *History of the Royal Society of London*, II, p.318: November 5 & 12th, 1668. Newton's *Principia,* 1687, p.21: Corollary 6 of 3rd law.

12. Westfall, R., 'Newton and the Fudge Factor', *Science*, 1973, 197,p.754.

13. Hanby, D., radio broadcast, 'London's Leonardo' 1987.

14. Schaffer & Hunter, Ed., *Robert Hooke, New Studies,* 1989.

15. Hooke's design for the Monument is now in the British Museum whereas Wren's design which was not adopted is now in All Souls College, Oxford. (Hanby, 'London's Leonardo,' The City University July 1987, p10

16. For a fine account of Hooke's genius in designing the dome of St Paul's, see Gribbin J&M *Out of the Shadow of a Giant* pp.79-81' whereby the catenary curve concept was applied: 'the best monument to Robert Hooke the architect is the dome of St Paul's cathedral.'

17. Only after that great theft of his ideas did he start to grow more cynical and embittered, Allan Chapmen has argued: '… a sense of intellectual betrayal in the way that the Royal Society had backed Sir Isaac Newton's claims for the discovery of universal gravitation, rather than his own. And it was this, I would argue, that gave him the meagre, suspicious, melancholy and reclusive aspect mentioned by Wallace.' (Robert Hoooke and the English Renaissance, Ed Kent & Chapman, p.20)

Chapter 7

1. Richard Hakluyt, *Principal Navigations*, 1598, Vol. 1.

2. Computer verification of the ephimerides of the period by Owen Gingerich demonstrated that such accuracy was first attained by the Nautical Almanac from 1779 onwards (O. Gingerich and Barbare Welther, *Planetary, lunar and solar positions, AD 1650-1805,* Harvard, 1983, Preface, p.xviii).

3. EVECTION - Horrocks devised an elliptical method for coping with this largest of the lunar inequalities, originally detected by Hipparchus. It was given its name by Ishmael Boulliau in 1645.

4. Whiteside, DT, *Vistas in Astronomy,* From high hope to disenchantment…1976, 19.

5. There is no simple answer, but my PhD grappled with the topic. James Gleick the chaos theorist kindly commented of my book, that the 'computer-assisted analysis *Newton's Forgotten Lunar Theory* is definitive.' (Gleick, *Isaac Newton* 2003 p.238.)

6. The story is told by Derek Howse, in *Greenwich Time and the Discovery or Longitude,* 1980.

7. Forbes, 'Origins of the Greenwich Observatory' *Vistas in Astronomy* 20 p.39.

8. Quoted in K. T. Hoppen, ' The Royal Society and Ireland: William Molyneux F. R. S. (1656-1698)' *Notes & Records of the Royal Society*, 18, 1963, p.127.

9. Chapman, A., *Three North Country Astronomers*, 1982 p.9

10. Forbes, E., *op. cit.* p26.

11. See Flamsteed bio by this author in the *Biographical Dictionary of Astronomers,* Ed. Hockey, 2007.

NOTES

12. 'I voluntarily offer myself as a witness of the barely credible certainty of your instruments...' Halley had testified writing from Leyden - though later on he changed his mind about the Dutchman's accuracy. 'Halley hath been too lavish in his praise' was Flamsteed's comment – confirmed by a modern analysis which found the standard deviation of errors in that star-catalogue to be two arcminutes (arxiv.org, *The Star-Catalogue of Hevelius*, Robert H. vn Gent 2010.

13. Forbes, E., *The Gresham Lectures of Flamsteed*, p38.

14. Baily, F., *An Account of the Revd John Flamsteed*, 1837, p. xxix.

15. See Kollerstrom and Yallop, 'Flamsteed's Lunar Data, 1692-95, sent to Newton' *JHA* 1995.

16. Flamsteed to Abraham Sharp, 4 May 1704: 'My discourse ...brought the subtle gentleman down hither.'

17. *1690 epoch: The Preface to John Flamsteed's Historia Coelestis Britannica*, Ed Chapman, 1982, p.181.

18. The other two being the periodic return of 'Halley's comet' and the relative movement or 'proper motion' of stars.

19. In the winter of 1694/5 the lunar and solar apses drew into alignment as the Sun crossed over them both at midwinter. Newton sought in vain for any perturbation linked to this nine-year cycle, absent from his *Theory of the Moon's Motion* (1702).

20. Whiteside, 'Newton's Lunar theory: from High Hope to Disenchantment' *Vistas in Astronomy*. 1996, p.321.

21. Whiteside never realised that these little 'ancillary equations' actually worked – nobody in modern times did until I got the whole thing to work in my PhD; also that it was the most widely-used lunar theory throughout the whole of the first half of the eighteenth century.

22. Westfall, p.546.

23. Baily, Ibid., p. xvi.h

24. Brewster, Vol. I, p.313.

25. Hawkins, S., *A Brief History of Time,* 1988, p.181.

26. Moore, P., *A History of Astronomy*, 1983, p.80.

27. Whiteside, *Mathematical Papers,* Vol VII, Introduction, p. Xxv.

28. These were the first-ever 'ancillary equations' i.e. added onto the major, traditional ones of 'evection' etc – by the nineteenthcentury there would be several hundred of them!

29. Baily, p.72.

30. Cohen, B., Intro. to Newton's Principia, 1971, p.176.

31. Flamsteed to Colson, 10.10.1698, *Corr.* Vol. IV.

32. Brewster, Vol. I, p.176.

33. When mapping the stars of the Southern sky, Halley had used the old co-ordinate system of Tycho Brahe, which was likely to err by four or five minutes.

34. Whiston, *Memoirs*, Ist Edn, p.294.

35. As Sharp wrote to Flamsteed, when informed of Newton's visit and the Committee's budget for publication: 'Printing the Catalogue without maps and constellations is to render the work lame and imperfect and it shews how little a genius Sir Isaac Newton has for such pieces of art, since, as before hinted, he looked but slightly upon your finest drafts, which will no doubt be as great an ornament and recommendation of the work as anything imaginable...' (Oct 1, 1705.)

36. Chapman, A., *The Preface to John Flamsteed's Historia Coelestis Britannica*, foreword, p.10.

37. Westfall, p.660.
38. Flamsteed to Pound, 15.11.1704: Baily, p.427.
39. Baily, p.83.
40. Ibid, p.246.
41. Flamsteed, Letter to Sharp, 22.12.1711.
42. Chapman, A. *Preface to Flamsteed's Historia*, 1982, p.176.
43. Abraham Sharp's doubtless astute commentary here was:
 Hereby am [I] rendered more sensible of the scope of their design, [of Halley and Newton] which undoubtedly was, out of envy, to wrest the honour and reputation of all your labours from you, and ascribe it to themselves, as far as with any pretence of reason they can. (11.6.1716, Baily p. 323)
44. Brown, B. *Astronomical Atlases*, 1932.
45. Baily, p339.
46. The Royal Greenwich Observatory dissolved in 1990. Two decades earlier it had moved from Greenwich down to Herstmonceaux in Sussex. Its archives were removed to Cambridge, and its telescopes migrated to clearer southern skies.

Chapter 8

1. Quoted in *'The Mathematical Discoveries of Newton,* H. W. Turnbull, 1945 p.30.
2. Whiteside, 'Patterns of Mathematical Thought in the later 17th century', *Archive for the history of Exact Sciences*, Vol 1, 1960, p368.
3. Augustus De Morgan, A. *the Life and Works of Newton*, 1914.
4. Hofmann, Leibniz in Paris, 1974, p192.
5. In July 1684 Leibniz wrote to his friend Mencke, about his new calculus article, saying: 'I do not believe either, that Mr Newton will claim it for himself, but only some inventions relating to infinite series which he has in part also applied to the circle.' (Jason Bardi, *The Calculus Wars*, 2006, p.117.)
6. Discussed by Hofmann in *Leibniz in Paris*, p.64.
7. Hall, R., *Philosophers at War* CUP 1980 p.9.
8. Whiteside, *Isis*, 1977, 68, p116-121.
9. Newton to Collins, *Correspondence* Vol. 1, 247-254.
10. De Morgan, op. cit. 1914, p.69.
11. Letter of 29 March 1716: *Corr.* VI, p.312.
12. De Morgan, op. cit. 1914, p.84-5.
13. See Hofman, *Leibniz in Paris*, 1974.
14. John Craig *Methodus figurarum ... quadraturas determinandi*, 1685; Craig *Tractatus Mathematicu de figurarum Curviliearum Quadraturis*, 1693.
15. John Craig, *Tractatus Mathematicus de Figurarum Curvilinearum Quadraturis* 1693, London, p.1.
16. to Dr. John Arbuthnot, on meeting De L'Hôpital: Westfall p.473.
17. This is 'Lemma II' of Volume 2, of the 1687 Principia, pp.157-8.
18. Expansion of $(x + a)^2$ where the a^2 term is ignored because it is too small.
19. Second term in the expansion of $(x + a)^n$, where all higher terms in the expansion are ignored as containing powers of a.
20. Bishop Berkeley, *The Analyst,* 1734 para 4.
21. Hall, R. op. cit., p.204: 'Remarks on the Dispute', 1713, reply to Keill's letter from London.

NOTES

22. Whiteside, *The Math. Principles Underlying Newton's* Principia. 1970, p10.
23. *Principia,* Book II, Prop 34, Scholium.
24. Rupert Hall took the view that, what Wallis published as sent to him by Newton displayed the method of fluxions 'and its use in problems of tangents, maxima and minima and the quadrature of curves' (*Adventurer in Thought*, 1992, p.258). One is startled that so careful a scholar could be so wholly mistaken – especially after he'd written a book on the subject (*Philosophers at War*, 1980).
25. Aiton, E., 'The Celestial Mechanics of Leibniz' *Annals of Science,* 1960,16, p.66.
26. In Leibnizian term, for the curve y=ax^{n-1}, area under it is given by $\int ax^{n-1}dx = a/n. x^n$
27. MP 8, p.5 This is the so-called 'branchistochrone' problem, .
28. Letter, Monmort to Brook Taylor, 7.12.1718,. *Corr.* VII pp.21-22.
29. Newton to Montague *Corr.*, 4, p226, then PT 97,19, 384-9.
30. Bernoulli, *Acta Eruditorum* May 1697 206-217; also a solution by De L'Hôpital 217-223.
31. Newton had merely submitted 'without proof… a method of describing the cycloid:' R. Woodhouse 'Treatise on … the Calculus of Variations,' Cambridge 1810 (MP 8:10. p.150).
32. The cycloid was what was called a mechanical curve, in that it was produced by a mechanical process, whereas describing it analytically was far from easy.
33. Ditto for Guicciardini: 'Newton had probably achieved this solution through a fluxional equation similar to …' (2011, p335). Science historians should not be allowed to indulge in such pipedreams, where nothing in the historical record supports their interpetation. He adds that 'Newton's fluxional analysis of the branchistochrone problem can be found in …' and gives a location, thereby reinforcing the impression of a modestly-unpublished text - neglecting to say that the text to which he alludes (MP 8:86-91) was only published years later in 1700, *after* Fatio had composed a book on the specific question.
34. Fatio Duillier *Lineae Brevissimi Descensus* 1699, 24 pp.
35. Whiteside, *Math Papaers*, 8:86, Appendix 2.
36. Some have contrasted the 'dynamics' of Leibniz with the 'rational mechanics' of the *Principia* (P. Costabel, 'Newton and Leibniz's dynamics,' The Texas Quarterly, 10: 119-26)).
37. See my online article 'The Birth of Calculus: towads a more Leibnizian View' (2012) for this list.
38. Charles Hayes *A Treatise of Fluxions* (315 pp) 1704, p.1
39. John Harris *A New Short Treatise of Algebra* (a last chapter, 'of Fluxions,') 1702, p.115.
40. See also George Cheyne, *Fluxionum* Methodus … of 1703, which alludes to the Newtonian text in Wallis' *Algebra, p.2*. It gives no curve gradients, it finds no maxima/minima.
41. See English translation of *De Quadratura* in John Harris's Lexicon Technicum of 1710, volume 2; or, English translation of various *De Quadratura* texts and manuscripts in Whiteside, Math. Papers, VIII.
42. A pleasant but illusory summing-up of the different views was given by Professor Ivor Grattain-Guinness, the distinguished historian of mathematics. Comparing 'Principal features of the calculi of Newton and Leibniz' in a table (Fontana *History of Mathematics* pp.244-5), for 'Basic derivative concept' he put under Newton' $\dot{x}/\dot{y}$ and under 'Leibniz' dy/dx. These are both to be doubted. Never did Newton write $\dot{x}/\dot{y}$ for

a gradient or derivative function, he never published any text with $\dot{x}/\dot{y}$; while the all-important dy/dx originated with the Bernoulli brothers in the early 1690s, then being clearly explained in the classic de L'Hôpital textbook, written in Paris as Marquis took math lessons from Johann Bernoulli. It's not in the 1684 & 1686 articles by Leibniz, which have dy and dx separate.

43. Westfall, p.721.
44. Hawking, S., *A Brief History of Time*, 1988, p.182.
45. Its text was composed in the 1690s: Whiteside, *Math Papers*,
46. Westfall, p.596
47. The authors had been discussing Westfall's *Newton and the Fudge Factor*, a trenchant exposeé of the systematic fiddling of data (See Appendix 4).
48. W. Broad and N. Wade 1985, *Betrayers of the Truth*, p.28.
49. Whiteside., *The Mathematical Principles underlying Newton's* Principia 1970, U of Glasgow, pp.9,10.
50. Writing in the third person, Leibniz declared that he was 'astounded not by their arguments but by the fictions that pervaded their attack upon his good faith.' P.27, Childs *Historia Et Origo*.
51. Leibniz to Editors of the Journal Literaire de la Haye, October 1713, in: *Correspondence* VI, 30-32, p.31.
52. For discussion here, see Guicciardini, N., *Isaac Newton on Mathematical Certainty and Method*, 2011, p.373.
53. Translation from *The Early Mathematical Manuscripts of Leibniz* J. M. Childs 1920, 22-58, pp. 23, 25; see discussion in R.C. Brown*, The Tangled Origin of the Leibnizian Calculus*, 2012, p.4.
54. This claim, that the actual world is the best of all possible worlds, is said to be a central argument of Leibniz' *Theodicy* (1710).
55. Newton, reply to Charta Volans (*Journal Literaffire de la Haye*,1713): Hall, p.206.
56. To help follow this arcane debate, readers may with to peruse the summary of contents of these two letters, helpfully given in Guicciardini 2011, pp.355,357.
57. Hall, A.R., *Philosophers at War*, 1980, p.270.
58. Isaac Newton *Universal Arithmetick* 2nd Edn 1728, trans from the Latin by Mr Raphson, p.227-8.
59. *David Gregory, Isaac Newton and their Circle* Oxford 1937, Ed Hiscock, p.18.
60. *Principia,* Book II, Proposition 34.
61. See discussion in Cajori's notes on the *Principia*, 1962, UCLA, p.657.
62. The nearest to such a reference in Raphson's book was a mention of Viète (1540-1603).

Chapter 9

1. Cajori, F., notes on the *Principia,* 1989 edition, p.627.
2. Sullivan, J., *Isaac Newton 1642-1727*, 1937, p. 75.
3. White, M. I.N. *The Last Sorcerer*, 1997 p221.
4. Hall, R., I.N. *Adventurer in Thought*, 1992 p.218.
5. Whiteside, F.T*., Introduction to Mathematical Works*, VI, p.20
6. J. W. L. Glaisher, quoted in *Math. Papers*, VI, p20.
7. *Principia* 1st Edn Definition 8, p.12.
8. *Corr.* II, p.467.

9. Hill, Ibid, p259.

10. William Whiston, *Memoirs*, p36; also see Cajori, notes on *Principia,* U. of California, p.630.

11. Cajori, Ibid., p. 631.

12. The title comes from an essay by Curtis Wilson, on 'From Kepler's Laws to Gravitation' (*Archive for History of Exact Sciences*, 1970, 6, p.97). He noted how the Trinity seemed to permeate Kepler's attitude towards cosmology. He then added 'Theology aside,...' and went on to discuss the physics of Kepler's laws.

13. Hill, C., *Intellectual Origins of the English Revolution*, 1987, p.171.

14. For 'divine arm' see Newton letters 'Containing some Argumentd for Proof of a Deity' in Bentley, *Sermons*, 1838, p.210.

15. Jacob, M., *The Radical Enlightenment,* 1981, p.92

16. Pitcairne to Gregory, 25.2.1706, op. cit. p.107.

17. Jacob, op. cit., p.83.

18. 'The late happy Revolution... has wonderfully increased Men's Prejudices against the Clergy' (*An Account of the Growth of Deism in England,* W. Stephens, p.8 1695)

19. Jacob, M.C., *op. cit.*, p.83.

20. Margaret Jacob, 'Newton and the French Prophets: New Evidence' *History of Science*, 1978, 16, 134-42, 139.

21. Buchwald & Feingold*, Newton and the origin of Civilization*, 2013, pp.335-338.

22. Leibniz, letter to Princess Caroline, Nov. 1715.

23. The Leibniz-Clarke Correspondence, 1998, p.11.

24. Margaret C. Jacob, *The Radical Enlightenment: Pantheists, Freemasons and Republicans*, 1981, p.96.

25. Shapin, 'Of Gods and Kings: Natural Philosophy and Politics in the Leibniz-Clarke Disputes' *Isis*, 1981, 72, p187-208)

26. Jacob, op. cit., p.112.

27. Castillejo, *The Expanding Force in Newton's Cosmos*, 1985, p.104.

28. Rob Iliffe, *Priest of Nature, The Religious worlds of Isaac Newton*, 2017, p.307.

29. Snobelen, S., 'Isaac Newton and the Devil' in Force and Hutton, Eds, *Newton and Newtonianism,* 2004, p.57.

30. Snobelen, Ibid., p.162.

31. Snobelen, S., 'Isaac Newton, heretic: the strategies of a Nicodemite' *BJHS* 1999, 32, 381-419, 387-8.

32. Christianson, *In the Presence of the Creator,* 1984, p.312.

33. Westfall, R., *Science and Religion in the 17ᵗʰ Century*,1973, p.208.

Chapter 10

1. Westfall *Never at Rest,* p.805. For the extent to which the *Chronology* may have emerged from an earlier unpublished manuscript, 'Theologiae,' see Ken Knoespel 'Interpretive Strategies in *Newton's Theologia gentilis origines philosophiae* in Force and Popkin, *Newton and Religion* 1999 p179-202.

2. Brook Taylor as a leading Freemason was instrumental in transmitting Freemasonry to France: Margaret Jacob, *The Radical Enlightenment*, p.112.

3. Jed Buchwald & Mordechai Feingold, *Newton and the Origin of Civilization,* 2013, p. ...; Cambridge, King's College Library, Keynes MS 139

4. Jean-Pierre de Bougainvill: Manuel, F. *A Portrait*, p352.

5. Brewster, *Memoirs of Isaac Newton*, II, 307.
6. Manuel, F. *A Portrait*, p.356.
7. Flamsteed then took 51' per annum as the rate of precession, whereas in his *Historia* in the next century it had become 50' i.e. one degree per 72 years.
8. 'Flamsteed, John' by NK, *Biographical Encyclopaedia of Astronomers,* 2007 Ed Hockey.
9. 'Newton refused to return the manuscripts he had received for a full decade:' Buchwald & Mordechai Feingold, Eds., *Newton and the Origin of Civilization*, 2013, p. 271. Francis Baily, in *his Account of the Revd John Flamsteed* 1835, never realised this, but B&M are surely correct.
10. B.L.van der Waerden, *Science Awakening II, The Birth of Astronomy* (Leyden and New York 1974), 'History of the Zodiac', p.228.
11. Edmund Halley, 'Remarks upon some Dissertations lately published at Paris, by the Rev. P. Souciet, against Sir Isaac Newton's Chronology' Phil. Trans. 1727, 34, p205-210.
12. Chronology, p.93.
13. Ibid.,p.26.
14. Newton, Chronology, p.57
15. Edmund Halley, 'Remarks upon some Dissertations lately published at Paris, by the Rev. P. Souciet, against Sir Isaac Newton's Chronology' *Phil. Trans.* 1727, 34, pp.205-210.
16. Newton, Phil. Trans. 1725, 33, p318.
17. De Revolutionibus, Trans. C.G.Wallis, *Great Books of the Western World* 1952, p590-621.
18. Mordechai & Feingold, *op. Cit.* pp.416, 436.

Chapter 11

1. The theme of this chapter was worked out with my colleague Peter Nockolds. Our attempt to co-author a paper foundered, alas, so my version of text is here included.
2. 'England was in fact on a gold standard from 1717 onwards' (C.R. Fay in 'Newton and the Gold Standard,' Cambridge History Journal, 1935, 5,1, 109-111), resulting from 'an intentional act by Newton.'
3. Anne and James Balakier, 'The spatial Infinite at Greenwich in works by Christopher Wren, James Thornhill and James Thompson, The Newtonian Connection' (free download).
4. Ibid, pp.72,73, 118.
5. Jed Buchwald & Mordechai Feingold, *Newton and the Origin of Civilization,* 2013, Fig 8.3, p.256.
6. A talk alas never published, by Ken Knoespel, Chair of the School of Literature, Communication and Culture, Georgia Institute of Technology, to the American Chemical Society in Fall 2006.
7. First noticed by Maev Kennedy *in The Guardian* 'Greenwich Painted Hall Shipshape after restoration' 2 May 2013.
8. Sir James Thornhill, *An Explanation of the Painting in the Royal Hospital at Greenwich* 1730.
9. Using the poster-photo on sale in the Great Hall, we estimate this angle as 23½° -24°.

NOTES

Appendices

1. Newton project (online) Keynes Ms. 130.04, King's College, Cambridge, UK.
2. D.T. Whiteside, *The Preliminary Manuscripts* 1989 p.X1.
3. Rupert Hall, *Isaac Newton Adventurer in Thought*,1992, p.33.
4. Westfall, *Never at Rest*, p.143: 'The story of the apple, set in the country, implies the stay in Woolsthorpe.'
5. Aubrey, J. *Brief Lives*, 1972, p18.
6. For an early estimate, see 1 Kings Chapter 5, Verse 23 where a value of 3 is taken for π.
7. MP Vol 8, p.479 (online); Whiteside, 'Newton's Discovery of the Binomial Theorem', *The Mathematical Gazette*, 1963 p.176.
8. The infinite-series expansion which he then sent to Leibiz, for finding the area of a circular segment, was the same as later appeard in the (posthumous) *De Methodis.*
9. Leibniz, *Historia at Origo Calculi Differentialis*, quoted in J. M. Child, 1920.
10. Hoffmann, *Leibniz in Paris, 1672-76, His growth to Mathematical Maturity* 1974, p.63.
11. Letter to Varignon, end of 1718, Corr. Vol. 5, p.18.
12. Hofmann, op. cit., 1974, p. 64.
13. Math Papers II 1968, 206-247: Newton *De Analysi per æquationes numero terminorum infinitas*, composed 1669 and published 1711.
14. Its full title was, *De analysi per aequationes numero termniorum infinitas.*
15. An English translation was published by John Harris in his *Lexicum Technicum* of 1710: Math Papers VII, pp. 258-297; reproduced Guicciardini 2011, p.228.
16. Guicciardini, N., 2011, p.228.
17. Having written a book on the subject, *The Development of Newtonian Calculus in Britain, 1700-1800* one might expect M. Guicciardini to have noticed that this phrase first appeared in the 1704 textbook by Hayes.
18. Whiteside, MP 2, *de Analysi* p.233. It is a translation of p.14 of *Commercium Epistolicum*, 1712. Actually, he wrote 'Let ABD be any curve…' but I've corrected this.
19. Whiteside, MP 2, p.232.
20. Harper, W., *Isaac Newton's Scientific Method*, 2011, p.220.
21. We've seen in Chapter 3, how the first germ of this computation appears the autumn of 1684, in *De Motu* as delivered to Halley: 'My calculations reveal that the centri*fugal* force by which our moon is held in her monthly motion about the earth is to the force of gravity at the surface of the earth very nearly (*quamproxime*) as the reciprocal of the square of the distance from the centre of the earth.' (Cohen 1980 p.266)
22. Densmore, D., *Newton's Principia: the Central Argument* Green Lion Press, Senta Fe, 1996, p.295-6.
23. This figure is equivalent to 7,936 miles diameter, as 1 Paris foot = 1.068 Imperial feet.
24. Corollary IX of Proposition IV of Book I of the *Principia* says: 'The arc which a body, uniformly revolving in a circle with a given centripetal force, describes in any time, is a mean proportion between the diameter of the circle, and the space which the same body falling by the same force would describe in the same time.'
25. Brougham and Routh, *Analytical View of Sir Isaac Newton's Principia*, 1855, p.40; Westfall, R., *Newton and the Fudge Factor,* Science, Feb 1973; Densmore, *Op cit.*; Harper, W., *Isaac Newton's Scientific method*, 2011, p.220.

26. Letter from John Wallis, 10 April 1695
27. Westfall, R., Newton and the Fudge Factor, *Science*, Feb 1973, p.751.
28. N.K., Newton's two Moon-tests *BJHS* 1991.
29. For these two different ellipses see Book III of the *Principia,* propositions 35 (Scholium) and 29.
30. Jean Bailly *Histoire de L'Astronomie Moderne* II, 1779, p.509.
31. Kollerstrom, N.,, 'A Reintroduction of Epicycles: Newton's 1702 Lunar Theory and Halley's Saros Correction', *Q. J. R. astr. Soc.* (1995), 36, 357-368.
32. 'De l'Orbite de la Lune dans le Système Newtonian', *Histoire de l'Academie Royale des sciences*, Paris 1746, p.128. For discussion, see Kollerstrom *Newton's Forgotten Lunar Theory, his contribution to the quest for longitude,* 2000, pp.230-1; or, 'A Reintruduction of Epicycles' (online) *QJRAS* 1995.
33. The mean length of the tropical lunar month (of 27.3 days) was cited by newton in 1702 as in excess by a mere 0.2 seconds. As I commented, 'It must have been the most accurately known physical constant of that period.' (*Newton's Forgotten Lunar Theory*, 2000, p.55). It was the most accurate physical parameter ever given by Newton (His sidereal month for comparison was far less accurate). However that 0.2 second error was cumulative and three decades later it had added up to this two arcminute error, here seen in Halley's data.
34. Curtis Wilson, 'The Newtonian Achievement in Astronomy', *General History of astronomy*, Vol 2, 1989, p.267: Halley like Flamsteed 'found errors in longitude as high as 8' or 9".

Select Bibliography

1. The authors of this book have used almost the entire content of my 25-page article in *Annals of Science,* 'Newton's late apprehension of the law of Gravity' (1999), with no acknowledgement.

Index

Abbé Conti, 186, 201
Acta Eruditorum, 27, 182, 194, 197
Aiton, Eric, 194
Algebra, John Wallis, 119, 189
Amsterdam, 29
Annus mirabile, 93
Aries, constellation of, 235
   Zero degrees of, 240
Arithmetica Universalis, 210
Aristotle, 82
Apple myth, the, 37-8
Approximation, method of, 119
Arithmetica Universalis, 23
Astronomia Brittanica, 69, 80
Astronomer Royal, the, 74, 149
Aristotle, 48
Aubrey, John, 137, 256
Aurora borealis, 130

Babington, Humphrey, 254
Bacon, Francis, 30
Baily, Francis, 154, 162
Bank of England, 1694
Baricentre, Earth-Moon, 264
Barrow, Isaac, 18, 46, 181
Barton, Catherine, 17, 30-2, 230
Bechler, Zev, 47, 60
Bentley, Richard, 226
Berkeley, Bishop, 29
Berlin academy of sciences, 115, 200
Bernoulli, Johannes, 23, 27, 180,
   197, 205

Bernoulli, Jacques, 267
Blake, William, 225
Borelli Giovanni, 96
Boyle, Robert, 72, 83, 137
   Lectures, 226
Brackenridge, Bruce, 116
Brahe, Tycho, 155
Brewster, David, 30, 55, 163-5, 202
British Museum, 145
Brouncker, Lord, 51
Burnett, Thomas, 74

Calculus, integral, 182
Cambridge, 76
Captain Halley, 130
Caroline, princess, 238, 248
Cassini, Giovanni, 166
Catenary curve, 179
Centripetal force, 71
Chapman, Allan, 169
Cheney, George, 23-4, 228
Charles II, king, 29
   Death of, 220
Chronology of the Ancient Kingdoms,
   36, 234, 237, 248, 253
Cohen, Bernard, 77, 113, 116
Collins, John 18, 148
Comet, of 1680, 34
Commercium Epistolicum, 169, 201
Conduitt, John, 23, 33-4, 254
Crabtree, William, 152
Craig, John, 188

Dampier, William, 117
De Analysi, 18-20, 114, 183-4, 259
De L'Hopital, Marquis, 189, 194
Descartes, 20, 46, 103, 123, 221
De Gravitatione, 20, 84
De Morgan, Augustus, 19, 30, 185, 187, 191
De Motu, 76-8, 215
De Quadratura, 23-5, 196, 199
Diamond (Newton's dog), 19
Divine Artificier, 225
Dryden, 31
Duillier, Fatio, 198

Earth, hollow, 129
    Size of, 262
Einstein, 40, 110
Elixir, the, 74
Epicycles, return of, 266
Equinoxes, precession of, 235
Eudoxus, 241, 244
Euler, Leonhardt, 60, 114
Evelyn, john, 135

Fatio de Duiller, 25-6, 228
Fire of London, 145
Flamsteed, 31, 40, 42-3, 53, 75, 91, 127, 161, 216, 223, 238
Fluxions, 104, 193
    Lemmap, 213
Fontenelle, Newton-biography, 37, 40
Freemasonry, 230

Galileo, 43
Gascoigne, William, 153
George, king, 253
Glorious Revolution, the, 20, 28, 227
Goethe, 98
Gold standard, 246
Gravity-ether, 17

Gregory, David, 42, 106-7, 157, 198, 228, 258
Greenwich, Observatory, 147, 155
    Painted hall, 246
Gresham College, 133, 137
Grimaldi, 53
Golden Age, 251
Guicciardini, Niccolo, 261

Halley, Edmond, 42, 85, 91, 93, 127, 174, 177, 237, 243, 268
Halley's comet, 75
Hanby, David, 142
Handel, 35
Hanover, archives, 181
    Dynasty, 205, 246
Hall, Rupert, 61, 186, 203, 208, 254
Hanover dynasty, 221
Hawkins, Stephen, 200
Harriot, Thomas, 59
Heresy, Arian, 21
Herivel, J.W., 106
Hevelius, Johannes, 155-6
Hipparchus, 236
Historia Coelestis Brittanica, 168, 173
Hooke, Robert, 45, 47-8, 78, 89, 133
Hooke's law, 97
Hollow Earth, 125
Horrocks, Jeremiah, 148-50, 152
    Theory, 159, 266
Huygens, Christiaan, 55, 57, 65, 95, 99

Iliffe, Rob, 73
Infinite series expansions, 184
Interference of light, 50
Io (Jupiter moon), 223

Judgement day, 231
Jupiter, satellites of, 222

Kepler, 99,
   Invents calculus, 180
   his laws, 68, 95
Kensington garden, 36-7
Keynes, Manyard, 41
Kit-Kat Club, the 32
Koyré, Alexander, 102

Laugh, of Newton, 34
Leibniz, 19, 28, 57, 116, 136, 182, 192,
   229, 258
Locke, John, 21, 23, 28-9
Lohne, John, 104
Lucasian professor, 17, 23
Luna (name for Moon), 223

Magi, last of, 41
Magnetic poles, four, 125
Manuel, Frank, 15, 30, 36, 78, 205
Maunder minimum, 132
Mechanical philosophy, 227
Memoirs of Europe, The, 32
Micrographia, 16, 65, 43, 84
Mint, the Royal, 27-8
Montague, Charles, 26-8, 177
   LordHalifax, 30-2
Moon, ye, 74
   Mass ratio, 124
   Test, 262
Moon-apple computation, 77, 111
Moore, Patrick, 106, 165
More, Henry, 73
Mother, death of, 97

Nell Gwyn, 150
Nervous breakdown, 99
New Theory of Light and Colour 1672,
   63, 65
Newton's first law, 71
Balls, 140
Newton, Humphrey, 18, 33

Newton-Raphson method, 122
Newton's rings, 51, 59
Noah, 21

Occam's razor, 52
Of Comets and Gravity (1682), 87
Oldenburg, Henry, 18, 47, 49, 148
Optics 1704 of Newton, 56, 61, 225

Patterson, Louise, 101-2, 134
Papish plot, the, 73
Pepys, Samuel, 87, 93, 220, 266
Philosophical Transactions, 47, 236, 259
Pi, finding it, 182
Pink, Paramore, the, 130
Portsmouth Collection, the, 33
Precession of equinoxes, 239
Primary colours, 64
Principia, 20, 34, 69, 79, 99, 112, 118,
   215, 250, 265
Ptolemy, Claudius, 169, 239

Quadrature, method of, 182, 256

Raphson, Joseph, 118-21
History of fluxions, 214
Rémond de Montfort, Pierre, 197, 207
Robur Carolinum, constellation, 170
Roemer, Ole, 56
Royal Society, the, 201
Russell, Bertrand, 205

Sabra, I, 61-3
Saros cycle, 269
Satan, 232
Sharp, Abraham, 171, 176, 267
Shapin, Stephen, 143
Simpson, John, 119-21
Sizar, 15
Sluse method, of fluxions 188
Stukeley, William 36

Solar vortex, 70
Star-maps, 157, 169
Star-catalogue, British, 176
St Helena, stars of, 130
Swift, Jonathan, 31, 3

Telescope, reflecting, 33, 58, 98
    Optics, 51
Thames, frozen, 220
Theologia gentilis origines, 22
Theory of the Moon, 42, 150, 165
Thornhill, James, 246-50
Tides, 125
Tower of London, 27, 29
Transmuting of metals, 71-2
Trinity, the Holy 21
    Denial of, 232
Trinity College, 15, 17, 21
Two notable corruptions (of
    scripture), 21
Two comets, ye, 76

Variation, the, of Moon, 266
Varignon, Pierre, 194, 207
Venus transit, 152
Virgil prophecy, 249
Virtuoso, the, by Shadwell, 135, 256
Voltaire, 29
Vortex-theory, 74

Wallis, John, 49, 119, 180, 193,
    259, 264
Wave-theory of light, 50
Westfall, Richard, 22, 111, 172, 201,
    208, 233-4, 262, 265
Westminster Abbey, 152
Whiston, William, 21, 23, 36, 125,
    167, 227
White, Michael, 215
Whiteside, Tom, 23, 53, 102, 192, 203
William of Orange, 20, 221
Woolsthorpe, 15, 38, 73, 255
Wren, Christopher, 68, 145